FAT CITY

FAT CITY
HOW
WASHINGTON
WASTES YOUR TAXES

DONALD LAMBRO

REGNERY/GATEWAY, Inc. *South Bend, Indiana*

Manufactured in the United States of America.

Library of Congress Catalog Card Number: 79-66498
International Standard Card Number: 0-89526-680-6

Library of Congress Cataloging in Publication Data

Lambro, Donald.
    Fat city.

        1.   Government spending policy—United States.
2.   Economic assistance, Domestic—United States.
I.   Title.
HJ7537.L35   336.3'9'0973   79-92080
ISBN 0-89526-680-6

SECOND PRINTING, 1980

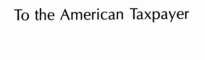
To the American Taxpayer

CONTENTS

Preface   xv

Acknowledgments   xxi

BOOK I   The Wastemakers   1

Chapter 1   Wasteland: Losing $100 Billion a Year   2

Chapter 2   The Hidden Bureaucracy   11

Chapter 3   Tracking the Beltway Bandits   16

Chapter 4   Paying the Special Interests   25

Chapter 5   The Forgotten Agencies   32

Chapter 6   Uncle Sam the Travelin' Man   38

Chapter 7   Henry Luce on the Potomac   47

Chapter 8   USDA: Where Are the Farmers?   54

Chapter 9   The Poverty Business   63

Chapter 10 Selling the Government   74

Chapter 11 Impact Aid: Making Rich Schools Richer   83

Chapter 12 The $100 Billion Paperwork Connection   87

Chapter 13 The Double Dippers   96

Chapter 14 A No-Frills Pentagon   101

Chapter 15 OSHA: Washington's Most Hated Agency   112

Chapter 16 HUD: The $76 Billion Disappointment   121

Chapter 17 Love and Passion at the National   134
            Science Foundation

Chapter 18 Cutting the Government: Jimmy Carter's   144
            Broken Promise

BOOK II *100 Nonessential Federal Programs* 153

Regional Commissions 154
U.S. Travel Service 157
The Pentagon's "Top Brass" Dining Rooms 159
U.S. Employment Service 162
Women's Bureau 165
Revenue Sharing 167
VISTA 170
Government Travel 174
VIP Lodges and Retreats 176
Federal Information Center 178
Personal Chefs for Cabinet Secretaries 179
President's Council on Physical Fitness 182
Government Film-Making 184
Beekeeper Indemnity Payments 188
Council on Legal Educational Opportunity 189
Automatic Elevator Operators 191
Consumer Information Center 192
814 Federal Advisory Boards, Committees,
    Commissions and Councils 193
House Gymnasium 195
Senate Gymnasium
Double Dippers 197
Economic Research Service 199
Alaska Railroad 203
Economic Development Administration 204
Congress' Florist Service 208
National Science Foundation Low Priority Research 210
National Institute of Building Sciences 215
Military Recreational Facilities 216
Mexican-United States Defense Commission 219
Inter-American Defense Board 220
Highway Beautification Program 221
Coast Guard Selected Reserve Program 222
Chauffeured Limousines 223

Federal Election Commission   226
Government Lobbyists   234
HUD's Office of International Affairs   236
Selective Service   237
Impact Aid To Education, "B" Category   240
HUD's Office of Interstate Land Sales Registration   242
USDA Costs of Inspecting, Classifying and
    Grading Cotton and Tobacco   245
Military Commissaries and Exchanges   246
Office of Technology Assessment   248
Minority Business Development Agency   252
National Institute of Education   254
Institute of Museum Services   259
Law Enforcement Assistance Administration   261
National Institute of Law Enforcement and
    Criminal Justice
Office of Juvenile Justice and Delinquency
Consultants   267
Civil Aeronautics Board   269
Japan-United States Friendship Commission   272
Bilingual Education Program   273
Military Servants   276
Youth Conservation Corps   278
Government Advertising   280
National Endowment for the Arts   282
National Endowment for the Humanities
Office of Consumer Affairs   291
Interstate Commerce Commission   292
Office of Small Pox Eradication   297
Advisory Commission on Intergovernmental Relations   298
Ethnic Heritage Studies   300
International Development Association   302
Community Services Administration   309
National Highway Traffic Safety Administration   312
Occupational Safety and Health Administration   318
National Institute for Occupational Safety and Health
Occupational Safety and Health Review Commission

BOOK II   *100 Nonessential Federal Programs cont'd.*

National Board for the Promotion of Rifle Practice	321
Small Business Administration	323
U.S. Parole Commission	330
Legal Services Corporation	332
Defense Civil Preparedness Program	339
Overseas Private Investment Corporation	341
Foreign Claims Settlement Commission	344
Educational and Cultural Exchange Grants	345
American Battle Monuments Commission	349
USDA Extension Service	350
HUD Urban Development Action Grants	352
Capitol Police	356
Franklin Delano Roosevelt Memorial Commission	358
Commission of Fine Arts	
Council On Environmental Quality and Office of Environmental Quality	360
Smithsonian Special Foreign Currency Program	362
Consumer Product Safety Commission	365
Department of Education	371
Maritime Administration	376
Federal Trade Commission	383
Amtrak	399
Council on Wage and Price Stability	404

Alphabetical listing

BOOK II   *100 Nonessential Federal Programs*   153

Advisory Commission on Intergovernmental Relations   298

Alaska Railroad   203

American Battle Monuments Commission   349

Amtrak   399

Automatic Elevator Operators   191

Beekeeper Indemnity Payments   188

Bilingual Education Program   273

Capitol Police   356

Chauffeured Limousines   223

Civil Aeronautics Board   269

Coast Guard Selected Reserve Program   222

Coastal Plains Regional Commission   154

Commission of Fine Arts   358

Community Services Administration   309

Congress' Florist Service   208

Consultants   267

Consumer Information Center   192

Consumer Product Safety Commission   365

Council on Environmental Quality   360

Council on Legal Education Opportunity   189

Council on Wage and Price Stability   404

Defense Civil Preparedness Program   339

Department of Education   371

Double Dippers   197

Economic Development Administration   204

Economic Research Service   199

Educational and Cultural Exchange Grants   345

Ethnic Heritage Studies   300

Federal Advisory Boards, Committees, Commissions, and Councils   193

BOOK II   *100 Nonessential Federal Programs cont'd.*

Federal Election Commission   226
Federal Information Center   178
Federal Trade Commission   383
Foreign Claims Settlement Commission   344
Four Corners Regional Commission   154
Franklin Delano Roosevelt Memorial Commission   358

Government Advertising   280
Government Film-Making   184
Government Lobbyists   234
Government Travel   174

Highway Beautification Program   221
House Gymnasium   195
HUD Urban Development Action Grants   352
HUD's Office of International Affairs   236
HUD's Office of Interstate Land Sales Registration   242

Impact Aid to Education, "B" Category   240
Institute of Museum Services   259
Inter-American Defense Board   220
International Development Association   302
Interstate Commerce Commission   292

Japan-United States Friendship Commission   272

Law Enforcement Assistance Administration   261
Legal Services Corporation   332

Maritime Administration   376
Mexican-United States Defense Commission   219
Mid-America Regional Commission   154
Mid-Atlantic Regional Commission   154
Mid-South Regional Commission   154
Military Commissaries and Exchanges   246
Military Recreational Facilities   216

Military Servants   276
Minority Business Development Agency   252

National Board for the Promotion of Rifle Practice   321
National Endowment for the Arts   282
National Endowment for the Humanities   282
National Highway Traffic Safety Administration   312
National Institute for Occupational Safety and Health   318
National Institute of Building Sciences   215
National Institute of Education   254
National Institute of Law Enforcement and
    Criminal Justice   261
National Science Foundation Low Priority Research   210
New England Regional Commission   154

Occupational Safety and Health Administration   318
Occupational Safety and Health Review Commission   318
Office of Consumer Affairs   291
Office of Environmental Quality   360
Office of Juvenile Justice and Delinquency   261
Office of Small Pox Eradication   297
Office of Technology Assessment   248
Old West Regional Commission   154
Overseas Private Investment Corporation   341
Ozarks Regional Commission   154

Pacific Northwest Regional Commission   154
The Pentagon's "Top Brass" Dining Rooms   159
Personal Chefs for Cabinet Secretaries   179
President's Council on Physical Fitness   182

Revenue Sharing   167

Selective Service   237
Senate Gymnasium   195
Small Business Administration   323
Smithsonian Special Foreign Currency Program   362
Southwest Border Regional Commission   154

BOOK II *100 Nonessential Federal Programs cont'd.*

Upper Great Lakes Regional Commission	154
USDA Costs of Inspecting, Classifying, and Grading Cotton and Tobacco	245
USDA Extension Service	350
U.S. Employment Service	162
U.S. Parole Commission	330
U.S. Travel Service	157
VIP Lodges and Retreats	176
VISTA	170
Women's Bureau	165
Youth Conservation Corps	278

PREFACE

Our federal government has become a bloated, extravagant, paternalistic, remote, cluttered, disorganized, inefficient, frivolous, duplicative, archaic wasteland. This is not a description one might expect to hear from the nightly television news, our political leaders, or our wisest academicians. They for the most part have presented us with a misleading picture of our government; misleading not so much in what they tell us, but in what they choose not to tell us.

What they have not told us is that America has an excess of government. And it is getting fatter and costlier with every passing year. If the average taxpayer were to spend one week touring the departments, bureaus, divisions, offices, commissions, institutes, boards, and other agencies of government, he or she would be led to one inescapable conclusion: Americans have more government than they need, more than they want, and more than they can afford. Like a riderless locomotive whose throttle has been pulled wide open, the federal government is running out of control.

The degree to which this excessiveness is growing can be seen in the speed with which our government has been increasing its budget and thus its demands upon our income. It took the government 175 years for its annual budget to reach $100 billion. That was in 1962, one year after John F. Kennedy became president. It then took *only nine years*, from 1962 to 1971, for the budget to pass the $200 billion mark. After that, only four years to hit $300 billion, and just two years after that to surpass $400 billion. By fiscal 1979 the government was spending nearly $500 billion a year and speeding toward $550 billion in fiscal 1980. The fiscal 1981 budget was expected to soar beyond $616 billion.

In 25 of the last 30 years the government has spent more than it took in and thus has had to borrow heavily to finance its deficit-ridden ventures. The year-end deficit for fiscal 1980 was expected to exceed $40 billion, while the government's total accumulated debt was estimated to rise to $839.2 billion, with *no end in sight*. Federal budget planners predicted the total debt would be $951.9 billion by fiscal 1982, close to $1 trillion.

Deficit spending has its cost. Each year a larger share of the annual budget must be spent just to pay the interest on our mounting debt. In 1979 federal interest payments alone totaled $52.7 billion. In 1980 interest payments rose to $57 billion.

All government spending and borrowing must of course be shouldered by the American taxpayer. At least 43 cents out of every dollar the government claims in taxes comes from individual income taxes, while 30 cents is derived from social security taxes paid by both individuals and employers. Another 13 cents out of each tax dollar comes from corporate taxes which all Americans must pay in the form of higher consumer prices.

All told, taxpayers are expected to pay more than half a trillion dollars in taxes to the federal government in 1980. And taxes are expected to rise sharply in future years as inflation pushes workers into higher tax brackets and the government taxes increasingly larger amounts out of their income. For most Americans of relatively modest means these taxes represent a substantial sacrifice for which they and their families must endure a lower standard of living *as a result of the government's insatiable demands* for their earnings.

A typical taxpayer earning $18,000 a year, for example, who supports a wife and two children, paid an astounding $4,814 in federal taxes in 1979, including income, social security, excise, and other levies.* (And this excluded state and local taxes.) Moreoever, Americans now find they must work for their government for nearly half the year before being allowed to keep the rewards of their own labors. To pay all of his taxes, the average taxpayer must now toil in behalf of the government from January 1 through the month of May.

Is this much taxation necessary? After a decade of covering Washington for a major news service, I am convinced it is not. And I am further convinced that taxes can be substantially and permanently reduced by cutting the size and cost of our government.

I fully realize that one of the most repeated political utterances of our time is that government has grown too fast, too big, too expensive, and too wasteful. This is something most Americans believe in the abstract, but know little about in the specific. (They are not alone. Government has grown so fast and so large that most of our congressional representatives know little of the specifics, either.)

Because of my suspicion that our government has become far more wasteful than our public servants have been willing to admit, I undertook an investigation that led me across the length and breadth of the federal landscape. I wanted to know what the government was actually doing with our money and who was really benefiting from its enormous expenditures.

To find out I interviewed hundreds of government officials, and examined thousands of pages of grants, contracts, travel vouchers, project summaries, studies, audits, testimony, memorandums, and other internal documents and papers. I talked to government contractors, congressional investigators, lobbyists, budget analysts, whistle blowers, as well as people in all walks of private life who have had to deal with the government's incessant demands, costs, regulations, penalties, and taxes.

Now certainly, a nation of 220 million people needs and demands a big government to manage its affairs, defend its people, and meet basic social needs. What my foray through the bureaucracy revealed was that our government has gone far beyond these basic needs— becoming involved in a multitude of esoteric studies, experiments, subsidies, services, pilot projects, and other schemes most Americans would find difficult to believe.

Somewhere along the way we have *lost sight* of the simple and basic purposes of government. We have allowed politicians and greedy special interests to grotesquely misshape our government into a cornucopia of excessive programs and redundant agencies. And because of this, Washington demands more tax revenue than is necessary for the government to fulfill its proper function in our society.

All told, I estimate that at least $100 billion a year in taxes is unnecessarily going to the federal government to be squandered on programs our country could better do without; wasteful programs that belong at the bottom of any national ranking of social priorities; programs whose original purpose for being no longer exists; programs that serve only a tiny fraction of the people at the expense of the nation as a whole; programs that duplicate what is already being done by the private sector. And by waste, I am not talking about losses the government accepts as routine and unavoidable. I am talking about a degree of waste and wantonness that permeates the very fabric of government; squandering, abuse, fraud, mismanagement, and extravagance so widespread as to raise the question of whether we can any longer allow our government to continue operating as it has without doing irrevocable damage to the economic foundation of our nation and the livelihood of every American.

This, then, is a report to the American taxpayer on the results of my investigation. I have chosen to divide my story into two parts. The first half deals generally with some of the worst areas of government waste and abuse, exposing government-wide practices and programs that have in large part existed decade after decade, administration after administration, Congress after Congress.

The second half presents 100 of what I believe to be the most wasteful, inefficient and unnecessary federal agencies, programs and expenditures in Washington today, accompanied by the reasons why each one should be abolished. It is my belief that the only effective way to cut federal spending is to simply terminate unneeded, unworkable, and outdated programs. The 100 proposed program terminations listed here would be a good place to start.

I use the word start advisedly because my list is in no way intended as a complete and exhaustive survey of the federal government. It is meant as a *departure point* for anyone wishing to conduct a more comprehensive examination with the purpose of sweeping out frivolous and highly dispensable agencies and programs.

Any attempt to cut big government down to size will invariably be met by stiff resistance from the special interests who feed off its programs, from the bureaucrats who run them to powerful lawmakers who want to protect pet programs whose demise would mean a loss of power and prestige for the congressional committees they chair. Thus, any budget-cutting effort is likely to be confronted by two fraudulent responses.

The first is the argument that federal spending cannot be cut significantly because most of it is "uncontrollable," cemented into law under certain entitlement programs for social security beneficiaries, black lung recipients, and the like. But, as this book seeks to demonstrate, major cuts can be made without harming truly needed programs. Laws enacted by Congress are merely words that can be changed or repealed by a simple majority vote. Such laws should never be used as an argument against evaluating acts of Congress which have piled program upon program, agency upon agency, in a bureaucratic extravaganza of confusion, duplication, and waste.

Would-be budget-cutters must also be wary of what I call the Orphans and Old People First response. Whenever anyone suggests slashing spending, congressional committee chairmen are sure to charge that any effort to cut their programs would seriously threaten services and benefits for the poor, the sick, the disabled, the jobless, i.e., the most disadvantaged groups in our country. (Somehow the waste, fraud, porkbarrel, and boondoggles escape their attention.) Similarly, when spending cuts are demanded by Congress, agency heads will likely cut the most sensitive and necessary programs— totally ignoring padded payrolls, exorbitant expenditures, and low-priority programs. All of this of course is calculated to frighten and intimidate anyone suggesting that government programs can be significantly reduced without hurting these needy constituencies. All too often, unfortunately, this kind of blackmail works, and proposed cuts are abandoned because most Americans—including most congressmen—are unable to pinpoint where wasteful spending and unnecessary programs can be easily cut.

To a large degree, this book was written to expose this flimflam game for the fraud that it is and to point to where federal activities can be deleted at considerable savings to the taxpayers. Government *can* be significantly reduced in size, and not a single truly needy American has to be denied benefits and services he or she truly deserves. This book was written to disseminate the arguments for these cuts as widely as possible among those who believe, as I do, that the government can be intelligently, prudently, and gradually *pruned back.* No longer should anyone be forced to remain inarticulate when challenged by the question, "Okay, where would you cut?" There are at least 100 possible replies to that question provided here.

I do not expect everyone to agree with me on each and every proposed cut. Each one of us has different beliefs about what government should be doing. Nevertheless, there are, I believe, enough examples of waste and ineffectiveness among my modest proposals to appeal to a consensus of Americans who believe that the time has come to tell Congress that enough is enough. Wasteful and unnecessary spending must stop.

One of the preeminent issues of our day is, How big do we wish our national government to be? Most Americans quite correctly believe that government must play an important role in insuring that the basic, human needs of all Americans be provided. But beyond that, surveys tell us that Americans are quite willing to see a substantial reduction made in nonessential federal agencies and programs, if that will mean providing more for those truly in need— along with a generous reduction in their federal taxes. Americans want to be responsible for their own lives, for their own successes and their own failures. But to do that they *must be allowed to keep more* of what they earn. That should be the overriding objective of any comprehensive effort to abolish unnecessary government. There can be no clearer nor more worthy goal for the future of our country.

DONALD LAMBRO
Washington, D.C.
December 1979

*According to the Tax Foundation, N.Y., N.Y.

ACKNOWLEDGMENTS

This book was written with the assistance of many people within the government, a number of whom must remain unnamed. Most of those who chose to talk honestly and candidly about their agency or program did so because they were disturbed by what the government was doing with the people's money. Many of them provided invaluable material and documentation. Almost all agreed to cooperate only with the understanding that what they said or provided would not be attributed to them. I am extremely grateful to all those within the bureaucracy who helped in this endeavor.

For permission to use previously published material, which I have revised and extended where necessary, I wish to extend my appreciation to the editors of the *Washingtonian, Free Enterprise, Policy Review,* and *Conservative Digest* magazines and United Press International. A special note of gratitude must also go to Grant Dillman, UPI vice president and Washington bureau chief, for recognizing the need for a closer, ongoing examination of the government and for giving me the opportunity to conduct that inquiry.

I also remain deeply indebted to Ryland Wiltshire of the National Journalism Center and Laurie Ingraham of the Heritage Foundation for their painstaking research. Without their enthusiastic assistance this book would not have been possible.

Finally, a very special bouquet must go to my wife, Jackie, whose help and encouragement provided me with the inspiration to complete this work.

FAT CITY

BOOK I
The Wastemakers

CHAPTER 1
Wasteland: Losing $100 Billion a Year

Tens of billions of tax dollars are lost each year by the federal government through fraud, mismanagement, abuse, waste, error, and sheer extravagance.

No one in Washington knows what the actual total is. What is even worse, the government *doesn't want* to know, for if it did, the total would be so unbelievably enormous that whatever little faith, if any, remained among taxpayers in Washington's ability to spend their money wisely would be destroyed.

It would of course take a veritable army of accountants to undertake a thorough audit of the $548 billion that Washington now spends annually. While a correspondent such as myself does not have access to such a force of bookkeepers, it has been possible for me to assemble some of the significant figures that have emerged, in recent years, from various government reports and audits, including Congress' auditing arm, the General Accounting Office. When I combined these figures—most of which are on the public record—with the spending loss estimates of other helpful sources (informed budget experts and investigators), the totals were beyond belief.

Simple addition of these statistics shows that the government is losing a *minimum* of $40 and possibly $50 billion a year. That is nearly 10 percent of the fiscal 1980 federal budget of $548 billion (add $12 billion in off-budget spending for the true $560 billion total). Yet even these figures represent *only a part* of the ultimate total. What that total amounts to, nobody knows; some experts say it could be double the $50 billion figure. This would mean that $100 billion is being lost through corruption, abuse, mismanagement, and wasteful, unnecessary, excessive government spending.

Major GAO audits and studies in recent years have given some insight into what is happening in our government today:

—Federal economic-assistance programs are being despoiled by white-collar cheaters and swindlers of an estimated $2.5 to $25 billion per year. (GAO experts estimate $15 billion to be the minimum annual figure).

—The government is losing more than half a billion dollars per

year from bad debts—as from small business loans, or from Veterans
Administration educational assistance overpayments—routinely
written off as "uncollectable."

—Nearly 14,000 audit reports are gathering dust on government
shelves, even though they document the loss of $4.3 billion annually
in unauthorized use of federal funds by contractors and grant
recipients.

The government admitted in 1979 that, over the last several years,
it had lost more than $3.5 billion as the result of debts written off as
uncollectable. These bad debt losses had been rising at a rate of
$500 million in a single year. By the end of 1978, a staggering $140
billion in loans and accounts receivable was owed to the government, an increase of $22 billion from the previous fiscal year. Said
a GAO auditor who has closely studied the problem, "I'd say we're
losing about a half billion dollars a year in bad debts that go
uncollected."

Wherever the GAO looked, it found loans and other funds receivable which had long been owed to the government. About one-fourth
of the Office of Education's $4 billion in loans was in default in
1979, and that default rate, it was determined, was increasing.

The Social Security Administration, with hardly any investigation,
regularly dismisses bad debts as "hardship cases." In one case they
wrote off a $1500 "bad debt" even though the person in question
had assets of more than $200,000.

The Interior Department has been substantially behind in its collection of more than $1.2 billion in annual oil and gas royalties owed
the government. Despite the fact that major oil and gas companies
may be seriously late in their payments, the Interior Department
never charges the companies a late penalty (as does the Internal
Revenue Service when an average taxpayer is delinquent with an
income tax payment).

In those cases where the Veterans Administration simply wrote off
educational assistance debts as "uncollectable," the GAO later found
that, in 58 percent of the cases, the persons *were* affluent enough to
have paid the loans. In one instance, the person had an automobile
loan exceeding $10,000. In another, the person had a $170,000
mortgage, but the V.A. *nevertheless wrote off* his $638 debt as
uncollectable.

Add to this a major GAO audit of the government's $3 billion a
year personnel travel bill—travel being one of the fastest-rising expenses in government—which found that about 15 percent of the

trips examined were unnecessary. Experts in Congress say that an annual minimum of $500 million—and perhaps as much as $1 billion—could be saved, if wasteful and unnecessary travel were stopped.

The government is also spending more than $32 billion a year on research and development studies in thousands of categories—from missiles to mint leaves. However, GAO investigators have said privately that as much as $1 billion or more of this research is wasted on "frivolous and ridiculously low-priority subjects."

In an eye-opening but, sadly, little-read 107-page report entitled "Federal Agencies Can and Should Do More to Combat Fraud in Government Programs," the GAO said that opportunities for defrauding the government are "virtually limitless," due to the number, variety, and value of federal programs.

"No one knows the magnitude of fraud against the government," the GAO study confessed, for—hidden *within apparently legitimate undertakings*—it "usually is unreported and/or undetected."

Grants, contracts, and loan guarantees are being acquired through corrupt means, such as bribery of public officials, false payment claims for goods and services not delivered, and collusion between contractors.

No agency or federal activity is untouched by the taint of fraud. The Labor Department, for example, has received reports in which it is alleged that in certain localities $40 million in fraudulent unemployment insurance benefits is being paid to claimants. The department's Comprehensive Employment and Training Act (CETA) program to combat unemployment has been so riddled with abuse, in state after state, that hardly a month has passed in recent years that a story has not surfaced, somewhere, revealing fraud or abuse or political favoritism in the granting of CETA jobs.

Another GAO investigation (into the $1.5 billion paid to federal workers for overtime) uncovered numerous cases of overtime abuses, including many instances in which false overtime was added to time cards. In the last two years, overtime costs have risen by more than $300 million. A great deal of it, investigators believe, is fraudulent. A second follow-up GAO study said that auditors discovered overtime abuses were widespread *throughout* the government.

Much of the problem in combatting fraud is getting the agencies to look for it in the first place. Pushed by Congress to get federal funds obligated and spent, most agency and department officials are devoted to "getting out the funds," and looking for the possibility of fraud, the GAO said, "takes a back seat."

But in those cases where investigations were conducted, fraud was found to be everywhere:

—When a Department of Housing and Urban Development insuring program—which had never experienced the slightest hint of scandal—began investigating itself, it came upon 30 cases of false statements. Twenty-four persons were convicted.

—When the Small Business Administration examined newly-licensed small business investment firms over a two-year period, it uncovered numerous schemes involving false statements.

—An investigation into a single Farmers Home Administration office found 19 cases of home loan frauds.

—In the past five years, there have been 841 convictions in the Federal Housing Administration's home mortgage program.

—Fraud was so prevalent in the government's disaster relief programs that the Carter administration was considering the creation of a *special strike force* to root out abuse and corruption.

—A random review of 40 Veterans Administration loan applications brought to light minor to substantial irregularities in more than 30 percent of such applications.

Some of the government's worst cases of cheating and abuse were found in the VA's GI educational assistance program which a GAO audit, in a classic case of bureaucratic *understatement*, labeled "a billion dollar problem." Sen. William Proxmire, (D., Wis.), chairman of the appropriations subcommittee which funds the VA, said that *more than $2.5 billion* in cumulative overpayments had been made to veterans under the program. (This "billion dollar program" stemmed in part from a 1972 law which provided for the advance payment of education assistance to veterans. What happened was that many veterans, after applying, decided not to go on to school, or dropped out once they had begun. However, due to school administrative delays in notifying the VA when a veteran had dropped out, and even further delay by the VA in halting payments, the checks often continued to roll out for many months. Veterans continued, therefore, to receive checks in amounts from a few hundred dollars to more than $1,000, and many kept them. The VA said it has tried to get control of the overpayments, but figures show they have made little headway. Experts on Proxmire's subcommittee said the situation had "not improved very much.")

In a related "problem," the National Direct Student Loan program's default rate has been about 20 percent—with some 700,000 students defaulting on loans totaling about $600 million. Cheating on this program was *so massive* that President Carter chose to exclude it from his overall student assistance expansion program. Yet the default rate was also high in the programs that Carter—and Congress—expanded. In the guaranteed student loan program, for example, the default rate has reached 13 percent.

In the past several years at least five congressional committees found that the $8 billion student loan program was debased by fraud, abuse, and default. Senate investigators came across so much official corruption and government mismanagement and individual cheating that even veteran committee members were stunned by its magnitude.

Thorough and repeated auditing is one of the best means for combatting fraud and uncovering costly mismanagement, error, and abuse, but GAO investigators said that all too often the auditors' recommendations are *ignored* by program officials and higher-ups. (Thousands of neglected reports—showing that at least $4.3 billion in federal funds were misspent by contractors and grantees—were found in the files of 34 federal agencies: rather than take steps to recover these funds, the agencies chose, in virtually every instance, to either *ignore the audit findings*—despite the fact that 80 percent of the total amount of money *was* recoverable—or reject them.)

Too frequently, the GAO noted, when government officials did act they resolved audit discrepancies in favor of the grantee or contractor without adequate explanation, "allowing them to claim and keep 62 percent of the amount which auditors reported as questionable." Even when officials agreed with the auditors, they collected "less than half the amount due the government."

Despite the obvious growth in fraud, investigators in the GAO, Congress, and elsewhere in the government agree that a major problem in combatting it is that, too often, the agencies *don't want to admit* there could possibly be any fraud in their programs in the first place. Frequently, government officials prefer to give defrauders the benefit of the doubt rather than take action against them. And clever little disguises and euphemisms are sometimes used to hide fraudulent losses of funds.

Thus, overpayment of VA educational benefits has often been categorized under "accounts receivable" instead of potential fraud. Similarly, housing loan applications are rejected for "minor infractions" when the real reason may be false statements that could be fraudulent.

The government has launched varying efforts, in administration after administration, to combat fraud and cut waste. But judging by the amount of fraud and waste unearthed in recent years, those efforts have been highly ineffective. More importantly, Congress for the most part has been reluctant to significantly cut funding from programs which have repeatedly been the victims—or perpetrators—of fraud and waste.

The stakes in terms of lost tax dollars are high—much higher than anyone has thus far realized.

Auditors for the scandal-plagued General Services Administration officially estimated that GSA has been losing about $100 million a year through fraud, and another $66 million through wasteful spending practices. These figures are appallingly understated. Knowledgeable GAO auditors have said, privately, that the agency is wasting at least another $100 million a year through inefficient leasing practices, poor procurement management, and extravagant purchasing policies.

A Civil Service Commission study found that 11.5 percent of all federal white-collar workers were being paid nearly half a billion dollars more per year than was commensurate with their positions; and it doesn't end there: an interminable stream of studies, reports, and memorandums gives still further documentation of the loss of federal tax dollars.

Certainly the largest *continuing* loss is in the (recently altered) Department of Health, Education and Welfare; HEW has calculated that between $5.5 and $6.5 billion is lost annually through waste and fraud.* My own estimate, based on conversations with HEW employes and non-HEW experts, puts that figure—when the full extent of welfare fraud and other abuses is factored in—closer to $10 billion a year.

With an annual budget of over $200 billion, HEW made history as a veritable smorgasbord for chiseling professionals and professional chiselers. The massive department, with its full-time staff of 300 auditors and investigators devoted exclusively to Medicaid and Medicare programs, still wastes nearly $2 billion a year on these programs alone.

Out of more than $5 billion spent for aid to families with depen-

*Congress in the fall of 1979 removed the Office of Education from HEW, which is now called the Department of Health and Human Services, and created a Cabinet-level Department of Education. References to HEW made here and elsewhere in the book were written prior to this reorganization.

dent children during the first six months of 1978, more than $414 million went to ineligible persons or overpayments. And, during this same period, more than $151 million went to ineligible persons or overpayments out of the $3.3 billion supplemental-security program for the aged, blind, and disabled. In all, $565 million was lost *in half a year* on two of HEW's largest welfare programs.

With the advance of the computer—increasingly being put into use by the government—it has become easier to detect fraud: one computer search for welfare fraud cases turned up 29,000 government employes who were receiving federal pay *plus* welfare payment; a computer probe into doctors' Medicaid billings revealed so many cases of fraud that HEW investigators *had to retard their investigation* in order to avoid clogging up the prosecuting pipeline; still another probe found 9,100 welfare recipients in 26 states to be drawing welfare checks from more than a single state. And yet, despite the relative ease with which these crimes are detected, it is virtually impossible for the government to prosecute any but the most flagrant offenses: the fraud is too vast, and the government's prosecuting resources too limited.

"The waste, fraud, abuses, and all the rest," said an OMB auditor, "make it obvious that the government is losing a hell of a lot of money." But it is "only in the last year or two," he said, that the true magnitude of the problem has hit home.

Watching Justice Department fraud prosecutions rising 27 percent in a single year, a Justice Department lawyer shook his head sadly and remarked, "The biggest problem is that when the consumer is victimized, he complains. When the government is victimized, nobody complains."

There is much our government could do if the federal tax-dollar losses were not so great: wasted tax dollars could easily pay for major new programs which many members of Congress now say the government cannot afford. The amount that is lost through fraud alone, according to even the lowest estimates, would easily be enough to fund a nearly five-fold increase in cancer research, or a 20-fold increase in air pollution control.

Better still, the lion's share of this money could be left in the pockets of the people who earned it.

It would be an enormous task to determine *precisely how much* of the government's budget is lost through wasteful spending, because no comprehensive federal study on government-wide losses sheerly due to waste has ever been made (incredible as it may be, the government has never undertaken such a study). But the task is not impossible; it would—for purely subjective reasons—be difficult, in the beginning, even to define what is wasteful, but it *could* be done. Getting government officials to overcome their reluctance to talk openly about waste in the programs they oversee is one of the biggest problems. As one middle-level Office of Management and Budget official remarked, "My head would be on the block if anything I said about these programs were attributed to me."

How much is wasted throughout the government? "Leaving out fraud, it is certainly in the billions, going by even the most charitable of percentages," an OMB official said.

When asked to evaluate the Justice Department's one to ten percent fraud estimate, a knowledgeable GAO investigator said:

> With everything that has been coming out, the GSA scandals, the overtime abuses, the many reports we've put out, there's no doubt that the overall fraud figure is closer to $25 billion a year than to $2.5 billion. And bear in mind that this was a Justice Department estimate compiled for GAO based on previous fraud cases, not on any thorough knowledge of what is really going on in these agencies and departments. Also bear in mind that these figures apply only to that portion of the budget involving domestic economic assistance payments of one kind or another which amounts to about $250 billion or so. This doesn't even cover defense spending. Add that into the equation and you're talking about an optimum figure of $50 billion in just fraud and abuse.

Another GAO official said, "No one knows how much is lost through waste and error, but my own guess is—when you add it up, fraud and waste—it is between $40 billion and $50 billion a year."

This official was talking about *obvious* cases of waste, such as errors and instances in which funds were spent either extravagantly or unnecessarily. Yet I would add another category—or perhaps another dimension—to the waste our government engages in with the federal taxes it takes from us all. This would include a plethora of programs and agencies and spending practices which, by any reasonable criteria, are nonessential to the nation's security and general welfare, and which ought to be brought to an end (these will be discussed in detail in the second half of this book.) When the cost of these unnecessary programs and agencies is added to the figures for waste cited above, it becomes apparent that *at least $100 billion too much* goes to Washington in federal taxes—$100 billion that could be invested in our nation's businesses, in our families, in plans for our retirement years.

Most of the figures cited here represent the largest and most obvious losses of federal tax revenues wasted through fraud and mismanagement. There are many others. We shall now examine in more detail further evidence of where the federal government is virtually throwing our money away.

CHAPTER 2
The Hidden Bureaucracy

Despite official government declarations that its civilian work force has been kept consistently below the 2.9 million mark for years, the number of people actually employed by Washington exceeds 14 million. This means that at least one worker out of eight owes his or her job to the federal government.

Your congressman won't tell you this, because he either doesn't know, or doesn't want *you* to know. Nonetheless, the government's official count of its civilian work force conveniently ignores millions of people both inside and outside the federal government whose salaries are paid directly or indirectly from federal revenues.

Not only are hundreds of thousands of workers employed by government-created agencies and programs excluded from the bureaucracy's monthly employment index, but millions of "outside" workers—who labor full time or part-time for the government, under a myriad of contracts and grants—are excluded, as well.

"The pressure is to keep the number as low as possible," confided one official of the Office of Personnel Management whose mission is to keep track of all government employment. He admitted that many federal workers fall into a "gray area" that is not counted by the official roll keepers.

A Senate Appropriations Committee staffer put it more bluntly: "The government payroll really includes millions more than the government says it does. It (Personnel Management's) is not an honest figure."

About 2.9 million civilians are employed by the executive branch, the Congress, the Judiciary, and the Postal Service. Another 2.1 million make up the military rolls. But another 9 million make up what the National Journal has called "Uncle Sam's Army of Invisible Employes" which, it said, are paid "either directly by the federal government or through intermediaries using federal grants, contracts, and matching payments." The Journal's survey was good as far as it went—it counted 8 million "invisible" employes. It failed, however, to include many federal agencies and programs whose employes—numbering at least a million—are not counted even though their income comes directly from the U.S. Treasury.

No one is actually aware of the precise number of workers who

11

are supported—in whole or in part—by federal funds, but here are details of what we *do* know.

While outside consultants, university researchers, contractors, and others are not, legally, federal employes, many do in fact work full time on government jobs, sometimes even administering government programs. Some major consulting firms earn almost all their income from federal contracts, year in and year out.

The Department of Health, Education and Welfare employs about 145,000 people inside its agencies. But, on the outside, HEW money pays the salaries of 1 million *additional* workers in state and local governments, in universities, in research firms and institutions, and among private contractors.

The Defense Department, in addition to its military forces, provides work for 2 million other people through research and development, procurement, and construction contracts and grants.

More significantly, there are a multitude of quasi-government agencies and government-created "corporations" whose workers are not officially defined or considered federal employes, even though they work full time in government programs and are paid with federal revenues.

In my own investigation into this category of federal employment, I found hundreds of thousands of workers who are not counted by the Office of Personnel Management (formerly the Civil Service Commission) simply because of the nongovernment definition Congress has chosen to apply to these programs. If Congress wanted to carry this approach to its ultimate absurdity, virtually every department and agency could be turned into a "nongovernment" corporation and the entire bureaucracy would, theoretically, disappear— at least as far as the Office of Personnel Management were concerned.

An example of this deceptive shell game is the Legal Services Corporation, whose corps of 4,795 attorneys and 241 administrative back-up personnel was established by Congress in the 1960s to provide free legal services to the poor.

Legal Services employes are *not counted* by the government—even though funds for all their salaries come directly from the Treasury. Officials argue that it was created by Congress as an "independent corporation" and is, thus, not a part of the executive branch of government. Legal Services workers consequently do not consider themselves to be federal employes.

Similarly, the Community Services Administration, the antipoverty agency created under President Johnson, provides operating funds for some 900 state and local Community Action agencies around the country which employ 38,000 people—in addition to another 6,000 in various related programs. None of these persons are considered to be federal employes, even though CSA funds go directly to these agencies to pay salaries.

Another so-called quasi-government agency is the 20,000-employe National Rail Passenger Corporation, which runs Amtrak and has another 6,500 workers on other rail lines. All of them remain un-counted, even though Uncle Sam pays the bulk of their salaries.

The government-created Consolidated Rail Corporation known as Conrail, which took over six bankrupt railroad lines, was created to someday become an independent, money-making corporation with the help of nearly $2 billion in federal aid.

This assistance, needed to cover Conrail's substantial annual def-icit, helps in part to pay the salaries of the Corporation's 93,000 employes.

In the same way, the 330 employes of the U.S. Railway Associa-tion, which was established to monitor Conrail and act as its banker, are *not* considered government workers, despite the fact that their paychecks come from the U.S. Treasury.

An examination of the more than 1.1 million people—a number greater than that of the United States Army—whose salaries have been paid in whole or in part by HEW reveals the extent to which federal employment has been substantially *hidden*.

According to then-HEW Secretary Joseph Califano, HEW em-ployed 84,600 in state government, 572,700 in local government, 87,700 people in universities, 33,400 people in nonprofit research institutions, 113,900 employes in private contractors, and 88,900 in other areas.

During a Senate Appropriations subcommittee hearing at which Califano presented his figures, a surprised chairman, Sen. Warren Magnuson (D., Wash.) blurted out, "This is the best public service job program I have ever heard of. That is more than we give them for public service jobs."

Sen. Ernest Hollings (D., S.C.), adding up HEW's total work force, exclaimed, "My God, we are over a million."

An example of HEW employment through private contractors would be the Medicare program, under which HEW paid Blue Cross and Blue Shield and other health care groups to administer the program. The department reports that 26,537 employes of these groups were paid with HEW funds.

The Commerce Department's Minority Business Development Agency lists only 207 employes on its rolls. This is because it does not count approximately 1,600 other persons employed within 188 self-help, business counseling organizations whose salaries it directly finances.

The Army Corps of Engineers, which has 36,000 civilian employes, pays billions of dollars annually to contractors to carry out maintenance and construction work on rivers and harbors, irrigation and flood control projects and other facilities. Corps officials say they have no idea how many workers these firms employ with federal funds, but that "it must be in the thousands and thousands."

The Labor Department officially lists 22,377 in its employ, but through the Comprehensive Employment and Training Act (CETA) the department is paying the salaries of 750,000 state and local government workers under its public service jobs program. In addition, Labor finances paychecks for 77,000 state employes who work in the U.S. Employment Service and Unemployment Service offices around the country. "They come under the state governments," said a government expert, "but their paychecks are 100 percent paid for with federal revenues."

The National Science Foundation, whose annual budget amounts to $1 billion, estimates that about 68,000 people—primarily college and university professors and researchers—are employed either full time or part-time under 19,230 contracts and grants. The salaries for principal NSF grantees may be for a few summer months or much longer, but—when figured on an annualized basis—many are being paid at a rate of up to $47,500 per year.

Similarly excluded from the tally of government workers are Peace Corps volunteers and the VISTA anti-poverty workers—all of whom receive a regular income from ACTION, the government's volunteer service agency. There are nearly 7,000 Peace Corps workers and 3,250 VISTA volunteers.

In recent years, officials have responded to critics of big government by maintaining that the federal work force has remained largely stable despite the rapid growth in the federal budget. Government statistics show that the civilian work force *rose* from 2.1 million in 1950 to more than 2.8 million in 1978—an increase of about one-third. Yet, as we have seen, this figure is deceptive at best.

It should be noted that, in this same period, the number of state and local employes tripled to more than 12 million, largely as a result of the growth and demands of federal programs.

At the same time, Office of Management and Budget officials report that there has been a sharp rise in the government's use of outside consultants and contractors—in large part because of White House-imposed hiring ceilings—which in turn has kept the official government payroll figure from growing significantly. (It should however be pointed out that, by the middle of 1979, federal employment was up by more than 34,000 persons since Gerald Ford left office.)

"If they won't give you the additional personnel to perform your mission, there is no other choice but to hire outside your agency," one bureaucrat said. "And that is what has been happening increasingly for several years now."

Said a congressional Appropriations Committee staffer, "The government's total work force has grown sharply. It's just that much of it has been hidden from public view."

CHAPTER 3
Tracking the Beltway Bandits

To the unknowing eye, the gathering of 142 professionals strolling about the comfortable Orcas Island resort looked and acted much like any other business group out on an all-expense-paid weekend where work and pleasure are painlessly blended in just the right proportions. The spacious and well-appointed suites overlooking the breathtaking waters of Washington State's fabulously scenic San Juan Islands, the shrimp and prime rib dinners, the yacht trips around the islands—all reflected that special attention to details and lavish frills which an IBM or General Motors might provide for their top brass on a similar "business" weekend in the spectacular grandeur of the Pacific Northwest.

Surely no one would have guessed that this was a gathering of well-paid consultants and federal and state bureaucrats who had been summoned together to grapple with the problems of the poor—who seemed a million light-years away from this pristine locale, which had once been the magnificent estate of a wealthy shipping magnate. Nor would anyone have suspected that the entire weekend's tab was being picked up by the United States Department of Health, Education and Welfare, courtesy of the American taxpayer.

The occasion for the conference was to discuss the results of the government's experiments on the poor in Seattle and Denver, where low-income families were provided with a guaranteed minimum income for five years. The project—involving nearly 5,000 families—was, in the words of one prominent consultant, "the biggest social experiment in the history of the human race." And indeed it was. Conceivably the biggest welfare program in the history of the nation hung in the balance, not to mention many millions of dollars in future revenue for the consulting firms that have been nurturing and feeding the guaranteed income concept for the past decade and more.

But, for the consultant companies that attended the Orcas Island conference on the Seattle and Denver Income Maintenance Experiments (SIME/DIME), along with the HEW and Labor Department representatives, more than just money was involved. For many of those who were there, SIME/DIME was more than a social experiment: it was a cause.

16

Most Americans have never heard of SIME/DIME and would be surprised to hear that the federal government was providing a basic guaranteed annual income to the poor. Wasn't this Richard Nixon's ill-fated Family Assistance Plan (FAP) which had died ignominiously in the Congress? Wasn't this, furthermore, the very proposal Gerald Ford had adamantly rejected in his campaign to retain the presidency? And, finally, wasn't this the type of costly proposal which Jimmy Carter had told HEW Secretary Califano that the nation *could not afford*?

And yet, here it was, being kept alive administration after administration, like some comatose patient who has been declared clinically dead, but whose life-support functions were being artificially sustained by machine. A very different kind of machine was keeping this proposal alive, however, one that is peopled by a shadowy network of liberal planners, economists, sociologists, data analysts, and thinkers. Most of them, at one time or another, can be found working in the type of consulting firms represented at Orcas Island or somewhere within the federal bureaucracy. And most of them, through the years, have moved with ease through a "revolving door" system that takes them from consulting into government and back again.

But to understand the enormous influence which major consulting firms have over government policy, it is absolutely necessary to understand how *pervasive* the government's use of consulting has become.

Though not widely perceived beyond the banks of the Potomac, government consulting in Washington has multiplied into a $2 billion-a-year growth industry in which major corporations like Rand, Brookings, SRI International (formerly Stanford Research Institute), Mathematica, Inc., and the Urban Institute, among others, have grown rich and powerful. And, by becoming increasingly dependent upon them, the government has been able to get around maximum personnel ceilings simply by farming out more and more of its work, research, evaluation, and even program administration. For all its importance as an experimental project, SIME/DIME was being fully administered, not by HEW, but by SRI and Mathematica. The National Institute of Health farms out much of its administrative work to consulting firms. So do many other agencies.

There are no accurate figures on the number of consulting firms doing business with the federal government. One partial survey found that 64 departments and agencies were paying consultants nearly $2 billion a year under some 34,000 contracts. In 1977 the government placed some 18,000 consultants on its payroll, but this represented only the tip of the iceberg. One of the problems in measuring the number of consultants who work for the government is in deciding on a common definition of *what a consultant is*. We have seen from the figures in the previous chapter that, whatever definition one uses, the number of persons or firms who provide advice, recommendations, analysis, data, and studies on a consulting basis number in the hundreds of thousands.

Yet the growth in government consulting remains in part a mystery because of the widespread unanimity, both in and out of government, that a great deal of their work is *of negligible value*. In its fiscal 1978 report on HEW's appropriation bill, the Senate Appropriations Committee confessed it was "unaware of any instance where a consultant's recommendation has produced a significant program improvement."

The committee stated:

"An analysis of the itemized contracts let during fiscal years 1976 and 1977 indicated that many of these contracts may have been inappropriate in the context of (a) agency missions and priorities; (b) previous contracts performed for the same purpose; and (c) duplicative contracts being let simultaneously within other parts of the Department and Federal Government."

Nonetheless, HEW's consulting costs, like those of virtually every other federal agency, continue to climb. In fiscal 1977 HEW's consulting bill was *at least* $94 million. By 1978 it had grown to $194 million.

"They are like parasites who feed off the government," one committee investigator said. "They keep coming back year after year."

Predictably enough, therefore, many consultants have earned the notorious nickname "beltway bandits," a title which accurately characterizes both the annual haul of tax dollars that fill their corporate saddlebags as well as their office hideouts—the beltway encircling Greater Washington, where many of them conduct their business.

Said one former HEW administrator:

> They have become like another branch of government, an unseen branch, advising bureaucrats, developing policies, propelling programs through the machinery of government. But what is most disturbing is the network they have formed among themselves, both inside as well as outside of government.

Another former HEW administrator, John Svahn, who headed the Social and Rehabilitation Service, found this network to be particularly pervasive within the field of *social welfare* policy. "You see the same individuals dealing with the same programs on literally a revolving door basis," he said. "And it's true that there has been a sort of interlocking directorate among them. The same people tend to stay within a penumbra of social policy, whether they are in government or the private sector—except the people who are awarding the contracts one day are picking them up the next."

Perhaps two of the most influential consulting firms in Washington in the field of social welfare are the Urban Institute and Mathematica, Inc.

Sparked by his then-special assistant, Joseph Califano, President Lyndon Johnson pushed for the creation of the Urban Institute more than 11 years ago, believing that the need existed for a liberal think tank in Washington to research and analyze domestic programs and proposals. With the help of several million dollars in federal seed money, the Institute was founded and is today one of the major contractors with Departments such as Housing and Urban Development, HEW, and Labor. In 1978 HEW gave the Institute about $3 million in consulting contracts.

With a payroll of almost $7 million a year, the Institute provides work for 300 researchers, data analysts and others whose work brings in $11 million annually in revenue. If the Institute is not exactly an extension of the federal government, it might as well be, because more than 86 percent of its income comes from 22 federal departments and agencies. The balance is derived from state and local governments, foundations, and private corporations.

Besides its prolific studies, the Institute is equally admired in Washington's upper circles for its elegant, catered dinners where government policymakers, administrators, members of Congress, academics, and fellow consultants gather to hear speakers and exchange views on everything from housing allowance experiments to microanalytic simulation.

A guest of the Institute recalled one of its "welfare symposia" affairs this way:

> Cocktails began at 6:30 p.m. There were bars everywhere. This was followed by a buffet served by tuxedoed waiters, most or all of them Spanish-speaking. The menu included boeuf bourguignon, watercress salad, eclairs. The silver was Reed and Barton.

Mathematica, Inc. was established in 1958 by a group of Princeton professors who occasionally did some data analysis for the government and found that consulting for the government was much more lucrative than teaching at Princeton. Last year the firm and its several subsidiaries in Washington and Princeton, New Jersey, earned $23 million—80 percent of it from the federal government.

Armed with a staff of 600 employes, Mathematica's annual report boasted to shareholders that the firm has "opened new business potential in information processing for government agencies."

Both the Institute and Mathematica have played a significant, though little-known, role in the shaping of welfare policy and welfare reform proposals over the past decade. Their influence is derived in large measure from their development of a highly sophisticated *data model* used to project costs of everything from food stamps to welfare reform to a guaranteed annual income.

Called the Transfer Income Model, or TRIM, the model was initially developed by a group of Urban Institute economists under a $1 million government contract. Many of these key economists— including Jodie Allen, who became a special assistant for welfare reform to Labor Secretary Ray Marshall—left the Institute for positions with Mathematica, and they took the TRIM model with them. With the support of additional government financing, primarily from HEW and the Office of Economic Opportunity, both firms improved the TRIM (Mathematica renamed theirs MATH) model and began selling its data to any federal agency needing cost estimates on income transfer programs. Thus, TRIM and its successors have been used to estimate, and in many ways shape, virtually every major welfare proposal for the past ten years. HEW, Labor, the Internal Revenue Service, HUD, the Congressional Budget Office, and the Library of Congress' Congressional Research Service are just some of the agencies which have used its data.

"There was enormous power being wielded here by these two consulting firms," one congressional investigator said. "The decisions that Nixon made on FAP and Ford on his income supplement proposal, plus other actions by the Congress on food stamp reform and social welfare, were by and large based on the figures derived from TRIM." Said another congressional staffer who has followed the battle over welfare reform closely:

> In every battle over a controversial proposal the side that usually wins is the side with the best information, the most convincing statistics. Right now consulting groups like the Urban Institute and Mathematica have control of the best data available.

Svahn agreed that those who control to a substantial degree the input of information control the decision-making process of government. "You can't argue with a computer," he said. "But the models are not totally objective because they are based on certain biased assumptions." These assumptions have been made by people in and out of government who are champions of the guaranteed annual income concept.

Even the most cursory review of the last ten years of welfare reform proposals finds the *same names* cropping up again and again, criss-crossing both government and consulting fields as if they were one and the same, and frequently in key positions of authority and influence. Virtually all of them represent one common point of view—a club within a club:

—William Morrill, HEW's assistant secretary for Planning and Evaluation between 1973 and 1976, whose office contracted for much of the research that contributed to the development of FAP, became a senior fellow at Mathematica.

—Henry Aaron held Morrill's old job as HEW's assistant secretary for Planning and Evaluation and has worked for several major consulting firms, including the Urban Institute, Brookings, and Rand.

—Jodie T. Allen served as chief of research and policy coordination for the Family Assistance Plan in HEW from 1969 to 1970, later becoming senior vice president at Mathematica from 1974 to 1977. She then became Labor Secretary Ray Marshall's special assistant for welfare reform.

—Richard Nathan served as a deputy undersecretary for welfare reform under HEW Secretary Elliot Richardson and was a major force behind FAP. Nathan returned to Brookings.

—Raymond Struyk, a former Urban Institute official, was a deputy assistant secretary in HUD's Office of Research and Demonstration (which in 1977 did *$3.1 million* worth of business with his former firm).

All of this has raised substantial questions about the appearance of conflicts as well as about the ability of top government officials to make fair and dispassionate decisions and judgments on tough and highly controversial issues. In an interview with Jodie Allen, during which she went to great lengths to demonstrate her total un-involvement with her former firm, she made a remark about her task in the Labor Department which I thought revealed a great deal about the approach being taken to test the jobs component of the Carter administration's welfare reform program. Said Allen, "I want to make it work. I want to see it succeed." One could not blame her for such enthusiasm, but neither could one help wondering how such an

"experiment" or "pilot program" could be truly impartial and un-
prejudiced, with one of its chief administrators actively working in
its behalf.

Four months after he took office, Jimmy Carter issued a memorandum to the heads of his executive departments and agencies saying,
"There has been and continues to be evidence that some consulting
services, including experts and advisors, are being used excessively,
unnecessarily, and improperly."

Among many areas of abuse, Mr. Carter cited "revolving door
abuses," whereby former government employes "may be improperly
favored for individual or contracted consulting arrangements." But
the abuses only began there.

A *Washington Post* investigation found top officials of the Appa-
lachian Regional Commission had received fat consulting contracts—as a sort of severence pay—when they left the antipoverty
agency. Harry Teter Jr., who resigned in July of 1978 as executive
director of the agency, was given $35,000 for a six-month review of
his years at the commission. Other top officials who resigned or
retired received similar consulting contracts, in one case as high as
$75,000.

At the same time, an HEW investigation revealed that *friends and
relatives* of officials at the National Institute on Drug Abuse had obtained millions of dollars in consulting contracts. HEW Inspector
General Thomas D. Morris said there was "a substantial appearance
of impropriety," and Secretary Califano stated he was "deeply disturbed" with the loose management practices and evidences of
cronyism.

"What bugs me about these consulting expenditures," said a House
committee investigator, "is the repetition. You find the same titles for
contracts every year. How many times has Head Start been evaluated? Or migrants? An enormous amount of money has been spent
on studying the aged."

The excessive degree to which consulting firms are being used by
the government can be seen in the planning papers of the Federal
Home Loan Bank Board's new $47 million building, whose ameni-
ties include a *skating rink* and an expensive *French restaurant*. The
consulting costs included $40,000 to negotiate leases for the build-
ing's retail space; $30,000 for "planning, developing, and market-
ing" of the commercial space; $9,300 to determine the eating facility

needs in the new building; $5,000 to go over the list of potential restaurant operators; $4,500 to "review and recommend" the restaurant operator's plans; $2,000 for an analysis of Washington area skating rinks; and $63,000 for a legal opinion on whether the FHLBB could lease out commercial space in the first place.

One of the questions I raised repeatedly during my own inquiry into this shadowy world of government consultants was whether the thousands of studies and reports prepared by this enormous industry were read by anyone. Many of them are widely disseminated to agency officials and appropriate congressional committees. Many others, contract officials said, are simply "dumped" into the government's data retrieval bank and forgotten.

Pointing to a three-inch thick computer printout of consulting contracts, an HEW official said, "There aren't enough people in the government to read all of these studies."

Said another government official, "That is a question I have been asking myself for eight years. We've been doing some of these studies time and again since the Johnson administration."

Clearly, the bulk of them are unneeded. Asked about a $24,000 analysis of the Work Incentive Program (WIN), the contracting officer replied, "It shouldn't have been done. We asked them to tell us whether the WIN program was having a net effect on hiring poor, unemployed workers. They (the Urban Institute) came back—after spending $24,000—and said, You can't answer that question with the limited program data available."

The Department of Housing and Urban Development spent $62 million on consultant studies of one kind or another in 1978. Congressional critics said a great deal of these contracted studies were unnecessary and constituted a waste of taxpayer's money. The HUD contracts included $143,000 for research and development of residential flooring systems; $189,000 to develop a citizen participation catalogue; $246,000 for a home improvement finance analysis; and $220,000 to produce a local government productivity handbook.

HUD has also issued $3.5 million in contracts, in part for the purpose of holding workshops around the country in order that state and local officials could discuss government finance problems. The U.S. Conference of Mayors got $49,254 for telephone interviews with mayors and other municipal officials on financial management needs. The International City Management Association got $43,000 to hold financial management workshops for city managers. The

Municipal Finance Officers Association obtained $96,280 for a financial management survey in six states—a program which a knowledgeable Senate budget expert called "ridiculous. It won't change any local or state financial capacity."

There is also a great deal of *duplication* in the bureaucracy's zeal to purchase consulting services. In one too-typical case, *four different* evaluation contracts were let by HEW's Office of Child Abuse, totaling $831,000, while the National Center for Health Services Research spent $300,000 to study the "abuse and neglect of children." And a third agency within HEW spent $49,000 to develop a guide for services to abused and neglected children.

A report to Congress on HEW's consulting activities said, "Nearly all the contracts let by the Office of the Secretary (of HEW) appear duplicative of operating agency activities." The report concluded rather appropriately, "So many of the contract descriptions throughout HEW smack of attempts to reinvent the wheel."

CHAPTER 4
Paying the Special Interests

We have heard a great deal about the rise of the "special interests" in recent years. What few people realize is that the federal government is financing a good many of them.

Indeed, the government is pouring hundreds of millions of dollars into a multitude of lobbying organizations, "public interest" law firms, and a wide assortment of associations and special interest groups across the country.

While the money going to these organizations, which number in the thousands, is increasing each year, little is known about how they spend these tax dollars, who receives these funds, and who ultimately benefits from their subsidized activities. Although their staffs are in many instances fully financed by the government, these groups are rarely if ever examined by Congress as to how they spend these funds. Yet their income is often used to influence federal legislation and government policies—affecting everything from food stamps to ERA.

As more and more funding is becoming available through grants, contracts, and awards, many of these lobbying and advocacy groups are establishing tax-exempt *spin-off groups* or so-called educational and research conduits, through which the federal funds are spent.

So many private groups and associations are receiving federal funding of one type or another that it is not uncommon to hear federal officials ask, "Do you know of anyone who *isn't* getting federal money?"

An examination of government records reveals a seemingly endless list of these subsidized organizations. Many of them are well-staffed, financially well-heeled, and often deeply involved in political action, grass-roots organizing, and various public advocacy and legislative lobbying activities and causes. More important, there is substantial evidence that our tax dollars are often indirectly supporting the lobbying programs of many of these special interest groups. This is occurring despite the fact that federal law clearly states that it is *illegal* for federal funds to be used "directly or indirectly" to influence a member of Congress in his legislative duties.

Among some of the biggest recipients of federal funding is the U.S. Conference of Mayors, which has a total budget of nearly $3 million;

the National Governors Association, whose total budget is over $3.5 million; and the National League of Cities, which receives over $2.7 million annually in government grants and contracts.

In federal funds alone, the Conference of Mayors received more than $1.6 million in fiscal 1978, while the Governors Association was expected to obtain, in 1979, close to $2 million in federal grants and contracts.

The Conference's well-appointed suites cover five floors of a modern office building near the White House. It employs 95 persons requiring a yearly payroll of $938,490 in addition to $738,000 in overhead costs. The organization's spokesman, Eugene Russell, explained that the federal grants and contracts are fulfilled by the Conference's tax-exempt and federally-supported Research and Education Foundation. (At the same time, its lobbying activities are handled by a separate staff, whose salaries and support costs come from the dues paid by some 600 cities who are members of the organization. The entire organization, however, works *together* like one well-oiled machine.)

As its executive director and chief lobbyist, John Gunther, explained, the Conference's lobbyists make frequent use of its federally-financed data, studies, and contract officers. "We do get a lot of information out of it (the tax-supported Research and Education Foundation) which we use in our lobbying efforts . . . I'm always looking up stuff in their reports."

What kind of contracts do these organizations receive? Here's a sampling from the Department of Housing and Urban Development contract catalogue:

—$75,000 to the National League of Cities to prepare and distribute a film about urban conservation.

—$90,000 to the U.S. Conference of Mayors to hold a series of seminars to discuss local financial management and other HUD-related topics.

—$35,073 to the National Association of Counties "to identify specific county government financial management needs and priorities and provide a forum for county officials to share information and resources in finance."

—$262,035 to the National Hispanic Coalition for Better Housing to provide, in part, "a channel for input from such groups to HUD," a project which one knowledgeable Senate Appropriations Committee aide called "nothing more than thinly disguised lobbying."

By using a little old free enterprise initiative to obtain as many federal bucks as possible, many of these non-profit organizations and other groups are getting funding *simultaneously* from dozens of different programs and agencies.

For example, the Conference of Mayors is funded by at least 15 different departments and agencies, including HUD, HEW, Commerce, Labor, Transportation, the National Endowment for the Humanities, the State Department, and the National Science Foundation.

As can happen under the circumstances, many agencies are totally unaware that they are all financing the same project, service or report. And these organizations take full advantage of this bureaucratic confusion by shopping around for as much funding as their bank accounts can hold. For instance, six different federal departments and agencies financed a conference of 60 women organized by a non-profit group known as Rural American Women (RAW), a small Washington-based organization that also got money from the Democratic National Committee. Each of these agencies gave Rural American Women about $5,000 and several expected to receive reports on what the conference accomplished; inquiries revealed that HEW (but also the Environmental Protection Agency!) received the group's 17-page report—most of which dealt with *how to hold a conference*. The Minority Business Development Agency spent $6,000 for the purpose of video-taping these proceedings.

The Washington-based National Association of Counties has 120 employes and receives about $2.5 million in various government contracts. And where does the money spent on these contracts go? County officials say about 25 percent of it pays for overhead costs, 50 percent goes for salaries, and the balance for travel, supplies, and printing expenses.

In addition to its $2 million in federal funding, the Governors Association receives about $1.6 million annually from the states to pay for its nine Washington lobbyists. The Association created the Center for Policy Research to act as its recipient of federal funds.

"There's no question that we are here to get more money for these programs (revenue sharing, block grants, etc.)," said one Center official, who took pains to point out that the research being done with federal funds is often "valuable to governors as lobbyists" when they testify and push for federal programs before Congress.

Are these grants and similar funding projects to these organizations worth while? The organizations who stealthily hunt for these federal dollars obviously think they are. But others disagree, including some

of the people who work for these very organizations. In the words
of one official from one of the groups singled out here:

> I happen to believe that a lot of it is a crock. But we didn't build the
> system. The Feds built it and we have to play the game, otherwise we
> would be opting out to the other special interests.

Thus, one can see the *predatory nature* of this expensive "game." It
is beat the other special interests to the bucks or be beaten.

A less understood objective in this game is the degree to which
these grants and contracts are geared solely toward building support
among special interest groups for certain federal programs.

"If I had to reduce it to its baldest terms," one organization official
said, "a number of the grants have been used by people in the federal
agencies who want a program started and want the support of our
organization." Said another special interest group spokesman, "Some
of this funding is obviously aimed at getting our support for certain
programs."

Yet one question persistently crops up. To what extent does federal
funding—no matter how well segregated—spill over into an organization's lobbying operations?

The National Conference of State Legislatures, with offices in Denver and Washington, gets nearly $1.4 million in federal funds, and
an additional $1.7 million from the states. It has 30 employes in
Washington, where the lobbying operation is run, and 60 persons in
Denver, where most but not all of its federal contract work is done.

While Karl Kurtz, director of operations, said the two activities
were kept totally separate, he added that "some of the rent here is
charged to those grants." Asked what would happen if federal funds
were cut off, Kurtz said, "It would probably change the level of
technical services we provide state legislatures." The question to be
asked is, Why should the federal government be providing state legislatures with *any* services?

"The purpose of most of these groups is to influence legislation
and public policies," said a prominent Washington attorney whose
career began in the public interest movement. This lawyer estimated
that public interest and consumer-oriented groups alone receive about
$100 million a year in federal grants and contracts.

"Their traditional sources of financing are drying up," he said,
"so the only place left to look to is the government."

Some federal funding for these and other so-called public interest
groups is being done, in part, through "public participation" grants.
The major premise for this program is that those groups who cannot

afford to present their views in a federal proceeding—such as a Federal Trade Commission hearing—shall be reimbursed for their costs. It just happens that the organizations being subsidized to present their views before the FTC almost universally support the position of the FTC.

While the Federal Trade Commission is the only agency specifically authorized by law to make such payments, other agencies are also issuing grants to similar groups under a controversial Justice Department opinion suggesting that an agency's authorizing legislation gives it the necessary authority to make such payments to whatever groups it chooses.

Meanwhile, an examination of groups funded by the FTC—some of whom have received more than $100,000 in legal and other overhead costs—reveals that many are *well-off financially*. It is also evident that much "public participation" money is going to lawyers. Out of a total of $1.8 million in FTC public participation funding, documents show that more than $813,000 went to pay attorneys fees and attorney-related disbursements, including travel costs and secretarial salaries.

Some of the recipients of FTC payments have included the liberal political activist group, Americans for Democratic Action; Consumers Union, publisher of the successful consumer magazine; the Consumer Federation of America, perhaps the nation's largest consumer group; and the National Consumer Law Center, which receives funds from a number of federal sources, including nearly $500,000 from Legal Services in a single year.

The ADA (Americans for Democratic Action) is listed on FTC records as the recipient of more than $177,000; this financed the ADA's participation in agency proceedings on everything from health spas to antacids. But appearances can be deceiving. ADA executive director Leon Shull said that "not one penny" of that money came to the ADA national office. According to Shull, it was channeled through the ADA's Consumer Affairs Committee, run by Ann Brown, an ADA national board member who operated the committee out of her home. But Ann Brown and her committee received little if any of the money either; it went instead to a busy Washington lawyer, who handled the committee's FTC presentations, and who received *and spent* virtually all of the money. The attorney in question employed nine other lawyers to handle this and other federally-funded accounts.

Has the ADA, with its seeming separation of responsibility between the parent group, a committee, and its attorney, benefited from these federal funds? Of course, because taxpayers are paying a lawyer to present—under the guise of representing some faceless, nameless group of consumers—the ADA's views before the government. The attorney, by the way, said in an interview that the views he presented before the FTC hearings also represented the views of the national ADA.

By now it should be clear that there is hardly a department or agency in the government that is not giving tax dollars to some group, association or special interest for one purpose or another. While I have chosen to concentrate here on some of the major lobbying groups, organizations of virtually every size, shape, and purpose have jumped aboard the gravy train.

For example, recipients of $33.2 million in yearly grants made by the International Communications Agency include such organizations as the American Bar Association, the American Political Science Association, the National 4-H Council, the YMCA, and even the U.S. Lawn Tennis Association. The grants run the gamut from conducting an exchange program for Latin American theatre critics to symposiums for South American journalists to world travel for young American political leaders, business executives, lecturers, and athletic directors.

ACTION, the volunteer service agency which runs the Peace Corps and VISTA, gives about $4 million annually to numerous leftist grassroots organizations and political advocacy groups. A House investigating committee in 1979 found many of these groups were involved in labor union organizing, political activities, and legislative lobbying.

A typical ACTION beneficiary, Midwest Academy, which is a training institution for community activists, was found to have issued federally-financed training brochures urging trainees to "give people a 'taste of blood.' Push your opponents so hard you can see them squirm."

Other legal research and social and political advocacy organizations around the country are also receiving funds from Legal Services, the government's corps of poverty lawyers. An examination of these grants and contracts shows that much of this money is supporting legal suits against the states. The special interest groups spending this money hope that, through the courts, they can achieve social changes they could not possibly win in the Congress or in the state legislatures. Funds to these organizations are financing suits against federal officials and state and municipal governments involving Indian land rights, hiring policies, welfare reform, food stamp regulations, student rights, and even due process in school discipline procedures.

In the final analysis, virtually all of this spending is *unnecessary and wasteful*. It serves only to further enrich many wealthy and profitable groups and companies whose bank accounts are kept fat with federal contracts and grants. It has acted as an irresistible lure to countless *other* special interest groups whose primary purpose for being seems to be to think up ways of snaring more and more federal money which the government is quite eager to give away for almost any conceivable purpose. It has also created a shadowy world of conduits, special interest organizations, and government-funded lobbyists who have to a large degree become an *unseen and unmonitored spending arm* of the government. All too often, this money— perhaps in the billions of dollars—is being frittered away on useless, ludicrous, and often self-serving programs which, by any objective measurement, have not improved the lives of our nation's citizens.

CHAPTER 5
The Forgotten Agencies

For more than 187 years, the Annual Assay Commission met to do the job it had been faithfully performing since April 2, 1792, even though government officials said it was an agency that no longer performed a useful function.

The four-member commission, one of the oldest agencies in the federal government, had the duty of measuring the precious metal content and weight of the nation's coinage since the days when money really was measured in silver and gold.

Since our coins contained primarily non-precious metal alloys, there was little if any need for the agency to assay coins as it had almost since the beginning of the Republic. Whatever testing was needed was done by the National Bureau of Standards.

"It was largely a ceremonial exercise," said a Treasury Department official. "It no longer served a useful function."

The commission had a budget of only $2,500 a year to cover the costs of its annual ritual, and Congress in late 1979 was considering legislation to abolish it. While in dollars and cents it didn't amount to a hill of beans, the agency was typical of many "forgotten agencies," large and small, which are scattered throughout the federal bureaucracy. Some, established on a temporary basis, have never met their original goals, despite decades of lethargic existence. Others have survived long after their original purpose was achieved. Some are so obscure they exist without full or regular congressional oversight of their activities and expenditures. Here are a few examples:

—The 12-member Franklin Delano Roosevelt Memorial Commission, created in 1955, was in 1979 still continuing its seemingly unending search for a suitable monument to FDR's memory, despite evidence that Mr. Roosevelt informed close friends he didn't want one. Yet after two decades of work and intergovernmental bickering, not to mention the spending of more than $400,000, it hadn't completed its designated task. Two different designs for a memorial have been rejected. A third is pending before Congress.

—Although it has been over a century since Uncle Sam last herded Indians onto reservations, the Navajo and Hopi Indian Relocation Commission was still moving Indians from one place to another in spite of considerable resistance from the two tribes.

—In 1942 President Roosevelt established the Joint Mexican-United States Defense Commission to coordinate defense activities against the Nazis. The commission still exists, holding what one Pentagon official described as "formal gatherings, formal luncheons" each year.

—An obscure office within the Department of Housing and Urban Development spends its time issuing studies on foreign countries and literature about the European influence on American communities and New Towns in the Soviet Union.

The American Battle Monuments Commission began in 1923 under General John J. Pershing. Today it oversees 23 military cemeteries abroad plus 14 monuments and memorials to our armed forces. The agency has a paid staff of 388, including eight U.S. Army officers. Congressional appropriations committee experts contend the commission's work could be handled by the Army.

Though not widely known, the federal government has been selling insurance abroad, providing policies to America's biggest corporations to protect them against the risks of war, expropriation of property, and currency inconvertibility.

Since the Overseas Private Investment Corporation was created in 1969 to provide both insurance and loan-guarantees for U.S. investors abroad, it has written billions of dollars' worth of policies, mostly for firms on *Fortune's* list of 500 wealthiest corporations and 50 largest banks in America.

Stung by reports about OPIC's low interest loans to resorts for the rich like Haiti's ultra-lavish Habitation Leclerc, Congress tried several years ago to end its insurance-writing function, but the agency managed to survive and grow, and continues to this day.

The Navajo and Hopi Indian Relocation Commission was enacted in 1974 to solve a complex and long-standing land battle between the tribes over grazing and other rights on some 2.5 million acres in Arizona. The commission was authorized by Congress to move some 5,750 Indians, voluntarily if possible, paying moving costs and other benefits to purchase new homes. Since 1974 the three-member commission has relocated only 80 families. The panel pays a $5,000 bonus to any family who voluntarily relocates now. What will happen to those families who refuse to move is anybody's guess. Thus, about a hundred years after the last Indian treaty was signed, the United States is still moving Indians from one land to another.

Each agency and program in the government must be fully reviewed, by both houses of Congress, for approval of its annual budget and for periodic renewal of its operating authority. But there was at least one agency that managed, for a time, to elude full congressional oversight. It was the Office of Minority Business Enterprise (now called the Minority Business Development Agency), created by President Nixon in 1969 as part of his "black capitalism" campaign. The office was budgeted at $50 million a year, but no Senate legislative committee had responsibility over the agency—that is, oversight responsibility to insure the agency performed the way Congress intended.

Incredible as it may seem, one committee official in the Senate confessed, "It just fell through the cracks. No one has authorization oversight over OMBE in the Senate."

OMBE had appeared regularly before the Senate Appropriations sub-committee for budget approval as well as the appropriate House panels. But the Senate Select Small Business Committee—which should have had jurisdiction over it—had never held hearings on the agency's program authority. The Senate eventually rectified this oversight, once it was brought to their attention, but it serves as an example of the way expensive and relatively ambitious programs can simply elude oversight by Congress.

Staffed by 207 workers, OMBE supports 188 business development organizations whose 1,600 federally paid employes provide consulting services for minority businessmen nationwide.

Other government agencies providing financial services and assistance for small businesses, including those operated by minorities, are the Small Business Administration, the Economic Development Administration, the Community Services Administration, the Department of Agriculture's rural development programs, and many others.

"There is no reason why the SBA can't perform this function, if indeed this function needs to be performed at all," said a Senate staffer experienced in small business programs.

Meanwhile, deep within the recesses of the Department of Housing and Urban Development lies the Office of International Affairs (OIA) which, HUD's promotional literature explains, has been "the pioneer in international urban development for almost three decades." Despite this evident longevity, several veteran congressional aides knowledgeable in housing programs expressed ignorance that HUD was involved in foreign matters.

With a staff of 13, OIA issues, among other things, housing and urban development profiles on foreign countries for American businessmen "interested in foreign business opportunities and investments."

One OIA booklet deals with the subject: "The Influence of the Foreign Heritage on the American City." Another analyzes the growth, organization, and resources of New Towns in the Soviet Union. The agency also maintains a computer bank filled with more than 7,000 documents on housing and urban development.

Significantly, the Office of Management and Budget has for several years urged that OIA's activities be turned over to the State Department which, after all, is responsible for this nation's foreign affairs. OIA's activities, however, might best be *dropped altogether*.

Since 1954 the Foreign Claims Settlement Commission has been adjudicating American repayment claims for property seized or destroyed in foreign countries. Now, after a quarter of a century of operation, many government officials say there are not enough remaining claims to warrant a separate agency.

Staffed by 30 employes plus three commissioners, each of whom are paid $47,500 a year, the agency's annual budget is about $1 million.

The commission had been focusing on East German claims, of which nearly 4,000 came in, but the deadline has since passed. It has completed processing 384 claims on property in China worth some $200 million, plus 5,911 Cuban claims totaling $1.8 billion. Once claims are cleared by the agency, they are turned over to the State Department for negotiation of payment. This is a perfect example of an agency whose usefulness has long since passed. It should be absorbed by either the State or Justice Department.

Has Congress seriously studied this agency and considered such an option? Of course not. Most members of Congress couldn't tell you a thing about the Foreign Claims Settlement Commission or the last time it was examined in any fundamental way. One top staff official of the Senate Foreign Relations Committee—which has oversight responsibility for the agency—told a reporter:

> We just don't have time to look at agencies like this. We have to be concerned with much larger subjects—SALT, the Panama Canal treaties, China. We have to let agencies like this one go by the board.

In the area of government duplication, one can find no better example than two of the government's oldest agencies which have been performing much the same function in related fields: the Bureau of Customs, created in 1789, and the Immigration Service, established in 1891.

Customs has some 5,000 inspectors at 300 points of entry checking for contraband, collecting duty fees, and verifying import cargo; 1,543 Immigration Service inspectors fulfill a largely similar inspection and clearance mission at border crossings and points of entry. There is no reason why their missions cannot be combined into a *single* agency.

"Their roles are very similar," said one budget official. "It's been demonstrated that both can handle the same assignment. There's no need to have two agents, in different uniforms, performing essentially the same kind of job."

The 26-member Advisory Commission on Intergovernmental Relations was begun in 1959 under the Eisenhower administration to recommend improvements in dealings between the federal and local governments. It has a budget of about $1.5 million a year and 35 employes. The commission meets about four times a year.

One of the commission's biggest accomplishments was a 14-volume study on federal grants and aid programs. The panel also publishes a quarterly magazine that goes to 25,000 federal, state, and local government officials, plus numerous studies like "Trends in Metropolitan America" and "Who Should Pay for Public Schools?".

The number of such "forgotten agencies" is seemingly inexhaustible, with many of them duplicative, unnecessary or outdated.

When I last looked there were at least five government committees for the handicapped: Advisory Council on Employment of the Handicapped; Committee for Purchase from the Blind and Other Severely Handicapped; National Center for Education Media and Materials for the Handicapped; National Planning and Advisory Council of the White House Conference on Handicapped Individuals; and the President's Committee on Employment of the Handicapped.

It must be pointed out that while many of these agencies appear relatively small in terms of their budgets and numbers of employes, there are many hidden costs associated with all of them which their budgets do not reflect. Their very existence generates other, *unseen* expenses which must also be borne by taxpayers—preparation of background investigations on appointed officials, reports, documents, travel costs, pensions and other benefits upon retirement, congressional as well as executive branch oversight responsibilities, civil service forms and other records which must be prepared and maintained, along with other costs inflicted by the bureaucracy.

Showing that a great deal of government deadwood exists is one thing, but getting rid of it is a different matter altogether.

"There is no agency so small or so poor that it does not have a group somewhere to support its function, whatever that may be," said a top Carter administration official.

He was of course right. Even the Annual Assay Commission had its supporters among coin collectors and vending machine operators.

Meanwhile, the federal bureaucracy can be so resilient that even agencies faced with total dissolution manage to spring back to life again.

A case in point was the Advisory Commission on Information, begun in 1948 under President Truman. It had a staff of three and a budget of $83,000 a year.

The five-member commission was about to go out of business as part of the Carter administration's merger of the U.S. Information Agency and the State Department's Bureau of Cultural and Educational Affairs. The new agency is called the International Communications Agency. But the advisory commission, which held only four meetings in 1978, and which issues only one report a year, was enlarged by Congress into a seven-member panel to continue dispensing the dispensable advice it has provided for more than three decades.

CHAPTER 6
Uncle Sam the Travelin' Man

When Secretary of Labor Ray Marshall and two of his top aides flew to conferences in Geneva and Bonn on official government business, they traveled—as do many high federal officials—first class all the way.

The spacious seats, champagne, and gourmet meals available in the first-class section to Mr. Marshall and his friends cost taxpayers $1,484 each. That was almost 40 percent more than economy class, which government officials, with rare exceptions, are supposed to use.

But Marshall is not alone in his upper class preference for the best in travel accommodations, though some top officials like Max Cleland, the triple amputee who heads the Veterans Administration, always travel economy.

An examination of government travel costs—which now total nearly $8 billion a year—reveals that many officials routinely travel first class. But that is *the least* of their abuses. My investigation also found:

—Officials of the World Bank, which receives much of its funds from the United States, took nearly 600 trips in 1977 on the costly supersonic airplane Concorde. It also frequently pays full travel costs for officials' wives.

—Many federal officials were found to have never filed a report of any kind with their agency detailing what they had accomplished on extensive trips abroad.

—Wives of federal officials were also found to have accompanied their husbands, at government expense, for so-called public relations purposes, solely to attend social activities such as banquets, cocktail parties, and other social gatherings.

—Government planes, equipped with every convenience, have often been used to fly officials to places which could have been reached more inexpensively if our public servants had flown commercial. Moreover, federal aircraft have been used to transport officials to conventions, air shows, and social events.

First-class travel continues to be predominant at the World Bank, which administers a $40 billion loan program for the impoverished countries of the world. In a single year, more than 7,800 trips cost the Bank over $12 million. Most routine travel remains first class, and in many cases it has been on the luxurious Concorde, the most costly commercial transportation available today. At the time, the Concorde's $1,683 round-trip fare to London, which the Bank gladly paid, was more than twice the $678 coach fare for a regular jet it could have chosen instead.

The Bank defended the use of the Concorde, arguing that the faster flight time reduced lost man hours spent in flight and thus saved money. But a Senate investigator who examined the Bank's travel practices said this rationale was "as phony as it could be. No one else in the government, no matter how important their mission, flies the Concorde." But perhaps nothing is too good for people who are seeking to help the world's starving poor.

According to the Bank's spokesmen, first-class travel was allowed when officials had to fly farther than 5,000 to 6,000 miles. Since most of the Bank's business is in Asia, South America, and Africa, at least 98 percent of its travel was first class. Tighter travel restrictions instituted by the Bank in March 1978 are said to have reduced first-class travel somewhat, but it still accounts for nearly 50 percent of their travel bill.

The argument for this extra luxury paid for by the American taxpayer goes this way: Since officials often spend up to three months of the year and more traveling, the more comfortable accommodations ease the burden of long distance flights. "After the first year or two, it's not a joyride anymore," one official said.

Yet State Department officials travel equally long distances, and just as often, but 98 percent of their travel is economy class.

"That's a lot of baloney," a State Department official said of the Bank's defense of first-class travel. "Many State employes travel three months or more each year but we still go economy."

But the Bank's little luxuries don't end there. It also provides free transportation for *spouses* of eligible employes—figured under a complex point system based in part on years employed—which it argues is needed "to keep up morale."

When a Bank official took his wife along on a global six-nation business trip to Honolulu, Tokyo, Manila, Jakarta, New Delhi, and Rome, the Bank gladly picked up the entire tab for their $3,250 first-class airfare.

In a single year the Bank spent more than half a million dollars on trips for spouses. Similarly, the Inter-American Development Bank, which receives more than half of its funding from the United States for loans to poor countries, also provides travel for wives of its officials.

In one case, the Inter-American Bank paid $4,000 so an official's wife could accompany him to the Philippines, India, Singapore, Japan, and France. On another trip, a wife traveled with her husband to Denmark, Belgium, Spain, Switzerland, and Yugoslavia, adding $1,879 in first-class air fare.

Congress has been unable to substantially curtail the travel of either bank since both were created as autonomous international bodies governed by directors representing member countries. Indeed, congressional committees have often found it difficult even to obtain information about their travel practices. Typically, when a reporter requested a list of trips by World Bank President Robert McNamara, he was turned down by a public information officer who said, "I don't think we ought to be accountable in detail to the public at large."

Meanwhile, within the executive branch agencies, where there is supposed to be some kind of accountability, bureaucrats are flying all over the place for all sort of reasons.

When 16 top Federal Aviation Administration officials flew to Oshkosh, Wisconsin, for the day aboard an FAA turboprop Grumman Gulfstream to attend the annual Experimental Aircraft Association show, they were of course just doing what comes naturally to any government bureaucrat.

Airplane buffs from around the country flock by the thousands to see the assortment of flying machines people have built in their garages and backyards. FAA spokesman Fred Fararr explained that the contingent of agency officials visited the show "just to get an idea of what's happening in the field." (They could have asked their regional officials to send them a report, because a flock of regional FAA officers also attended the air show.)

But the air fair must have been terribly important, for FAA Administrator Langhorne Bond also flew up to Oshkosh in an FAA Cessna twin jet, which comfortably seats five, to speak and present an award. Bond's only other passenger on his gas-guzzling jet was an aide to a California congressman who is a member of the House aviation subcommittee which has jurisdiction over Bond's agency. When questioned, the aide said he accompanied Bond because of his boss' work on the aviation panel, but a subcommittee official said the panel had never examined the subject of home-built aircraft. The aide, however, who is also a licensed pilot, confessed that, while at the show, he picked up some plans to build a single engine Christen Eagle.

It was a very expensive shopping trip. Bond's excursion round trip cost taxpayers $1,381. Commercial tickets would have cost $352.

Another FAA plane trip—which took the Department of Transportation's number two information officer, Robert Holland, and two other officials to Fond Du Lac, Wisconsin, to attend the National Aerobatic Competition—cost $1,332. Commercial would have cost $528. An FAA spokesman said that regional FAA safety enforcement officials were also at the aerobatic show.

Meanwhile, one warm July weekend, Deputy DOT Secretary Alan Butchman flew to Boston on a Friday to inspect the Transportation Systems Center, a DOT-funded research and development facility.

After four hours at the center, Butchman flew to nearby Martha's Vineyard where he spent the rest of the weekend, returning to Washington on Monday. A spokesman for DOT said Butchman reimbursed the department $30 for the added cost of his sidetrip to the resort island. But the trip hardly seemed essential in the first place. An official at the Boston center noted that, four days before Butchman's trip, two other DOT officials had also toured the center in what he described as "a fairly extensive visit."

In the grand scheme of things, few will remember that trips like these ever took place. Thousands like them are made every day by officials throughout the government. It is estimated that there are probably more than 20,000 federal bureaucrats in the air on any given day. The administration's spending budget for fiscal 1980 called for $3.1 billion in personnel travel and $4.8 billion for moving office materials, federal property, and the household goods of civilian employes and military personnel.

Much of this travel, government investigators found, has been unnecessary and wasteful. In an audit of the travel practices of five departments and agencies, the General Accounting Office found that 15 percent of the trips they examined were unnecessary. At the time, the House Government Operations Committee calculated that at least $375 million per year was spent on travel that should never have occurred. More recent estimates put the figure of wasteful and unnecessary travel at $500 million a year.

Like Ray Marshall, many of our top government officials prefer to travel first class when the taxpayer is picking up the bill. Officials choosing first-class travel over economy while on government business have also included Attorney General Griffin Bell, Agriculture Secretary Robert Bergland, and Treasury Secretary Michael Blumenthal. Commerce Secretary Juanita Kreps usually flew first class, while associates of HUD Secretary Patricia Harris said she flew first class about half of the time.

While first class appears to be routine among many federal officials, they are in fact violating a government prohibition against it. Regulations enforced by the Office of Management and Budget state that first class travel is to be avoided except in cases of medical disability, unavailability of economy seats, or when first class is deemed "necessary for the conduct of the mission."

It is this last provision which officials have liberally interpreted to mean first class always. Nonetheless, an OMB official couldn't have been any clearer about what the policy has been: "The general policy is that it will be less than first class. You don't travel first class unless you have a vital reason to do so."

Perhaps there should also be a rule that you *do not travel at all* unless you have a vital reason to do so.

Take the cases of Alan Ehrlich, an official of the Consumer Product Safety Commission, who flew to Paris to discuss lawnmower standards, and his colleague, Bert Simson, who flew to Moscow to attend an international conference on television sets.

On his way back Simson stopped off for two days of vacation in Frankfurt, Germany. Ehrlich, who was to have returned in eight days, stayed over an extra day in Paris. In both cases they used their own funds on the days off. But when a reporter inquired, five months after their return, if either of them had filed a report with the Commission on their trips, the answer in both cases was no.

Were the trips necessary? "I must admit, that Soviet Union trip I have to scratch my head over," said Barbara Franklin, a Commission member at the time. "I can't see it did any good whatsoever."

While not always requiring formal reports, the Commission does require that "logs"—summaries of where the officials have been and with whom they met—be filed on trips considered to be "of substantial interest matter" (though what good these logs do is a mystery to everyone, including those who work for the Commission). Thus, while trips are taken to the four corners of the world, what transpired on them is not communicated in any formal way to the Commission.

In one year, for example, George Nichols, who headed the agency's foreign operations, traveled to London, Buenos Aires, Rio de Janiero, Paris, and Tokyo. He filed no reports on any of these trips. In fact, Mrs. Franklin said of Nichols' operation, "I can't figure out what that whole damn office does."

But Nichols was not alone in keeping Commission officials in the dark about his travel accomplishments. Commission Chairman John Byington enjoyed considerable travel, as did Mrs. Franklin. Byington took trips to Brussels, Bonn, Hamburg, Geneva, Tokyo, Hong Kong, and Taiwan. Mrs. Franklin went to Ottawa, Paris, Cologne, London, and Berlin. Byington attended a European Consumer Leader Group meeting. Mrs. Franklin met with various consumer leaders. Both gave some speeches. But neither of them submitted reports on what the trips had achieved. In fact, Mrs. Franklin failed to even file logs of her trips.

"I can see from your own standpoint that it looks a little bit funny," she told this reporter, "but we have no requirement that a report be filed." She said she could not recall ever having received a report on any of Byington's trips abroad. As to her own neglect regarding the filing of even cursory logs on her own trips, she remarked, "I think I screwed up by not having all the logs filed," adding that she "wouldn't like staff people flying around without filing a report of some kind." The Commission spends $1.2 million a year on travel.

Many agencies and departments within the government maintain their own fleets of small executive aircraft. These range from the jet fleet used by the Coast Guard and top Transportation Department officials to the 72-plane fleet maintained by the Federal Aviation Administration at a cost of $23 million a year.

As noted earlier, these planes are often used to fly officials to places which could be more cheaply reached by flying commercial. Frequently, these trips are less than vital to an agency's responsibility or mission.

For example, when a Coast Guard jet flew three top Guard officers and their wives to Seattle and back from Washington in order to attend the Reserve Officers Association convention, the fuel costs alone exceeded $3,000. While Guard regulations allow wives to travel with their husbands "for public relations purposes," a Coast Guard official said that, in this case, "these ladies do not satisfy the criteria for official functions."

On a five-day tour of Los Angeles and Seattle to inspect Guard installations, Admiral Owen W. Siler, the Guard commandant, and two other rear admirals were accompanied by their wives. Officials said the wives were needed to attend various social affairs with their husbands. On another trip, Siler, accompanied by two aides, flew to New York City to speak at a New York Times luncheon. The round-trip fuel cost for the Coast Guard jet was $291. The commercial shuttle fare would have been $78 round trip.

The Air Force's 89th Military Airlift Wing maintains a fleet of executive aircraft, including Air Force One, for use by the White House, Cabinet secretaries, other VIPs, and members of Congress. The wing had 25 planes until President Carter cut it back to 16. Some believe even that number is too many.

An examination of Pentagon flight manifests for a two-month period revealed the following use of the fleet by officials of the government:

—Sen. Barry Goldwater (R., Ariz.) was flown on Air Force jets to Sawyer, Michigan, and to Yuma, Arizona, to speak at military bases. Cost of both flights: $5,282.

—Sen. Daniel Moynihan (D., N.Y.) was flown by the Air Force from his home in New York to Washington. An aide said Moynihan—who had requested the trip because of a back ailment—was flown on a stretcher. He added that the senator went to work as usual the next day, voted in the Senate and chaired a morning hearing. The one-way trip cost $850.

—Then-Treasury Secretary Michael Blumenthal and two aides were flown to Cleveland on an eight-seat Jetstar to deliver a speech to a group of businessmen. Cost: $1,413.

—An Air Force major was flown alone on an eight-seat military jet from Washington to Wilmington, North Carolina, and back. It cost the government $1,488 round trip to fly him there, compared to $112 for a commercial flight.

The plane used for many of these trips is the VC140, a small but sleek four-engine jet that seats eight passengers and is described by one Air Force official as "plush." Another officer said there was "no reason in the world why we should keep planes on standby for members of Congress. They should be required to travel commercial unless there is some emergency."

One knowledgeable government auditor who has extensively investigated government travel abuses said, "There's just too much travel that is unnecessary. They (the agency and department heads) are not looking closely enough at it."

Indeed they aren't. One congressional survey found that in a disturbing number of cases federal officials are *approving their own* travel. This survey found that 71 percent of the traveling employes in one agency and 44 percent of the traveling employes in another were signing their own travel requests.

Still further abuses were uncovered by a Senate Appropriations Committee investigating team when they began probing the travel activities within the Environmental Protection Agency. Some examples of what they dug up include the following:

—When an EPA official went to Paris for a three-day meeting on "Management of Industrial River Basins," he took two days off which he did not charge to his annual leave. Then he returned to Paris eight months later to attend another conference, taking another eight days of leave without charging it to his annual leave allowance.

—EPA management "retreats" were held outside of the Greater Washington, D.C., area even though two-thirds of those who attended were from Washington. These meetings were held in such places as Denver and Big Canoe, Georgia, costing taxpayers nearly $12,000 for the Denver retreat and over $4,600 for a meeting in nearby Warrenton, Virginia.

—An EPA assistant administrator frequently took his secretary along on field trips, despite the fact that EPA regional or area offices were present at most of his destinations. Taxpayers paid the additional $3,000 to have the secretary accompany the official on at least eight trips.

—Another official took a 23-day vacation immediately after traveling to Hawaii on EPA business, which followed a three-hour visit with a contractor in Menlo Park, California.

Is it any wonder that government travel costs have shot up so sharply in recent years—rising from $1.8 billion in 1973 to $2.5 billion in fiscal 1977 to more than $3 billion in fiscal 1980, solely for the travel of our public officials. An increase exceeding $1 billion in six years!

Although a great deal of media attention is paid to junketing by members of Congress, legislative travel—costing about $22 million a year—actually accounts for less than 1 percent of the government's total travel bill.

The departments and agencies of the *executive* branch are the big spenders in the travel business. Agriculture spent over $100 million annually; Treasury, more than $95 million; HEW, $86 million; Transportation, $81 million; the Veterans Administration, $80 million; with other independent agencies collectively spending more than $100 million a year.

The last time Congress seriously attempted to do something about excessive travel was in 1975, when it approved a mandatory 10 percent cut in travel spending offered by Sen. William Roth (R., Del.)

in 1975. But two months after enactment, it was quietly repealed after a howl of protest from agencies who claimed they could not function under such strict reductions. Congress substituted a milder Roth proposal which called upon the president to enforce tougher regulations to cut unnecessary travel. But that has proven largely ineffective.

What is the solution? Many say only agency heads and supervisors can put a halt to needless travel and its abuse, but GAO investigators found that would be putting the problem in charge of the solution. "These are the people who are supposed to be setting an example for the rest of the government," a Senate Appropriations Committee staffer said. "Instead, they are among the worst offenders."

Still, for some jetsetters, old habits are hard to break. An assistant to then-Secretary Blumenthal, the former Bendix Corporation board chairman, explained why the Treasury secretary always insisted on flying first class.

"See," he said, "when Blumenthal was doing corporate work, he traveled in his own jet. He's become accustomed to something a little better."

For most taxpayers, that "something a little better" is a luxury they can no longer afford.

CHAPTER 7
Henry Luce on the Potomac

The buxom blonde in the short shorts and white T-shirt standing seductively in front of her new Subaru sedan wants the readers of *Driver* magazine to know she can change a flat under any circumstances.

Soldiers magazine tells its readers that television reruns of Star Trek are "back in orbit" and that Buffalo Bill's liquor bill was "tremendous." Hardly heart-pounding stuff, but if you turn to the magazine's inside back cover, you can eat your heart out over a full-page pinup of a sultry, sensuous woman seated in a fanback wicker chair. Her evening dress, slit to the thighs, is tucked alluringly between her shapely legs.

Meanwhile, the blue-jeaned cowboy in the black Stetson hat being propelled from the rodeo chute on top of 2,000 pounds of bull tells *Airman* readers (and perhaps the bull), "I'm the boss—the king."

Law Enforcement Bulletin spills the beans on everything you have ever wanted to know about "the massage parlor problem," including that parlors in Chicago have advertised "nude manicures, nude shoeshine, nude keymaking, nude wrestling and nude sex consultations."

Sealift's glossy pages contain a special feature about Charlie Brown, a crusty-looking seaman aboard the survey ship USS Wilkes who is the author of a book titled *Around the World with Charlie Brown*. This incredible memoir, we are told, tells about Charlie's old flames, like the "tall, redheaded lady" from San Francisco who was so well endowed that "when she removed her bra all the wrinkles were dragged from her face."

These magazines and their contents have one common denominator: they are produced, published, and distributed by the federal government.

Along with hundreds, possibly thousands of other thick, slick, full-color magazines and periodicals of one type or another, they are part of an ever-growing government magazine empire that surpasses anything Henry Luce could have dreamed possible when Time-Life, Inc. was just a gleam in his eye.

No one in the government knows precisely their total numbers or cost, nor how many government workers are assigned—fulltime or part-time—to produce them. Even the Office of Management and

47

Budget, responsible for auditing and justifying government expenditures, has no idea how extensive or how costly this magazine madness has become. "I guess there's not as close a scrutiny as we would
like to have," an OMB official admitted.

But one thing is known: Uncle Sam is undisputedly the world's
biggest magazine publisher.

Government officials privately estimate their total annual cost in
terms of employe salaries, overhead, benefits, and production and
printing costs to be in the hundreds of millions of dollars. One OMB
survey found that the executive branch departments were spending
about half a billion dollars a year in printing bills alone.

How this magazine jungle proliferated along the Potomac is "still
a mystery" to OMB investigators. "They're everywhere," one of them
said. "From the biggest department to the smallest bureau, they all
have their publications. And most of them are unneeded."

The degree to which the government seeks out specialized markets
for its magazines is perhaps best demonstrated in *Driver*, published
by the Air Force as "the traffic safety magazine for the military driver."

The full-page blonde pinup beside the shiny Subaru was "Miss
Driver" who, after examining her new car, exclaimed, "You'd never
believe where the jack and spare are located—under the hood with
the engine!" Miss Driver said she made a point "to right away have
a practice run" at changing a wheel. "It's a good thing I learned how
to do it in the daylight and not under emergency conditions," she
told the magazine's readers.

Other *Driver* features include interviews with racers like Mario
Andretti ("Tell your readers I use seat belts," Mario says) and Emerson
Fittipaldi, who says he feels safer on the track than in ordinary street
traffic. Other vital pieces of journalism abound, such as a piece on
foiling motorcycle thieves, plus "A Day in the Dirt," a story about
cross-country motorcycle racing, photos about Go-Karting, and tips
on "automobile restoration."

An issue of *Airman*, the official air force monthly, features "Air
Force Cowboys" on one of its four-color covers, illustrated by a
denim-clad officer, his cheek bulging with a chaw of Red Man chew-
ing tobacco. Inside, there is an eight-page extravaganza on how
America's western airmen spend their weekends calf roping and bull
riding at rodeos. An adjoining two-page spread on Lieutenant Dennis
Snee's talent as a joke writer explains that his stuff has been used in
Playboy and *Mad* magazines, and even by comedian Rodney
Dangerfield.

Sealift, the magazine of the Military Sealift Command, isn't resting on its laurels with the Charlie Brown exclusive. The issue also includes a photo essay on the "tall ships" that came to celebrate the Bicentennial, plus a history of the four naval vessels named after the battle of Yorktown.

Worklife, published monthly by the Labor Department's Employment and Training Administration, is printed on stock that would make *Fortune* magazine look cheap. One issue contained a puff piece on—you guessed it—the Labor Department, as well as stories on the Great Depression, labor leader John L. Lewis, and the first Labor Day parade.

A glossy, full-color photo layout on the International Azalea Festival in Norfolk, Virginia, was lavishly featured in *All Hands*, published by the navy, and an issue of *Progressive Fish-Culturist* revealed the effects of water salinity on the eggs and fry of goldfish.

An examination of the weekly, monthly, quarterly, and yearly government magazines, newsletters, newspapers, and even books reveals that many are duplicative; others are provided primarily to members of Congress who pass them out to constituents; many contain articles that are merely the previously published speeches and congressional testimony of the heads of the agencies producing them.

When asked to provide a copy of each magazine and periodical published by the United States Army, a public information officer said, "I'd almost have to send them over in a truck."

A spokesman for the Commerce Department said that if his department tried to catalogue every periodical it published, "We would have a catalogue that looks like the Washington phone book."

It takes 1,168 pages in Andriot's *Guide to U.S. Government Serials and Periodicals* to list all of the government's publications. The "best sellers are in the U.S. Government Printing Office's booklet, *Government Periodicals*, some of which include:

Federal Design Matters—A quarterly providing information on "the progress and accomplishments of the President's Federal Design Improvement Program."

Problems of Communism—Information on "various aspects of world communism today."

Public Roads—Contains articles on highway research and surfacing.

Postal Life—A bimonthly that keeps America's postal employes "informed and abreast" of developments in the U.S. Postal Service.

Outdoor Recreation Action—The government says this publication "should help to keep professionals, public and private leaders in outdoor recreation abreast of significant developments."

Our Public Lands—Tells how to buy public lands, and where to hunt, fish, and camp out.

Other choice selections include: *Plant Disease Reporter, Population Sciences, Guidelines for the Control of Weeds, Background Notes on the Countries of the World,* and *Schizophrenia Bulletin.*

What strikes one immediately about these magazines is the overwhelming *unimportance* of their contents. In addition to stories on Star Trek and Buffalo Bill, one issue of *Soldiers,* the official U.S. Army magazine, included pieces on cigarette smoking and the joys of sailing. It costs the Army more than $1 million a year to publish and distribute the monthly magazine free to about 200,000 servicemen.

In addition to the massage parlors story, the FBI's monthly *Law Enforcement Bulletin* runs articles on the speeches and views of its agency's director, firearm silencers, an oil and gas investment fraud scheme, and a promotion piece on the new FBI Academy.

The FBI publishes 70,000 copies of the magazine each month and sends them free to police and other law enforcement agencies around the country at an annual cost of over $414,000. At least seven employes work on the magazine.

An examination of previous issues of *Treasury Papers,* which is no longer published by the Treasury Department, showed that all contained at least one, and sometimes two or more of the speeches given by former Secretary William Simon. The remainder of the issues were filled with previously published speeches, testimony or statements by other Department officials.

Numerous other publications similarly feature the comments and photographs of the people who head the agencies that issue the magazines. For example, one issue of *All Hands,* put out by the Navy, included a full-color cover photo of Navy Secretary W. Graham Claytor, Jr., plus a seven-page profile that was sprinkled with 10 photos of him, in addition to a story on his wife. An issue of *Airman,* published by the Air Force, devoted a cover photo story to its boss, Secretary Thomas C. Reed, with a six-page article that said, "Neither the forest nor the trees blocks Secretary Reed's vision."

Perhaps one of the most expensive publications is the Interior Department's Annual Yearbook, generously illustrated with brilliant color photographs depicting the nation's rich natural resources. The Department's 160-page bicentennial issue devoted to America's 200-year history took two years and the full and part-time work of two dozen employes to prepare, costing almost $100,000 just to print. Of the 55,000 copies initially printed, more than 12,000 were given to members of Congress to distribute to constituents and friends. Another 25,000 were sent to Department field offices for distribution "as they wish," an official said.

It cost the Government Printing Office $1.25 to print each copy. It then turned around and sold them for $5.55 to the tax-paying public—more than four times their cost. "They're making a big profit," one Interior official said, noting that lower-income Americans "probably could not afford to buy one." When asked if it was necessary to print the magazines on such expensive paper, with costly color pictures, the official said "The photographs are the biggest appeal. We couldn't sell it if we didn't have them."

Like the Interior Department, the Agriculture Department—which issues thousands of publications each year—also promotes and distributes an annual yearbook. Each senator and House member gets several hundred copies to distribute.

"In some offices they are used like currency," an aide to a southwestern congressman said, "and are traded for office supplies, stationary, etc. They're nothing but giveaways used for political purposes."

As could be expected, there is *rampant duplication of effort* among the agencies' publishing activities. Interior's Fish and Wildlife Service, National Park Service, Bureau of Land Management, Bureau of Outdoor Recreation, Bureau of Reclamation, and Office of Territorial Affairs all issue publications concerning recreation.

There are at least three magazines on fish. The U.S. Navy alone issues at least three magazines concerning safety.

While virtually every department and agency issues periodicals of one variety or another, none can compete with the Pentagon for publishing enterprise. One study on military magazines, conducted by the *Armed Forces Journal* (a private enterprise) in 1975 found that the Pentagon was spending at least $57 million a year to publish 371 different magazines.

Indeed, the military was producing "eight times as many magazines as the nation's biggest trade magazine publishers," the *Journal* said. Prodded by the *Journal* study, then-Defense Secretary Melvin Laird launched his own investigation which found a total of 1,402 different magazines, newspapers and newsletters being published by the various military services and divisions. The study came up with a publishing cost of nearly $13 million a year, but the *Journal* said the Pentagon could never pay its 259 fulltime and 6,429 part-time writers and editors for that amount of money, not to mention the other overhead costs not included.

The Air Force said it spent $3.6 million in fiscal 1975 to issue its magazines; this excludes the cost of newspapers published at various bases in the field. Figures for fiscal year 1978 showed that costs now exceed $4 million a year for the Navy, according to the Pentagon.

The military's publishers "seem to have gained a new principle of war," the *Journal* remarked in its investigation of the government's magazine mania, "Publish or Perish." Notably, the *Journal* isn't willing to dismiss all military publications as wasteful, but it argues sensibly that many of them wouldn't be missed and many more could be combined. A review of dozens of military magazines confirms that the *Journal* is right on target.

Who reads these magazines? It is often impossible to tell.

The only known government survey was conducted by Laird's task force study, which sampled reader reaction to several military magazines.

Asked how familiar servicemen were with *Commanders Digest*, a biweekly that was published by the Armed Forces News Bureau, more than 44 percent said they seldom if ever read it. Other periodicals, the survey showed, had good readership among enlisted men and women and officers. Nonetheless, an examination of numerous magazines indicates that many are issued solely for public relations purposes and actually reach very small audiences.

For example, the Department of Transportation's full color quarterly, *Transportation USA*, had a distribution of about 12,000 and cost $100,000 a year to produce. Articles in the magazine included stories about the popularity of bicycles, minibuses in Westport, Connecticut, and experiments with "people movers"—subjects that have been widely written about in nongovernment magazines and newspapers.

Are these magazines filling a need?

One OMB official, who asked not to be identified, said, "Many of them are probably not needed, but have become status symbols of a sort and public relations vehicles. And that type of activity is hard to curtail."

It should also be noted that many special interest groups and businesses benefit from many government magazines. The weekly *Internal Revenue Bulletin*, which costs subscribers $40 a year, keeps tax lawyers abreast of the latest IRS decisions and tax rulings. This magazine, however, would be difficult for the layman to use in calculating his or her taxes.

The monthly *Journal of the Federal Home Loan Bank Board*, which costs subscribers $24.50 a year, is published specifically for "the savings and loan industry," according to the Government Printing Office's listing of periodicals.

And of course one of the most popular journals is the Commerce Department's *Commerce Business Daily*, which provides a complete summary of the government's procurement, sales, and contract awards, all for $105 a year.

The extremes the government has gone to in seeking specialized reader markets is extraordinary. The classic example of this is *Direction*, a monthly public relations magazine published by the Navy. It contains articles showing naval personnel how to deal with the media, plus instruction on producing films and photographs, and writing copy for newspapers and magazines. Thus, there is even a government magazine on publishing magazines. Articles in *Direction* have included "The Myth of the Adversary Press" and "The Don'ts of Photo Releases," which instructs the proper way to crop photos for publications. And there is advice for the beleaguered public information officer. As one of the magazine's editorials suggested, "The media are not always fair or fully responsible. You are the ones who must go more than 50 percent of the way to meet the media, if necessary: not for their sake, but for ours."

Asked about the government's publishing industry, one budget expert said, "There's just too many of them. It's out of control."

As we have seen, many of these magazines are frivolous and unneeded. Many duplicate the work of others. Many more are dripping in self-glorification for agency programs and for the people who run them. And they're doing it with taxpayer's money.

CHAPTER 8
USDA: Where Are the Farmers?

The Department of Agriculture has discovered the "most popular vegetable grown" by Americans in their backyard gardens. It is the tomato.

It was nothing, really. All USDA had to do was to poll over 1,400 households across the country to come up with this startling discovery.

While you might be of the opinion that this is a rather silly exercise for the United States government to be undertaking, let me hasten to add that the Agriculture Department is up to its plowshares in a great deal more than just tomatoes. In fact, after wading through hundreds of USDA reports, studies, surveys, booklets, brochures, fact sheets, and other assorted documents, I'm beginning to wonder whether the Department has any time left for farmers.

Did you know, for example, that in 1975, 17 percent of all households used their ovens less than in the previous year? That's one of the findings produced by a USDA survey in that year; it also found that "one out of three households" canned fruits and vegetables at home.

USDA's insatiable curiosity leaves no field unfurrowed. Another survey found that fast-food chains are among the nation's most popular eating places. "When Americans eat out," USDA's Economic Research Service discovered, "they're likely to head for a convenient and inexpensive fast-food restaurant." Now this is *really earth-shattering research*, of which we should all stand in awe. The subject is *really exhausted*. Consider:

"The quick-service, low-priced food outlets aren't the only popular eateries, however. Sixty percent of the respondents said someone in the family bought food at a restaurant that offered a main course for less than $5," and "nearly half" said someone in the family had patronized a restaurant offering a main course costing *more* than $5.

"What determines where families will go out to eat?" the survey asked. Income seems to be a major factor. However, there are "no hard-and-fast dividing lines—all income level households show some amount of purchases in all types of restaurants."

But it's the location of the family garden that USDA was most concerned with for many years: Department researchers went to

54

extraordinary lengths, discovering finally that "around 85 percent of the gardens were located in the household yard." Where are the remaining gardens located? Sadly, USDA said its survey "did not determine the exact location of the home gardens that were located elsewhere." But they intend to find out: "In the second phase of the study, we are planning to investigate who provides the land for the away-from-home fruit or vegetable gardens."

If, perhaps, "Demographic Changes on U.S. Food Consumption" is more your cup of tea, USDA has prepared a report alleging that potatoes are "one of the few foods consumed at a low rate by single-person households." It also informs us that persons living alone "consume more vegetables and fruits per capita than persons in larger households"; that children and large households "are the high consumers of cereals and pastas"; and that the "high consumers of soda pop" are teenagers.

The question is, of course, Why is the government telling us this? More to the point, Why should USDA be spending millions of dollars on studies about the location of backyard gardens, the most popular vegetable, and whether single people watching their weight steer clear of potatoes?

No one in the government seems to know why USDA became involved in these studies, or when they first began branching out from the corn and wheat crop reports into the secret life of the home-maker and the territorial imperative of the backyard gardener.

When Congress created an agriculture agency in 1862, with nine employes and a $64,000 budget, its primary mission was to distribute seeds to farmers. Today, with 81,000 employes, a $23.6 billion budget (including a $2.5 billion payroll), the average farmer can no longer be considered the dominant responsibility of the United States Department of Agriculture. In fact, USDA has largely been turned into a *welfare* agency, spending more than half its budget to help feed poor and low-income families, as well as the nation's school children, rich and poor.

Nearly $14 billion of USDA's budget is now consumed by food stamp and school lunch programs, with much of the remaining $10 billion going to assist businesses and corporate agricultural interests far removed from the traditional family farmer. Indeed, some USDA programs have been responsible for the decline in family farms.

The last time Congress bothered to take a close look at the Department of Agriculture was in 1953. Since then, our lawmakers have heaped new programs upon the Department, and expanded old ones, year after year. USDA now has 923 employes devoted solely to explaining its programs and agencies to the press and the public.

Obviously, like many federal agencies, USDA's original purpose has been substantially enlarged since Congress turned the modest seed program into a Cabinet-level department in 1889—a time when the nation had more than 4.5 million farms and 26 million farmers. Today, America's farm population is down to 3.1 million people on 2.8 million farms; for some inexplicable reason, while our farm population dwindled the government's farm program expanded.

Perhaps the most noticeable—not to mention the most wasteful— of all USDA undertakings is its publishing activity. The Department spends $18 million a year to publish 58 million copies of its magnificent research findings, publications and paperwork.

USDA literature includes 6,120 regular publications, including ones on bark mulch landscaping, lawn maintenance, how to clean bathrooms, refrigerators, and dishes—everything from "Growing Perennials" to "Handling Your Big Game Kill."

With a staff of 1,000 employes, including 600 economists, the $29 million-a-year Economic Research Service has been a major source of reports, studies, and seemingly endless publications.

An examination of almost 800 ERS documents shows numerous reports were prepared for trade organizations. Examples of their output include an analysis of the potato industry presented to the Ohio Potato Growers Association; a report on tobacco production given to the United States Tobacco Association; and the "Domestic Situation and Outlook for Cotton" presented to the Southern Cotton Association. Thus, it is not surprising that a top ERS official said that about one-fourth of ERS' work benefits major food and fiber industries.

"No more than 10 to 15 percent of our publications go directly to farmers," he said. Most of ERS' market analysis is aimed at commodity traders, agribusinesses, and the scientific and academic communities. Another ERS official characterized ERS' "Outlook-Situation" reports, which analyze and forecast food production and prices, as "giveaway publications," saying they went to "few farmers, a lot of commodity traders, a lot of the agribusiness firms."

"If we didn't do this, they (agribusinesses and big traders) would have to do it for themselves," said another ERS official. *The poor dears*.

There are some in ERS who insist that the farmer is still the agency's "basic mission," but a list of ERS reports and studies shows such far-removed efforts as "Fast Food In Japan—A Billion Dollar Industry" along with "Fast Food Franchises." These marketing studies do nothing more than explore the market potential, both here and abroad, for huge corporations such as McDonald's and Kentucky Fried Chicken, both of whom have recently made lucrative inroads into Japan and other Asian countries. Companies like these, of course, are fully capable of financing their own marketing research studies. But, as one government food expert put it:

> In almost every case, if business can get the government to pay for any of its costs, they'll find out about the service and milk it to the limit.

A Senate Appropriations subcommittee, looking into the matter, concluded that few of the continuing publications produced by USDA were helpful to farm producers in making decisions relative to managing their increasingly costly operations.

At one hearing, Sen. Henry Bellmon (R., Okla.) scolded top USDA officials: "It looks as if the information you are putting out is primarily geared either for economists or other statisticians, and not really for the farmers." Complained a member of the House Agriculture Committee:

> The Department often puts out more information than the farming industry can possibly use. We need to be more selective in the type of information and data USDA churns out.

Farmers agree, according to a survey of 5,000 of them conducted by *Successful Farming Magazine*. Seventy-five percent said USDA crop and livestock reports were not helpful to them, while 58 percent said they did not get their money's worth from government agricultural services. More than 25 percent either didn't get USDA literature or said that what they got was "useless." And 54.6 percent found USDA materials only "moderately useful."

But beyond USDA's excessive and wasteful output of reports, studies, and other materials, there is a far more explosive controversy over the effect of agricultural research on rising farm costs, and ultimately on the price of food.

USDA's research budget is more than $1 billion a year and rising. It pays for a broad range of research—from developing hybrid strains of cucumbers and carrots to finding out where homeowners' gardens are located.

Perhaps the most bizarre—though by no means an isolated example of this research—was the widely-publicized $113,417 study which questioned 2,161 mothers to find out if they preferred children's clothing that requires no ironing. Other research projects have examined "Men's Attitudes toward Cotton," "Consumers' Preferences for Fresh Tomatoes," and, as we have seen, even discovered that many families patronize fast-food restaurants because they can afford them!

Quite understandably, congressional investigators call such studies "nonsense." Among the most critical of the way USDA manages its agricultural research dollars are GAO food and farm-research experts, who warn against USDA research policies that neglect human nutrition; thumbing through an inch-thick USDA report on food research spending, one knowledgeable official held half a dozen pages together and said, "Look at this. Out of thousands of research programs this is all they've devoted to food nutrition."

Through the years, an enormous portion of our food research budget has emphasized crop yields—through better fertilizers, pesticides, herbicides, and elaborate farm equipment. Such research policies have imposed significant "social costs" upon our country, and particularly upon our farming community, according to an internal government memorandum on food research programs.

"Government research has produced a capital-intensive, technological farm industry that has driven out the small and medium-sized farmer," one veteran House Agriculture Committee official said. "We've created better, more productive grains and vegetables that require elaborate machinery and expensive fertilizers, herbicides, and pesticides. Only the big corporate farmer can survive in this kind of system."

USDA's impact on the broiler industry is a good example of what has happened. Federal research developed disease-control procedures that allowed poultry to be raised by the thousands in a minimum of space. But the result was that "the economics of scale" pushed small chicken producers out of the market.

Moreover, the degree to which food research programs have been duplicated throughout the bureaucracy is significant. A Library of Congress study found food-related research programs in such diverse agencies as the Commerce and Defense Departments, the Tennessee Valley Authority, and the National Science Foundation.

Meantime, much USDA research spending has no clear relevance to our country's food and fiber needs and often serves to benefit only highly profitable commercial industries. In one recent fiscal year, for example, nearly $100,000 was sought from Congress for research on spearmint and peppermint. The prime users of mint are the chewing gum, pharmaceutical, and toothpaste industries. Other examples of USDA research include $4 million for ornamental plant and turf research; $4 million for peanut research; $66,000 for English walnuts research.

Is USDA research helping the American farmer? *Successful Farming*'s poll found 65 percent of farmers were relying "more on research results from private companies."

But there are other USDA programs whose original purpose appears to have been stretched far beyond what Congress originally intended for them to accomplish in the first place. Consider the fact that USDA's Motion Picture Division spends over $431,000 annually producing movies, plus more than $84,000 for outside filmmakers. There are films promoting pest-management and conservation practices along with others entitled "Bicycling for Sport or Pleasure," "How to Buy Natural Cheese," and "Hiking Trails in Alaska."

One five-minute USDA film entitled "Secretary Butz—Conduct and Ethics" was released several months before the former USDA secretary was forced to resign after telling a joke that was offensive to blacks.

USDA, which has been producing films longer than any other federal agency, has made thousands of movies, most of them unnecessary, during its 50 years of movie-making.

There are many programs and agencies within USDA that are simply bureaucratic vestiges of a bygone era. No doubt they were needed and useful when they were established several decades ago, but now they are curious relics that seem out of place in a computerized, high technology age. One of these is the USDA's Extension Service which has agents and offices located in each and every county in the country—all 3,000 of them, *including real farm-intensive areas like Manhattan, Chicago, Boston, Detroit, and Los Angeles.*

Operating with a $500 million annual budget, partially shared by state and county governments, and a force of 19,000 workers, the program provides educational, research, and financial services to farmers and nonfarmers alike, in addition to its 4-H and home economics program for rural and urban poor housewives.

The entire Extension program needs to be reevaluated in terms of whom it is actually helping and whether or not those people receiving services of one kind or another really deserve them or whether they ought to obtain them from other sources, for, in many cases, the Extension Service appears to be offering services and advice that Congress never intended at all. One of these services is advice on lawn care. "People can phone in their county agent who will plug in a three-minute cassette that deals with problem lawns," said an information officer for the agency. "That's what the county agents are there for."

USDA figures its county agents annually spend over 500 man-years dealing with "lawns, home gardens, and house plants." There are USDA plans to conduct a survey of the extent of lawn and garden problems among homeowners.

USDA began its network of county agents in 1914, an era when the lack of adequate communication required that the USDA make agents accessible to every county in the land. It was also a time when America was still heavily populated by commercial farmers, as well as by people who fed themselves by farming.

Yet, despite substantial changes in our society, Congress to this day has made no comprehensive evaluation and overhaul of our agricultural program to decide whether a coast-to-coast county system of offices and agents is still warranted.

In addition to the Extension Service outposts, USDA maintains other offices throughout the country, resulting in duplication of operational expenses and manpower. For example, the 20,000-person U.S. Forest Service, USDA's largest agency, operates out of some 900 offices nationwide, while the Soil Conservation Service has 13,000 employes located in virtually every county. Additionally, the Agricultural Stabilization and Conservation Service runs some 2,700 county and 51 state offices, while the Farmers Home Administration operates 1,783 fulltime and 936 part-time offices nationwide.

Some movement has been made to consolidate these offices into unified centers, but thousands of fragmented USDA facilities still exist. Individual evaluation also needs to be applied to each of these other programs to determine whether their many programs and activities are necessary and relevant to today's needs.

USDA duplication also extends to a mountain of paperwork, which adds a burden to the farmer as well as to USDA's budget. Eleven agencies within USDA require information of one type or another from farmers through 169 different forms, producing more than 12 million responses annually.

The Federal Paperwork Commission calculated that these 169 forms annually consume more than seven million man-hours from farmers at an estimated cost to them of $35 million a year. Is it any wonder that food prices are going up?

Previous administrations have tried to strip some USDA programs, but with little or no success. President Nixon once proposed dismantling USDA altogether by dividing its numerous programs among different super-departments. But opposition from the farm lobby was so intense that the plan was quickly abandoned.

Every president since Dwight Eisenhower, including President Carter, has recommended either abolishing or curbing the $110 million special milk-subsidy program which provides a second carton of milk to certain youngsters as part of the USDA's $4 billion-a-year school lunch program. Since school children who receive this extra pint of milk are already getting free school lunches, which also includes a half-pint of milk each school day, that additional pint of milk has a very low "nutritional priority," as one USDA official admitted.

Congress has always rejected proposed cuts in the milk program, but this has less to do with claims about improving the nutrition of our children than it does with bolstering dairy prices. It is also a policy that is totally out of kilter with what we now know about good nutrition and the dangers of fat-saturated diets.

The Department's school lunch program is providing hot lunches to many deserving children, but the program also benefits millions of middle- and upper-income children, too. USDA figures that nearly $800 million will be spent in the fiscal 1980 year to buy lunch and milk for wealthy and middle-class children whose parents are financially able to buy their own lunches, or pack them at home.

USDA is also spending about $1.6 billion on assistance programs for rural businesses and residents. But many of these programs duplicate—or overlap with—loan programs in a myriad of other agencies elsewhere in the government, such as the Small Business Administration, the Economic Development Administration, the Office of Minority Business Enterprise, and the Housing and Urban Development Department.

Moreover, the Rural Electrification Administration—created in 1935 to make loans to bring electricity to rural areas—is another example of a program that has survived its now defunct purpose for being. It is an agency, according to one of Carter's top reorganization chiefs, whose original purpose "has long since been achieved." All but about 1 percent of the nation's farms have been powered under the program. The REA has a budget of nearly $26 million a year.

A great many USDA activities are undoubtedly vital to the nation's food and fiber needs, particularly in areas such as meat and grain inspection, environmental safeguards, soil conservation, and disaster relief assistance for farmers who are constantly facing the risk of ruin through an act of nature. But many of USDA's programs are no longer needed or have gone considerably beyond the original intent of Congress.

There is obviously a great deal going on at the Department of Agriculture that could be terminated tomorrow without hurting American agriculture. As for the country's major agricultural industries, surely they have the financial resources to provide the research, marketing analysis, and forecasting now being provided "free" by taxpayers.

The enormity of the task facing both the Congress and the executive branch—if ever they get around to cleaning house, down at USDA—is summed up by one USDA worker, who said: "There are a ton of changes that need to be made down here. A lot of it is *as outdated as hell.*"

CHAPTER 9
The Poverty Business

Since President Lyndon Johnson declared "war on poverty" in 1964, the federal government has spent *more than $30 billion* in a misguided effort to turn LBJ's grandiose dream into a reality. While LBJ knew a thing or two about making war, he had forgotten everything he learned firsthand about rising out of poverty. By every possible objective criterion, his war on poverty has been an abject failure.

Since the 1960s—according to economists, social scientists, and some members of Congress—the government has spent enough money on this and all the nation's other social welfare programs to lift every man, woman, and child out of poverty *three times over*.

Yet, despite an armada of government poverty-fighters and a host of federal programs created to "eradicate poverty" once and for all, an estimated 29 million Americans remain below the $6,700 official poverty income line. Many millions more hover near it.

While there is evidence a few of the programs created under the Economic Opportunity Act of 1964 have helped some of the poor, particularly disadvantaged children, the overwhelming evidence available reveals that much of the so-called antipoverty money spent under this act has not alleviated the grim day-to-day reality within America's urban slums and among the rural poor.

On the contrary, a major share of the government's antipoverty spending has been consumed by an industry of government workers, consultants, special interest groups, lobbyists, researchers, and other firms and individuals who have been greedily feeding off the program at the expense of the poor.

The mistaken belief persists, to this day, that Johnson's ambitious war plans were all but destroyed by President Nixon, who dismantled the Office of Economic Opportunity, which housed the special poverty programs, slashed their budgets, and even tried to abolish the core of OEO: the Community Action Agency. But such is not the case.

Virtually all of OEO's programs spun off, under Nixon, to different departments and agencies; they are not only alive and healthy, but their budgets are bigger than ever—cumulatively spending more than $4 billion a year. (At its peak, in 1969, OEO's total budget was but $1.9 billion for all programs.)

An examination of the core of this antipoverty program, now called the Community Services Administration, reveals the shocking truth about where much of our "poverty money" is going:

—Millions of dollars are being spent on studies, surveys, research reports, literature, and other materials, a great deal of which ends up gathering dust on government shelves, or is buried within costly data retrieval systems.

—Costly duplication is widely evident among competing programs, departments, and agencies in the fields of housing, nutrition, energy, and economic development.

—Overhead costs on many projects and spending activities are swallowing 50 percent or more of grants and contracts.

—Neither the executive branch nor the Congress has ever tried to thoroughly evaluate the contribution of these programs toward the reduction of poverty.

A look at the budgets of the Community Services Administration, Legal Services Corporation, Job Corps, Head Start, and Summer Youth Employment, among others, reveals that most have gotten substantial budget *increases* from Congress since the Nixon administration.

Job Corps went from $274.1 million in fiscal 1977 to nearly $500 million in fiscal 1979. Head Start, a program for poor preschool children had shot up to $680 million by 1979. Legal Services, intended to provide legal services to the poor, jumped from $157 million in 1978 to an estimated $280 million for fiscal 1980. And Community Services went from $511 million in fiscal 1977 to $668 million in fiscal 1979. All these programs were born out of the original OEO created under President Johnson. The figures show that they are hardly being "starved," as some critics would argue.

Since its inception, OEO, now CSA, along with some of its spin-off programs, has been steeped in controversy and marred by abuse, corruption, and waste.

Political clashes erupted in the 1960s between establishment political leaders and representatives of the poor and the antiestablishment advocacy groups and activist leaders who, for the first time, were largely in charge of delivering services to the poor through local Community Action Agencies.

Along with the infighting came numerous cases where funds were used for activities clearly *not envisioned* nor authorized by Congress. In many cases, for example, Legal Services lawyers were encour-

aging rent strikes, boycotts, and picketing, and were actively lobbying state legislatures in behalf of legislation and political reforms.

It was federal poverty money, through Legal Services attorneys,
which initiated and funded the 1972 Indian land claims suit arguing
that two-thirds of the state of Maine belongs to the Passamaquoddy
and Penobscot Indian tribes.

However, the focus of the government's antipoverty effort has always been on its core Community Services program, under which
a network of 900 local poverty agencies was established to coordinate and deliver a myriad of services for the poor—everything from
social counseling, food shopping tips, nutritional guidance, job training, and outreach programs to make the poor aware of the kinds of
government assistance programs available to them.

The program provided jobs and experience for poverty workers
employed by the program, but—as the House Government Operations Committee discovered—it also produced "inexperienced or
self-seeking local boards which in turn led to instances of mismanagement and outright graft."

Twelve years after the local agencies were established under OEO,
the committee said it was still uncovering "major areas of weakness,
inefficiency, and ineffectiveness."

In recent years the committee has issued nine separate reports
dealing with abuses and mismanagement within the antipoverty
agencies.

In the beginning, the local poverty agencies received from OEO
up to 90 percent of their money, which they used to fund programs
like Head Start and Job Corps. Today CSA provides administrative
funds to the local agencies which, in turn, must seek their own project money from other federal and state sources. (These local Community Action agencies are currently spending *nearly $2 billion a
year* in local, state, and federal funds.)

In addition to providing the local agencies with operating expenses, CSA has provided them with some funds for planning, research, and some new projects. While some local agencies spend
their funds wisely and prudently, there is little evidence they are
lifting families out of poverty. Meanwhile, many others have mis-
spent and squandered their funds.

But it is within CSA's headquarters in Washington that we can see
most clearly how poverty funds are being wasted, year after year.

A 1975 internal study of the agency found that a hefty 21 percent of its funds were being consumed by administrative costs, which the report said was "considerably higher than expected."

Said one former CSA worker, "Too much of our money is going into administrative costs, both here and in the field, and a lot more into private groups that do not directly benefit the poor."

It is difficult to accurately trace where CSA's money is really going and who actually benefits from it. The agency has no figures or studies analyzing how much of its funds benefit the poor, in real terms. However, an examination of CSA's contacts, grants, and other expenditures shows that much of the agency's funding is helping to finance the operations, salaries, and other overhead costs of hundreds of private, sometimes nonprofit organizations known within CSA as "conduits."

Many of these conduits use CSA money to lobby Congress; publish magazines, newsletters, and other materials; bring suit against the government; and organize groups for political action. Others are engaged in research projects and studies which few people, *least of all the poor*, will ever read.

"An industry of associations—particularly here in Washington—has sprung up around the poverty program," said one Senate staffer who closely monitors poverty programs. "All of them are feeding on it in one way or another."

What has been happening can be seen in a $1 million grant to the National Association of Farmworker Organizations for energy training and technical assistance. A CSA official said nearly $600,000 of the grant would go to local farmworker groups for research and development projects to develop skills among the poor in the energy field. At least 40 percent of the grant went to program directors, research professionals, training staff, and other middle class specialists, together with literature, conferences, and travel.

In fiscal 1977 CSA spent more than $9 million on energy-related research and development, funneling the money to outside professional firms. Here's where some of the money went: $366,000 to the Urban Institute, a federally-funded think tank, for an analysis of its winterization program; $45,000 to study fraud among energy companies; $72,380 to produce a television film on energy conservation; $700,000 to a Massachusetts legal research firm to produce studies promoting utility rate structure reform; $40,000 for an energy conservation motivation study. It is impossible to see how the poor benefited from the expenditure of any of this money.

Like most federal agencies, CSA often hastily approves grants and contracts because it does not want to be caught with any unspent funds at the end of the fiscal year. (It is very hard to convince Congress that you are doing your job and need a bigger budget when you end up with a *surplus* at the end of the year.)

A typical case involved two $73,000 grants to Farmworker Groups in Rochester, New York, and Boise, Idaho, to increase participation by women in their organizations. More than $26,000 of each grant went for administrative costs. Another $29,000 of each grant was earmarked for development of a data collection system.

Did these two projects measure up to any strict test of need? Were the projects thought out carefully? It didn't appear so. "Their project was not fully delineated," a CSA official admitted, "but we approved it anyway. We have to have all of our money out by the end of the fiscal year or else we must return the balance to the Treasury." (God forbid!) The official continued, "It was getting down to the deadline. Congress doesn't like it when you have money left over at the end of the year."

In past years CSA has spent about $30 million annually in the field of food and nutrition. Much of this money goes to groups and organizations for reports on nutrition programs and "advocacy assistance"—lobbying—for federal food programs.

One recipient of this CSA funding is the Washington-based Food Research Action Center (FRAC) which in one year got $550,000 from CSA. The money went, in part, to help FRAC lobby Congress for expansion of the food stamp program and other assistance programs.

But a FRAC lobbyist in Washington can better describe what this CSA-supported organization does:

> We testify at hearings, meeting with members of Congress and their aides to influence legislation, draft amendments, and help with speech-writing for members. We try to get as many benefits as we can (in federal welfare assistance legislation), and seek to expand those benefits through appropriate legislation.

Among its many federally-subsidized activities, FRAC brought a successful lawsuit against proposed food stamp cuts during the Ford administration.

There are many other examples. The Community Nutrition Institute got $200,000 "to develop a national strategy for Indian programs." A CSA official said the project amounted to "making contact with Indian groups around the country" in order to organize support for CSA programs.

Some of those who have received CSA money were former OEO

officials or groups like the National Center for Community Action, Inc., once a training arm of OEO. In 1977 this organization got $750,000—$360,000 went for salaries and overhead, and $55,000 was spent on travel. The Center also used this funding to publish a monthly magazine, *National Center Reporter*, which contained articles about welfare, consumers, and the poor. In addition, it issued publications such as *Legislative Update*, a newsletter, plus catalogues like "Where the Money Is," which listed federal funding programs. Printing costs exceeded $132,000.

One of the CSA's richest conduits was the National League of Cities and the U.S. Conference of Mayors. The joint organization developed a system of counseling centers for disadvantaged Vietnam veterans into which CSA funneled $2.3 million. According to CSA officials, overhead alone for this project ran to more than $617,000— $170,513 of which was spent by CSA just to handle paperwork. The organization also spent $229,000 on staff salaries, $160,000 for consultants, and $58,000 on travel. Other expenses from this contract included $90,000 for a computer firm in Detroit and another $70,000 in additional consultant costs.

Not only are many of the research grants awarded by CSA *totally useless*, but the report the money paid for usually *ends up on a shelf or in a computer* and is quickly forgotten.

One grant for $8,155 was awarded to an organization in Washington for a study on poor rural women in Appalachia. According to the CSA official in charge of this contract, the researchers were to "go out into the community, find out who are the community leaders, how many went to college, the jobs they have, and identify those women who are active in organizations." Not exactly the kind of government project that a poor person can relate to, unless he or she is the recipient of the contract—and there is little if any chance of that happening.

What will happen to the report? It will go directly to her, the official said, and after she has read it, it will be fed into CSA's computer.

Perhaps no antipoverty program has drawn more fire than CSA's Office of Economic Development. Costing $48 million a year, this CSA program offers capital to local businesses to provide jobs for the poor.

"It was a lousy program then and it still is," scowled Sar Levitan, a George Washington University economics professor who was one of the antipoverty program's chief architects. "It has never worked out."

By October 1976, OEO was operating 36 special-impact economic development programs that had received more than $300 million in federal assistance.

OEO has estimated that local Community Development Corporations employ more than 770 people directly, but the businesses they develop and back financially provide 5,516 jobs. A House Government Operations subcommittee chaired by Rep. Cardiss Collins (D., Ill.) figured out that each job was costing taxpayers $18,000. "I am absolutely shocked," Ms. Collins told government auditors. "I find this figure to be absolutely appalling."

One OED venture was a bankrupt pool table company acquired in 1972 after a private consultant had warned the firm's financial projections and management were faulty. The business has lost $300,000.

CSA initially rejected a proposal to acquire a produce wholesale company because of the firm's insolvency and shaky management capability. A consultant hired by the sponsoring agency confirmed CSA's judgment. The agency, however, convinced CSA that with enough capital, the company could make a go of it. The antipoverty agency approved a $196,000 investment in the firm—which remained insolvent.

New York City's Bedford-Stuyvesant district represents one of the poverty program's most persistent efforts to restore an economically depressed community. In the last 12 years more than $55 million has been poured into the area to refurbish abandoned housing, save declining businesses, and boost employment. In spite of this, unemployment increased from 6 percent in 1970 to more than 15 percent in 1976. Vacant houses increased to 2,000 in 1976, twice the number of vacancies existing in 1972. More than 24 percent of the area's businesses, employing some 6,000 persons, pulled out between 1969 and 1974.

Almost half of all money spent in Bedford-Stuyvesant has gone into construction and housing rehabilitation. Unfortunately, officials say that, because the cost of totally gutting and rehabilitating the dwellings is so high, local residents "cannot afford to buy these homes."

"The more I learn about it, the more it becomes clear to me that it is like throwing a tablespoon of water on a fire," Rep. John Conyers (D., Mich.) declared at a hearing on the program.

"We expect an economic organization in a devastated area that is suffering from a depression to come in and do what private entrepreneurs have chosen not to do," Conyers said.

Meantime, the program is duplicating a rash of other government business assistance programs aimed at helping economically depressed areas, including the Small Business Administration, the Economic Development Administration, Minority Business Enterprise, along with other similar programs in USDA and HUD.

Rampant duplication also extends to CSA's community food and nutrition program, which seeks—through outreach activities—to insure that the poor participate in government nutrition programs like food stamps and school lunches.

However, the Department of Agriculture spends $50 million a year on *similar* outreach activities, $20 million more than CSA. The USDA program uses more than 6,000 Extension Service paraprofessionals in half of the nation's counties who go door-to-door in cities like Detroit and Newark, as well as in poor rural areas.

"We're delivering essentially the same service," a USDA official said. "There is obviously considerable overlap in what we're doing."

Overlap is also fully evident in CSA's minigrants, averaging $2,000 each, to establish community gardens for the poor. The Agriculture Department operates a similar service.

These and other criticisms and abuses have seriously weakened congressional confidence in the antipoverty program. (It is difficult to find *anyone* in Congress, of *any* political persuasion, to speak enthusiastically about the program's accomplishments.)

Even Rep. Collins, one of the agency's staunchest supporters, says the agency should not be expanded "until it first cleans up its act." Knowing what we know now, the chances of that happening appear to be remote.

Certainly no one in Congress has criticized the antipoverty program more than Sen. Abraham Ribicoff, one of CSA's original and most enthusiastic supporters. In his 1972 book, *America Can Make It*, the liberal Connecticut Democrat declared:

> Our antipoverty efforts failed. The philosophy of the 1960s—to provide a vast array of services to the poor—must be judged by results. There are 26 million poor Americans—not because they lack social services, advice and counseling but because they lack money, the great equalizer.

It was the "middlemen—not the poor," Ribicoff said, who were prospering under the antipoverty program. "Scores of former anti-poverty officials, and hundreds of private management consulting firms they go to work for are living off the poor," he said. "There is big money in poverty—big money for everybody, that is, except the poor."

Ribicoff found that in OEO's first six years of existence, some $600 million was spent solely on contracts with private consulting firms for evaluation, technical assistance, and consultation.

Asked to update the views he spelled out in his book, Ribicoff said during an interview:

> I wouldn't change a single word I wrote. I started with high hopes. It sounded good. But when you analyzed what's been accomplished, the balance sheet indicates they have generally been failures.

One of the antipoverty program's major architects, Sar Levitan, believes the program has been a key factor in easing poverty in America, but admits there is no concrete evidence that it has had anything to do with the gradual lessening of poverty in our nation. "What you want to measure is not measurable," Levitan said when asked to provide proof of his exhuberant evaluation of CSA's record over the past 15 years.

On the other hand, it is interesting that Levitan credits the Vietnam War, with its jobs, as having been "the most important single thing that brought people out of poverty," not CSA.

Howard Phillips, whom Nixon chose to abolish OEO, said the program was used as a political vehicle by left-wing activists. "I visited health programs where the main concern was registering voters," Phillips said. "The war on poverty program had no impact on poverty, except for the people who were employed by it." At its height, he said, "81 percent of OEO's funds went in one form or another to overhead costs."

One of the few economists to have studied federal poverty programs is UCLA Professor Thomas Sowell, who has written:

> To be blunt, the poor are a gold mine. By the time they are studied, advised, experimented with, and administered, the poor have helped many a middle-class liberal to achieve affluence with government money.

Writing in the *New York Times Magazine*, Sowell said, "The total amount of money the government spends on its many antipoverty efforts is three times what would be required to lift every man, woman and child in America above the official poverty line by simply sending money to the poor."

CSA employes 110,000 people in its 900 local Community Action Agencies, half of whom are said to be from the poor. Forty-four percent of those working in Metropolitan area agencies are making between $10,000 and $15,000 or more a year. A sampling of salaries paid to major Community Action directors in the cities ranges from $22,000 to $48,000 a year.

More than 1,000 people work in CSA's Washington headquarters and its 10 regional offices nationwide. CSA regional directors earn from $36,171 up to $47,500 a year. The director of CSA in Washington earns $57,500 a year. These are astronomical sums to many Americans, who work and scrimp and save all their lives just to keep their head above the poverty line. Is it any wonder that the belief is growing that the poverty business has become a *lucrative career* for thousands of Americans in and out of government?

Meanwhile, it must be underscored that severe criticism of the government's antipoverty programs has not been limited to economists and members of Congress. Many of CSA's own employes and some top officials privately have voiced doubts and criticisms about the program.

"So much of what I see here," said one, "has little impact on the day-to-day lives of the poor. A lot of what is spent is going to an entirely different group of people organized to help the poor. I'm not sure how much of that gets to the poor."

Said another long-time CSA employe,

> We see these contracts getting approved, spending hundreds of thousands of dollars on one project, and we wonder how in the hell does this grant or this study or this report help anyone who is poor. The answer is that it hasn't.

Much of the disillusionment, many poverty workers say, has stemmed from case after case of abuse and mismanagement which numerous congressional committees have uncovered in the program. In one investigation, the House Government Operations Committee charged that CSA had "not served the nation's poor adequately"; that, too often, funds are "not properly accounted for"; and that CSA programs have shown "an unacceptably high number of failures and serious problems."

In another report the committee declared, "Despite its 10 years of experience, there is still confusion in some quarters about the mission of CSA and its priorities." The same report also found the agency had been filled, in recent years, with politically appointed and overpaid employes whose jobs had little relation to their salaries. "The agency's seeming inability to recognize or correct deficiencies identified throughout the course of this investigation raises questions about its abilities to correct existing management deficiencies without external assistance," the committee said.

President Carter's reorganization team began their examination of CSA with good intentions, determined to take a tough-minded approach to this scandal-plagued agency. "The question we have to ask," said one administration official involved in the reorganization study, "is whether there is a role for a community-based, federally supported organization that would complement the regular services provided by the other departments. The proliferation is incredible." In the end, however, political considerations prevailed. The agency wasn't touched.

When all is said and done, has the war on poverty program been successful, even to a limited degree? No one can tell.

Despite interviews with more than 60 experts in the poverty field, *not one* could provide any data to show that anyone rose out of poverty—outside of those who worked for the program—as a result of the program's services and other expenditures.

It is noteworthy, in fact, that when some of the top experts in the field were questioned on this very point, all pointed to those who had worked or now work for the poverty program as proof that the war on poverty has been successful in economically elevating the disadvantaged. But Sen. Ribicoff is not fooled by this flim-flam argument, and neither should anyone else. "That's a very insidious use of logic and a very poor justification for a program," he said. "I would be more impressed if anyone could point to someone who was poor who elevated himself out of poverty because of the program's services."

One knowledgeable congressional investigator, who has spent more than six years examining the CSA program, put it this way:

> Some Community Services Agencies do virtually nothing with their funds. Others are very effective. It's a mixed bag. Has it reduced poverty? Frankly, it's impossible to tell.

CHAPTER 10
Selling the Government

The federal government is spending more than $1.5 billion each and every year solely to promote, communicate, and sell its programs and accomplishments to the American people.

Each year hundreds of millions of tax dollars are spent to run an "army" of nearly 20,000 public information and public affairs workers, movie-makers, broadcasters, writers, editors, and Madison Avenue-type advertising specialists. And every year this public relations army is becoming larger and more expensive.

Salaries for top government press officers—some of whom have been elevated to the rank of assistant secretary—now reach $50,000 a year. Most make more than $30,000 a year. But money isn't everything; Ernest Lotito, who headed the Commerce Department's public information office, with a salary of $47,500 a year, said, "I'd take the job if it paid $5,000 less."

Despite numerous audits and surveys, no one in the government knows precisely how much is being spent for all public information programs. However, officials in several sectors of the government, including the Office of Management and Budget and the Office of Personnel Management, privately maintain that the annual cost is somewhere around $1.5 billion and possibly much higher.

The estimates include $500 million for audio-visual programs, more than $200 million for advertising, and about $400 million for all other public relations and public information programs, including the salaries of the employes who operate them.

While some of the government's public information functions may fulfill necessary and often vital educational and communication needs, an enormous amount of it is extravagant and unnecessary.

Hundreds of "news" releases are issued daily to promote statements and speeches by agency officials. Costly exhibits are placed in federal office buildings displaying larger-than-life pictures of department and agency heads. Agencies are even providing news broadcasts and voice feeds to radio stations around the country, implementing expensive video-tape and play-back systems, and running other ambitious film and audio programs as well. Brochures, booklets, leaflets, and other glossy, full-color literature are produced by the millions. And government "PR" types sit around daily trying

74

to think up promotional stunts to get their superiors and programs featured in the newspapers and on the 7 o'clock evening news.

Hardly an agency of government, no matter how tiny it may be, is without a public relations program. Even President Carter's government reorganization task force, formed to cut waste from a "bloated" bureaucracy, operates a press staff and regularly issues material touting its accomplishments.

As expected, the Defense Department has one of the largest public information and public relations forces in the government, costing more than $25 million a year—excluding advertising for recruitment. Within this operation is a press and public affairs staff of more than 316 people in the Pentagon, plus more than 1,200 military and civilian workers scattered throughout the services and Defense agencies.

Despite its smaller size, the Department of Agriculture virtually matches Defense with a nearly 1,000-worker information-media force—costing $26 million a year.

USDA's information army includes 311 public information officers and specialists, 90 writer-editors, 50 general information officials, 19 illustrators, and 59 film specialists.

USDA writers turn out a mountain of material each year—everything from the annual USDA yearbook to literature on "How To Grow Strawberries."

The Department of Health, Education and Welfare, Washington's largest department in terms of expenditures, has a public affairs staff of 459 whose salaries and activities cost $25.4 million a year. This total includes 96 media information specialists, 57 writers who turn out speeches, articles, and statements, 90 who work full time on HEW publications, plus 44 who handle film and broadcasting projects.

The Commerce Department, which encompasses many unrelated agencies like the U.S. Travel Service and the Census Bureau, has a yearly public affairs budget of $5.6 million.

The department's Office of Public Affairs, serving just the Office of the Secretary, maintains 20 employes under a budget of nearly $800,000. One of the Commerce Department's subagencies, the Maritime Administration, boasts a public affairs budget of nearly half a million dollars, with a staff of eight, while the National Oceanic and Atmospheric Administration (NOAA) has a public affairs budget of $1.1 million which finances about 30 employes. Stanley Eames, director of public affairs for NOAA, which includes the U.S. Weather

Service, says that one-third to one-half of his staff's work is concerned solely with safety and education.

Although the Interior Department is the third smallest department in terms of expenditures, it has a total public affairs staff of 341 people requiring a budget of over $9 million a year.

The Labor Department, meanwhile, feeds an $8.3 million public information budget, excluding printing costs, for a staff of 162 public relations employes, which includes 55 information officers, 35 writers-editors, and 20 editorial and publication assistants.

One of the government's newest departments, the Department of Energy, has over 100 public affairs employes who consume a budget of $2 million a year.

An OMB official summed all of this up by saying, "When you look at the functions of each department and what needs to be communicated, and then see what is being put out, there is clearly more being done than is absolutely necessary."

To get an idea of what our government's PR people spend their time doing, *Wall Street Journal* reporter James M. Perry provided a glimpse into a brain-storming session at the Department of Transportation, where public affairs officials were kicking around some promotional ideas for a prototype gas-efficient vehicle:

> *Terrence Bracy* (assistant secretary for governmental and public affairs): We're getting close. We really are. They say the Moody car got to Washington from Florida on $6 worth of gas, though I don't believe that.
>
> *Ernest Warner* (director of intergovernmental affairs): We gotta blow it up a little more.
>
> *Bracy*: Let's think of having an off-beat auto show. The industry has regular auto shows all the time; why couldn't we have one of our own? We'd let every crazy inventor bring his car here and we'd display them in the plaza (of the Department's quadrangle).
>
> *Susan Williams* (Bracy's deputy): It would be terrific. Think of all the people.
>
> *Warner*: What fun.
>
> *Bracy*: Let's think about it.

Clearly, in every public information program there are excesses. The bigger and more costly the program, the bigger and more costly the excesses. Consider, for example, the 44-member White House press office which issued a 33-page report just to defend the barroom behavior of presidential assistant Hamilton Jordan; President Carter's entire State of the Union address totaled only 15 pages.

Yet public information officials believe the nation would crumble without them. "We're here to get information out to the public," said Commerce's number one press flack, Ernest Lotito. "The news media couldn't survive without us." Among Commerce's newest innovations, without which the country's media couldn't survive, is a Spanish-language broadcast that, according to Lotito, includes "radio feature material, informational stuff, where to go on a vacation, how to save energy." Hardly life-sustaining information.

To his credit, however, Mr. Lotito confesses that, if it had to, Commerce's public relations operations could be run "for less than we're spending now." He also admits that in the process of disseminating public information, he is actually out to shine the department's image: "If I can make the department look good in the process, I'm happy to do it." No one of course wants the Department of Commerce—or any other agency of government, for that matter—to look bad in the public's eyes. But the question is whether we need to spend hundreds of millions of dollars annually to promote the government's image.

Through the years, public information jobs have been elevated in both rank and pay. The rank has been boosted so high that chief information officers at Defense, Treasury, HEW, and State now hold the title of assistant secretary, a post that pays $52,750 a year. (As an assistant secretary of defense for public affairs, Thomas Ross outranked everyone in the active military, except the members of the Joint Chiefs of Staff.)

Meanwhile, Washington in recent years has been turning increasingly to a more direct form of communication with the public: advertising. Consider this television spot:

The children are gathered in the parlor around their grandmother, a small, Italian-looking woman who is happily showing them pictures, presumably photographs of relatives and ancestors from "the old country," in a family album. A distraught husband barges into the kitchen and angrily asks his wife what this woman is doing in his house. "I don't want her here," he shouts. "I want her out of here."

The little old woman—it is never made clear whether she is the man's mother or mother-in-law—obviously is an embarrassment to him. She probably is an immigrant; she certainly is a reminder of his beginnings and an object of his prejudices.

This minidrama is professionally played out in a sixty-second film spot produced under the auspices of the United States Office of Education and aired by television stations around the country. It is only one example of Uncle Sam's investment of tens of millions of dollars in media advertising.

It may not be widely known, but the government is among the top 20 advertisers in the country, right up there with Coca-Cola and Playtex bras, spending more than $200 million a year to "sell" the public on everything from stamp collecting to the beauty of our national parks.

And like Norman Lear, the above excerpt suggests that the government has learned to package prejudice, in a sophisticated attempt to teach people it is wrong.

The Italian grandmother spot, which I have seen several times on television, always leaves me blinking in disbelief. At first, it is not clear what the film is trying to say. The point, however, sinks in when you've seen it several times and pondered its significance (if in fact it has any). Suddenly, you begin to realize that the government is leaving no stone unturned in its zeal to root out prejudice. I mean, on a list of 30 or 40 prejudices, hatred toward one's mother or mother-in-law must rank low. Moreover, like Lear's rather controversial treatment of bigotry (many believe *All in the Family's* Archie Bunker confirms people's prejudices rather than exposes them), the government's ads *may actually foster* prejudice in young people.

In one animated Office of Education ad directed at children's programing, the dialogue goes like this:

> *Boy 1:* We just hired a new man, he's in our training program—name's Kowalski.
> *Boy 2:* Polish fellow, eh? You may end up calling it your *training and training* program. (Both boys laugh.)
> *Boy 3:* I hear you've got a Bernstein in your neighborhood now.
> *Boy 4:* So they're Jewish?
> *Boy 3:* A psychiatrist, you know. Now you can have your head shrunk—wholesale! (Both boys laugh.)
> *Announcer:* Seems when kids play grown-up they copy the grown-ups they know best. Their folks.

Now, isn't this in part how prejudices are fed on the playground and among adults—through cheap racial and ethnic jokes? And of course we cannot ignore a more central question: Why is the government in this business at all? There isn't, after all, a scintilla of evidence that such advertising reduces racial, religious, ethnic, or sexual prejudices.

These messages are of course just a fragment of Uncle Sam's running account with Madison Avenue. The Defense Department has the largest and perhaps most necessary advertising budget because of the need to maintain military recruitment, but advertising can also be found in dozens of other agencies.

Amtrak, the government's rail passenger corporation, spends more than $10 million a year trying to convince Americans to ride its trains. The ads were total failures. The gasoline shortage, in the end, sharply boosted service, until gas once again appeared to become more plentiful. Similarly, Conrail, the quasi-government freight line corporation, spent over $1 million in advertising merely to promote "public awareness" of its existence.

The Consumer Product Safety Commission has run radio spots to remind skiers to keep their bindings tight, and created "Grandma Nature," an elderly woman in lace and tennis shoes who lectured television viewers about safety in the nursery. What mothers did before the Commission created this advertising campaign is hard to say, but apparently they weren't as dumb about taking care of their infants as the Commission assumes.

The Postal Service has run a $4 million ad campaign to get people to write more letters and thus increase the sale of stamps, which drew a "Golden Fleece" award for wasteful spending from Sen. William Proxmire. The Service has also advertised heavily to get people interested in stamp collecting and to convince them to mail their Christmas cards early.

In one spot dreamed up by the Postal Service's ad agency, Young & Rubicam, a mother and her young daughter get a letter from a faraway friend:

> Daughter: But couldn't she call?
> Mother: Of course, but when I get a letter from her, I guess I feel like you do when you get a gift.

Everyone agrees that alcoholism is one of the nation's more disturbing problems, and—according to all the available statistics—it is getting worse. But any intelligent person must seriously question the effectiveness of the television and radio spots produced by the National Institute on Alcohol Abuse. One ad shows a couple out on a picnic. The young lady finishes a glass of wine and asks for another. But her companion talks her out of it, saying it's "because I care about you." This agency budgeted about $350,000 for its ads, but one must raise serious questions whether the ads have done anything to alleviate the problem of alcoholism, particularly among young people.

The Food and Drug Administration's Nutrition Labeling Program launched a nationwide mass-media education program geared toward getting Americans to "Read the label, set a better table." Radio and television spots were recorded by such stars as Dick Van Dyke, Pearl Bailey, and Bob Newhart. Tapes were sent out to hundreds of television stations and thousands of radio stations. Did it improve the nutrition of Americans? We'll never know because FDA has no way of knowing who aired the spots, how often, who listened, and, more importantly, who followed FDA's advice. Still, anyone who has spent any time in a supermarket knows American shoppers do not spend much time, if any, reading food labels, as important as that might be.

Despite the government's prolific efforts to produce radio and television ads in enormous quantities, the reality of it all is that their efforts are usually reaching very few people. Most stations play the ads late at night or in the early hours of the morning between the late-late shows, when they have few commercial spots and need to fill in time. At these hours, very few Americans are awake to hear the government's messages.

The National Highway Traffic Safety Administration produced a 30-second commercial, which was one of five spots that were produced by an advertising agency under a $150,000 contract. The actors were dressed in "Star Wars" costumes, and in a rowdy barroom scene the public is told that, even on some intergalactic planet, it is not safe to let a friend drive home drunk. The agency's audiovisual specialist, Robert Marx, distributed 900 prints of the commercial to television stations. But Marx told the *Journal*'s Perry, "We have no way of knowing how many times they are shown. It is a public service and we don't want to bother them with a lot of reporting requirements." But the agency's administrator, Joan Claybrook, appears to be realistic about it all: "We are competing with thousands of other people . . . and our spot—like the rest—gets on so late at night hardly anyone is watching."

The Office of Management and Budget audited the advertising expenditures of 62 agencies and found $122 million in annual outlays. However, an OMB budget analyst called the figure "understated." It is now "easily over $200 million a year."

Perhaps the most criticized yet most persistent of government public information efforts is filmmaking, a government-wide activity which President Carter's media adviser, Barry Jagoda, says has grown into a $500 million a year enterprise.

The government owns more than $1.5 billion in film, television, and other audio equipment and has, over the past 40 years, produced thousands of films on everything from how to brush your teeth to the thrill of hydrofoil racing.

While some government films may serve important educational and training functions, the vast number of them are made solely to glorify each agency's accomplishments and programs—such as the 14-minute film on the skills of the U.S. Navy's bobsled team.

"We found persistent agency self-promotion in these films," Jagoda said.

How did the government's film industry grow so large?

Jagoda explained that, when Congress legislates certain programs, it also says there will be public information programs about these government efforts, "and that becomes the basis for making films and disseminating information about the program."

It is this kind of vague "public information" directive by Congress which has allowed the government's public relations programs to become bloated quite out of proportion to any justifiable need.

After completing his government-wide film investigation—one of many that has been conducted over the last 10 years—Jagoda said Carter issued strict rules to all department and agency heads "to prohibit the use of government films for self-promotion." But the distinction between what is self-promotion and what is educational or informational is extremely fuzzy when federal bureaucrats are interpreting it. Thus, the saga of Hollywood-in-Washington goes on.

Elsewhere, however, there are extensive self-promotion activities throughout the government, though many departments and agencies won't admit it.

When the General Accounting Office reviewed some of the more than 3,000 publications issued annually by the Department of Agriculture, they were told by officials that none of the material was produced to promote their agencies and programs.

But the GAO thought otherwise. After reviewing the material, they concluded that the USDA's publications were directed "more to enhancing Agriculture's image than to informing the general public."

Careful examination of news releases and other statements and reports issued daily by HEW, HUD, Agriculture, and other departments found numerous cases in which the government's press "flacks," as they are called by media people, were disseminating speeches of officials, congratulatory statements, and other less than vital announcements.

In one of them, HEW Secretary Joseph Califano was congratulating the chairman of a House committee for reauthorizing the elementary and secondary education program. In a USDA release, an assistant secretary announced that canned peaches and cranberry sauce were being purchased for child nutrition programs. *Now, really*. But this type of so-called "public information is being poured out of the bureaucracy, produced, written, and typed by highly-paid federal bureaucrats, and mailed by the millions to seemingly endless media lists within the nation's capital and elsewhere.

Millions of dollars are also spent each year for "congressional liaison" employes throughout the government whose primary job is to sell their agency's programs to Congress and to help insure that future budget requests will be supported by a majority of lawmakers.

It is estimated that more than $68 million is spent annually for salaries of these federal liaison specialists, which may be the ultimate in the "selling of the government"—tax dollars being spent to insure that Congress spends even more tax dollars.

It is difficult to imagine a government activity or expenditure that is more wasteful or more unnecessary to the efficient operation of our government than these exaggerated press and public information programs. This is not to say that some of them are not valuable. But they have been allowed to grow to such grotesque excesses that their curtailment should be *one of the first priorities* of any effort to cleanse the government of its most wasteful manifestations. Federal programs that perform efficiently and effectively *do not need to be sold* to the American people. Only bad ones.

CHAPTER 11
Impact Aid: Making Rich Schools Richer

Fred Foster works in Washington for the federal government. He is married, has three children, and lives in nearby Fairfax County, Virginia, in a comfortable four-bedroom house. He pays property taxes on his home which amount to about $1,400 a year.

Foster, which is not his real name, also pays state income tax, state sales tax, plus a personal property tax and other local levies and taxes—all of which finance local government costs, including those for the public schools which his children attend.

Still, because he is a government employe, his children—along with millions of other children of federal workers—are considered by law to have placed an inequitable burden or "impact" on local school costs. This, according to federal law, makes Fairfax County schools eligible for additional federal school aid—$18 million in fiscal 1980—to offset the costs of educating federally-connected children. The program is called "impact aid" and in the 1980 fiscal year the government will pay out $816 million to 4,340 of the country's 16,000 school districts to fund it.

Every president from Dwight Eisenhower to Jimmy Carter has tried to cut the impact aid program, but Congress has resisted, largely because school districts in 400 of the nation's 435 congressional districts receive money from it. In other words, the program is virtually "locked in" politically, because, unfortunately, members of Congress rarely vote against programs which bring federal dollars into their states or districts.

Impact aid's original purpose—begun when Harry Truman was in the White House—was simply to provide school aid to communities where non-taxable military installations, many in rural areas, added to local school costs without providing tax revenues to meet them.

The original program provided a flat payment for each student whose parents worked and resided on military bases. In 1951, this amounted to a modest $29 million a year. But as Congress added new groups of recipients to the program, its costs multiplied 28-fold. More than $9 billion has gone into the program since it began.

One of the key departures from the program's original rationale

83

was to extend aid to communities where federal employes worked on government property, but lived in private residences, which of course were taxed to support local schools and other government programs within the communities.

But communities argued they were still losing money because they were getting no property or business taxes from the federal installations.

This part of the program grew so rapidly that, by 1970, President Nixon said his administration had found 70 percent of all federal impact payments to schools were "for children of federal employes who live off-base and pay local property taxes."

In a message to Congress, Nixon said that "nearly twice as much federal money goes into the nation's wealthiest county through this program as goes into the 100 poorest counties combined."

Thus, while Fairfax County, with a median family income of $28,000, may get up to $18 million in impact aid, less affluent communities are getting little or nothing. Examples include Buffalo, which receives only $350,000 in impact aid; Cleveland, $398,000; and Jersey City, $263,000.

On the other hand, other Washington, D.C., suburbs, like Maryland's Prince George's County and Montgomery County, receive $10 million and $6 million, respectively, in federal impact aid. Affluent communities like New York's Westchester County and Connecticut's wealthy Fairfield County also are getting hundreds of thousands of dollars because they educate the children of usually well-paid federal employes.

A top official of the U.S. Office of Education who lives in Fairfax County said, "For the life of me, I can't see why my child should generate a payment just because I work for the government."

At one time in the growth of this program, things had become so ridiculous that reporters who worked in the Capitol covering the Congress found they were counted in their counties as eligible for impact aid simply because they worked on "federal property," even though they owned their own homes and were in fact working in the private sector.

But let us examine some of the arguments for this *extended* form of impact aid. Does the presence of federal facilities and employes indeed result in an adverse impact upon local school costs? Counties receiving impact aid say that it does, but many others reject that contention. In 1974, Duane Mattheis of the U.S. Office of Education said:

Literally hundreds of the eligible districts . . . suffer no appreciable ad-verse effect on the ability to support schools due to the presence of federally-connected children. On the contrary, a federal activity is often a major and much-prized economic benefit.

Out of the $816 million in impact aid, over $320 million is being spent for children of federal employes, the vast majority of whom own their own homes and pay property taxes to support their schools in addition to other local and state taxes.

In 1974, Congress voted to eliminate payments in this category—but "hold harmless" provisions were added to insure that school districts continue to receive most, if not all, of their impact money.

Local officials argue strongly that, despite any economic benefit the federal government may bring into an area, whether it is a civilian or military facility, there are also many unseen losses in revenues.

For example, they say that while off-base military personnel may pay property tax on their homes, many can legally avoid paying a number of other taxes which denies the school district revenue.

In Fairfax County, out of a total of 26,400 federally-connected students, 1,200 live at the Army's Fort Belvoir. Of the remaining 25,200 children who live on private property, 15,800 are from mil-itary families. The rest are children of civilian government workers.

"Most military personnel in this area," says a county official, "maintain their original residency in states like Florida, where there is no income tax, and thus avoid paying one here.

"Moreover, they are exempt from paying personal property tax, full county and state vehicle fees and, since they shop at the military commissary, they avoid sales taxes" on food, which represents "quite a bit of lost income and shows there is an impact."

But while school officials are able to detail the negative impact of government facilities and workers, they are unable to provide any figures on any positive economic benefit.

One county official was asked which side would come out ahead if all negative federal impact costs were compared to the total state, property, sales, and other taxes paid by government employes, plus all other forms of income their higher-than-average salaries poured into the area's economy. His answer couldn't have been more re-vealing: "Certainly overall there is a positive economic impact. If there were no federal employes in Fairfax County, it would be des-titute. It would have a severely negative economic affect on the county."

And when presented with the figures of who gets what, many local school officials react with surprise and bitterness.

"I don't think it's fair," said Gene Stockdale, an assistant school superintendent in South Bend, Indiana, which gets virtually no impact aid.

South Bend's 30,000-student school system has many of the same educational problems of other medium size cities, including special inner city needs, Stockdale said. "If one gets it, everybody ought to get it," he added, calling the impact aid system "outdated. We have 70 different aid to education programs, with all the paperwork and costly overhead that goes with it. It drives you nuts. What we need is a single uniform aid to education program in which the money would go to the states and then be redistributed back to the local school districts." Such a simple, money-saving approach to aid to education would be rejected out of hand by Washington. If it isn't complex and almost impossible to understand and administer, the government wouldn't consider it.

With yearly impact aid expected to go over $1 billion by 1982, President Carter followed the lead of his predecessors and proposed a number of reforms to gradually phase down what he considered to be the least necessary elements of impact aid. Specifically, Carter wanted to eliminate payments for children whose parents worked on federal property outside the county in which the school district was located. But that was rejected by a House subcommittee, which in fact voted to relax restrictions on the program that Congress had imposed three years ago.

Then-HEW Secretary Joseph Califano testified that the administration's reforms could have saved $76 million in 1979, money which, he believed, would be better spent to meet "other educational needs such as those of the handicapped and disadvantaged." He might have added that complete elimination of impact aid for children of parents who live on their own private, residential property and support their schools through local and state taxes, would free hundreds of millions of dollars more to improve the poorest and most needy school systems in our nation. Such a reform, however, would require a degree of unselfishness in our lawmakers that, thus far, has not been detected by the public they are elected to serve.

CHAPTER 12
The $100 Billion Paperwork Connection

Bob Hansen is a small, independent agricultural wholesaler in Omaha, Nebraska. He works hard, pays his taxes on time and, like most Americans, believes in obeying the law. But when the federal government recently sent him yet another bureaucratic form to fill out, Hansen decided that he would at last "find out what the penalty is for not complying."

Ed Gaffney, who manufactures products for the handicapped in Waukesha, Wisconsin, says the government's paperwork demands have become so intolerable that when he received another form from the Federal Trade Commission, "We just decided not to fill it out." Gaffney backed down, however, when he began getting telegrams and phone calls from the FTC, which threatened to fine him $50 a day until he filed the form.

John Pauley is vice-president of Gala Industries of Eagle Rock, Virginia, which makes centrifugal dryers for the plastics industry. "I don't understand half of what I'm reading on these forms," he says, and, in fact, Washington's incessant demands for information have become so heavy that Pauley was forced to hire an extra employe just to handle the deluge of paperwork. Complying with the increased reporting requirements of the new pension-reform act alone costs Gala Industries $2,000 a year "and God knows how many hours," Pauley says. "And this is money you can't give to your employes in raises or bonuses—you're giving it to the government."

These are just a few reactions from a nationwide survey of increasingly frustrated businessmen and women now actively protesting the enormous cost, in time and money, of fulfilling the government's rising paperwork requirements—from Census Bureau questionnaires to IRS forms to Department of Energy surveys to FTC data reports.

Despite the avalanche of protests, however, things now seem to be getting worse instead of better. In fact, they may be getting out of hand altogether. Thomas McIntyre, when he was a senator from New Hampshire, studied the problem and calculated that "the paperwork generated in one year by Washington alone would fill Yankee Stadium from the playing field to the top of the stands 51 times."

And still the paperwork comes piling down upon all of us. The Department of Energy, the newest and perhaps most prolific contributor of federal paperwork, sent service station owners a monthly form accompanied by four pages of complex, small print instructions, part of which read:

> Calculate the average pump selling price for each of the motor fuels listed in Item A and Item B by dividing Column (a) by Column (b). Enter results in Column (c) rounding to the nearest tenth of a cent.

Complained Charles Kahl, a regional representative for the National Federation of Independent Business (NFIB) in Hampton, New Hampshire, "These service station forms are designed to monitor just about everything the owner does. This is nothing but asinine harassment."

If it is any consolation to the service station owners (and it probably isn't), banks are also notable sufferers. Thomas Masilla, Jr., assistant treasurer of the Hibernia Corporation, a New Orleans banking firm, says that filling out federal forms cost his company between $200,000 and $300,000 a year.

Big corporations, of course, also have reason to complain about this increase in regulatory red tape. A major oil company, for example, estimates that it has to file more than 400 reports (excluding tax forms) each year with at least 45 different federal agencies, but at least the major companies have the resources to handle the federal paperwork demands—the costs of which are of course passed along to consumers.

Small companies, on the other hand, with fewer than 50 employes, must complete some 75 federal forms annually (plus required state and local forms), and they are, therefore, the ones who suffer most from this "paperwork blizzard."

James McKevitt, chief counsel for the NFIB, says his organization's 445,000 member firms complain that they "have to spend 15 percent to 20 percent of their time every week simply filling out various forms requested by an endless variety of federal agencies."

One complaint that was registered bluntly and publicly came from Bob Hansen, the Omaha agricultural wholesaler who employs only 15 workers. "We just don't have time to screw around with this stuff," he said. "We're trying to run a business. I've had a census form on my desk for several months. It was supposed to be done in February. There are six pages of detailed questions, asking sales by commodity lines in the millions, by percentages. Unless you have a computer it's virtually impossible to break out this kind of information."

Hansen says he spends a total of four days, perhaps as much as a week out of each month, "making out a report to someone. This census form says I must comply under penalty of law. So I'm going to find out what the penalty is."

Daniel Slade, who runs Crickett Press, Inc., of Massachusetts, says that the census form "takes 10 to 15 hours of my time and that of my staff." Then, on top of that, there is the pension plan paperwork which, alone, caused Crickett Press to hire an extra clerk. "The forms are so intricate that even the accountants and lawyers are having trouble interpreting them," Slade complains. "Our girl had to call Washington the other day to clear up a question."

Ed Gaffney, the Wisconsin manufacturer, says it takes him three to four hours just to fill out a quarterly FTC survey. Gaffney got the same census form which Hansen and millions of other businesses received. He calls it "horrendous."

"A lot of the reports we must fill out are duplicative," Gaffney says. "The FTC report was almost identical to a Commerce Department survey I received."

Last year, Gaffney's company, Ortho-Kinetics, Inc., did a little over $3.2 million in sales of products for the handicapped. He provides work for 50 employes, one of whom was hired full time just to handle the government's forms.

If I didn't have to comply with all of this," he says, "I could pass that savings along in lower prices or in bonuses and salary increases for my employes. I've been complaining about government paperwork since we were one-tenth the size we are now. But it never does any good."

Some businessmen, like Hansen and Edward Richard, president of Magnetics International of Maple Heights, Ohio, have tried to resist the paperwork onslaught, but so far they have been no match for the powerful bureaucracy.

Richard's firm, a small manufacturer of motors, magnets, and generators, must file 56 different forms with various agencies of the government. For him, the last straw was a Federal Trade Commission quarterly report form which sought data on his company's sales, securities, assets, and liabilities. What did the FTC do when he refused to comply?

"They threatened court action if I didn't complete it," he told a New York Times reporter, "and even implied imprisonment. The government bullies people. Those people are working for us—but the way they came on, it was as though I was working for them."

Government paperwork "has definitely increased and increased every single year," says Portland, Oregon, businessman Wayne Kuhn. "And the reason it is getting worse is because the government is telling you how to live, what to do, how to conduct your business."

Kuhn, a member of the boards of directors of several businesses, estimated that 8 to 10 percent of their costs relate to federal paperwork. "And these costs are passed on to the consumers. That's what few people realize."

Robert Stewart, Jr., manager of Gulf Oil's Business Economics Corporate Planning Department, singles out federal regulatory agencies like the Equal Employment Opportunity Commission, the Occupational Safety and Health Administration, and the Environmental Protection Agency as among the worst paperwork offenders.

"Some paperwork is necessary to develop the kind of statistics industry and businesses need to make intelligent decisions," Stewart says. "But agencies like these are requesting data to help the regulatory agencies devise more regulations. This is where a tremendous expansion has occurred since the early 1970s in paperwork demands."

The government's own statistics on its paperwork demands are staggering. The Agriculture Department, for example, annually spends $150 million producing various forms—forms that have produced *989,224 cubic feet* of records, filling almost 37,000 file drawers. The Labor Department estimates that respondents annually complete 44.8 million of its forms, requiring 17.2 million hours of effort. The General Accounting Office reports that Americans fill out 424.8 million federal forms each year—consuming 127.7 million hours of work.

Translating this time into money, the best available estimates are that business annually spends $32 billion to comply with the paperwork demands of Washington—but experts say this official figure is probably underestimated by a factor of four. It costs individuals nearly $9 billion a year to meet their own paperwork requirements, primarily tax forms. Eventually this total overall cost of paperwork is borne by every American, in the form of higher taxes and rising prices.

To put it in its simplest terms, the paperwork blizzard has increased the cost of virtually everything in our economy—from health care to energy to education. It has gotten so bad, in fact, that it is not uncommon for businesses to turn down government bids on work contracts, no matter how lucrative they may at first appear, because of the cost of the paperwork.

State and local governments are finding themselves in the same dilemma. The state of Maryland once rejected a $60,000 grant for a consumer education program because the costs of complying with the paperwork requirements would have consumed 75 percent of the grant. State highway officials around the country have testified that federal paperwork eats up 25 percent of their program costs. One school turned down a $4,500 grant because the paperwork would have cost $6,000.

Even when it is successful in soliciting bids, the government itself must often pay exhorbitant sums for equipment and other contracted services because of the paperwork it imposes upon the business contractor. One noted example involved a government agency that sought to buy about $4,000 worth of fire fighting equipment. The agency's solicitation bid was 155 pages long and included 23 pages of foldout diagrams. Forty-one firms were solicited, but only two responded. The successful bid, grotesquely swollen by the cost of filling out the required forms, was $15,497—or about four times the estimated cost of the equipment.

In addition to driving up the cost of everything the government buys with our money by many billions of dollars, the paperwork blitz is also forcing up many consumer costs the government supposedly wants to keep down. Thus, a hospital in Tennessee complained that federal paperwork demands were adding $4 a day to the cost of a hospital room. In Massachusetts, paperwork is costing hospitals between $60 million and $80 million a year.

In the energy field, the General Accounting Office has reported that energy-producing companies spent 1.5 million hours in 1975 responding to requests for data from congressional committees and federal agencies. Again, for all of this, consumers foot the bill.

After Congress enacted the pension reform act (ERISA), the mandatory reports became so intolerable that firms began terminating existing plans and refusing to establish new ones, thereby jeopardizing the pensions of thousands of workers. In one case, said a government report, "Fifteen employes lost their pension plan because the small company could not handle the paperwork."

Every year the government spends more than $43 billion to print, process, compile and store federal forms. In all, an estimated $100 billion a year—and many believe the figure is higher—is sucked from our economy to comply with this paperwork passion.

Is anything being done to curb the federal paperwork mill? And who is really to blame for this mess?

Congress wrestled with the problem as far back as 1942 and came up with the Federal Reports Act, which gave the Budget Office veto power over new federal forms proposed by departments and agencies. Its aim was to weed out unnecessary paperwork and minimize costs to the public. But, according to every available study, the act has been a failure.

"One of the problems is that the Office of Management and Budget isn't adequately staffed to do this job," says David Marsh, executive director of the Business Advisory Council on Federal Reports. Marsh says OMB has only 11 professional reviewers who must evaluate thousands of forms each year.

In 1974, Congress tried again and created the Federal Paperwork Commission which churned out a considerable amount of paperwork of its own and even produced a movie about the problem. The commission made over 770 paper-cutting recommendations valued at more than $10 billion and managed to talk a number of agencies into accepting some of them. Still, when compared to the magnitude of the problem, the number of recommendations actually implemented by the bureaucracy as a whole was relatively small.

"It was like trying to put out the Towering Inferno with a garden hose," a former commission official confided to a friend.

Under get-tough orders from President Carter, then-OMB Director Bert Lance attempted a fresh paperwork purge but made no discernible dent in the problem. Although the administration claimed to have cut federal paperwork by 12 percent, few if any in the business community believed it.

"We think we're heroes if we just hold the line," says Marsh, whose advisory council represents 120 business associations and 75 companies.

One of the big problems, he notes, is that the most prolific producer of paperwork, the Internal Revenue Service, is exempt from OMB review procedures. "For small businesses, tax forms represent about one-third of their reporting burden," Marsh says.

Yet even while the paperwork thicket worsens each year, there is some evidence that the private sector is beginning to fight back, or at least resisting long enough to require the government to impose penalties. One survey by the National Federation of Independent Business shows that about 400,000 businesses are fined by the government each year for violating federal rules and regulations, many of them requiring reports of one kind or another. After studying the survey's startling findings, Sen. Lloyd Bentsen, A Texas Democrat, noted that most of the violations were "due in part or entirely to confusion or ignorance of federal regulations and not with premeditated, willful intent to break laws."

Small businesses, Bentsen added, simply "cannot afford the cost of complying with every nit-picking federal paperwork requirement." And Bentsen says there are a lot of them, spread out over 70,000 pages of the *Federal Register* every year.

Often it is just cheaper to pay the fine than comply, businessmen say. One firm chose to pay a $500 fine rather than assume the cost of paying $750 to an attorney or accountant in order to complete a complicated federal form.

And, as one paperwork expert says, "It's not only business. I think everyone has had a bellyful of this."

Some are taking the government to court. The FTC's "line of business" reports were being challenged because businesses complained they demanded too wide an assortment of data. "For companies with a product mix," Marsh points out, "the line of business is not the way they keep their books."

Other court suits have challenged the government's violation of confidentiality of business data, which has allowed other agencies to have access to the data, as well as the Environmental Protection Agency's efforts to collect similar economic data by plant in order to develop industry-by-industry regulatory guidelines. The FTC is fighting more than a dozen lawsuits against its paperwork requirements.

While all of this legal battling is going on, however, the real source of rising federal paperwork continues on its merry way. For if the executive branch is the pipeline for the continuing flow of paperwork, it is the Congress that has been turning on the spigot without restraint.

Former Sen. Thomas McIntyre (D., N.H.) placed the blame exactly where it belonged: "The biggest culprit in paperwork is *us*," he testified. " 'We have met the enemy and the enemy is us'," he said, quoting a famous Pogo observation.

And he was right. Although most members of Congress piously excoriate the horrors of mounting paperwork, there are few on Capitol Hill who have not voted for or proposed legislation that did not mandate new reporting requirements. Lobbying disclosure reforms, the Arab boycott bill, the Humphrey-Hawkins full employment measure—all of these pieces of legislation and thousands more require that more forms be drawn up and filled out by business, state and local governments, public interest groups, and just ordinary citizens.

More than 9,000 laws enacted by Congress require reports of one type or another. Just between 1965 and 1968, for example, when Congress was racing to enact President Johnson's Great Society programs, the number of government reports grew by 30 percent. By almost every account, that trend continues today. Rep. Frank Horton, the New York Republican who chaired the Paperwork Commission, says the paperwork mountain has risen by a factor of five in the past decade.

The solution is elusive at best—unless someone can find a way to not only convince the Congress to enact fewer laws but also eliminate many of the unnecessary ones now on the books. The Senate once adopted a feeble rule which required that bills sent to the floor be accompanied by a paperwork-impact assessment. But the rule is rarely complied with. As one congressional veteran put it:

> Asking congressmen to curb paperwork is like asking them to enact fewer bills. They're just never going to do it.

When William Proxmire asked government agencies to send him a copy of every form they used, reactions from the bureaucracy ranged from bemused frustration to paralytic shock. Proxmire might just as well have asked a confetti manufacturer to send him a copy of everything he had shredded since day one.

"My God," shrieked one Census Bureau official. "It would take three people two days just to pull all the forms."

"If we start now and worked until doomsday, we could never get all the forms," an exasperated official replied.

"You know what everyone did when I told them of your request?" an Internal Revenue Service official asked Proxmire. "They laughed."

They shouldn't have. It's an expensive joke. In terms of both dollars and wasted productivity, the federal government's avalanche of paperwork has become a Kafka-like nightmare for private businesses, local governments, and individual citizens. In fact, in a time of disaster epics, it is easy to imagine a movie spectacular in which the nation's capital is *smothered to death* in a blizzard of paperwork produced by a bureaucracy gone berserk.

While the anguished cries of businessmen around the country reach crescendo levels, at least one entrepreneur has found a way to turn federal paperwork to his own profit.

Wayne H. Robbins, who runs Conva Care Services, Inc., a Bedford, Indiana, medical-equipment rental company, says that Medicare and Medicaid paperwork have been "adding a terrific cost" to his rental prices, which the sick and the elderly must bear. In 1970, it cost him $4,096 to process claims on rental equipment. Today, his paperwork costs have soared to more than $23,000 a year.

"This Medicare is so complex," he says, "it takes an Einstein to understand it. The elderly just can't hack it."

So Robbins has gone into the business of helping the poor and the elderly process their federal paperwork claims by creating his own H&R Block-type business called Medical Insurance Claims Service. Robbins' answer to the government's paperwork mess is, "If you can't beat 'em—join 'em."

CHAPTER 13
The Double Dippers

Under an obscure 1964 law, thousands of "retired" military officers are getting big federal pensions plus regular government salaries that provide some with dual incomes totaling $80,000 and more a year.

The practice is called "double dipping." It benefits about 180,000 military retirees who have taken civilian government jobs, often performing the same job they had in the military but at sharply higher incomes—frequently higher than those of their superiors and far higher than those of civilians in comparable government jobs.

Some double dippers are getting paid more by the government than members of Congress ($60,662), Cabinet secretaries ($69,630), U.S. Appeals Court judges ($57,500); they even surpass the $72,500 salaries paid to associate justices of the Supreme Court and the $75,000 a year paid to Supreme Court Chief Justice Warren Burger and Vice-President Walter Mondale.

The biggest double dipper anyone has found thus far is CIA Director Stansfield Turner who, by beating a deadline, won a 41 percent government pay increase which boosted his total federal income to nearly $81,000 a year.

Turner's pay boost was the result of his decision on the last day of 1978 to retire from the Navy as a four-star admiral, which immediately made him eligible for a $23,390-a-year pension, to be added to the $57,500 he earned as CIA chief. Had Turner waited just a few days to retire, he would have had to forfeit his pension while in his present government job.

This was because Congress, in 1978, placed a ceiling of $47,500 on the combined federal pay plus federal pension which future military retirees could receive. The law, which contained a generous "grandfather" clause, took effect on January 11, 1979. Turner, however, retired officially on December 31, 1978, in plenty of time to beat the "date of retirement" deadline.

Defense Department statistics show that the Dual Compensation Act of 1964 has been a powerful retirement incentive for officers who take advantage of early 20-year retirement in order to substantially increase their government income while working toward a second federal pension under the civil service system.

For example, between 1972 and 1975 there was an 83 percent increase in the number of military retirees who went to work for the government. More than half of all retirees left the service after 20 years. Experts say this trend continues today.

Moreover, the lucrative "revolving door" transfer from the military to the civilian payroll has often been manipulated by a little-known "buddy system," through which the new job is tailored exactly to meet the qualifications or specifications of retired applicants.

The annual cost of providing retirement pay to double dippers is over $1 billion, part of the military's pension costs which now add more than $10 billion annually to the federal budget. Sen. Thomas Eagleton (D., Mo.) has warned that if nothing is done to curb runaway military pension costs, they will end up costing "more than $30 billion a year at the end of this century."

Here is how the system works:

Retired military enlisted people and reserve officers represent the biggest group of federal employes who get both paychecks and full pensions from the government. Retired "regular" officers must take a partial pension cut while double dipping. Retired federal judges, career diplomats, Tennessee Valley Authority employes, and a relatively few other retired federal employes can also engage in double dipping with full or partial pensions.

For almost everyone else, however, double dipping is prohibited. Retired civil service workers who return to government are required to forfeit all or part of their pensions while on the federal payroll. Social Security beneficiaries find their benefit checks cut when their income exceeds $3,480, if they are under 65 ($4,500 if they are over 65). Welfare and food stamp clients have similar restrictions on income.

Even reservists called back to active military duty are prohibited from receiving both retirement benefits and service pay. They must choose one or the other, but if they take federal civilian jobs they can get full pensions and regular salaries.

"We know of no business, company or corporation that retires its executives or other employes and then rehires them in fulltime, permanent, second-career jobs paying them both a full pension and salary," said Sid Taylor, research director for the National Taxpayers Union.

There are 16 former admirals now earning an average of more than $60,000 a year in government, with a combined $34,500 pension and $25,900 salary. Elsewhere in the government, there are more than 8,600 former lieutenant colonels and Navy commanders getting double paychecks which average almost $33,000 a year.

The National Taxpayers Union estimates that about 3,000 retired military personnel in second-career jobs on the federal payroll are earning from $50,000 to $80,000 per year in combined pay plus pension income.

A case in point was Admiral Daniel J. Murphy, a former deputy to CIA Director Turner, who "retired" to take a $47,500 a year civilian post in the Defense Department as an under-secretary in charge of intelligence. For Murphy, the change in jobs meant boosting his annual income to $60,000 because he immediately began receiving about $12,500 of his estimated $20,000 retirement pay.

Alfred D. Starbird, a retired lieutenant general who devoted 37 years to the military after graduation from West Point, was also among the champion double dippers who earned at least $71,000 a year from the government. Starbird served as an assistant administrator for national security for what was then called the Energy Research and Development Administration (since folded into the Department of Energy) at a salary of $50,000. Because he was a "regular army" officer, he was, like Murphy, limited while working for the government to only a partial pension—$21,000 of his $36,000 entitlement. Still, at the time he held his post, Starbird's total compensation far exceeded the salary of his superior, who was earning "only" $52,500 a year and ran all of ERDA.

There are also 33 members of Congress receiving dual compensation, including Sen. Howard Cannon (D., Nev.), a retired Air Force major general who receives $14,026 a year in retirement pay while on the congressional payroll, bringing his annual federal income to more than $71,500.

Until the combined pay-pension ceiling of $47,500 went into effect at the beginning of 1979, attempts in Congress to institute a total ban on dual compensation, or at least a deferment of pension, all met defeat. A House Appropriations Committee effort to ban dual compensation for future federal employes—though avoiding any change for present double dippers—was rejected by the House 220-173 after heavy lobbying by retired military groups. A similar amendment offered by Eagleton also failed.

Some, like Rep. Les Aspin (D., Wis.), would like to go even further and postpone all military pensions for future retirees "until a more normal retirement age," perhaps between the ages of 55 and 62.

Aspin asked, "Is it fair, to millions of taxpayers who don't collect military pensions, that we pay so much 'retired pay' to so many 'retirees' who aren't retired at all?"

Originally, there was a $10,000 a year combined pay and pension ceiling for military retirees who held civilian government jobs, but Congress opened up the pension floodgates when it passed the 1964 Dual Compensation Act. This allowed a "double dipping" windfall that has been escalating pension outlays throughout all government agencies for years. This single law has cost taxpayers about $9 billion to date.

While enlisted and reserve retirees who take civilian government jobs have no limitations placed on their retirement income, retired "regular" officers are limited to the first $4,532 (which is indexed) of their pensions, plus half of the balance.

According to a House Civil Service Committee study, based on 1975 data, about 80,000 retirees hold civilian jobs in the Defense Department, many of them performing in the same office or job they had before they "retired." Another 35,000 work for the Postal Service, most of them as blue collar postal workers.

The study found that an average civil service salary of $21,660, when combined with an average $10,865 pension, provided some 27,600 retired military officers with an annual income of $32,525.

The study also found that more than 111,600 retired enlisted personnel earned an average of almost $20,000 in pension and pay.

Because these sums are automatically adjusted upward each year to keep pace with inflation, a study by Aspin found that a 20-year officer who retired in 1977 received pension benefits totaling 144 percent of what he made in the previous two decades.

This is in sharp contrast to the average private-sector worker who will receive pension checks totaling 20 to 30 percent of his earnings over the same period.

Helping military officers to retire into lucrative civil service jobs is a little-known civil service regulation loophole called the "unassembled exam." This is how it works, according to government workers.

Under a "buddy system," the pending retiree files a job qualification sheet with the Office of Personnel Management. Then a military superior (or a friend in the department where the job is located) carefully draws up a "job description" statement that is, according to one federal worker, "amazingly identical" to the applicant's qualifications, experience and background.

The hiring officer (or computer), when presented with a list of all top candidates whose qualifications closely match the job, invariably selects the *rigged* applicant.

But the real controversy over dual compensation goes much deeper than this. The real heart of the issue is early retirement.

"The whole retirement system has to be worked over," former House Appropriations Committee Chairman George Mahon (D., Tex.) told me.

"The problem is letting them get pensions immediately upon retirement," said Dick Lieberman, a knowledgeable Senate Appropriations Committee official. "The flaw in the system today is the 20-years-and-out philosophy, and that is what has to be changed."

Figures indicate that about half of all double dippers today are between 40 and 50 years of age. Defense Department calculations show that if the minimum age at which military pensions are paid were raised to age 45, the government would save at least $1.2 billion a year. If the qualifying age were raised to age 50, a nearly $2.3 billion savings would be realized. And if it were raised to age 55, the result would be an almost $3.8 billion savings in pensions costs.

Thus, the answer to this outrageously wanton expenditure of public funds is not just to end the practice of dual compensation, but to totally reform the retirement system so that pensions are not paid to military personnel *until they truly reach* retirement age.

CHAPTER 14
A No-Frills Pentagon

It is easy, and sometimes politically rewarding, to criticize military spending. That is why the Pentagon's highly visible budget is usually the first to take it on the chin from members of Congress looking for some fast media attention and plaudits from America's antimilitary spending critics.

That also, in part, explains the growing public perception that defense spending has been swollen wholly out of proportion to other budgetary expenditures. Despite evidence to the contrary, the belief persists that the Pentagon's budget is consuming the lion's share of the federal budget at the expense of America's so-called human needs.

To set the record straight, the Defense Department's slice of the federal budget has been shrinking for years, while that portion directed toward those "human needs"* has risen dramatically, and continues to grow.

Consider the following. Between 1952 and 1976, military spending increased from $46 billion to $90 billion, an increase of about 50 percent over 24 years. At the same time, however, spending on health, education, and welfare rose from $5 billion to $128.7 billion, an increase of 1,346 percent. Put another way, total federal spending rose over this period by $158 billion, but, of that sum, 51 percent went to the Health, Education and Welfare Department, and 19 percent went to the Defense Department.

In 1952 military spending accounted for 49 percent of all federal outlays. By 1968 the Pentagon consumed 45 percent of the budget. President Ford's fiscal 1976 military budget request of $94 billion (which Congress cut to $90 billion) represented 26.9 percent of the total budget. Ford's fiscal 1978 budget, his last, dropped the defense share to 25 percent of the budget. President Carter subsequently reduced the Pentagon's slice to 24 percent of federal outlays.

The point of all this is not in any way to belittle the Pentagon's fiscal 1980 $130.9 billion budget. By any standard, it is an enormous sum of money. But it must be kept in focus in relation to other federal

---

*I find this abstract social welfare term somewhat mystifying, since it rests on the assumption that America's defense has nothing whatsoever to do with human needs—which is most obviously not true.

expenditures. For while 24 cents out of every federal tax dollar now goes to national defense, 38 cents out of each dollar goes to direct benefit payments to individuals, with an additional 16 cents of each dollar going to states and localities—all of which provides abundantly for those "human needs."

Still, having said all of this, even the most cursory examination of military expenditures reveals an alarming degree of wasteful spending which in no way contributes to America's military strength. Much of it can only be described in one word: frills. Yet many of these frills and other special benefits are so cemented into military practices and life-styles that a nuclear bomb couldn't dislodge them. Moreover, much of the Defense Department's costliest excesses are the product of long-outdated manpower management practices, particularly the Pentagon's ritualistic worship of early retirement.

The Pentagon has produced a bloated civilian bureaucracy of one million men and women to support some two million military personnel. An incredible 55 percent of the Defense Department's budget went for personnel costs in fiscal 1979, not for weapons development and procurement, or for other military needs.

The General Accounting Office revealed how these personnel costs have become unnecessarily swollen when it focused on one tiny military facility as an exercise to see how military funds were spent. The GAO uncovered a classic example of military bureaucratization, finding that 65 out of 68 military personnel working at the Naval Weapons Support Center in Crane, Indiana, were *unnecessary*. In fact, the auditing agency concluded that the U.S. Navy could save $858,000 a year by simply replacing the military personnel with civilians.

The Navy, it turned out, was spending $1.2 million a year to keep 19 officers and 49 enlisted men at the Center. But only 23 of the military personnel—or one in three—worked at jobs related to the mission of the Naval Center. The GAO discovered that the other 45, plus 10 civilians, were providing services for the 23 personnel who did all the Center-related work. Such services included food preparation, maintenance, commissary and exchange store facilities, recreation programs, and health care. The GAO recommended that 65 military positions be cut, and that one officer and two enlisted men be retained for overall supervision of an enlarged civilian work force. The Defense Department balked at the suggestion, but agreed to review its commercial and industrial activities to see if military personnel could be reduced. (Over 10,000 military men are assigned to 90 commercial and industrial military support activities run by the Defense Department. A great many of them are probably unneeded.)

This of course represents a miniscule item in the Pentagon's multi-billion-dollar budget. But the Defense budget is *crammed* with miniscule items like this one—virtually all of them examples of bureaucratic excess and extravagance.

For example, in a perhaps all-too-typical case of wasteful Pentagon spending, the Navy was found to have assigned five of its bachelor enlisted men in Norfolk, Virginia, to live off-base at government expense, despite the fact that there were 675 unused housing units for bachelors right on their base. In a study conducted for Rep. Les Aspin, the Navy was found to be assigning a wing or a floor of the bachelor enlisted quarters to a particular unit. When that military unit had too many bachelors for its assigned quarters, it simply housed the men off-base. Whether another military unit in the next wing—or on another floor—had dozens of empty rooms was immaterial. Bachelor enlisted persons assigned off-base housing received a housing allowance which ranged, according to rank, from $66.60 to $204 a month.

Aspin's study disclosed that the practice was costing an extra $3.4 million a year at the 11 bases he investigated. Worldwide, however, Aspin estimated that the practice could be costing taxpayers more than $50 million annually.

The use of chauffeurs by military officers has continued to be one of the Defense Department's most wasteful practices. A 1979 GAO study discovered Army officers were misusing this service in Europe, and concluded that soldiers used as drivers "are wasting considerable time chauffeuring vehicles and waiting for passengers."

The GAO found one military driver spending 80 percent of his time driving and the rest of his "work" period doing nothing. In another case, a driver spent 50 percent of his time driving and the remainder studying college courses. And a third driver spent only 30 percent of his time driving and the other 70 percent doing nothing.

The GAO found several instances in which staff heads were being provided with transportation "from their offices to the command office building" at headquarters, a distance of 200 to 300 yards. In one case, the former chief and acting chief of the National Security Agency in Europe "were provided chauffeur service between their offices and the European Command Conference Center—a leisurely 3.5 minute walk," the GAO said.

Though repeatedly exposed as an unnecessary and wasteful practice, the "selling of the Pentagon" continues unabated. A vivid example of this inexcusable activity was found in the Navy and the Air Force, which were spending at least $42,000 a year to bring more than 3,500 community leaders from around the country to free "orientation trips" on 31 military bases in the United States and Puerto Rico. This obvious public relations campaign included free transportation to the bases, lectures, sightseeing, and heavy exposure to the military's position on controversial defense issues. Sen. William Proxmire saw the trips for what they were, "A clear case of lobbying of local citizens for military programs." Why this type of activity is needed when the military is spending $25 million a year on its regular public relations programs, plus another $20 million annually for legislative affairs to promote and support its programs before Congress, is anybody's guess.

Perhaps one of the most shameful expenditures of public funds in behalf of the military was the $1 million a year taxpayers shelled out to subsidize a luxury hotel in Hawaii's Waikiki Beach. The government-run Hale Koa Hotel provided military people and retirees with rooms at a rate 40 percent lower than that of other hotels in the area. More than half of the $100 million hotel's customers were retired military personnel, with active-duty personnel making up about 33 percent. One might have been more sympathetic to this expenditure if it had been provided as a means of rest and recreation for our Vietnam War wounded, but the hotel did not open until two years after the last of our troops had been withdrawn from Southeast Asia.

Military travel abuses are also among the worst in the government. According to one Defense Department audit, the Pentagon's civilian and military brass have misused military aircraft to the tune of $52.3 million. The misuse involved using military transport planes for low priority missions, particularly for travel in cases where cheaper commercial transportation was readily available. Most significantly, the audit discovered that the Air Force pilots were being required to fly so many so-called administrative and support missions that they were not putting in the necessary number of combat flight training hours required.

DOD auditors found that 55 percent of the domestic flights and 17 percent of the foreign flights they reviewed could have been taken on scheduled commercial airlines at considerable savings. Sen. William Proxmire, who made the audit public, said:

What we have here is the picture of every high-ranking officer or civilian in the Pentagon simply being able to request government transportation free, regardless of its cost or mission—simply on the basis of rank. This internal audit puts the lie to the age-old excuse of the military services that transportation of the generals and admirals is appropriate because the aircraft have to fly anyway, and there is no additional cost if the brass go along. In fact, there are substantial additional costs; the cost over the price of available commercial transportation; the cost of having extra aircraft on hand; the price we pay in not having our pilots trained for wartime missions.

The Pentagon's system of perks for our military men and women includes a cornucopia of benefits—from cosmetic plastic surgery for military wives (which, it is argued, is necessary to bolster military morale) to free warehouse storage and payment of moving expenses when retirees leave the service. America's military, depending upon the individual's rank, can receive free or subsidized housing, free legal services, free travel on military aircraft, reduced interest rates on home mortgages, and a pension equal to from 50 to 75 percent of base pay upon retirement—which can begin as early as age 37.

There may once have been legitimate reasons for many of these benefits to compensate our military in time of war, when salaries were shamefully low. But the time is long overdue when the entire military compensation system—benefits, pay, and retirement costs— should be completely overhauled. According to Martin Binkin, a senior fellow in the Brookings Institution's Foreign Policy Studies program:

> The system used today to compensate armed forces personnel, a system geared to meet the needs of the military establishment of an earlier era, is a costly anachronism.

Supporters of moves to expand military compensation and benefits argue that the military has been suffering an erosion of benefits, due to inflation and congressional cuts in military programs. However, a comprehensive study of military pay and benefits conducted for Rep. Les Aspin by the Congressional Research Service found that *exactly the opposite* was true.

In a nutshell, this study—which was completed in December of 1977—found that, while there have been some cuts in benefits, overall improvement in pay plus benefits far exceeded those reductions. According to the study, per capita military pay rose 30 percent from 1968 to 1976 and the value of fringe benefits rose 90 percent, after allowing for inflation. In all, the study found, total pay and benefits increased 43 percent per capita. The study did find that per capita pay and benefits had increased slowly for the military since 1972, but nonetheless it found the military was substantially better off than were those in the civilian sector, who suffered more from the recession. At the same time, the study made clear that per capita comparisons were not altogether the best, because they assumed that a military officer remained at the same rank from 1968 through 1976. As Aspin wisely noted, "A real person is getting promoted, and he's getting regular longevity pay increases."

The Library of Congress study, which took one year to complete, was conducted by a team of three military specialists, two of whom were retired military career officials. They concluded that what happened to military pay and benefits during the last decade "was neither all positive nor all negative," but the sense of their findings was that military personnel "have received favorable compensation treatment."

The military commissaries are, undoubtedly, one of the most outrageous perks provided to our military; they sell tax-free, cut-rate groceries and other goods with the help of a $566.4 million a year federal subsidy. To anyone who has had to pay higher and higher grocery prices, perhaps while living on a fixed income, this is a government-subsidized benefit that should make a person's blood boil.

Housewives of active or retired military officers, some of whom live in $100,000-plus homes, do their grocery shopping in these facilities to take advantage of subsidized food and other supplies that are 20 to 25 percent cheaper than in commercial stores.

While nonmilitary people paid $3.99 for a carton of cigarettes, for instance, military people paid only $2.65 at their commissary. A family-size loaf of Wonder Bread, which costs 63 cents at commercial supermarkets, cost them 44 cents; porterhouse steak, which ran around $2.94 a pound elsewhere, cost them $2.29 a pound; a box of egg noodles that retailed commercially for 57 cents cost 38 cents at the military store; 95 cents for a one-pound package of all-beef frankfurters costing $1.45 elsewhere.

Both Republican and Democratic presidents have urged that the subsidy be phased out of existence. In fact, President Carter told a retired Navy serviceman at one of his celebrated town meeting sessions, "I don't think it's unreasonable for the taxpayers to demand that the military at least pay enough for goods they buy to cover operating expenses."

Not only are active and retired military people and their dependents allowed to shop the cut-rate commissaries, but the privilege is also extended to 3,146 diplomats of foreign countries "recognized as friendly to the United States." (Diplomats from Soviet-bloc countries are ineligible, however.)

The commissaries were first established back in the 19th century as support facilities at remote frontier posts. Congress passed legislation in 1866 to authorize the Army to establish the first commissaries. Marine and Navy commissaries followed after the turn of the century, and the Air Force got them in 1947. As American military forces spread over the world in the post-World War II era, the need for commissaries grew with them. Their numbers, however, grew far beyond the nation's frontier posts and into the nation's most populated metropolitan areas.

In 1948, when Congress began questioning their growth, a law was passed requiring the Defense Department to certify that each commissary was needed because commercial facilities were either inconvenient or were charging unreasonable prices. Yet "somewhere during the past century" the original purposes of commissaries "gradually faded from view," a Senate Appropriations subcommittee report observed.

Today they are available at every major military installation in the country—with five in San Francisco, four each in San Diego and Norfolk, Virginia, three in Honolulu, and six in Washington, D.C. There are 418 commissaries in operation worldwide, 279 of them in the United States, with annual sales of $3 billion. Another 55 new commissaries are being planned.

The stores required an annual subsidy of $100 million in 1964 to pay the salaries of civilian and military personnel who run them. Today that subsidy has grown enormously. The administration's budget for fiscal 1980 contained requests for $336.2 million to pay the salaries of 25,000 military employes who operate the stores; $70.2 million to pay for transporting goods to commissaries overseas; $160 million in indirect costs for exterior painting, snow removal, personnel benefits, and other administrative services.

It is estimated that this subsidy will cost taxpayers more than $5 billion in the course of the next decade.

Over the years, the issue of commissaries has been subjected to numerous congressional and Defense Department studies. In one study, the GAO concluded that the location of commissaries in large metropolitan areas could not be justified. Sen. Thomas Eagleton (D., Mo.) said:

Commissaries were a necessity for military families in the frontier days, when military posts were isolated and going into town to buy groceries would have meant a trip of hours or days. Those days are gone, however. There is really little justification for maintaining six military commissaries in metropolitan Washington, for example. I doubt if there is a single military family in the Washington area living more than a few minutes from a commercial grocery store.

Warren Nelson, a top aide and military adviser to Rep. Les Aspin, told a *Washington Post* reporter:

You'd think we were paying these guys $100 a month and a cup of coffee. People just bitch and scream whenever there's a proposal to eliminate the subsidy. It used to be that commissaries were compensation for low pay, but we changed the whole basis for that in 1967 when pay comparability was instituted.

While it has been argued that Army sergeants with low pay cannot afford to buy their food at commercial rates, the fact remains that military pay for all ranks, as I have noted, has increased significantly in recent years. Equally significant is the fact that the commissaries are open to all active and retired military personnel whatever their income.

For example, a Navy captain who earned over $33,000 a year, lived in an upper middle class Maryland suburb of Washington, owned three cars, and belonged to the local country club, bought the bulk of his family's groceries at the commissary right along with lower-paid personnel. *Washington Post* reporter Sandra Boodman, in an article on commissaries, chose another example: a wife of a retired admiral who lived in a Washington suburban neighborhood in a $120,000 home. This couple also shopped in the commissary.

A Senate Appropriations Committee report, which urged elimination of the commissary subsidy, noted that from 1964 to 1975 military compensation increased 127 percent, while the consumer price index rose only 74 percent in the same period.

The report also noted that, when the salaries of military personnel were compared to the pay of civilian workers (who receive no such comparable benefit), including fringe benefits, the average military employe "receives $4,257 per year more than the civilian employe."

Commissary supporters claim that phasing out the subsidy would hurt retirees. Yet a Defense Department study which examined the income tax filing of nearly one million military retirees found that the vast majority reported adjusted gross incomes ranging from $10,000 to $35,000 or higher. Only 136,000 were found to have annual adjusted gross incomes of $7,000 or less. (It should be noted that this study, the first of its kind ever conducted of military retirement incomes, did *not* include Social Security benefits—which would significantly raise the income of the older retirees, since Social Security is not taxable.)

The commissaries, in the words of a knowledgeable Senate Appropriations Committee aide, "are indefensible." Yet there are other innumerable areas where the Pentagon could cut costs and, at the same time, provide the "tough, lean, efficient fighting force" that Jimmy Carter once promised.

Here are several areas where major cost savings could be made:

—Thin out the top-heavy bureaucracy of officers brought about by the "grade creep" under which lower-grade officers are boosted to higher pay levels by having their job description reclassified to make it appear that their job carries more work and responsibility than it really does. It is estimated that the Pentagon could save $1 billion annually if the grade creep of the past 10 years were rolled back.

—Cut nonessential Defense Department civilian personnel who now exceed in numbers all of the employes of the Department of Health, Education and Welfare, Treasury, Agriculture, and the U.S. Postal Service combined. DOD's 1500 public information and public relations specialists would be a good place to begin cutting.

—Curb wherever possible military transfers and substantially extend the average tour of duty. For every month the average tour of duty is extended we could save $200 million annually. The bill for rotating military transfers was more than $3 billion in fiscal 1980. Much of this could be saved simply by requiring that personnel fulfill their full tour of duty time. One of the services was found to be transferring men eight months before their tour of duty was over. Besides saving money, this simple reform would significantly raise military morale and no doubt improve job performance. No one in the military likes being shifted around as often as they now are.

—Undertake a hardnosed review of unneeded bases and facilities both at home and abroad, leading to the closing of those found to be superfluous to our defense and the defense of our allies. There is a potential savings here of more than $1 billion.

—As suggested in the previous chapter, end the practice of double-dipping. The Civil Service Commission said there are 141,817 persons drawing dual government compensation. The National Taxpayers Union estimates there are actually 150,000 of them, when the CIA, White House, and about 800 congressional employes are included in the totals.

—Require that the military contribute to their pensions. In contrast to federal civilian employes, the military pay nothing into their pension fund. Requiring that they do could cut defense costs by as much as $2 billion a year.

These are just a few of the places where defense spending could be significantly reduced without cutting into our military muscle. There are many, many more, including a laundry list of smaller expenditures which pad the Pentagon's budget and gobble up hundreds of millions of dollars annually. For instance, why must our top military and civilian brass be provided with elite, private dining rooms in the Pentagon where they can dine on $2.65 Delmonico steak dinners, leaving taxpayers to foot the $1.3 million a year subsidy for the cut-rate meals? Why should wives of military personnel be provided with free face lifts, nose bobs, and breast enlargements by military plastic surgeons at the taxpayers' expense? Why, indeed, should taxpayers be asked to shell out $300 million a year to provide military officers with an assortment of recreational facilities and activities, including 300 military golf courses, tennis courts, bowling alleys, marinas, stables and riding trails, a ski resort, and other fun and games which they should pay for themselves. Why must Uncle Sam continue to employ more than 300 servants to serve at the beck and call of our highest military brass as well as junior Navy and Marine Corps officers—at a cost of more than $4.5 million a year? Throw in another $1 million for subsidized veterinarian care for military pets. Add $13 million for the costs of publishing more than 1,402 military magazines and other periodicals. Kick in an additional several million for all those military chauffeurs the top brass say they can't do without. Well, you get the point. There are a lot of frills that need cutting, and they can be cut *without hurting our military needs*.

But if the Defense Department were to implement one costcutting reform above all others, it would have to be the institution of a modernized retirement program that would completely replace the early 20-year-and-out pensioning system that has been in place for more than 30 years. With an annual $10 billion bill for retirees staring us in the face, we can no longer afford to let our military men and women retire early on half-pay pensions for life. It is a waste of costly training, experience, and manpower. President Ford once urged Congress to "strengthen the incentives to serve a full 30-year term," before allowing retirement and pensioning. There is no reason why we cannot go even further than that, deferring all pensions for our military until age 55 or 60 when they will, most likely, be truly retired, not moving into second-career jobs. The argument that we would no longer be able to draw competent military people is ludicrous on its face. The government's civilian sector isn't retired on full pension until age 55, after 30 years of service, yet it continues to draw highly qualified careerists into its ranks. And figures show that our military—once pay and benefits are factored together—are paid *better* than civilian employes, on the average. Ending the costly and wasteful 20-year-and-out ritual would save billions of dollars in military pension costs, strengthen our military capability and resources, and keep our most talented and experienced military men and women in service to their country.

CHAPTER 15
OSHA: Washington's Most Hated Agency

"They made me feel like a crook," said Jim Clark, a successful Dallas businessman bitter over his experience with the Occupational Safety and Health Administration.

Ross Goddard, president of Speed Check Conveyor Company of Decatur, Georgia, said OSHA was "out to drive the free enterprise system out of business."

Betty Hanicke, who runs a prosthetic and orthopedic manufacturing company in Kansas City, Missouri, thought OSHA's habit of "coming in and slapping penalties on private businesses is as bad as Hitler's Germany or Castro's Cuba."

The resentment and anger these three business executives registered toward OSHA is not unusual among most business people of today. In fact, their remarks were mild compared with those of many owners of small businesses whose views about OSHA are often unprintable.

The scorn and contempt for this federal agency, strongly evidenced in interviews with business leaders across the country, vividly illustrates why it has become the government's most hated bureaucracy.

The reasons for this are at once numerous and tragic, for OSHA was begun with the best of intentions: to curb injuries and fatalities among the nation's workers. However, statistics show both that the agency has failed to protect workers and that it has significantly worsened the deeply adversary relationship between government and the business community.

In the last year or so, however, businessmen and women have begun to fight back, in Washington and in the courts, challenging OSHA at every turn—and winning.

The Occupational Safety and Health Act of 1970 was the culmination of years of lobbying efforts, principally by organized labor. The Senate voted for it 83 to 3, and the House, 383 to 5. President Nixon signed the measure into law with little fanfare.

OSHA's birth may have been all but ignored by the media, but it didn't take long before the full impact of the new agency was felt at the local level. OSHA—whose broad domain covers over six million businesses having one or more employes and whose rules and regulations are enforced nationwide by more than 1,400 compliance officers empowered to call on and inspect business premises *without notice*—fell upon business with a thud. (All federal, state and local government workers are exempt from OSHA regulations as might be expected. Bureaucrats never want to be subjected to the rules and regulations they impose on others.) OSHA is authorized to inflict heavy penalties: it can levy a maximum of $1,000 for every violation and up to $10,000 for willful or repeated violations. Failure to correct violations within a given period of time can result in further fines of up to $1,000 a day.

Even a failure to post the official OSHA poster can net an employer a $1,000 fine.

Since its enactment, OSHA has been busy, to say the least. In 1976, OSHA officers inspected 90,369 businesses and cited 61,000 of them for a total of 380,356 separate violations. The fines then levied, plus the costs of complying with OSHA's orders, were of course passed on to consumers.

A survey by the National Association of Manufacturers computed the cost of complying with OSHA's requirements at an average of $35,000 for firms of between one and 100 workers, $73,500 for companies of up to 500 employes, and $350,000 for firms of up to 1,000 workers.

Beyond just the costs of complying with OSHA, businessmen have been enraged by what many consider to be the sheer *idiocy* of OSHA's demands. Consider these examples.

—An OSHA inspector told a Florida meat-packing company that a safety railing had to be put up around its loading dock to keep workers from falling off. After the company put up the railing, an Agriculture Department inspector ordered it removed as an obstacle to sanitation.

—A Massachusetts supermarket was ordered to install a nonslip grating on its workspace floor. Then along came the USDA again, and the market was forced to rip out the grating and install a sanitary tile floor. Cost to the store: $25,000.

—The Continental Can Corporation was ordered to construct sound shields around machinery at its Pittsburgh plant at a cost of $33.5 million. This OSHA directive was eventually overturned in court, however, after Continental proved it had spent $100,000 a year to provide its employes with ear protectors which reduced noise levels to far below federal standards.

—A small South Carolina manufacturer with only 12 employes was informed that his machinery needed a safety gear. The manufacturer protested that, while his machines had every protective device known to the industry, the precautionary device demanded by OSHA inspectors simply did not exist. He was thereupon forced out of business. But even after his plant was closed down, OSHA slapped him with a $500 penalty, declaring that this businessman must serve as "an example" to other employers.

—The University of Illinois was forced to spend $557,000 when OSHA ruled that railings along an elevated walkway connecting campus buildings were a few inches too short. OSHA required all such railing to be precisely 42 inches high.

Not even farms escape OSHA's reach. One of its decrees required that toilet and handwashing facilities be erected on all farms of at least five employes "within a five-minute walk of each employe's place of work in the field." These facilities, OSHA said, must be equipped with towels, soap, inside door locks, signs, and toilet paper fixtures.

OSHA has also managed to enrage farmers with the rank paternalism of its worker-safety pamphlet series. These illustrated pamphlets—ultimately withheld from the public—instructed farmers that "bare feet aren't safe around cattle," and warned them that "when floors are wet and slippery with manure, you could have a bad fall."

Needless to say, the agency's rulings are also frequently inconsistent. Rep. Steven Symms (R., Idaho) told of a firm in his state and another in Montana with four identical machines. OSHA inspected the Montana plant, found one machine to be safe and the other unsafe, and levied a $125 penalty on the company; another OSHA inspector found both of the machines in Idaho to be unsafe, and ordered a $600 fine.

Similarly, two log cabin manufacturing plants in Texas were inspected by OSHA agents, and both were cited for almost identical violations. One plant was fined $750, the second $100.

Employers across the country say they are willing to correct unsafe conditions in their businesses but object to *arbitrary* determinations of OSHA violations and the imposition of fines even when they are more than eager to comply.

Rep. George Hansen (R., Idaho), chairman of the American Conservative Union's Stop OSHA Committee, is among those who believe that Congress went too far with the agency's mandate over the nation's workplaces. Said Hansen:

> Never before has there been so much arbitrary power given to one official: the OSHA inspector is free to walk into any place of business in the United States, decide what, if any, violations exist, and then force correction of the violations through penalties and fines.
>
> The businessman has no day in court unless he appeals to the Occupational Safety and Health Review Commission. Never is he allowed a jury trial, and never is there any need of a search warrant to enter his premises. In the interests of federal administrative efficiency, the American businessman is denied rights afforded to all criminals. Indeed, a criminal is considered innocent until proven guilty. He is guaranteed a jury trial. If a judge ever discovered that a criminal's property had been searched without a warrant, his case would be dismissed immediately.

In Kansas City, Betty Hanicke, who runs the P.W. Hanicke Manufacturing Company, which makes surgical prosthetic and orthopedic devices, also cites constitutional perils. OSHA inspectors, Hanicke said, "are like the Gestapo."

One morning Hanicke was greeted unexpectedly by an OSHA agent who ruled that a machine needed a side guard on a grinding wheel. Although she immediately agreed to install one, she was shocked to discover the following Friday that she had been fined $60.

Said Hanicke:

> I protested. They didn't give us enough time to correct the problem before they fined us. We've used this machine for 30 years or more and no one was ever hurt. It's un-American. They do this sort of thing in Communist countries. The $60 is not going to make or break us, but it is the principle of the matter. We feel we should have been given reasonable time to correct the situation.

According to Ross Goddard, president of a conveyor belt company in Decatur, Georgia, most OSHA inspectors are inexperienced and don't know what they're doing. "They sent a boy out here who didn't know anything about engineering. They have about 6,000 rules and regulations that a half-dozen lawyers together couldn't understand," Goddard said. "Then they refer you to some rule that's in a book at the Library of Congress."

Goddard said the guard device that OSHA agents ordered him to put on a punch press would not have allowed its operator to feed material into the machine. On another occasion, he recalled, an inspector

... had me put a guard on an ironworking machine that wasn't necessary. They fined me $60, which I paid, and then later told me that no guard was needed. I never got my $60 back.

Goddard said he had "two books of OSHA's rules and regulations, but when they came and I asked them to explain one page to me, they couldn't."

Jim Clark, president of Metals, Inc., of Dallas, said:

OSHA inspectors don't know what they're doing. They don't understand our machinery. They told us we had to put a guard on this piece of equipment. Since there was no such guard made anywhere for it, we had to make one ourselves. I contacted every manufacturer in this country who uses the machine, and they said they had never had any accident using them. Then they sent me affidavits to show the OSHA people that this was the case.

OSHA was unmoved. It fined Metals, Inc. $500. But Clark's story didn't end there:

One employe refused to work on the machine after the guard was put on, and others said the guard made it dangerous. Within two weeks one employe almost completely severed a finger, which he still doesn't have complete use of. This is the first accident with that machine, and it happened because of the guard.

Clark removed the guard after the accident and has had no problems with the machine since. However, he estimated that business delays and other expenses associated with the OSHA order cost him about $5,000, and this sum, he said, "will be passed on to the consumers."

C. L. Vines, a Santa Barbara, California welding contractor, said that OSHA inspectors were unnecessary:

We already have state safety inspectors, plus state worker compensation inspectors, as well as insurance inspectors, not to mention fire and building inspectors. How many inspectors do we need?

He continued, "Every time we turn around we get slapped with more controls. And it's coming out of our pockets as taxpayers."

Donald Bauder of Colorado Springs, Colorado, agreed. OSHA inspectors, he said, are "a pain in the neck. I don't like government trying to tell me how to run my business." Bauder, who runs RBM Precision Metal Products, Inc., said that OSHA inspectors made him get rid of his punch presses because "they didn't meet OSHA specifications. So now I have an 80-ton press that meets the requirements, but it's always breaking down because it requires more wiring. It's supposed to be safe, but one fellow got his finger chopped pretty bad."

Rus Hensley, president of a small manufacturing concern in Dallas, called OSHA inspectors "a bunch of imbeciles who don't know anything about industry. They're ill-trained. Most have never been in a manufacturing plant before. There's one woman inspector who expects the place to look like a doctor's office.

"I've seen them walk past a machine that could eat you alive and head for a wall socket that might need replacing," he said.

Clearly, from the aforementioned, business people are angry. And many have fought OSHA in the courts. One of these litigants was Jan Bosang, secretary-treasurer of Hardwood Dimension and Mouldings, Inc., of Richmond Hill, New York. She charged that OSHA wanted her company to replace metal guards on her machines with plastic ones which broke easily. She said agency officials threatened that "if we contested the fine they would close us down."

When she persisted in her decision to contest OSHA's decree, however, the agency quickly backed off. Bosang said the inspectors offered to reduce the $600 in fines levied against her company "if we didn't contest" the penalities. She flatly rejected the deal, and the litigation continued. It cost her more than $6,000 in legal fees and other related expenses.

"People are afraid of OSHA," she said, "and afraid of being closed down."

Principally, however, it has been the government's policy of punishment first and correction later that has most angered this New York businesswoman. She said:

> There are better ways of doing things. The state inspectors come in and say that something needs correcting, and they give us a reasonable amount of time to comply. We have never had a problem with them. But OSHA is a nightmare.

Indianapolis attorney John Raikos represented Blocksom and Company, a firm that fought OSHA for over two years. The company, which manufactures mattress filler, sought a permanent injunction against the agency, arguing that the legislation which created it was unconstitutional. One of the complaints in OSHA's 83-page report on Blocksom said that the bottom rung of a ladder needed repair. To fight this and other charges, Raikos estimated the company had spent approximately $72,000 in legal and business costs.

But by far the most significant and far-reaching court action in OSHA's history successfully challenged the constitutionality of the agency's inspection practices. The case was initiated by 61-year-old Ferrol G. (Bill) Barlow who runs a heating and plumbing company with his four sons in Pocatello, Idaho. Barlow employs a total of 33 people.

Barlow is a husky man with short steel-gray hair, a warm smile, and a handshake that can crack a walnut. His little man fights city hall story reminded one of a movie Jimmy Stewart might have starred in 30 years ago. The real story began at 11 a.m. on September 13, 1975, when OSHA inspector Daniel T. Sanger walked into his shop, unexpected and unannounced, to conduct an inspection. Barlow politely refused him admission, saying he knew Sanger was just doing his duty but that he, Barlow, believed that the Fourth Amendment means exactly what it says about the rights of people to be secure "against unreasonable searches." He added that he would be happy to comply if the agent could produce a search warrant that provided a probable cause for OSHA to believe that some violation existed on his premises.

The dispute found its way to the U.S. District Court in Idaho, where a three-judge panel ruled in Barlow's favor, holding that warrantless OSHA inspections "are unconstitutional as being violative of the Fourth Amendment."

OSHA appealed to the Supreme Court which ruled in Barlow's favor, saying that the agency must obtain a search warrant giving it authority to conduct a search of a businessman's premises, if the employer demands it. Since most business employers do not bar OSHA inspectors from their premises, the agency has not been forced to seek court warrants with any significant frequency. But the protection is there to be used whenever businesses feel their rights to unwarranted search and seizure are being violated.

But the fallout from Barlow's landmark suit—which cost him more than $100,000—raised other questions about the fundamental concept behind OSHA, and whether the agency was achieving its stated goals.

Has OSHA been effective? Has this nationwide army of federal inspectors actually reduced work-related injuries and deaths? And at what cost to business and consumers?

There is no convincing evidence to show that, in more than nine years of existence, OSHA has had any significant impact on worker safety and health. In fact, the Bureau of Labor Statistics has said the number of work days lost per 100 workers due to injuries has increased 15 percent since 1972.

An exhaustive study funded by OSHA in the state of Wisconsin found that 75 percent of all accidents were caused by behavioral problems or momentary carelessness, resulting in injuries such as strains, sprains, cuts, backaches, and hernias—hardly the kind of injuries which would seem to require the intrusion of the federal government. "It would be extremely difficult to control these types of accidents with an inspection system," the Wisconsin study properly concluded.

Another study by Idaho's Industrial Commission similarly stated, "It becomes apparent that the major cause of occupational injuries and illnesses in Idaho is a self-inflicted injury brought about by an unsafe act by an employee."

And still another survey by the California Department of Industrial Relations concluded that no more than 18 percent of all accidents throughout the country might be avoided by some type of government inspection system. In other words, an army of federal inspectors spread out across the length and breadth of our land, imposing penalties and demanding costly alterations of equipment and plant facilities, could hope to affect only 18 percent *at the very maximum*.

And what would all this cost? Since its inception, OSHA has cost taxpayers $872.7 million, but the cost in terms of business investment and consumer costs is in the billions of dollars. The annual McGraw-Hill survey estimated that industry spent over $3.2 billion in 1976 to comply with the agency's regulations. Since 1972, McGraw-Hill's survey said businesses had spent a total of $15 billion to comply with OSHA.

For a moment in late 1976 and early 1977 it appeared that the Carter administration was beginning to respond to the complaints of business people against OSHA. The administration had announced at the end of 1977 that some 1,100 unnecessary OSHA rules were being eliminated from the regulation books. These included ludicrous rules such as those governing the common step ladder. However, the vast majority of OSHA's 800 pages of complex, nit-picking regulations remained, along with the arbitrary rulings that OSHA field inspectors continue to make on a daily basis—making life more difficult, more costly, and less profitable for American business—but not very much safer.

How necessary is OSHA's work safety function? An internal White House memorandum in 1977 revealed that three top Carter administration officials had begun to explore ways of abolishing the agency's occupational safety responsibilities. But their work toward this goal was stopped dead in its tracks once organized labor got wind of these intentions. It was too bad, really. Because the overwhelming evidence is clear that this is a superfluous federal agency that for all its hundreds of millions of dollars, has not achieved its stated objective—and never will.

As far as the clearly angry reaction by America's businesses against OSHA is concerned, one more outraged voice might be helpful to sharpen the focus of this entire debate. It comes from a former Georgia peanut farmer who said, "If I were an employer, I'd like for all my employes to be safe. But with the mention of OSHA, there kind of rises something up in me to resist it and not cooperate with it." The angry speaker was President Jimmy Carter at a White House Cabinet meeting.

CHAPTER 16
HUD: The $76 Billion Disappointment

Since the Department of Housing and Urban Development was established in 1965, it has spent more than $76 billion in pursuit of the official national goal of decent housing for every American. Today that goal remains unreached. Despite all the billions HUD has spent, millions of Americans still live in grossly substandard urban and rural housing.

Over the years, according to the government, federal housing programs have financed the construction of more than one million housing units. Yet had the government simply spent HUD's $76 billion to purchase housing for the poor, it could have bought—at today's inflated prices—more than 1.5 million new $50,000 single-family homes. What has gone wrong? Where did all that money go?

My own investigation into HUD's expenditures finds that much of its $10 billion a year budget has been going into the following activities:

—More than $50 million a year is being spent on worthless, low-priority research and study projects and reports—a great deal of which duplicates work that has been done repeatedly in the past by HUD and other agencies.

—A large chunk of HUD's billions is not benefiting the poor or even low-income groups, but instead is going to banks, private investors, and rich and influential consulting firms.

—HUD's $3.9 billion a year Community Development Grant program has thrown its money lavishly at communities across the country, irrespective of whether they deserve such funding or not.

—Hundreds of millions of dollars have gone into pipe-dream housing schemes from Model Cities to New Communities, most of which have ended up either bankrupt or decaying into slum housing.

—HUD has wasted tax dollars on needless public-relations schemes and promotions, bloated salaries and personnel, marginal housing programs that have long outlived their need, excessive travel, and extravagant grants and contracts to municipalities and organizations *which do nothing* to improve the lives of the poor.

I first began looking into HUD's expenditures when I received a

121

tip, in 1978, from a HUD employe that the department was about to embark on a $13 million public-relations campaign to improve its sagging image. The blueprint for this Madison Avenue blitz was conceived by a Philadelphia consulting firm at a cost of $64,000. The company developed what became known, inside HUD, as the "National Communications Program."

In developing its plan, the company interviewed 91 top HUD officials to solicit their views about the department's overall image. One would think that their views would be of intense interest to HUD's top public relations officials. However, senior public information officers in the department said they didn't have time to read what their own program managers had to say about HUD, so they hired *another* consultant to boil down the interviews into a summary report.

The final plan—as presented to then-HUD Secretary Patricia Harris—said, "Too often the perception is that the department is fragmented, scandal-ridden, inefficient, and an agent of last resort whose clientele is on welfare."

The image-building campaign, which had Harris' full support, included a "nationwide urban promotion encouraging community and private industry support" for the administration's Urban Development Action Grant program. It further proposed a nationwide communication effort "to disseminate basic energy conservation information," and "promotion of greater public awareness of assisted housing developments which are successes."

The entire multi-million dollar PR campaign was to run the gamut of Madison Avenue's most sophisticated promotional techniques, including fairs, expositions, conferences, symposia, exhibits, a speakers bureau, and broader use of the news media. Other activities were to include surveys of consumer attitudes toward HUD, and a series of interviews with "important HUD constituency groups" to measure their attitudes toward HUD programs. The plan also called for development of "a new system to identify, categorize, and prioritize primary audiences for messages needed to communicate HUD programs." Translation: Organize lobbying and other special interest groups in HUD's behalf.

Said one HUD official who was intimately familiar with what the department was about to do: "This has got to be one of the biggest boondoggles around here."

But bureaucrats can get greedy. Not only was the department planning to plunge $13 million into this promotional extravaganza, but it was considering adding another $14 million for the following year.

However, just a few days before I was about to break this story, HUD's top public information officials notified me that the program had been suddenly trimmed down to $3.5 million, and most of the projects and programs contained in the master plan had been laid aside indefinitely. While $3.5 million—on top of the $3 million HUD normally spends each year on promotion—is still too much, the taxpayers had been saved $10 million.

I reported the story about what HUD intended to do anyway, and, as was expected, top HUD officials from Mrs. Harris on down called the story "a cheap shot." But there was nothing cheap about the waste and mismanagement which exists throughout HUD's numerous programs.

The Department of Housing and Urban Development was created during the Johnson administration, in an effort to pull together dozens of housing and community development programs that, over the years, had been scattered across the federal landscape by Congress.

One of HUD's chief goals was outlined in the National Housing Policy Act of 1949:

> The elimination of substandard and other inadequate housing through the clearance of slums and blighted areas, and the realization as soon as feasible of the goal of a decent home and a suitable living environment for every American family.

Toward this end, HUD is spending $741.5 million a year in public housing operating subsidies, more than $368 million a year in rental subsidies for low and moderate income people, and $830 million in housing assistance for the elderly.

Yet like other omnibus departments formed to combine and coordinate a multiplicity of related government programs, HUD's overhead costs, along with other budget items, have grown sharply.

Salaries now total $268 million a year for a full-time staff of more than 16,000 (which was authorized to rise by a full 15 percent, by 1980, to 17,400.) At least 2,440 HUD employes currently earn more than $30,000 per year. When rents, utilities, and other overhead and administrative costs are added to salaries, HUD's yearly operating costs total more than $530 million. The department is growing so fast, in fact, that it has already filled a relatively new $26 million, 10-story building—with no room to spare.

Now, spending $10 billion a year isn't as easy as it may sound, even with over 16,000 people to help spend it. But HUD's bureau-crats are constantly thinking up new ways to get rid of our money.

A prime example was a $4.8 million "Urban Observatory Pro-gram," launched by HUD to funnel research money into local uni-versities for work on community problems. Much of this money was spent on a lot of half-baked public opinion surveys conducted by telephone to produce reports like "The Supply and Demand for Small Boats and Associated Services in Northeastern New Jersey." It said a survey of local marinas and boat manufacturers showed "a large demand exists for recreational boat facilities." What did they expect this special interest group to say? That boats are no longer popular? Other studies conducted under this program overlapped or dupli-cated work being done by the Law Enforcement Assistance Admin-istration, and the Departments of Interior and Labor, among others.

So much of HUD's money is wasted on projects like these that it is not uncommon to hear HUD officials privately call many of its studies "turkeys." They also say that a significant number of contracts let by HUD are either "misdirected or unnecessary." One of these contracts paid $184,000 to study the feasibility of undertaking "post occupancy evaluations" of HUD-financed housing projects. The study's final report weighed 5 pounds, 12 ounces and numbered 466 pages. Almost 200 pages contained nothing more than a list of per-sons and organizations with purported expertise in related fields. Two of those listed were dead. Others were listed with no address.

In defense of the study, HUD officials said the report was man-dated by Congress. While this is true, a HUD official who was highly critical of the report said it ignored what Congress had specifically asked for: a study of the special housing needs of the elderly and the handicapped.

Said Al Louis Ripskis, an official within HUD's Office of Evaluation and one of the department's most vocal critics:

> The report is a complete waste of the taxpayer's money. It is nothing more than propaganda for post occupancy evaluations which under this proposal would be undertaken by consultants like the ones who prepared this report.

Indeed, had HUD accepted the report's recommendations, such evaluations could cost as much as $750,000 each and "add consid-erable red tape and millions of dollars to housing costs," Ripskis said. Moreover, the study's proposal would have violated HUD's own findings, issued in early 1978, which found that "poorly con-

ceived and cost-inducing regulations" were adding millions to housing costs throughout the nation.

HUD spends $8 million a year on printing, issuing a voluminous
quantity of reports, booklets, brochures, and pamphlets, including
literature on how to use grasses and palm leaves to build huts, and
on Europe's housing subsidy systems. The report on "Palms—Their
Use In Building," issued by HUD's Office of International Affairs,
tells us that, among plants, the palm family "may be conceded to
rank second only to the grass family from the standpoint of its usefulness to native tropical man." It advises prospective palm hut
builders:

> The fan-leaved types do not require special preparation other than flat-
> tening and drying. They are then tied or otherwise fastened to the frame-
> work like shingles with the blade pointing downwards.

HUD's report on grass hut building advises potential home builders:

> The longer the grass the better. It should be cut after the seed has
> ripened, but before it has dried out and become brittle. It must be
> combed to remove the soft leaf and short pieces and should be dried.
> The grass should now be tied in bundles about the size of a double
> handful and the butts cut off square with a panga.

Directories are also popular in HUD's vast publishing enterprise,
particularly the 175-page "Community Development Block Grant
Program," which lists every community in the country that acquired
money under this program in fiscal 1977. The book is useful in at
least one regard, in that it reveals how wealthy communities like
Santa Barbara, California, among many others, get community development money. The law that established this program says the
money is intended "principally for persons of low and moderate
income." Yet its grants are shoveled out to well-to-do communities
such as Mount Kisco, New York, $389,000, and Stamford, Connect-
icut, more than $2 million. These are communities that have ade-
quate tax resources to finance virtually any community development
program they might imagine.

It was for this very reason that HUD Secretary Harris proposed
changing the program's formula so that 75 percent of the grants
would be concentrated on the nation's neediest communities. Unfortunately, her commonsensical proposal was rejected by Congress
when lawmakers realized that less-deserving communities within
their own districts would lose grant money.

Meanwhile, a House Appropriations subcommittee investigation into the block grant program found large portions of the funds often are eaten up by excessively high overhead costs.

The panel found that in Houston, for example, nearly 47 percent of grant funds went for planning, management, and administration. Nearly 75 percent of funds spent by Buffalo in 1977 went for similar "nonprogram" costs. Washington, D.C., spent more than 51 percent of its funds in the same period for administrative and planning costs.

Is the Community Block Grant Program effective in improving conditions in America's poorest cities after the appropriation of over $15 billion thus far? No one really knows. A two-year, 527-page study by the Brookings Institution said it could not answer that question, because "different observers will interpret the history of a given program differently." But HUD is determined. The department extended the Brookings contract for four more years to continue evaluating the block grant program.

In terms of its "investments," HUD has been involved in more losing propositions than most departments in the government. In the last six years, HUD has had to pay nearly $8 billion to banks and other lenders for defaulted housing loans. As a result of these defaulted loans, HUD in the past half-dozen years has had to take over some 2,000 housing projects totaling more than 241,000 dwelling units. By the middle of 1978 HUD owned 28,658 single-family residences and 386 multi-family projects containing 39,443 dwelling units. At the beginning of 1978 HUD had approximately $6 billion in loans outstanding.

Many of HUD's programs, like Urban Renewal, Operation Breakthrough, Model Cities, New Communities, Urban Beautification— projects that were launched with high hopes, much money, and inflated rhetoric—are now considered among the government's biggest bombs.

Said one congressional housing expert:

> HUD has been a monumental experiment to see if the federal government could provide suitable housing for the nation's poor and make its cities a decent place in which to live. Yet many of its biggest projects have been abject and utter failures.

Other projects have simply outlived their usefulness. One of them is the Federal Housing Administration, whose continued need is seriously being questioned. For one thing, fewer people are using FHA's Guaranteed Mortgage loans because of the increasing development of private mortgage companies and the availability of money through other lending institutions. FHA's guaranteed loans in recent years have accounted for less than 10 percent of the mortgages being made available for home purchasing. Moreover, FHA's foreclosure rate has been growing. In fact, Congress in fiscal 1978 had to give FHA nearly $2 billion to make up its losses from mortgage foreclosures, and the agency had to ask for another $352 million in fiscal 1979. "A lot of people are now questioning the need for FHA," said a top official of the Senate Appropriations subcommittee which oversees HUD's funding.

HUD's "New Communities" experiment was undoubtedly one of the Department's biggest disasters. Under this program HUD purchased bonds, debentures, and notes from private and public developers to finance land acquisition and housing development to build totally new communities. Thirteen projects were begun, with HUD loan guarantees totaling about $300 million. All but four of the projects completely folded, and the entire enterprise was being phased out of existence in 1979. One top HUD official in charge of the program called the project's history "sad, painful, and expensive." The government lost at least $150 million on the experiment.

"Model Cities" was begun in 1966 as a "comprehensive attack on social, economic, and physical problems in selected slum and blighted areas." Millions of dollars in grants were issued to transform some of the nation's worst urban ghettos, but the program flopped. Eventually it was merged into the Community Block Grant program. In all, 145 cities received $2.5 billion in federal funds, but critics said *planning costs* used up a hefty portion of the money. Needless to say, the nation's worst cities remain much as they were before the program was launched.

The bulk of HUD's budget is being spent in "Section 8" assisted housing which includes rent subsidies for the poor and the elderly. In 1977, 64 percent of all assisted-housing money went to provide housing for the aged. But there is reason to question how much of the assistance is actually helping the elderly.

HUD has created some of the most complicated financial transactions in the history of housing finance, but its "Section 202" housing assistance for the elderly may be one of the most bizarre. It works like this: HUD loans the money to the developer, who builds the housing project for low-income elderly residents. The developer then pays off the mortgage with the help of the federal operating subsidies approved by Congress to keep the apartment rents affordable to the aged.

"What you have here is government money being used to pay

back the government for the mortgage money it lent in the first place," said one HUD employe.

In program after program, one finds case after case illustrating how hundreds of millions of dollars, our dollars, are being wasted each year.

HUD asked Congress for $130 million in fiscal 1980 for its housing rehabilitation loan program, despite the fact that a GAO study found 53 percent of the total amount due on loans in previous years was not collected. According to the GAO, this was because of the way in which HUD charged interest on defaulted loans, the result of which was to lower "the effective interest rate from 3.0 percent to 2.3 percent upon default, resulting in a 31.5 percent savings in interest actually paid by the borrower." Even more incredibly, there have been numerous reports showing how this program has been used to benefit wealthy and upper middle income people. The *Washington Post*, for example, found instances in which $50,000-a-year homeowners were getting rehabilitation loans. Some of these wealthy recipients were using HUD's 3 percent interest loans to install home greenhouses and skylights.

HUD also proposed spending about $5 million on a new Liveable Cities program in 1980. Would this attractively named program make the plight of America's slum housing inhabitants more bearable? Fat chance! Here's a description of the program from HUD's justifications for its budget request:

> Projects will include programs for neighborhood and community based arts, urban design, user needs design, and the encouragement of the preservation of historic or other structures which have neighborhood or community significance. Specific examples of eligible projects include a traveling community exhibit, documentary films, and designing a neighborhood cultural facility.

What else would this money be used for? A letter from the mayor of Lewiston, Maine, to Rep. Edward Boland (D., Mass.) sought a grant to fund the city's winter carnival whose activities were to include building a snow palace, ice sculpture contests, taffy on the snow, snowshoe races, parades, and French cuisine. Fortunately, the Congress turned thumbs down on this fledgling boondoggle.

HUD plans to spend $4.3 million to continue its work on its Experimental Housing Allowance Program in 1980, even though GAO concluded that this $163 million experiment *could never answer* the research questions being posed.

HUD is also spending nearly $900,000 a year on its Fair Housing and Equal Opportunity research program. Yet, according to Sen. William Proxmire, this HUD program funded a $350,000 unsolicited proposal from Columbia University Law School to conduct a demonstration program to train law students in fair housing law. HUD explained that the project was aimed at testing whether the "clinical seminar approach" can be successful in inducing law students to study fair housing law. Yet the Legal Services Corporation, created by Congress to provide legal services to the poor, was spending $11.4 million on research and evaluation. And, as Proxmire pointed out, most law schools maintain affiliations with legal defender programs which provide similar training experience.

As part of its $3.5 million Housing Needs of Special Users Program, HUD awarded a four-month, $17,046 contract to the Rehab Group to conduct a "document check" of HUD programs affected by the Architectural Barriers and the Rehabilitation Acts to insure HUD's compliance with those statutes. In other words, HUD was spending $4,100 a month to see if it was complying with the law, something its own Office of General Counsel should have done. At the very least, as Proxmire instructed HUD officials, this was a project that would make "a good summer job for a HUD intern."

HUD is spending $3.8 million a year on its State and Local Policy Analysis Research program, from which they awarded a $50,000 contract to the National Association of Schools of Public Affairs and Administration to conduct an evaluation of professional master's degree programs at 175 member schools. What this has to do with providing better housing for America's poor is anybody's guess.

The Treasury Department, as we all know, is responsible for New York City's Loan Guarantee Program. At least $250,000 under this program was spent on consultants and other contracts to evaluate the city's financial status. Nonetheless, HUD still felt it was necessary to dish out over $100,000 to Columbia University to conduct a fiscal impact analysis of the long-term implications of the city's budget as part of a $1.6 million HUD program of economic development and public finance.

Meantime, monstrously excessive overpayments continue to be made by HUD's state and regional offices for operational and other administrative costs. A GAO investigation of HUD's Cincinnati Service Office found the department was paying $1,020 to mow a 2.2 acre tract of lawn for which it should have paid a little over $100. It also paid $1,050 to paint a three bedroom apartment when comparable work actually cost $200. The GAO also uncovered cases in which apartments were painted twice within a two-to-four-month period. In all, the GAO found that work which cost HUD about $2 million *should have cost half* that amount.

But HUD is as sloppy and wasteful with its own internal expenditures as it is with the housing and urban development programs and projects which it funds, all too often, with little auditing or cost-benefit evaluation.

A case in point concerned the installation of four huge glass security-doors in the two corridors leading to the offices of the HUD secretary who, at that time, was Patricia Harris. It cost taxpayers nearly $60,000 for the purchase and installation of the doors, or about what it would cost to build a three bedroom house. They were put in to improve security leading to Mrs. Harris' suite of offices, but not before the General Services Administration—which supervised their installation—informed the department that, to be effective, the doors must be guarded full time. HUD rejected the idea, however, and the expensive glass doors remain open to this day to anyone who wishes to pass through them. White lettering was also purchased, under the same contract, to identify to passersby that the doors led to the "Office of the Secretary." But this simple lettering was rejected by HUD senior officials who said that it "didn't go with the image of a Cabinet secretary." Gold leaf lettering, which cost eight times more, (about $1,000) was substituted. Costs involved in the entire project included $4,000 in administrative overhead to handle federal paperwork; $3,470 for overtime—because HUD officials wanted the work done in a hurry; and $3,312 for two small desk-sized counters to be placed by the doors. Although custom made, they have never been used.

Like everything else at HUD, its travel budget—about $22 million a year—is filled with waste. Compare HUD's $22 million for 16,000 employes with that of the Veterans Administration, which spends $23.5 million on travel, but has over 227,500 employes, 14 times that of HUD.

Out of 192 first-class trips taken by HUD officials in 1978, 27 of them were justified because of "exceptional circumstances for the successful performance of the agency mission." All of the others claimed they flew first class because "no coach was available," for "medical reasons," or because they did not wish to spend an additional night on the road. Secretary Harris led all other HUD employes by taking 17 first-class trips, in each case citing "exceptional circumstances." On seven trips William Wise, then the department's chief public information officer, also chose to travel first class.

Moreover, HUD officials appear to be spending more of their time on housing problems *abroad* than right here at home. HUD asked for $160,000 for international travel in fiscal 1980, or two and a half times what it spent in fiscal 1978. Much of the overseas travel seems unnecessary: $4,824 to send two HUD officials to Copenhagen, Denmark, and to Godthad, Greenland, to attend a "symposium on Human Settlements Planning and Development in the Arctic." In another instance HUD sent an official to Ottawa, Canada, to study Canadian Federalism with White House Fellows for three days.

Despite continual newspaper and television "horror" stories about slum housing throughout America, HUD operates a College Housing program in which millions of dollars are spent on dormitories. Cornell University, under this program, received more than a quarter of a million dollars to *renovate the bathrooms* in one of its dorms. Moreover, by the end of 1978, 83 institutions of higher learning that had received these low-interest, federally-subsidized loans were delinquent in their repayments to the tune of $14.3 million.

Though not widely publicized, the HUD secretary maintains a $15 million kitty which is officially described as a "discretionary fund for demonstration-innovative projects." A House investigation was harshly critical of the way this money has been spent. And there was much to be critical of, particularly in the way funds for unsolicited projects have been "wired" by HUD officials who appear to be currying favor with city officials and other groups in behalf of the administration in Washington at the time. A case in point concerned a $1.8 million HUD grant to Savannah, Georgia, to restore homes in the city's historic area. A House investigative report disclosed: "A top HUD official announced the grant to Savannah at a meeting there, before the application for the funds had been submitted." HUD's Office of General Counsel called the project "so imprecise as to make it impossible to determine such basic matters as identity of the proposed grantee . . . and the activities for which innovative block grant funding is requested." The report even found the city's commitment to the project questionable, noting that a top city official vowed to fight the grant and described the Savannah businessman who was pushing the project as a "dilettante who won't communicate with the city's government and hasn't accomplished anything."

Perhaps the most questionable of HUD's spending is in its $675 million Urban Development Action Grant program. When the GAO investigated 18 of this program's grants to cities, they questioned the necessity of four (or more than one-fifth) of the grants reviewed.

The idea behind the UDAG grants was simply to act as an economic lever to encourage the commitment of private capital for building projects and developments within depressed urban areas. Yet more than 10 percent of the HUD-assisted projects which GAO examined were found to have no private commitments of funds whatsoever.

HUD boasts the UDAG grants have encouraged private investment in the nation's economically depressed inner cities, estimating that each UDAG dollar (which was removed from the economy in the first place) stimulates six non-federal dollars in private investment. Proxmire, however, questions whether many of these projects "would have gone forward without any UDAG support." There is much evidence that many HUD-assisted development projects would indeed have gone forward. For example, the GAO found that an $8 million grant to build an underground parking garage in Boston was not needed to encourage the private developer of a commercial development above the facility. In fact, HUD's own area office economist said, "Without UDAG funding this proposal will quite probably be completed as planned."

But it is within HUD's public housing projects that we see its worst failures—separate little worlds of decaying, boarded-up, rat-infested, garbage-strewn developments, some of which look like World War II landscapes. Here is what *Washington Post* reporter Jackson Diehl found out about HUD projects in a 1979 story, entitled "Ghostly Remains":

> Billions of tax dollars were spent nationally—and millions were poured into the Pumpkin Hill Apartments (in South Laurel, Maryland)—in pursuit of this Kennedy-Johnson dream of decent, affordable housing for every American.
>
> What millions of tax dollars bought in the case of Pumpkin Hill are apartments that Prince George's County Executive Lawrence J. Hogan recently called "threats to human life."
>
> Pumpkin Hill, moreover, is one of six federally subsidized housing fiascoes in Prince George's County. Almost $35 million—five times the amount the government set out to spend—has been poured into the Pumpkin Hill, Central Gardens, Washington Heights, Baber Village, Nalley, and Glenarden apartment projects.
>
> What HUD has to show for that $35 million today are six ugly and dangerous suburban slums.

The big losers—besides the taxpayers—are the very people that the 2,140 apartment units were built to help.

Low and moderate-income families in Prince George's—who in some cases could only watch helplessly as their homes were deliberately condemned as a way of herding them into the projects—have suffered through their swift decline. Some of these families are worse off than they were before.

In all too many cases, the winners have turned out to be the private developers who snapped up federal loans and subsidies designed to encourage construction of these apartments. Some of them, with little or no investment, have walked away from these projects millions of dollars richer.

Diehl's investigation concluded that "government specialists must take a major share of the blame for the waste of tens of millions of dollars in Prince George's County alone." For, he found, the government agencies responsible for these housing monstrosities "allowed or forced developers to build poorly designed buildings in impractical locations, failed to report or detect decay, and permitted substandard buildings and grounds to exist that way for years.

"Most incredibly," he added, "HUD officials confess they have no real idea how much government money has gone into these six projects—or any one of them, for that matter. No such accounting has ever been made."

The list of wasteful, unnecessary, ineffective, and extravagant spending at HUD is seemingly endless. The grants, projects, expenditures, and other programs touched on here *only scratch the surface* of this $10 billion-a-year bureaucracy. The most disappointing thing about HUD is that while it has been spending billions of dollars year after year to improve the lives of the poor, in many areas of the country—whether in the inner cities or in rural pockets of poverty—America's slums have remained largely *unchanged*. In many cases they have become much worse. Ask anyone who lives in Harlem. The tragic part of Jackson Diehl's article is that essentially the same story can be written—indeed, *has* been written—in most major cities in the country. And the greatest tragedy of all is that, instead of the poor, it is the banks, private developers, investors, consultants, contractors, and their own employes who have been among HUD's most successful beneficiaries.

CHAPTER 17
Love and Passion at the National Science Foundation

"Can I speak frankly with you?" the young lady replied after being asked precisely how government-sponsored researchers could accurately measure sexual arousal among college men.

The volunteer collegiates were given joints of marijuana to smoke while viewing porno flicks. The idea was to see what effect, if any, the drug had on their manly capacity to become sexually excited. The sexual experiment was funded by the government's National Institute on Drug Abuse for a mere one hundred and twenty-one thousand bucks.

"Please do," I quickly responded over the phone as I positioned myself at a typewriter to take notes.

"Well," the agency spokeswoman said after a lengthy pause, "while they show them erotic movies they measure . . . this is crazy, but . . . they used a device that goes over the male organ to measure its size, by using a ring."

"Now let me get this straight," I said. "You mean they placed a ring over the penis?"

"Yes, that's right," she said somewhat nervously, though apparently relieved that she had managed to explain how the whole thing was done without going into any further detail.

She was right. It did sound crazy. How can the government be funding research projects like these?

There was, of course, a case to be made for the pot-porno-penis project. A statement by Dr. Robert L. Dupont, then the director of NIDA, said the project was conducted

> . . . to study the effects of marijuana on human sexual response. Interest in this area has arisen because of earlier evidence suggesting the possible impairment of male sexual response related to chronic marijuana use despite the belief that marijuana enhances sexual arousal. If indeed it interferes with such functioning, such information may be an important deterrant to use.

Now, there are a lot of things that can be said about this kind of nonsense by the government, but no one said it better than Sen. William Proxmire, the Senate's penny-pinching spending critic who called the study "one of the most shocking examples of the 'federal

134

love machine' I have ever found. With the level of drug addiction doubling in only the last 3-4 years, the funding of these so-called scientific studies constitutes an appalling disregard of any reasonable system of priorities."

As it turned out, Proxmire's blast was fatal. The project "just never got off the ground," a spokesman said later.

But the effort was, and is, symptomatic of a larger problem. The government's "love machine" continues to crank out sex-connected studies and other research projects of dubious worth. Many of the projects have almost zero priority, and indeed many of them are laughably ludicrous.

Take, for instance, the government's inquiry into sexual activity between 1971 and 1976 among unmarried teenagers between the ages of 15 and 19. The National Institute of Child Health and Human Development found out, among other things, that most initial and subsequent sexual encounters "took place in the home of the girl or her male partner's home." For other locations, "whites favored automobiles, blacks favored motels," according to the government study. Why we must know where teenagers had sexual encounters, and which race prefers motels over automobiles escapes me. Worse, the entire study amounted to a rank invasion of privacy by the federal government, which clearly *has no right* to make such inquiries.

In another sex-related study, Dr. Ellen Berscheid of the University of Minnesota believed it was important to test her theory that "psychological dependence is a key ingredient in interpersonal relations ranging from 'liking' to 'romantic love'."

The National Science Foundation evidently thought so, too, because they shelled out more than $212,000 to find out if her theory held water. To this day, no one really knows for sure. For her theory, like love itself, defies any degree of certainty.

Dr. Berscheid's experiment used a pool of student volunteers who dated one another over a period of weeks. The NSF's official project summary explained:

Some students never date the same person twice, while others date only one person during the experiment. In this way psychological dependence is varied from couple to couple, with maximum dependence arising where only one person is dated. The actual level of dependence produced in these varied dating patterns is measured by the time the partners spend "tracking" one another. It is hoped that measurements of such attentiveness will provide the kind of evidence necessary to confirm the role of dependence in such relationships. This may lead to a better scientific model of human interactions with real predictive power.

The summary suggests Dr. Berscheid's theory could produce "scientific insights" useful to marriage counselors and psychiatrists. It says nothing about people who cannot afford to see a psychiatrist, or the millions of couples who would never see a marriage counselor.

The experiments produced an outpouring of papers and reports by Dr. Berscheid and her colleagues. Among them was an edited book entitled *Romantic Love and Sexual Jealousy*, plus a report on "the relationship between male height, attraction, and the 'cardinal principle' of date and mate selection." No doubt to be made into a sequel to "Moulin Rouge." Worth noting, too, is the fact that the grants partially supported three doctoral dissertations.

Washington's version of "Love Among The Ruins" has many sequels, such as a $261,000 NSF study by a University of Wisconsin sociologist who sought to test whether an "equity theory" of love can predict "human reactions in deeply intimate relationships."

The study concluded:

> Professional counselors have failed to recognize or to impress upon their clients how important equity considerations are in mate selection and for marital stability. Generally, counselors imply that if a person is careful in mate selection he can find an attractive, successful, respected, well-adjusted mate. Young couples share their confidence . . . Surprisingly, young couples seem to be most concerned about capturing a beautiful or handsome partner, but they expect "the best" of everything else as well. Unfortunately, such expectations are not very realistic. In fact, people almost always end up with partners whose social assets— whose physical appearance, social background, intelligence, and personality—very closely "match" their own. A massive scaling down of aspirations is in order.

Now, this is pretty pedestrian stuff. I mean, it is the kind of thing one expects to find, and often does, in *Redbook* or *Cosmopolitan*.

Obviously, sex research at NSF is in vogue. One $82,000 study even sought to quantify masculinity and femininity by placing some kind of socially acceptable index on each. The study also examined self-esteem, sex role stereotypes and self-analysis of whether individuals consider themselves masculine or feminine. Chalk one up for gay rights.

But lest we become too caught up with NSF's preoccupation with love and passion, let us not ignore some equally remarkable examples of the agency's other research priorities. Chili, for instance.

This research effort was attempting to create a strong preference for chili pepper or coffee among laboratory rats, food tastes which the rodents quite understandably abhor. Cost: $50,000.

NSF explained the project this way:

Humans in most cultures add a characteristic flavoring to their basic foods, and develop strong preferences for substances which they find initially unpalatable, such as coffee or chili pepper. Both the flavoring and the preference for initially unpalatable foods seem to be virtually unique to humans in the animal kingdom. This study is directed toward an understanding of these aspects of human behavior, through a search for their biological roots in another omniverous animal, the laboratory rat.

I'll resist the temptation to suggest that the search for one's biological roots would leave even Alex Haley incredulous. Proxmire, who questioned the study's value at a subcommittee hearing on NSF's budget requests, was equally disbelieving:

Proxmire: Let's assume these rats really go mad for coffee and chili; prefer it to anything after they have developed a taste for it. What have you got besides hungry rats?

Richard Louttit (NSF director for behavioral and neural sciences): You have a rat whose food preferences have now become more like those of human beings, and now we can look at the biological changes which have led to that strange choice of diets on the part of this animal in a way that we can't do in the human being. It is simply using the laboratory rat as an animal model to look at the kind of process that is known to occur in human beings.

Proxmire: I still don't see where we are getting. I don't see that you have determined, no matter what the finding is, that is of any value to human beings. I gather that if we find there are rats and other animals that are able to cultivate a taste as we cultivate a taste, then you feel you have advanced along the road toward determining what it is in human beings that enables us to cultivate a taste. If we have advanced along that path, still what do we have?

Dr. Richard Atkinson (NSF deputy director): If we can understand the biological mechanism, the changes that occur in the cells or the brain structures that give rise to this change in the rat's behavior, that create these unique tastes, that is a step toward understanding why human beings have these peculiarities.

Proxmire: It seems to me that a direct study on human beings would be feasible. As I say chili and coffee are harmless foods.

Atkinson: These types of studies with laboratory rats and the like open up these areas. For example, many of the issues of hunger and obesity are areas that cannot really be studied with the human organism. We are now breaking through into dramatic ways of understanding obesity and hunger.

Proxmire: If you wanted to study obesity, coffee would be the last thing you would look at because there are no calories in coffee at all. I haven't seen many people who have gotten obese on chili either.

If the chili study doesn't bring tears to your eyes, consider a $200,000 study on speech patterns of the people of Philadelphia. W. C. Fields, who knew a thing or two about Philly, would have been speechless.

Investigating the linguistic patterns and variations of Philadelphians, including the effects of class and ethnic composition on their speech, may be ground-breaking stuff at NSF, but Professor Henry Higgins proved the point, at least in a fictional sense, about 100 years ago.

As if to press their contention that most Americans are incapable of judging the significance or value of their studies, the NSF described the project this way:

The results so far confirm many general principles of sound change in other communities, and have also produced new and unexpected findings such as the reversal of the direction of the glide in the dipthong aw—as in pound—as the nucleus rises to high position.

Boiled to its essentials, the study seeks to show that one cannot only alter the way people speak—like "The Rain In Spain"—but, by changing their speech characteristics, one can also change their self-esteem and behavioral attitudes.

"Isn't this something that George Bernard Shaw wrote about 80 or 90 years ago?" Proxmire blurted out, as NSF officials sought to explain the study in highly scientific terms. Their brisk answer, "Yes sir." Eliza Doolittle, thanks to NSF, may be rediscovered in Philadelphia.

It goes without saying that there is much that NSF has done and is doing that is of inestimable value and importance to the advancement of science and for the benefit of mankind. A $104,000 grant to a Wisconsin laboratory which was examining the possibility of getting safe red food color from beets is one example of useful, goal-oriented research worthy of the taxpayer's support.

One of the chief arguments repeatedly employed against efforts to trim NSF's burgeoning budget is the warning that vital, life-saving research could be denied federal support in the process. This was the expected line of reasoning in March of 1979 when Rep. John Ashbrook (R., Ohio) offered an amendment in the House to cut a modest $14 million from NSF's Biological, Behavioral, and Social Science research.

"How many people here would vote for $100,000 to study the growth of viruses in monkey kidney cells?" asked Rep. Tom Harkin (D., Iowa). While this NSF-funded research had no immediate payoff, Harkin said, Dr. Jonas Salk, a few years later, used the study in his own research and came up with his polio vaccine.

But Harkin and Ashbrook were clearly talking about apples and oranges. Ashbrook was not attacking medical research. Instead, he was criticizing studies which, he argued, were indefensible and simply wasted tax dollars.

A classic example of what Ashbrook was getting at was the $83,839 NSF gave to the American Bar Association to study the social structure of the legal profession. The study, according to NSF, sought to examine "the extent and nature of social differentiation within the profession" as well as "the social, economic, political, and legal values of the various segments of the profession."

Other NSF research criticized by Ashbrook and other members of Congress included $52,338 to study the cooperative breeding habits of the white-fronted bee-eater, a small African bird; $43,000 to study "the development of the sense of taste in sheep"; and $90,000 to examine "patterns of facial muscle activity accompanying low-intensity emotional states."

"My amendment does not deal with basic valuable research," Ashbrook told his colleagues. "It deals with the foolish, fringe folly of researchers who use our tax money like the dilettante squandering his inheritance—recklessly and with little meaning or value except to pander to their own snobbish tastes." Ashbrook's amendment won, 219-174, but was unfortunately knocked out of the NSF authorization bill in a House-Senate conference committee which met to iron out differences over the measure.

Created in 1950 to support basic research and education in the sciences, NSF modestly began with a budget of only $250,000. In fiscal 1979 Congress gave the agency $911 million. Their budget in fiscal 1980 exceeded the $1 billion mark for the first time, representing a $76 million increase over the previous year's budget. From 1970 to the present, NSF's budgets have increased at an average annual growth rate of about 8.5 percent. This money—in salaries and expenses—supports the work of 68,000 college and university teachers and researchers, and in many cases supports some of the operational overhead of the institutions themselves.

Needless to say, these grants are providing substantial additional income to college and university professors and teachers, when the research—as it often is—is done in the summer vacation period. In fact, some grantees may have two or three grants going at the same time.

Before Congress imposed a ceiling of $47,500 in 1978 on payments to researchers, at least 8 percent of NSF's principal grantees were getting that or more in payment for their work. And those gravy days may be returning, for the House Appropriations Committee in 1979 proposed abolishing the ceiling on grant money.

Beyond this, however, an examination of NSF grants reveals that enormous sums of money are being spent on research projects of little if any value.

Why, for example, must we spend $80,000 to conduct a systematic analysis of the decision-making processes through which presidential candidates seek and win their party's nominations? NSF is spending $3.5 million a year on political science research. In 1979 it gave $33,000 to the State University of New York to study over 2,000 contributors to the 1978 congressional campaigns, trying in part to find out why people contribute to certain candidates.

NSF justified the grant this way:

> Contributors are an important segment of a candidate's constituency. Therefore, this study explores their motivations and political expectations in order to test theoretical hypotheses from previous work on Congress, representation and political participation.

One of NSF's recipients in this research program was the National Governors' Association which received a $60,000 grant to study the transition problems of four newly elected governors.

As should be expected, NSF's research spending often duplicates the work of other federal agencies. For example, NSF budgeted $2.1 million for its Science for Citizens: Health and Safety program, $48,285 of which was spent to hold a series of seven health and safety forums for copper smelter workers and to produce an occupational safety handbook. The National Institute for Occupational Health and Safety spent $61.4 million on similar work.

NSF was also spending about $10 million a year to study economics, surely one of the most inexact of the sciences. Grants in this field of research included a University of California researcher's examination of Dutch labor markets and wages from the 1580's to the middle of the nineteenth century. Cost: $65,300. Another grantee, a Columbia University professor, was studying the social impact of credit allocation by a single bank in Keene, New Hampshire, from 1833 to 1955. Cost: $10,581.

As noted earlier, NSF, like the Legal Services Corporation, is conducting law research. In 1978 NSF paid over $51,000 to an Arizona State University researcher to study the effects of advertising on legal services pricing. According to NSF's justification, the money paid for an investigation into:

... the potential for scientific studies to make a contribution to this important public issue by testing strategies for an economic analysis of legal service advertising.

Translation: The money went to study whether or not there should be a study.

In May, 1978 NSF spent over $61,000 to "examine the practices and attitudes of librarians and individuals placing, renewing and cancelling periodical subscriptions." For this project, which involved sending out 6,400 questionnaires to subscribers, the researcher wanted $57,328. NSF increased the request by another $4,000.

The agency asked for $7.3 million in fiscal 1980 for Atomic, Molecular and Plasma Physics, or $500,000 more than the previous year. Almost $60,000 of the funds available in this field went to a University of Michigan researcher to study the acoustics of the piano and the violin. In 1978 NSF spent $30,000 to study the "accoustical behavior of the orchestral wind and brass instruments." The agency said it hoped these studies would have "a real impact on the technology of musical instruments."

As part of its $7.4 million a year anthropological science program, NSF awarded a $30,500 grant to a University of California-Berkeley researcher to conduct a survey of the ways colors are classified in 130 languages.

These examples are not isolated ones. An examination of thousands of NSF studies repeatedly finds similar grants throughout NSF's research portfolio.

How does the government justify spending $40,000 on a study of the origins of the Polynesian culture when so many more pressing problems cry out for support? Do we really need to spend $124,000 to investigate abusive behavior at recreational parks and playgrounds in Boston? Or $54,400 to study the dynamics of family lives in a peasant Alpine village? Or $92,900 to study the distribution of wealth in the United States during the late 1700's?

The list of wasteful or just low priority research goes on and on: $22,000 on a study of polygymy among birds; $24,000 on the reproductive strategies in milkweeds; or $81,300 on the sociosexual behavior of the dabbling African black duck.

Each of these projects, and thousands more like them, represent comparatively small sums of money, but *when viewed cumulatively*, year after year, we are talking about hundreds of millions of dollars, eventually billions.

When Sen. Henry Bellmon of Oklahoma asked NSF officials at a hearing on their budget what would happen if Congress simply decided to "totally end funding" for the entire agency for five years, a stunned Dr. Atkinson replied, "I can't tell you—that is a matter for conjecture."

Later, in a more elaborate answer submitted in writing, Atkinson said such a termination would result in "an abrupt and dramatic disruption of academic research in all areas of the nation"—which seemed to many observers at the time to be a predictable, somewhat parochial, not to say hysterical reply. The federal government now spends $31.2 billion a year on all its research programs. NSF's share of that research is only about 18 percent. It, therefore, seems rather inconceivable that the nation's academic community would just shrivel up and die if reasonable and careful restraints were made on future NSF research spending alone.

It is a sacred rule of government that for programs to be considered successful, they must without fail seek bigger and bigger budgets each year. The government's religious devotion to that rule is most vividly demonstrated by the continually rising budget of the National Science Foundation. Perhaps in no other agency of government can taxpayers see more clearly how their earnings are being frivolously spent on so many so-called "scientific" studies. Many of the studies being funded are about as scientific as the Wizard of Oz. This does not mean, however, that worthwhile, goal-oriented research should not be pursued with the vigorous financial assistance of the federal government. But it does mean that intelligent choices and priorities must be assigned to that research.

When the Senate Appropriations Committee met in the summer of 1979 to vote on the agency's fiscal 1980 budget, Sen. Proxmire proposed a modest $30 million cut in its requests. Not a single member of the committee could be found to support the Wisconsin Democrat's spending cut.

Ventured one veteran Senate committee staffer:

The only way to cut out this nonsense is to cut their budget. We're not going to be able to tell NSF which projects do and which do not have value. They alone must decide that. However, we can force them to make better use of their money by simply giving them significantly less money to begin with. And Congress sure as hell hasn't been doing that.

CHAPTER 18
Cutting the Government: Jimmy Carter's Broken Promise

Despite President Carter's campaign pledge to "cut the bureaucracy down to size" and throw out wasteful federal programs, few government agencies have actually been abolished since he took office.

One of Carter's major campaign promises in 1976 was to consolidate nearly 2,000 federal agencies and programs down to about 200 tightly-organized units of government.

While much of the reduction, Carter said, would be achieved by reorganization, he also vowed that zero-based budgeting—under which each program must justify its existence—would be used to cut "unneeded or obsolescent programs."

"The challenge before the nation is to cut the bureaucracy down to size," Carter said in Columbus, Ohio, on September 9, 1976. If elected, he promised he would "shut down out-dated agencies and programs once and for all."

How has the president succeeded?

Despite ambitious plans, only a few functioning agencies have actually been abolished, and most of them represented very small savings in budget cuts. By virtually every measurable criterion, the government continues to grow substantially.

By fiscal 1980, yearly spending had increased by $97 billion since Gerald Ford left office—to nearly $548 billion. Since January 1977, the federal payroll had risen by over 34,000 workers. But this was only the *visible* part. What was not seen was $12 billion in off-budget programs and agencies such as the Federal Financing Bank, the Postal Service, the U.S. Railway Association, the Rural Telephone Bank, and other agencies, all of which—when added to the fiscal 1980 budget—pushed the real government spending total up to $560 billion.

As for Carter's campaign pledge to shrink the government down to 200 consolidated units, White House officials would rather forget he made it.

"I don't know where that figure actually came from," said Carter's reorganization chief, Harrison Wellford, in an interview. "Frankly,

I wish it had never been used." (It came from Carter, who said on a "Face the Nation" interview, March 14, 1976: "But we now have about 1,900 [agencies], perhaps more, in the federal government, and I intend to cut those down to no more than 200. It's a goal that I've set for myself that I think is achievable.")

Actually, a White House inventory found there were 1,846 departments, agencies, boards, commissions, administrations and advisory committees, which alone numbered more than 1,000. (Excluded from this count were hundreds of interagency committees spread throughout the government which the White House said would be "impossible" to tabulate.)

From this master list the Carter administration said it had successfully abolished a total of 760 agencies or units of government, but had added another 348 for a net reduction of 412 agencies. (The term "agencies" is used here in the generic sense and is meant to encompass virtually every type of government program or organized entity.)

Carter's so-called cuts, however, were not as substantive as they at first appeared. This was because 677 of them were carved from the government's myriad of informal advisory committees and commissions which meet only occasionally, rarely involve any permanent staff, and represent very little cost to a budget that is now spending $1.5 billion a day.

Yet even though Carter cut the number of advisory committees, their cost still increased—up from $64.9 million in 1978 to an estimated $74.1 million in 1979. The blame for this rise lay with Congress as well as the White House, both of whom continue to create new committees, even as the old ones were being abolished. In 1978, for example, 204 new advisory committees were added to the government's cluttered bureaucracy.

So excluding these 677 committees, we are left with 83 actual Cabinet and non-Cabinet agencies the White House claimed to have terminated.

Closer examination, however, revealed that most of these 83 were not in fact abolished, but were merged into other, larger agencies and programs—their missions and payrolls still intact, and very often enlarged.

In point of fact, only about a dozen functioning governmental units or agencies were actually terminated as a result of President Carter's efforts to trim the bureaucracy. Most of them, it should be noted, were small advisory offices or councils, some with little or no staff.

And in most of these instances, the employes were simply moved into other government jobs.

One of these so-called abolished agencies was the White House Office of Telecommunications, which was originally established under President Nixon to research and coordinate communications policies and technology. In truth, OTP was transferred lock, stock and barrel to the Commerce Department and merged there with the department's Office of Telecommunications. The newly consolidated agency, together with some programs from HEW, was renamed the National Telecommunications and Information Administration.

Did the merger result in a net savings to the taxpayers? Before consolidation, the combined cost of the two agencies was less than $10 million a year. Their cost in fiscal 1979 was nearly $12 million.

"It certainly cannot be considered a termination," a Commerce official said. "The program was simply lifted out of the White House and moved over here." Thus, while the White House agency was eliminated on paper, its functions, employes and costs continue.

In the same way, while the White House maintains that it has abolished the Domestic Council created under President Nixon, the unit—function, job slots, and all—remains *alive and well* in Carter's Domestic Policy staff.

Other White House offices abolished by Carter, like the Energy Resources Council, the Federal Property Council, and the Economic Opportunity Council were nothing but "shadow agencies," according to one White House official who said they were "pretty moribund by the time we got to them."

Beyond all of this, several independent agencies listed on the White House termination list were ended solely because Congress chose not to extend their authority. In some cases the White House had originally sought their continuation.

One of these was the Renegotiation Board which expired March 31, 1979, despite President Carter's support for its continued existence. The board died when Congress failed to reauthorize it for another year. The President's fiscal 1980 budget had asked for $7.3 million for the now-defunct agency, an increase of $1 million over the previous year's budget.

What happened to the Board's 180 employes? Some sought early retirement or got jobs elsewhere in the private sector, but many went to work for the White House Council on Wage and Price Stability, among other federal agencies.

Other agencies like the Commission on Federal Paperwork and

the American Revolution Bicentennial Administration also appeared on the White House death list. But President Carter can make no claim to having rubbed these agencies out of existence. Both went out of business as scheduled because Congress had set "sunset" expiration deadlines for them when they were originally enacted, not because the White House sought their demise.

This was also the case with the Indian Claims Commission which went out of business in September, 1978, because Congress in 1976 had set a deadline for the agency to cease operations.

The National Center for Productivity And Quality of Working Life, for which Carter had provided $3 million in his fiscal 1979 budget, officially closed its doors on September 30, 1978—again, because Congress had placed a termination date in its authorization law. When the time came to consider its continuation, Congress chose to let it die in dignity. Yet the Center hasn't totally disappeared. Two employes continue part of its work at the Commerce Department's National Technical Information Service, and in October of 1978 President Carter created a "National Productivity Board."

Far more important, however, is the fact that many other agencies which the White House placed in its "loss" column were simply renamed and moved wholesale into larger agencies which in effect act as "hiding places."

The National Fire Prevention and Control Administration was moved from Commerce, renamed the U.S. Fire Administration, and placed in a new agency called the Federal Emergency Management Agency (FEMA). FEMA has in fact become the new repository for a number of small agencies, including the Federal Disaster Assistance Administration, the Federal Insurance Administration, the Federal Preparedness Agency, and the Defense Civil Preparedness Agency.

Similarly, the Agriculture Department's 1,000-employe Economic Reserve Service, which produces marketing reports for big agricultural industries, was merged with the Statistical Reporting Service and renamed the Economic Research and Statistics Service. A spokesman at ERS said that no one lost their job as a result of the merger.

Likewise, many of the old energy programs, like the Energy Research and Development Administration and the Federal Power Commission, now called the Federal Energy Regulatory Commission, were moved into the new Department of Energy. These agencies appear on the White House list as "losses," yet their functions, and the employes who perform them, continue to live within the Energy Department.

Similar transfers of agencies occurred when the Civil Service Commission was abolished and renamed the Office of Personnel Management. The new agency inherited at least seven sub-agencies from the old Commission under Carter's reorganization shifts.

This is why veteran government watchers were not fooled by this bureaucratic version of musical chairs which the Carter administration had been so adroitly performing. Said a veteran staffer on the Senate Appropriations Committee:

I don't see too much evidence of programs being knocked out. Instead of getting rid of old programs, they are starting new ones.

In the first two years of the Carter administration at least 68 separate grant programs were abolished, but in that same period Congress and the administration put an additional 62 grant programs in their place.

Essentially, Carter applied the same approach to reorganization of the federal government that he used while governor of Georgia when he consolidated 300 state offices, boards, and commissions into 22 superagencies. This effort, however, resulted in the state payroll going up from 34,322 employes to 42,400 and the state budget rising by 58.5 percent.

As could be expected, the White House was sensitive about keeping its list of 760 "abolished" agencies and committees intact, believing the list represented the truest picture of what the administration's reorganization efforts accomplished. When asked to provide a distilled list of those agencies actually terminated—deleting the advisory committees and those agencies whose functions were just transferred elsewhere—a top reorganization task force official replied that such a list would be "impossible to compile." Why? Because it would be so small. Everyone would know that Jimmy Carter had not, as promised, "cut the bureaucracy down to size."

However, White House officials spoke bluntly about the obstacles they had to combat in their bureaucracy-cutting crusade:

"The reality is that there is no office so humble or useless that it doesn't have some passionate defender," Wellford said in an interview with this reporter. "You don't have anyone lobbying for the elimination of unnecessary agencies. You never feel any pressure on that. But there is always someone pushing for one of these limp-along, useless groups.

"The zeal for pruning the bureaucracy in general never matches the resistance against cutting the specific," he continued. "That's just the way it is. This is a bad season for reformers. Interest groups are flourishing. It's very difficult to marshall grass roots support and opinion on Congress. Look at them: Common Cause, Ralph Nader's Citizens Lobby, the Fortune 500. There's an extraordinary imbalance here. They are all protecting some program or privilege."

This was why, Wellford continued, the administration's focus on bureaucracy pruning moved from program termination, which Carter emphasized in his campaign, to one of program consolidation.

"The focus has widened," he said. "The emphasis is on improving efficiency—on consolidation. We feel this is the emphasis that is the wisest and best approach."

Why the change? "Obviously we are influenced by what the market will bear on the Hill," he said. While admitting that there were still many more "programs and agencies we could get rid of," Wellford stressed "the amount of political capital required to eliminate a government agency that has a congressional subcommittee chairman as its protector is very, very large."

By that he meant that any fight to abolish some obscure program or agency inevitably leads to opposition in Congress, sometimes making permanent enemies of lawmakers whose votes the administration needed for major legislative battles. That was why, he explained, Carter was better off conserving his "political capital" for major congressional battles, rather than waste them by alienating lawmakers in an attempt to erase some obscure $25 million agency that performed no useful function.

Wellford's frustration, perhaps reflecting that of the administration, was clear: "It doesn't make sense to alienate them (Congress)," he said. "Carter came here with high ideals and came up against a wall of congressional resistance."

Has the President fulfilled his campaign promise to cut back the bureaucracy? Has the government been, in Carter's words, "cut down to size"? The administration's own answer to that question, when stripped of rhetoric and bureaucratic excuses, was clearly in the negative. Said Wellford, "Within the realm of the political climate and the political realities, I think he has." Yet Wellford easily admitted that, by any objective measurement, the government's overall "growth is up," though he argued weakly that the pace of that upward growth has been slowed. This sounds like the airline pilot who announced to his passengers that he and his crew were completely lost but that, nevertheless, he was making "excellent time."

Still, there is reason to believe that Carter and his crew did not undertake a very vigorous effort to prune the bureaucracy. This was particularly evident when Carter—quite apart from the sleight of hand reorganization cuts we have discussed thus far—presented his fiscal 1980 budget which contained $4.5 billion in proposed program terminations. On the surface, it appeared to be a valiant effort to end unneeded programs. Unfortunately, the administration never made a concerted follow-up effort to go over the heads of congressional committee barons to argue for their abolition. The proposed deletions ran the gamut from $3.6 million in beekeeper indemnities (payments for dead bees) to $1 billion in unnecessary or low-priority public works projects. According to White House insiders, Carter's suggested program cuts were substantially reduced from an original list more than twice as ambitious. However, it was whittled down, according to one White House aide, "because it just would have created more enemies on the Hill than we could afford."

Yet despite the best of intentions, Carter's $4.5 billion in proposed cuts may have been one of the best kept secrets in Washington. When a reporter in mid-1979 went to the White House and asked to see the written justifications for making these cuts, he was told by Carter's high command that no such package of justifications existed. A few fragmented briefs in behalf of some cuts were produced after much searching, but if the administration was truly serious about cutting unwanted and nonessential programs, it would have had a book full of ferocious and devastating arguments ready and waiting for anyone who wanted to use them. If the ammunition against these programs had been gathered together in a comprehensive fashion and persuasively presented to members of Congress, special interest groups, the news media, and taxpayers generally, the Congress would have been much more receptive to proposals to eliminate them than it was. But the administration made no such attempt. Carter lost the fight against cutting the bureaucracy because he never entered the battle.

It is traditional in the government budget process that for every program expenditure sought from Congress, the executive branch must submit its justifications to the Appropriations Committees of the House and Senate who review and approve all funding. However, when the administration submitted its fiscal 1980 budget containing wholesale program terminations, no justifications for them were presented to Congress. This was a pity. Because as one savvy Senate Appropriations Committee staffer remarked, "Unless these senators have the arguments for or against something right in front of them, there is no way you are going to win their support."

When this reporter suggested to a White House adviser that the packaging and promotion of arguments supporting Carter's budget deletions would have produced a devastating and effective offensive on Capitol Hill, he replied, after some thought, "You know, that's not a bad idea," then turned to his aide and said, "Let's think about that for next year."

My own view is that Carter's expressed desire to prune the bureaucracy was never serious to begin with. The lukewarm, half-hearted treatment the administration gave to what was Carter's principal campaign issue suggests strongly that the man from Georgia was a captive of too many political factions to carry out his exuberant campaign promises about cutting waste and trimming bureaucratic fat.

Thus, we see that few federal programs of any substance have been erased by Jimmy Carter. The bureaucracy, fat and frivolous as ever, *continues to grow* and to consume the fruits and labors of an increasingly weakened private sector. The job of cutting back on needless, ineffective, and wasteful government programs and agencies must await a new and more determined administration.

BOOK II
100 Nonessential Federal Programs

PROGRAMS 1–11

Coastal Plains Regional Commission
Four Corners Regional Commission
New England Regional Commission
Old West Regional Commission
Ozarks Regional Commission
Pacific Northwest Regional Commission
Upper Great Lakes Regional Commission
Southwest Border Regional Commission
Mid-America Regional Commission
Mid-Atlantic Regional Commission
Mid-South Regional Commission
TOTAL — $67.7 Million

In a fit of candor President Jimmy Carter called these commissions "a waste of time and money." Then he turned around and approved requests to boost their funding, and supported a decision to expand their numbers and their cost to the taxpayers. Such is the power of politics over common sense.

Carter made his private thoughts known in an internal White House memorandum prior to publicly announcing his decision in January, 1979, to create three more commissions in addition to the eight which already existed.

The president's written comments, leaked to a reporter for the *St. Louis Post-Dispatch*, couldn't have been clearer: "Reluctant agreement," he wrote on the decision memorandum prepared for the proposed establishment of the Mid-America, Mid-South and Mid-Atlantic Commissions. Then he added:

> But in general I consider the regional commissions to be a waste of time and money—very top heavy under the federal and state co-chairman—a source of a few $ for governors. Maybe it's improving—I hope so.

The president was right. They *are* a waste of money—big money. Since 1966 they have cost taxpayers $530.5 million. Yet virtually every significant study done on the commissions found that the nation got back little if anything for the more than half billion dollars invested in them.

In many respects they are a regional extension of the idea behind

154

the Economic Development Administration (which will be discussed later) to initiate and spur long-range economic development in areas of severe unemployment and low income, primarily through an assortment of business and public works grants and loans. As originally envisioned, the commissions were to combat economic depressions on a regional basis, working in concert with state and local officials to see that federal money was placed where it was most needed. But it hasn't worked out that way. They have largely been ineffective bodies, in many cases duplicating similar federal programs.

In 1974 a joint study* by the Commerce Department and the Office of Management and Budget, which Congress requested, concluded that the commissions

> . . . have had very limited influence on the allocation of resources in their regions to create jobs for the unemployed in areas of persistent and substantial unemployment. Although many of the commissions have developed broad plans for dealing with unemployment problems in their regions, they have had little success in directing resources to help implement those plans.

Like many economic assistance programs of this sort, it is almost impossible to determine exactly how a tangle of technical assistance and demonstration projects, planning assistance grants, and public works financing, among the hundreds of projects funded by the commissions, are supposed to help an area's economy. When I attempted to trace one economic impact grant through a maze of bureaucratic dollar shuffling, I found the regional commission had given the money to the state of Arizona which in turn gave most of it to an Ohio research firm in payment for a planning study. Similarly, in case after case, I found research and various consulting firms receiving the major portion of the federal dollars spent by these commissions.

A 1974 study* of these and other federal regional programs by the Brookings Institution concluded that the regional commissions "in general . . . have been organizations of limited accomplishment."

The Brookings study also concluded that "as a superstructure upon the more traditional structure of federal-state organization, they are a complicating feature, attractive to the states for whatever money and services they yield, but not for their own sake." While at times there may be specific areas of the country in which dire poverty and severe unemployment—complicated by other economic condi-

*"Report to the Congress on the Proposal for an Economic Adjustment Program," February 1, 1974, OMB-Commerce.

*Martha Derthick, Between State and Nation, Brookings Institution, Washington, D.C.

tions—demand a regional approach, "it should not be extended to the whole country," the study said. Such a coast-to-coast application of the regional concept has in effect placed "the needy region on a par with others, while giving extraordinary help to places whose need for it has not been demonstrated."

More recent studies on the commissions have not exactly been effusive in praise for their works. In 1977 the Center for Social Analysis of the State University of New York concluded:

> Overall, they suffer from such resource anemia that they struggle to find something useful that relates (sometime vaguely) to their mandate. They are monuments of administrative adaptation to adversity.

The study went on to observe, "No commission has succeeded in accomplishing the legislative intent of bringing the overall allocation and administration of public funds—federal, state, local—into conformity with a regional plan," adding that their "economic development impacts have been small."

Originally, these commissions were meant to be temporary, organized to stimulate depressed economies on a regional basis and then go out of business. But by late 1979 Congress was considering new legislation that would make them permanent, broaden their authority and powers, and substantially increase their funding. The proposed cost from 1980 through 1983 would be $3.8 billion, although this would also include the Appalachian Regional Commission.

The governors of the states, who serve on the commissions together with federal co-chairmen appointed by the president, have lobbied strongly for their expansion, because they like what little federal assistance and benefits the commissions provide. But the overwhelming evidence clearly shows that the commissions have been creatures of waste and embarrassingly little accomplishment. They should be abolished.

PROGRAM 12

U.S. Travel Service — $8 Million

This is an agency that should take a long trip—into oblivion. It is a perfect example of the government getting involved in an activity the private sector does infinitely better.

The U.S. Travel Service was created in 1961 to promote travel to America from abroad. However, there is no convincing evidence that it has had any effect whatsoever on increasing travel to the United States. Besides the fact that the government shouldn't be subsidizing U.S. travel promotion, there are other reasons why the Service should be shut down. Discount air fares have made overseas travel considerably more affordable. Airlines, shipping lines, and other travel-related businesses have substantially increased their travel promotion. The diminished value of the dollar has improved foreign purchasing power for U.S. products.

The agency, which was created under the Kennedy administration, had a staff totaling 123 employes in addition to six foreign offices around the world. The Service has conducted research, issued volumes of literature on tourism to the U.S., and promoted travel to this country at international fairs and exhibitions. It has also conducted widely popular familiarization tours to the U.S.A. for foreign journalists. Such "theme tours" cost the agency $100,000.

The Carter administration, which urged Congress to terminate the agency in fiscal 1980, has testified that taxpayers

> ... can no longer afford—given the current economic situation—to fund programs which are not effective, no matter how small.

Franklin D. Raines, an associate director with the Office of Management and Budget, said OMB conducted a study of the agency's activities and found that there were "serious inconsistencies and inadequacies" in the analytical justification supporting the effectiveness of various travel program activities. Raines noted, for example, that the Travel Service's data involving the number of foreign arrivals generated through direct federal promotional activities is "highly questionable and very difficult to validate."

Moreover, the study found that the Service's promotional activities

> ... in many ways overlap with those already performed by numerous non-federal government and private sector organizations.

OMB's analysis of the Travel Service, Raines said, came to the conclusion:

Federal funding of promotional activities in support of tourism is just not a cost-effective expenditure of the taxpayers' money. The declining value of the dollar relative to other foreign currencies does far more to influence our travel deficit than any promotional efforts. We can find no correlation whatever between what we have spent on promotion and shifts in the deficit.

Testifying before the Senate Commerce Committee, Raines said OMB concluded that

... promotion of destinations and forms of travel is something which clearly is not a federal responsibility. Promoting the United States as a destination for foreign travellers is a job that can be left to the private sector (tour operators, car rental companies, hotel chains, banks, and carriers) which already has very substantial resources, expertise, and commitment to develop marketing strategies to attract foreign travellers to the United States, thereby increasing its profit potential.

Past administrations have rarely if ever sent spokesmen up to Capitol Hill to urge the elimination of some federal agency, least of all the Carter administration. But in this case, OMB's suggestion was long overdue.

U.S. carriers are currently spending more than $300 million a year on advertising, plus another $40 million on other forms of promotion annually. U.S. airlines serving foreign countries spend an estimated 30 percent or more of their advertising budget to encourage foreign travellers to visit the United States. Other parts of the tourist industry similarly expend large sums of money to promote travel to America. By any reckoning this should be adequate. The Travel Service should go out of business.

PROGRAM 13
The Pentagon's "Top Brass" Dining Rooms — $2 Million

There are some exclusive restaurants in Washington where you can dine on a perfectly broiled Delmonico steak for $2.65, or a baked filet of flounder for a paltry $1.60. Or would you prefer sirloin slices au jus, with a soup appetizer, and Bavarian-style beans and Spaetzle, plus buttered peas and onions, all for $2.75. If your tastes run to more continental fare, might we interest you in "Steak a la Ritz" topped with an egg and choice of vegetable for $2.50?

How can they do this at these prices in these days of double digit inflation? you ask. The answer is that the restaurants are subsidized to the tune of $1.3 million a year by the taxpayers. But don't bother making reservations, because their clientele is restricted to top military brass only. The restaurants, you see, are in the Pentagon.

The restaurants consist of five private dining rooms in which about 400 admirals, generals, and top ranking civilian Defense Department officials elegantly lunch each day on entrees and dinners prepared and served in crisp military fashion by about 100 enlisted men.

The menu prices, according to the Defense Department, pay for the food, beverages, laundry, silverware, and other supplies, while the taxpayer foots the bill for personnel salaries, utilities, and other costs of maintaining the physical space of the dining rooms. The subsidized costs, according to official figures, break down this way: Army Dining Room, $269,760; Navy Dining Room, $320,845; Air Force Dining Room, $227,846; Joint Chiefs Dining Room, $186,670; and Secretary of Defense Dining Room, $235,275.

The Defense Department maintains the exclusive facilities are needed so that top brass and high civilian officials can dine and conduct official business "without undue concern for the security of their conversations," which is "often classified or of a highly sensitive nature." However, staff people who have worked in these dining rooms say that the talk

   . . . is usually about golf, some movie they saw last night, just social conversation.

If the Pentagon's panjandrums need to discuss top secret matters over lunch, surely they can have food brought up to their offices or conference rooms.

It has also been argued that the executive dining rooms are a necessary "fringe benefit" that encourages generals and admirals to

159

stay in the military. Yet it is difficult to imagine that our top defense leaders would ever base any decision to remain in the military in whole or in part on the existence of these dining rooms.

Blue-jacketed Filipino stewards are recruited by the Navy to dutifully wait upon their military brass. They are also employed in the dining rooms operated by the Joint Chiefs. The Air Force and the Army prefer to use their own enlisted men. And the dining rooms' exclusivity is never broken. The rooms are restricted to admirals and three-star generals and their immediate deputies, in addition to civilian Defense Department officials at the assistant-secretary level and their chief deputies.

An examination of the menus in each of them shows the prices are bargains by any comparison. In the Secretary of Defense Dining Room, the secretary and his highest ranked colleagues pay 50 cents for cold avocado soup, 25 cents for a fruit juice appetizer, $1.70 for a ham omelette, 50 cents for a fresh fruits and cottage cheese plate, 45 cents for a hearts of lettuce salad with choice of five dressings, $2.65 for a broiled Delmonico steak cooked to order.

In the Air Force Dining Room, our highest paid brass can dine on broiled filet of sole for $1.65, broiled breast of chicken for $1.50, or fresh fruit and cheeses for 65 cents. The Navy's bigwigs, on the other hand, pay 35 cents for the soup of the day, which on one menu was "beef royale," $2.25 for brochette of pork tenderloin with double baked potatoes, and a paltry 40 cents for apple pie a la mode. Elsewhere on the Navy executive dining room menu, top brass officers pay 25 cents for chilled fruit juice, $2.50 for steak, and $2.25 for "Chicken Liver au Vin Blanc," served with the vegetable of the day (plus rolls).

Meanwhile, the Joint Chiefs of Staff and their well-paid colleagues (who earn between $45,000 and $60,000 a year) pay $1.75 to dine on baked fillet of perch, or $2.65 for broiled Delmonico steak. A tossed salad with sliced boiled eggs and choice of dressing goes for 50 cents. Chilled watermelon is 40 cents.

The House Appropriations Committee has been sharply critical of the subsidized dining salons. In one of its reports the committee said the $2 million being spent on the five Pentagon dining rooms and 18 other private military bistros in Washington and throughout the world was clearly excessive and the amount of the subsidy should be substantially reduced. "There does not appear to be any reason why some of the Executive Dining Rooms operating in the Pentagon cannot be consolidated for use by the various services rather than each service having its own facilities," the panel said.

But this rather aristocratic practice continues as it has for years, without any sign from the military that they are prepared to tighten their belts and eliminate the facilities. There is of course no reason why our top military leaders cannot eat in the regular cafeterias used by the Pentagon's 25,000 other employes—though the food, I am told, is admittedly worse and in some instances more expensive.

With the country's military budget under continuing attack, it would be a worthy gesture if our top brass were to set an example in cost-cutting for the Defense Department by simply abolishing the highly elitist dining rooms and eating with lower ranked military personnel and civilian employes in the regular mess facilities. It would no doubt boost military and civilian morale to see their superiors dining along side them instead of in their restricted "country club" restaurants. It would be a dramatic gesture to the public too, showing that the military was sincerely trying to cut unneccessary and frivolous expenditures. The dining rooms should be closed down.

PROGRAM 14

U.S. Employment Service — $738 Million

The federal government has been operating an employment service of sorts ever since 1918. But it wasn't until the Great Depression that Uncle Sam plunged into the employment business in a big way to find work for the nation's jobless. Yet like everything else the government does in response to a national emergency, the government's employment service has continued long after that crisis faded into history.

The U.S. Employment Service was begun under the Wagner-Peyser Act of 1933 which authorized a nationwide service to act as a labor exchange. State employment offices were to serve both employers and employes, matching job seekers with the available jobs.

Today, however, there is good reason to question why we need a national personnel placement service financed by the federal government. The country is virtually awash with national, state and local job recruitment and placement companies of all sizes and capabilities. The economy for some time now has been producing employment for job seekers at an energetic pace. In fact in recent years the job market has been producing job openings in record numbers.

The national headquarters for the U.S. Employment Service is in the Department of Labor where 571 federal employes oversee the operations of the 54 state and territorial employment agencies which employ 37,000 people in 2500 state offices.

However, the Employment Service is actually sort of a half-breed government creation, financed completely through federal tax revenues although its offices are still considered agencies of the states. Those who work in the state offices are state employes not federal employes, even though their salaries are derived from the U.S. Treasury.

Here is how the financing for the U.S. Employment Service works. Its budget for fiscal 1979 totaled $719.6 million, with 97 percent of that sum raised through the federal unemployment tax on employers which is paid into the Treasury's Unemployment Trust Fund. The remaining 3 percent of that sum, $21.6 million, comes out of the Treasury's general revenues which all of us pay. However, this pays only for the 37,000 "state" employes and the operation of the state offices in which they work. It does not pay for the 571 U.S. Employment Service employes within the Labor Department. The em-

employes and operation of this headquarters have a budget of an additional $18.2 million, with $17.2 million of it coming from the Unemployment Trust Fund and nearly $1 million from general revenues.

The Employment Service found jobs in 1978 for 4.6 million people (1.4 million of them were placed more than once), but many of these job seekers were not placed in permanent positions of employment. In fact, officials said a great number of them were given only temporary jobs lasting from one-to-three days. Thus, their overall success in finding jobs for the unemployed—when compared to thousands of personnel agencies and temporary manpower companies across the country who find jobs for many millions more each year—is rather negligible within the context of the nation's total workforce of more than 70 million people.

On the other hand, supporters of the Employment Service argue that the agency performs many other tasks such as registering food stamp and welfare applicants for job placement, but officials admit the agency does not verify whether these people do in fact go for the job interviews they are sent for. Indeed, it is really more of a pro forma ritual than anything else.

In addition, the Employment Service's work in many instances has been duplicating the employment services of the Comprehensive Employment and Training Act program. "In many ways they duplicate each other," said a congressional committee expert in Labor programs. "In some cities they fight each other and run totally separate and duplicative services."

The General Accounting Office, in one study on government employment programs, found in the spring of 1979 there were half a dozen federal agencies and at least a dozen state and local agencies providing essentially the same services for job seekers. CETA alone was costing taxpayers $4.4 billion a year to provide jobs for the unemployed.

Clearly, the U.S. Employment Service has outlived its need. With the jobless picture varying widely throughout the country, it is ridiculous to have a coast to coast, state-by-state, city-by-city bureaucracy of personnel offices. Officials argue that the need is particularly great for unemployed minorities, veterans, and the disadvantaged. Perhaps a scaled down, highly focused effort might make some sense for these groups. But their number is so small overall that it would be a waste to continue mounting a national employment service in every state just for them.

The Service should be eliminated and that portion of the unemployment tax which finances it should be reduced accordingly. If the states wish to continue the employment service out of their own revenues, that is their prerogative. But it wouldn't be surprising to see many states, where unemployment is low and where private employment firms are vigorous and effective, decide that the program is just not needed.

PROGRAM 15

Women's Bureau — $2.5 Million

When the Women's Bureau was established by Congress back in 1929 there wasn't a shred of doubt that women needed all the help they could get to obtain better paying jobs in every sector of American life. Today, however, with all of the advances made by women, particularly in the area of equal pay for equal work, this agency has become a bureaucratic anachronism.

In its literature, the Bureau employs high-sounding rhetoric about its aims, declaring that it is primarily concerned with women's employment "and their employability," working with "target groups of women with special employment-related needs to develop programs to meet those needs."

In reality, however, the Bureau has become nothing more than a legislative lobbying outfit that uses the taxpayers' money to mobilize support for such controversial proposals as the Equal Rights Amendment, helps to provide women speakers for various organizations, and issues useless but expensive literature about careers for women and statistics on the female labor force.

The Bureau rarely develops fresh information of its own, preferring to use that which has already been put out by the Labor Department where it resides. As one official told me frankly, "We're really an information and referral service. We are constantly referring people to other agencies" for information, data, or other types of assistance.

Financed with an annual budget of $2.5 million a year to run its Washington headquarters and 10 regional offices, plus pay the salaries of 85 employes, the Bureau is a perfect example of bureaucratic redundancy. There are numerous bureaus and offices within the massive U.S. Labor Department and all of them conduct programs concerned with both men *and* women. The Employment Standards Administration, the Office of Federal Contract Compliance, the Occupational Safety and Health Administration, the Bureau of Labor Statistics, and the separate Equal Employment Opportunity Commission—all are agencies concerned with the labor force, and that of course includes women. By the Bureau's own admission it either passes on complaints and inquiries by women to these and other federal agencies or else uses data and services supplied by these agencies.

As to its own agenda, the Bureau lists "enforcement of laws and regulations which prohibit discrimination in employment," but this is clearly the responsibility of other agencies such as the Equal Employment Opportunity Commission and the Justice Department. The Bureau also states it has worked in behalf of the Equal Rights Amendment and legislation to expand child care facilities, measures which are highly controversial in our nation and on which women of various political persuasions hold differing views. Yet this agency lobbies actively for these and other controversial legislative proposals.

At one time, when admittedly not enough women were employed in either the private or public sector, this agency may have been necessary. Today that is no longer the case. Women must not be placed by government on a separate work reservation all their own. They are a part of the total work force and their problems should be the concern of the entire Labor Department as well as the nation.

PROGRAM 16

Revenue Sharing — $6.8 Billion

The federal government gives away billions of dollars a year in no-strings-attached assistance to state and local governments even though many of them have enormous budget surpluses. Nonetheless, every governmental jurisdiction in the country—large or small, rich or poor, well managed or mismanaged—gets a slice of the money. It is called revenue sharing.

Enacted in 1972, revenue sharing now gives out nearly $7 billion a year to states, cities and towns who can spend the money anyway they please. Sen. Gaylord Nelson (D., Wis.) was among those who opposed the program at the time, asking "Where in the hell do we get the money to pay for it?"

The question was manifestly appropriate because the federal government was running a deficit that averaged $28 billion annually during the first four years of the Nixon administration which pushed the program. Washington was paying $20 billion a year at that time in just interest on the federal debt, which rose more than $110 billion in Nixon's first term in office. The answer to Nelson's question was that the government would borrow the money. Yet in spite of this, and other warnings to the contrary, Congress went ahead and blissfully approved revenue sharing which then began sending a total of $6 billion a year in checks to the states and localities.

Also among those opposing it was then-Senate Democratic leader Mike Mansfield who was against giving money away without "some quid pro quo such as requiring matching funds, supervision of the money's use, and congressional oversight. I'm concerned also about some of the uses the money is being put to," he said in an interview, "bridle paths and the like—a lot of things like that which I think are questionable. I'd rather see the money used to decrease the national debt."

Mansfield was right. The program was an unmonitored pork barrel program, riddled with abuse. Some of the uses this money has been put to included the purchase of a pooltable for an Alaskan village and construction of two municipal golf courses. Since the money could be spent on anything, much of it has gone into raising state and local government salaries.

The idea even soured some of its most enthusiastic supporters—men like Sen. Edmund S. Muskie of Maine. One of the program's chief problems, Muskie eventually came to realize, was that it gave money.

> ... to more than 38,000 jurisdictions, some of which have neither demonstrated a need nor provided a use for it. In the spirit of compromise necessary to secure passage of the act, the program was transformed into a streamlined form of federal aid to virtually every local government in the nation—regardless of size, function or relative need.

One of the chief questions to be asked about this program is that if federal funds are as finite as we are told they are, why are we giving so much money to the least in need? Why, for example, are we sending $2.3 billion a year to wealthy state governments that had a $13.3 billion budget surplus in fiscal 1977, a $9 billion surplus in fiscal 1978, and a projected $4.3 billion surplus in fiscal 1979? Meanwhile, in each of these years the federal government ran deficits of $50 billion, $48.8 billion, and $37 billion respectively.

While some state governments are obviously in better financial shape than others, Sen. Lloyd Bentsen (D., Tex.) has pointed out that "not a single state is expected to have a deficit in fiscal 1980." Although state governments are on the whole doing pretty well financially, the Joint Economic Committee of Congress found that local governments were even better off. Bentsen, chairman of the committee, said a study the panel conducted found that "the fiscal condition of local governments has improved more than that of state governments since the 1960s."

Meanwhile, Rep. Jack Brooks (D., Tex.), another revenue sharing opponent, said in House debate over the issue in 1979, "I think revenue sharing is a badly conceived program in which Congress has abdicated its responsibilities and its control over federal expenditures."

Brooks' argument concerning Congress' Constitutional responsibility for both raising taxes and for expending them is a particularly crucial one, because revenue sharing destroys the concept of governmental accountability. While the federal government is raising the money through taxes and borrowing in order to give it to the states, it has lost responsibility for how the money is spent. And those on the local level who spend the funds do so by avoiding the responsibility for raising it.

In point of fact, revenue sharing is nothing more than a copout for state and local officials who have spent their governments into the red but fear the political consequences of either raising taxes or telling their constituents that cutbacks are needed. If the federal government can bail them out, they can have their cake and eat it too.

Clearly, each state and local government must be responsible to its citizens for taxing and spending those taxes prudently for needed government programs. If additional revenue is so badly needed, then the voters will surely approve the taxes to raise it. But if the people will not approve increased taxation, then it is reasonable to assume they are quite willing to do without certain programs, or to reduce those programs they can no longer afford.

When Congress passed revenue sharing, and later extended it to 1980, our lawmakers had in effect caved in to the political demands of the cities and states—particularly the large, bankrupt, urban giants—and agreed to do what the states and localities would not: borrow the money at high interest rates.

Revenue sharing has been a program without direction, one over which the federal government has been unable to exert any degree of auditing or control. There are nearly 800 pending complaints of civil rights violations in state and local programs funded through revenue sharing. Its distribution of funds, according to Treasury officials, has been inequitable under federal standards. But officials say the government has been unable to sort out the inequities.

Revenue sharing is clearly a program the nation can do without. If the federal government wants to provide the states and localities with more money to finance important local needs, the Congress should reduce Washington's tax take to allow the option of raising taxes at the lower levels of government where taxpayers can keep a better eye on how their money is being spent.

And don't for a moment believe the states and localities will be thrown out into the cold if revenue sharing were summarily abolished. In fiscal 1980 local and state governments were to reap $83 billion in federal assistance of one kind or another, representing nearly 24 percent of all their expenditures.

If the states and localities so desperately need additional revenue, they can surely raise it on their own far more cheaply than the federal government. Federal borrowing in fiscal 1979 was estimated to cost $52.7 billion in interest payments. Congress should have the courage to honestly announce, "There is nothing to share. Our Treasury is deeply in debt."

PROGRAM 17

VISTA — $30.8 Million

VISTA, the government's domestic corps of poverty workers, has become an unfortunate symbol of Washington's misguided efforts to assist the poor through a panoply of services they neither need nor want. Nonetheless, VISTA has been a program that journalists, politicians, grass-roots activists and others concerned with social welfare programs have rushed to defend whenever it has strayed into troubled waters which has frequently been the case. Yet anyone taking the time to examine VISTA's activities would come to understand how cruelly unrelated they are to the day-to-day needs of the truly poor.

Housed in ACTION, the government's collection of volunteer agencies which include the Peace Corps, Foster Grandparents, and Retired Senior Volunteer programs, VISTA has become a home for political activists, ideologues, and social revolutionaries who see the program not as a people-to-people attempt to assist the poor and disadvantaged, but as a vehicle for social and political upheaval and reform.

In an eye-opening 113-page report written by investigators for the House Appropriations Committee at the end of 1978, the agency was accused of engaging in political campaigns, legislative lobbying, and labor-union organizing. The investigators, who interviewed more than 200 persons in 22 states, found VISTA had often been involved in wasteful, illegal, and improper activities.

One of the activities focused on by the investigators was VISTA's $4 million a year National Grants program which channeled money to an assortment of leftist activist organizations around the country. Much of the money, the report charged, went to radical grass-roots and so-called public interest groups. But instead of being used to help the poor—which is the overriding objective of VISTA's corps of poverty workers—a great deal of the money was spent in middle income neighborhoods on blatantly political activities.

Among some of its most damaging revelations, the report charged that:

—VISTA workers who were assigned to a community research project worked in an Arkansas primary election in 1978, while other VISTA workers in St. Louis and New Orleans lobbied the state legislature and organized household workers in behalf of a labor union.

170

—VISTA workers organized jewelry workers in Providence, R.I., in behalf of another labor union, and the ACTION state director who knew about it "made no effort to stop it."

—The National Public Interest Group Clearinghouse, a Ralph Nader spin-off, which received nearly $300,000 in VISTA training funds, was actually the headquarters of a public interest advocacy group specializing in consumer legislation, utility rates and voter registration. The investigators found that in this particular project the group did not use its VISTA workers in low income neighborhoods, nor did it focus on "poverty issues, but rather problems of middle class families."

—The National Association of Farmworkers Organization, a registered lobbying group, received a VISTA National Grants award of $50,000. The investigators found that in this case the money was being used "to sustain a lobbying organization" in which at least one of its affiliates was engaged in labor union organizing of farmworkers in Ohio.

The House report made clear that all of the organizations VISTA had chosen to give these grants to—without competitive bidding— were peopled and led by political activists and reformers whose views and political philosophies were consistent with those of Sam Brown, the radical antiwar activist of the 1960s who heads ACTION. Many of these groups operated under the guise of seeking to alleviate poverty, but in reality they were often bent on fomenting political upheaval and combating the existing political establishment.

Examples of their radical goals and tactics were laid bare in the House report. Here's an excerpt from the kind of typical literature and training materials issued by one of VISTA's grant recipients, Midwest Academy:

> The Third Principle of Direct Action organizing is that it attempts to alter the relations of power between people's organizations and their real enemies. The enemies are often unresponsive politicians, tax assessors, utilities, landlords, government agencies, large corporations or banks.
>
> You may want to assign some people to be "inciters" and move about to heat up the action getting people angrier and encouraging them to show their anger. You may at other times want some "calmers" to stand near people who may be disruptive to the focus of the action.

Midwest, which was awarded a grant of more than $500,000 by VISTA to train the program's volunteers, bills itself as a training institution for community activists. Its literature shows it favors affirmative action, abortion, the Equal Rights Amendment, and a score of other "Women's Lib" goals. The Academy also says it teaches "the job of redistributing social wealth and power."

Reviewing the often-inflammatory statements and language contained in taxpayer-supported documents provided to VISTA workers, the House investigators suggested that Congress should consider if the above philosophy for training VISTA volunteers "is in keeping with the intent" of the legislation which authorized the program.

A prime example of VISTA's involvement in labor union organizing was found in a grant of more than $470,000 to the Community Organization Research Action Project (CORAP) which is a spinoff of the activist Association of Community Organizations for Reform Now (ACORN). In fact, CORAP was expressly set up for the purpose of receiving and administering VISTA money.

"Five VISTA volunteers in New Orleans," the report said, "were actively engaged in organizing a labor union for household workers in the area until directed by the ACTION Office of Compliance to terminate the assignments." However, the report went on to note that

... all VISTAs assigned to the grant are still indirectly involved in labor organizing activity by collecting ACORN membership dues which are used, in part, to pay the salary of the chief organizer, who is personally responsible for the household workers' union organizing drive.

A $290,000 grant to the National Public Interest Group Clearinghouse was intended to train and place 45 VISTAs in poor community neighborhoods. But the investigators said they interviewed VISTAs in New York City and Albany, New York, who were trained and placed by this group and found they were "not working in low income neighborhoods." Further, the problems being addressed were "not typically poverty issues, but rather problems of middle class families and declining neighborhoods." These included property taxes, redlining, and small claims actions.

Moreover, the Clearinghouse was found to be operating out of the headquarters of the Public Interest Research Group, a Nader-type public interest advocacy organization which works on consumer legislation, utility rate restructure, and voter registration. The New York PIRG "supports an active legislative lobbying program at the state level," the report said, adding that

... while there is no evidence of any direct volunteer involvement in these activities, the availability of VISTA resources may make it easier for the organization to divert manpower to the lobbying effort.

In an example of VISTA's labor union organizing, the House task force found two VISTAs who were assigned to the Rhode Island Workers Association (RIWA) in Providence. Both were "engaged substantially full time in proscribed union organizing related activity," the investigators said. "Their target was the jewelry workers."

Incredibly, neither the VISTAs nor the project supervisor thought they had done anything improper. "In their view, getting workers together is not necessarily union organizing," the report said.

Part of the VISTA efforts were directed at producing a monthly newsletter called "Links and Chains." Its first issue declared:

> Although we may be working in different factories, our wages, benefits and working conditions are the same everywhere—they stink. We aim to change that, we can improve our situation—but only if we work together, we can't let management separate us on the basis of sex, race, or language barrier.

Other areas of VISTA dealt with in the report concerned travel expenditure abuses, unauthorized obligations of funds, a poor accounting system, and general mismanagement of personnel, procurement and finance programs. One of the report's chief recommendations was to abolish VISTA's National Grants program:

> The findings . . . not only demonstrate the inefficiencies in administering the $4 million program, but also the improper use and ineffectiveness of grants in meeting intended goals to reach low income communities.

When VISTA was created in 1964 it was commissioned by Congress to provide opportunities for concerned Americans who wanted to devote their time and energies to relieving poverty within the United States. Over the years VISTA has moved far from that worthy goal and is now promoting political confrontation, social upheaval, activist, grass-roots organizing, lobbying, and a broad range of other *questionable* activities which have nothing at all to do with the real needs of the poor: good jobs with adequate income. VISTA should be dismantled and the money that is being wasted on this agency should be turned back into the economy in the form of lower taxes. That, in the long run, will help the poor more than anything VISTA could do even if its budget were multiplied one hundred fold.

PROGRAM 18
Government Travel — $500 Million

When I examined government-wide travel expenditures in 1975 the total bill was $2 billion a year. Today the cost of our traveling public servants exceeds $3 billion and it continues to climb. The Carter administration requested $3.1 billion for "transportation of persons" in fiscal 1980. It also asked for $4.8 billion for nonpersonnel transportation—moving furniture, supplies, equipment and other things. That pushed the total travel bill to nearly $8 billion a year. As we saw in Chapter 6 an enormous amount of this money is being wasted.

Each year members of Congress piously beat their breasts over this needless expenditure of funds, but when legislation has been offered to curb wasteful travel, it loses for lack of a majority vote. True, one travel-cutting measure offered by Sen. William Roth (R., Del.) did win approval several years ago but it was quietly repealed by Congress a few months later as a result of a howl of protests from the bureaucracy.

Numerous examples of wasteful travel expenditures were given in BOOK I, but the temptation to provide just a few more is irresistible. Consider the following:

—The Consumer Cooperative Bank Self-Help Development program in HUD proposed boosting its travel expenses from $150,000 in fiscal 1979 to $512,000 in fiscal 1980. This worked out to an expenditure of nearly $8,000 a year in travel costs for every member of the staff, including secretaries.

—The Economic Development Administration raised its travel budget by 100 percent between fiscal 1979 and fiscal 1980, which figured out to $2,000 in travel per EDA employe.

—The Railroad Retirement Board took 39 first class trips in six months. Three of the Board's employes accounted for 28 of them.

—A survey by Sen. James Sasser (D., Tenn.) found that out of 241 government trips 53 percent of them had been authorized by the same person performing the travel.

—The government completely ignores supersaver and other discount fares which could cut fares anywhere from 25 to 45 percent per flight.

There are an estimated 20,000 federal bureaucrats traveling somewhere in the world on any given day and this doesn't include non-

governmental employes who are traveling on federal grants and contracts which could add several billion dollars more to the yearly
travel bill.

It should be clear to anyone who has examined the government's
day-to-day travel eccentricities that nothing would be lost if more of
our public servants were told to stay in their offices and to use the
phone, mails, and other forms of communication instead of their air
credit cards. Several members of Congress who believe this area is
ripe for the budget-cutting scalpel agree that at least $500 million
could be cut in wasteful or low priority travel. True, bureaucrats
would have to give fewer speeches, attend fewer seminars, and rely
more on their state and regional offices, but no one believes this will
in any way harm our nation's important federal programs and agencies. Whether the cut is made selectively in each of the appropriations bills, or done through an across-the-board percentage cut, this
is an expenditure that has been grotesquely bloated out of all proportion to the efficient operation of our government. Government
travel should be immediately slashed.

PROGRAM 19

VIP Lodges And Retreats — $28,000

How would you like to spend your summer vacation for $39.50 a day for two in a huge log cabin with beamed ceilings, a great stone fireplace, and a magnificent view of Jackson Lake in the midst of Wyoming's Grand Teton National Park? Or would you prefer spending your winter in a seashore house in the Virgin Islands for $8.50 a night? Well, you can't, not unless you are among the elite few who count themselves among the government's VIPs.

The bargain basement rates being charged to our top level bureaucrats are of course subsidized by taxpayers who would pay many times these amounts if they used comparable lodgings in these magnificent vacation settings.

The above examples represent just two of the government's special VIP lodges and retreats run by the National Park Service. The Grand Teton hideaway is Brinkerhoff House where President Carter, among other VIPs, has vacationed. Travel agents say there is nothing comparable to Brinkerhoff's $39.50 rate in the area. Two bedroom cabins in the private sector, providing breakfast and dinner, would cost Teton vacationers $230 a day.

The Park Service's one-room cabins in the Virgin Islands, with bath and kitchenette, have been rented to such government officials as White House aide Jack Watson, State Department spokesman Thomas B. Reston, Justice Department official Timothy G. Smith, and others on the White House staff. None of them complained about shelling out $8.50 a night for these comfortable accommodations, not when the public must pay $18.50 a night for the Island cottages. A privately rented waterfront cabana in the area, travel agents say, would rent for $45 a day in season.

The 146-acre Camp Hoover lodge nestled in Virginia's Shenandoah National Park on the trout-stocked Rapidan River is one of the most popular VIP retreats. It has been a popular vacation site of Vice President Walter Mondale, Secretary of State Cyrus Vance and Interior Secretary Cecil Andrus whose department runs the place. Other VIP hideaways include Pink House at Cape Hatteras National Seashore in North Carolina, Good Luck Lodge at Catoctin National Park in Maryland, and Overlook Quarters in Prince William Forest Park. VIPs pay anywhere from $40 a night at Camp Hoover to $10 a night for a lodge in the beautiful Catoctin Mountains near the presidential Camp David retreat.

Do the VIP rates at least provide for the maintenance and operation of these places? National Park Service Director William Whalen told a House subcommittee, "We would be lucky if we break even." The Service provides these figures on the annual operating costs of these facilities: Camp Hoover, $11,654; Brinkerhoff House, $3,540; Pink House, $4,246; Good Luck Lodge, $4,211; Overlook Quarters, $4,764. No figures were available on the operation of the Virgin Islands facilities and other retreats that may be operated by other departments and agencies of the government. Thus, the $24,000 figure used as a cost for this activity is only fragmentary.

The government has a rather bizarre rationale for maintaining these retreats. Ira Whitlock, an Interior Department official responsible for making VIP reservations for these hideaways, told *U.S. News and World Report*:

> The big corporations can do it and, by heavens, considering the amount of money these people represent, the U.S. has a high investment. If these places stop somebody from having a heart attack or suffering from exhaustion, they are well worth the price. We feel VIP houses are good for the country.

Mr. Whitlock's heart attack argument to the contrary (which is ridiculous on its face because the government is one of the most insulated, secure and risk free places to work in the world), these VIP lodges and retreats should be closed down. If our government elite want a place to vacation, let them choose from the nation's many vacation spots and pay what every other hard working American must pay to enjoy a few days or weeks away from home and work. Americans want to provide adequate pay and benefits for their public servants, but subsidizing the vacations of our highest paid officials is going a little too far.

PROGRAM 20

Federal Information Center — $4 Million

This relatively new agency is tucked into the General Services Administration where it provides the public with information about the federal government. The fact that every agency of government already expends considerable time, money and effort to fulfill this same function is apparently irrelevant to the GSA, which runs it, or the Congress who decided to make the Center permanent in 1978.

There are 38 centers nationwide serving 75 cities, 47 of them through toll-free lines. Last year about 3 percent of the nation's population bothered to use the Center's services. The bulk of their inquiries, 75 percent, were by telephone. The rest were walk-ins. Many, though not all, were from people seeking the telephone number of a specific agency or office. The Center employs 157 people to do this work. Their salaries consume 80 percent of the Center's $4 million a year budget.

The problem with this agency is that it isn't needed. To a large degree, it is the government's version of the telephone company's information service. It is for people who are *too lazy* to use the telephone book which, as a matter of fact, contains the names, addresses and phone numbers of all federal agencies in each area anyway. Moreover, every local, state, and regional federal office already provides the public with a variety of information services through the telephone, a monumental assortment of literature, and in person responses to citizen inquiries. Ask Washington reporters who spend their time making thousands of inquiries about the government each year and they will tell you they have never heard of the Federal Information Center. The entire government is their source of information.

With the government already spending $1.5 billion a year to disseminate information about itself, this little agency is redundant. Since, according to its own figures, so few Americans bother to use this service, it should be *shut down*.

PROGRAM 21

Personal Chefs for Cabinet Secretaries — $200,000

In what must rank as one of the most elitist and self-indulgent acts by our public servants, at least seven Cabinet secretaries employ personal government chefs to cook their breakfast and lunch. It is one of the most inexcusable expenditures in Washington today.

For HEW Secretary Joseph Califano, who was fired by President Carter for entirely different reasons, it was perfectly natural that a "public servant" who earned half a million dollars a year as a top flight lawyer be allowed this one little luxury at the taxpayers' expense. Surely, even the poor would allow him this. And to the distress of those who believed Carter would cut wasteful spending as he promised, the president let Califano have this much-prized aristocratic perk.

To those who remember that week in April 1977 when the story about Califano's $13,000-a-year chef leaked out, Carter's sanction of this indefensible expenditure of public funds said everything one needed to know about the new administration. If Carter could excuse this kind of bureaucratic foolishness, he could make a case for any kind of wasteful and unnecessary spending.

But Califano wasn't alone in playing Louis XIV with the taxpayers' money. As the former HEW secretary told Tom Snyder, host of the NBC television program *Tomorrow*, "I'm not the only one. They all have them."

It costs taxpayers more than $200,000 a year in salaries and other costs to provide these meals to department heads and their chief assistants and deputies. In many cases the chefs prepare the meals in the secretaries' personal kitchens and serve them in their private dining rooms, many of which adjoin their offices. The cost figures are fragmentary at best because they do not include fringe benefits for the chefs, such as pensions, nor do they include the costs of janitorial services, and the salaries of the messengers and mail room clerks who are occasionally used as waiters.

Although Cabinet secretaries—who earn $69,630 a year—and their equally well-paid senior subordinates say they pay for these meals, the nominal prices charged do not in any way cover the costs of operating these private dining facilities. In many cases it is doubtful that the prices charged cover even the costs of the food.

My own survey found that personal government chefs were being provided for the secretaries of the Departments of the Treasury, Defense, Justice, Commerce, Labor, Health, Education and Welfare, and Transportation.

Attorney General Benjamin Civiletti's two chefs, who are paid $23,000 and $17,000, serve him and his special assistants in a handsome Williamsburg-style dining room adjacent to his spacious office. Civiletti and his associates pay only $1.50 for a full breakfast that may include juice, eggs, bacon, grits, sausage or pancakes. According to one menu prepared by Civiletti's chief chef, the attorney general during one week lunched on broiled white fish, deviled crab, and swiss steak, all of which were served with vegetables, salad, dessert and a beverage, all for a paltry $2.50.

At the Commerce Department the secretary's chef, who earns $17,035, prepares breakfast and lunch each day in a large well-equipped kitchen adjacent to an English Tudor-style, dark-paneled dining room, lined with oil portraits of past secretaries.

Former Commerce Secretary Juanita Kreps and her top deputies paid $2.50 to $3 for their lunches which included flank steak, chicken a la king, or beef stew, plus vegetables, rolls, dessert, and beverage. The secretary's cook, Ethel Warr, said, "She loved my apple pie, and especially my blueberry muffins for breakfast."

At HEW, Secretary Patricia Harris and her highest officials are served by a cook, who now earns $18,171, and a helper, who earns $11,054. A typical light lunch for Mrs. Harris, including homemade chili, tossed salad, iced tea or coffee, costs only $1.50. But the secretary can also enjoy a heartier lunch of baked chicken, or some other entree, plus vegetables, rolls, dessert, and coffee for only $4.50.

Labor Secretary Ray Marshall's personal chef is paid $17,867 to prepare breakfasts as well as lunches which include roast beef, soup, salad, dessert, and beverage, all for only $3.50.

Over at the Transportation Department Secretary Neil Goldschmidt and twenty other top officials are catered by three Coast Guard cooks in his private dining room, while at Treasury, Secretary G. William Miller's chef is paid $22,000. A Treasury spokesman said "the top people in the Treasury" paid $4 per meal which could include anything from lasagna to roast beef, including salad, vegetables, dessert, and beverage.

The Defense Department's special dining facilities were discussed earlier in a chapter on the Pentagon's "top brass" dining facilities. But it might be worthwhile to point out that a Pentagon spokesman figured out that Defense Secretary Harold Brown's average lunch cost him only $2.96.

All of this suggests that some of our highest government officials are working in a world that is inflation-proof. To the average American who must buy his meals in the real world, *these prices are unreal*, especially when one considers the personal services that go with them.

A check of Washington area restaurants gave clear proof that luncheon prices being charged Cabinet officials are ridiculously low when compared to what the typical restaurant patron must pay. At one moderately priced restaurant on Capitol Hill, for example, a hamburger and french fries cost $2.95. Beef stroganoff, soup, and a salad cost $4.75. According to the manager, "An average lunch with beverage, tax, and tip would cost $6." At another popular moderately priced restaurant in downtown Washington the cheapest item on the menu, spaghetti with meat sauce, cost $2.95. Dessert and beverage are extra, the restaurants said.

All of the secretaries work in buildings with large employe cafeterias where regular department employes eat. If department heads are so busy that they must eat in their offices, or in adjoining dining rooms, as many of them argue, then let them—like any other busy government worker—have cafeteria food sent up to their offices. As for breakfast, let them eat at home before they leave for work, like the rest of us.

Americans want to provide Cabinet secretaries with fair and adequate compensation for their work, but providing them with their own personal chefs and *subsidizing their meals* is ridiculous. This is an outrageous example of wasteful spending and it must stop.

PROGRAM 22

President's Council On Physical Fitness — $818,000

Despite the expenditure of millions of dollars by this agency since 1956, there is no evidence that it has improved the physical fitness of Americans in any measurable way. From the beginning this program has been an "image" effort to associate the President of the United States with everything that symbolizes vigorous good health and athletic competition.

Like many other programs of this sort, its officials would make you believe that, if it didn't exist, the nation would be all the poorer physically for its demise. The truth is that America is on an athletic and sports binge. There is hardly a community in the country that isn't populated with softball, soccer, baseball, football, basketball, and tennis teams, among other sports activities for all ages, boys and girls, men and women. These sports activities are promoted, financed, and run by an assortment of local, state, and national associations, leagues, and clubs. Their strength comes from millions of interested and concerned private citizens who believe in good sportsmanship, athletic achievement, competition, and physical fitness. All of these activities would exist with or without the Council.

The activities of the Council are not terribly important to the promotion of physical fitness to begin with. The Council, which has only 11 fulltime employes, conducts a public service advertising campaign on radio, television, and in specialized journals and magazines. In addition, it gives approximately 18,000 men and women Presidential Sports Awards for participating in 43 sports activities. The ads, however, are usually broadcast late at night when few Americans hear them. The awards, let's face it, are meant to associate the White House and its occupant with the politically beneficial image of being supportive of sports activities.

The Council's awards, of course, are not the only sports awards given in the United States. Not only do the above organizations mentioned issue their own awards along with their local, state, regional, and national programs of competition, but virtually every public school system in the country conducts similar programs on its own and also issues letters, certificates of achievement or other types of awards for outstanding sports participants.

The Council might be nice for the president's image, but physical fitness is going on all around the country without any assistance from the federal government, thank you.

PROGRAM 23

Government Film-Making — $500 Million

The government is spending at least half a billion dollars a year to produce movies and other audio-visual programs on every conceivable subject—from dental care to sea sponges. Since World War I it is estimated that 100,000 films have been produced, most of them frivolous, self-promoting, and duplicative. Although this activity has been studied and criticized repeatedly administration after administration, the result has always been the same. The bureaucracy ends up producing more movies than ever before. And the costs for this celluloid extravagance continue to rise.

A study by the White House Office of Telecommunications in 1974 found the government was spending $375 million to produce and distribute films and other audio-visual programs out of at least 653 federal facilities throughout the government.

By 1978 another study by the Commerce Department's Office of Telecommunications Policy said this figure had grown to an astounding $500 million a year and might be even higher than that since a good deal of the government's film-making was going on without the knowledge of any central authority. "The estimate of yearly expenditures of $500 million is conservative," the study said, adding that a previous study by a private industry publication* had estimated that more than $632 million a year was being spent on movie-making by the government.

Quite often, the Commerce report said, "three or four bureaus or agencies within a single department have separate studios, sometimes in the same building. Many of the facilities are in use less than one-third of the time. Often, money to purchase equipment comes out of unrelated program budgets, or from quickly-spent funds at the end of the fiscal year."

Duplication in film-making was also found to be rampant. The Air Force produced 11 films on driving safety, four of which were released in a single year. During the same period the Health, Educational and Welfare Department made two films on driver safety, while the Army, the National Aeronautics and Space Administration, and the Transportation Department produced films on the same subject.

*The Hope Reports, 1977

Here are some choice examples of what the government is doing for you in the film business:

Your Teeth Are in Your Hands. No, this in not a film about the denture problems of the elderly. It is a $35,000 film series made by the Navy to instruct recruits on how to care for their teeth.

In *Mulligan Stew* the Agriculture Department spent $300,000 to teach children about good nutrition, a subject that is being taught in virtually every public school system.

HEW made *America on the Rocks*, a $375,000 movie which discovered that alcoholism is a middle-class problem.

In *Games*, the Army spent $60,000 to explore racism.

How to Succeed with Brunettes was part of a $64,000 film series by the Navy on etiquette, not for enlisted men, but for officers. This film taught the art of assisting milady with her coat, while another Navy epic, *Blondes Prefer Gentlemen*, told officers how to maneuver suavely through a dinner party.

The government has produced nearly 600 dental films in what would appear to be a chronic oral fixation by Washington officialdom. At least a dozen of these films, made by the Veterans Administration, tell how to brush your teeth. An additional 14 federal film classics will tell you everything you have ever wanted to know about venereal disease. The Navy made one called *The Return of Count Spirochette*.

The Commerce Department produced a series of five films called *The Great American Fish Story* which the study described as nothing more than public relations "for the fish industry." Their cost: $125,000. Other Commerce movies include *Sponge Treasures from the Sea*, *Outdoor Fish Cookery*, and *See More of America*. Their total cost, $70,000.

For a mere $22,210 the Bureau of Mines produced *Wealth out of Waste*, while the Bureau of Reclamation made *Miracle of Water* for $25,000 and *Of Time and a River* for $50,000, both of which were considered "public relations" efforts by the agency.

The National Park Service produces history films of all things, including *The Extraordinary Creation*, $37,192, *Winter Encampment*, $46,634, *Seige of Fort Stanwix*, $95,399, and *Jamestown*, $16,412. The Park Service also makes nature movies such as *Age of Alaska*, *Capulin Mountain*, *Mt. McKinley*, *The Land Eternal*, and *California Gray Whale*, all of which cost taxpayers $163,000.

NASA has produced such films as *Partners with Industry*, $27,000,

4 Rms, Earth View, $55,000, Down to Earth, $36,000, and Mars—
The Search Begins, $75,000.

The Department of Transportation made Flight 52 for $141,000
which the Commerce study described as "agency P.R." The Federal
Aviation Administration produced a history of the age of flight, In
Celebration of Flight, for $55,000, one of a number of flight films
made by a host of government agencies. The FAA also produced
such unremembered films as Aloft, $10,000, and Microwave Landing
Systems, $37,000.

The Treasury Department has made many films too, including Hey,
We're in Business, An American Partnership, and A Simple Matter of
Deduction. It cost taxpayers $173,000 to make them.

The list goes on and on: Sauce for the Gander, Ready for Edna,
Project Slush, View from the Sky, Safe Refuse Collection, Solving a
Problem with Sedation, You Can't Bite Back, Tent Flaps and Flapjacks,
One Bug Too Many, Sanitary Design for Drinking Fountains, and Talk-
ing with Dolphins.

Who sees these films? In most cases, their audience is extremely
limited when compared to similar productions within the mass media. One agency made a 30-minute bicentennial film at a cost of
$454,463. The agency said 500,000 people saw the movie. Compare
that to the average cost of producing a half-hour prime time commerical program for television which in 1978 was $177,000. It was
probably seen by an average of 30 million people.

Very few government films are even seen by more than two million
people. While a typical agency motion picture might estimate its
films are seen by one million people at a cost of about $100,000,
the study noted that no one has bothered to consider that $100 to
reach 1,000 people is "a comparatively expensive form of communication, or that the primary audience often consists of school
children."

Many of the government's films are distributed to schools, civic
associations, social clubs and other special interest groups. However, the Commerce study noted the government "does little, if any,
research into whether the needs of the students are being met by its
films, or whether the government's needs are met by reaching students." More importantly, the study said the government's limited
reporting data on film distribution suggested "that the vast majority
of Americans never see a government film." And the report correctly
pointed out that there was nothing to indicate "what those who have
seen the films think of them."

As expected, the Defense Department is far and away the government's biggest producer of audio-visual programs. The best available estimates put DOD's costs at a stunning $350 million a year. In fiscal 1976 DOD produced 1,141 motion pictures, 5,560 television titles, and 3,412 audio and mixed media presentations. The Commerce report broke down DOD's total cost this way: Products and services, $147 million; new equipment, $40 million; salaries, $163 million.

Like everything else in the military, movies run into cost overruns, too. In one case, the Army set about to produce a series of training films titled *How To Fight*. The Army approved the making of eight films between July, 1974 and February, 1975 for a total cost of $400,000. By July, 1977 three of the movies had been cancelled after $77,000 had been spent on them. The others were in various stages of completion. In the end, the films cost a total of $620,000.

All of this *only skims the surface* of Washington's Hollywood on the Potomac. The total costs cited here are decidedly below the true totals, which are probably several hundred million dollars higher. The Commerce study showed a pattern of waste and squandering that may be unparalleled anywhere else in the government. The government should sell its movie equipment, phase out its audio-visual employes, and get out of the film business lock, stock and barrel. If Washington's entire film-producing efforts ended tomorrow, no one would notice. Its existence is the classic example of unending government extravagance and outrageous duplication. It must stop.

PROGRAM 24

Beekeeper Indemnity Payments — $2.9 Million

This program, begun in 1970, is run by the Agricultural Stabilization and Conservation Service. Essentially, it pays beekeepers in the event their bees are killed, through no fault of the beekeepers, by federally registered and approved pesticides. Thus, it came as no surprise when a deadly serious official of the program told a colleague of mine:

> You know, since we began making these payments we have not heard of a single bee dying from natural causes.

The beekeepers are reimbursed for their losses by direct cash payments determined by the market value of the bees. The average claim has been $3,000. But, according to published reports, five Arizona beekeepers received more than $1 million between 1967 (payments were made retroactively) and 1974. In one case a beekeeper received a $225,000 payment in 1974.

In fiscal 1978 a total of 1,826 beekeepers filed for claims amounting to nearly $4.5 million. In all, $23.8 million has been paid out under this program since it began.

Government budget officials who have evaluated the program said there is evidence it has been abused. It has also served to discourage beekeepers from taking necessary steps to minimize the threat of pesticide use. Moreover, officials concluded that the nature of the problem is such that the program "cannot be administered in a way that is fair to both the intended beneficiaries and to taxpayers."

One study discovered that the 20 largest recipients (representing 0.009 percent of the beekeepers) ran 3 percent of all of the nation's bee colonies. The program is inherently unfair and *should never have been enacted* in the first place. The payments should be terminated.

PROGRAM 25

Council On Legal Educational Opportunity — $1 Million

The Council On Legal Educational Opportunity (CLEO) was established in 1968 to get more students into law schools, even though our law schools are bulging and job opportunities for lawyers have become increasingly tight.

The professed aim of CLEO is to help "persons from disadvantaged backgrounds to undertake training for the legal profession." It was begun under the Office of Economic Opportunity's Office of Legal Services (now the Legal Services Corporation) but is now operated as a "nonprofit private agency," although it is funded totally by the Department of Health, Education and Welfare.

Created at the urging of the American Bar Association and the American Association of Law Schools, the program helps a relatively small number of economically and educationally disadvantaged students gain entry into law school—despite inadequate achievement scores. The program has established seven summer institutes at law schools to help select those students with legal potential. For six weeks the prospective law students are taught the basics of legal research, writing briefs, etc. Those who do well are usually admitted. To be accepted into CLEO's program one need only be disadvantaged (whatever that means nowadays) and "interested in" law school. CLEO gives a $1,000 stipend to those who are accepted into law school which in turn is expected to further assist students with a tuition grant.

However, the program flies in the face of some overwhelming statistics. A record number of law students are jamming our schools right now—121,606 were enrolled in ABA-approved law schools in 1978. Nearly 10,000 of them were minority students. A grand total of 37,660 men and women were admitted to the bar to practice law in 1977.

But another issue is whether students should be accepted into law school—or *any* school, for that matter—on the basis of his race or economic background, and not on scholastic achievement. The average CLEO student accepted into law school had a Law School Admission Test score of 425 (the typical range is between 350-525). The average LSAT of a student accepted by the University of Virginia Law School in 1978 was 696. Many nonminority students who applied to UVA law with an LSAT in the low 600s didn't get accepted.

189

But the CLEO student with a 425 LSAT, with the help of the federal government, made it. The point is, of course, that entrance into law schools, as crowded as they are, should be on the basis of academic achievement, not on one's race or benefactor, even if it happens to be the federal government.

In addition, the government is encouraging more lawyers than this country needs or wants. The 1978-79 Pre-Law Handbook, published by the Association of American Law Schools and the Law School Admission Council reported:

> The dramatic increase in the number of lawyers entering the profession during the last five years has affected the placement opportunities for this increased number of law school graduates. . . . In 1978 and 1979 the market for graduates is tight. Prospective law students should be aware of this problem.

The same is true of 1980 and beyond. That was why former ABA president Chesterfield Smith estimated that, by 1985, there would be twice as many lawyers as there are today, and expressed doubt that the present American legal system "can profitably employ them all."

There are many professions that desperately need more manpower today. Lawyers are not among them. Indeed, there are about 11,000 black lawyers in the United States today. (Most of them no doubt became lawyers *without* benefit of this program.)

Meanwhile, the government is giving away billions of dollars in scholastic and educational assistance each year to help young people, including the disadvantaged, get into college. About $8 billion a year is being spent through work-study assistance, supplemental grants for needy students, direct loans, loan guarantees, and other aid programs. All of this should be enough.

PROGRAM 26

Automatic Elevator Operators — $893,000

According to the Architect's Office, all of the elevators in the Capitol and the adjoining congressional office buildings are automatic. So why do they need 94 elevator "operators"? Patronage, that's why. It's been around since the days of George Washington.

Congress employs 46 operators in the Capitol, 28 in the House office buildings, and 20 in the Senate office buildings. Their job is to push the automatic buttons for the members and other visitors to the Capitol. The elevator does the rest, automatically stopping at the right floor. For this task the operators are paid $9,536 a year. They work 6-hour shifts but are paid for 8 hours. Elevator operators in other federal office buildings in Washington earn from $10,000 a year to $11,024. By comparison, elevator operators working in commercial buildings in the nation's capital earn from $7,280 to $7,436 a year. *Moral*: If you want to be an elevator operator, work for the federal government.

By September 30, 1980 the House planned to reduce its contingent of operators to 36, but that would still be 36 too many. The senators, apparently, were still afraid to try running the things by themselves. Only the Congress would employ operators to run automatic elevators. Only they can get rid of them.

PROGRAM 27

Consumer Information Center — $1.2 Million

Interested in growing your own bonsai tree? How about attracting and feeding birds? Having problems selecting luggage for that trip to Europe? Well, the Consumer Information Center has government-produced literature to answer questions about these and thousands of other "problems" confronting the American consumer.

Operating with a budget of nearly $1.2 million, this rather nebulous agency is really a middleman for the government's brochures, booklets, pamphlets and other assorted literature. Its mission is to take what hundreds of departments, agencies, and offices churn out and sell or give it away to the American public. You've probably heard their ads on radio and television urging people to write to Pueblo, Colorado, where 100 government employes are eager to fill requests.

For anywhere from nothing to $2.60 you can obtain booklets on *And Now a Word about Your Shampoo, Beautiful Junk, Safe Brown Bag Lunches, Dealing with the Angry Child, Feeding a Crowd, How to Select Used Furniture, Firewood for Your Fireplace, Imaginative Ways with Bathrooms, Making Your Own Terrarium, Backpacking Gear, Skiing and Skiing Equipment, Snowmobiles, Above Ground Archaeology, Investing in Gold,* and *How to Pack and Wrap Parcels for Mailing.*

Created under the Nixon administration in 1970, this agency has a staff of 20 at its Washington headquarters within the General Services Administration. Its literature proudly boasts a testimonial from that arch-economizer himself, President Ford, who says the government "has an obligation to share this information with the public in a useful form."

In addition to requesting federal agencies to write still more booklets which their research has shown a "need" for, the Center also sends out speakers and displays to consumer meetings.

Most of this literature shouldn't be issued by the government in the first place. But since it is, each agency should be responsible for distributing its own materials. The government doesn't need a middleman to peddle what most consumers don't want anyway. In fact, most of this type of information is already available to them in magazines and other publications from the private sector.

This is a trivial and wasteful expenditure and should be stopped.

PROGRAM 28

814 Federal Advisory Boards, Committees, Commissions and Councils — $74 Million

Despite some reduction under the Carter administration, the federal government is still drenched in advisory committees—more than 800 of them at the end of 1978.

The late Sen. Lee Metcalf (D., Mont.) called them "a headless monster," and frequently called attention to the fact that they were stacked with representatives of big corporations, universities, organized labor and other powerful special interest groups who sought to influence the policies and programs of the government.

Congressional investigators who have studied them for years privately admit that 90 percent of them could be abolished tomorrow without so much as a ripple in the machinery of government.

While the Carter administration did make an effort to carry out the law, which requires that unnecessary committees and boards be either consolidated or terminated, an examination of the remaining panels shows that many of them are unnecessary. Here is a sampling of what remains tucked away in the bureaucracy:

Secretary of the Navy's Advisory Committee on Naval History; Theatre Advisory Panel; National Boating Safety Advisory Council; National Advisory Council for Career Education; National Professional Standards Review Council; National Council on the Humanities; National Council on the Arts; National Public Advisory Committee on Regional Economic Development; National Arboretum Advisory Council; National Advisory Research Resources Council; Music Advisory Panel; Model Adoption Legislation and Procedures Advisory Panel; Media Arts Advisory Panel; National Mobile Home Advisory Council; Social Sciences and Population Study Section; Travel Advisory Board; Visual Arts Advisory Panel; National Advisory Council on Women's Educational Programs; National Commission on Neighborhoods; and the Small Business Advisory Committee.

The first known federal advisory committee was used by George Washington to assist him in dealing with the Whisky Rebellion. Like everything else in government, the committees grew—so large and so fast that, by 1970, when congressional concern over their population began to peak, no one in the government had the slightest

193

idea how many there were, who served on them, and what they cost to operate.

When I last examined this activity in 1975, there were more than 1200 panels and they cost an estimated $75 million a year to run. Today, that number has been cut to a little more than 800, but their annual cost still remains about the same. Inflation is the primary reason, but a number of the special commissions created by Congress have budgets of a million dollars or more.

Moreover, despite the cuts, new ones are being created all the time. While OMB in 1978 terminated 205 committees and consolidated 58 others, both Congress and the administration created 204 new panels and commissions. Thus, the total hasn't changed that much over the past year or so.

Most of these committees and other advisory panels meet very rarely, sometimes once or twice a year, and few of them have any permanent staff. The departments or agencies provide necessary personnel when needed and members of the committees are paid per diem for their expenses. In addition to these costs, they require regular oversight by the Office of Management and Budget, which must submit an annual report to Congress giving their titles and location, plus any statistics on terminations or consolidations.

Some of these committees, such as those dealing with health and diseases, as well as military matters, are obviously important and should be preserved—though no doubt a number of them could be consolidated. The rest, however, *should be abolished.* An arm of government has evolved where none was ever intended. If the government needs advisory experts, it can employ them as the need arises. If a problem is a legitimate, long-range one, taxpayers expect their taxes to pay the cost of hiring the best brains available to grapple with it on a fulltime basis.

PROGRAM 29–30

House Gymnasium — $114,485
Senate Gymnasium — $97,801

Cloistered within the winding recesses of Capitol Hill's sprawling congressional office buildings are two of the most exclusive health spas in the world—the House and Senate gymnasiums. Secure from tourists, constituents, lobbyists, and prying reporters, the gyms provide a comfortable retreat where our 535 lawmakers can sweat, exercise, and bathe away their political cares. Here, a senator or representative can float in blue-green swimming pools, relax under the skillful hands of a masseur (for male members) or a masseuse (for female members), engage in a fast game of paddleball (a congressional version of handball), work out with an armada of expensive gymnastic and exercise equipment, work up a sweat in a steambath or sauna, or just bask under a sunlamp to keep up that mid-winter tan for the folks back home.

It is one of the most restricted athletic clubs in the country. No one—friends, family or staff members—are allowed to use the gymnasiums—only members of Congress. (The only exception to that is in the House, where members can bring their children in on weekends.)

The House gym has a professional staff of seven, including one full-time masseur who earns $20,000 a year. A woman physical therapist who runs the Ladies Health Facility for female House members, and who also provides massages, is paid $17,513 a year.

The Senate gymnasiums, called "the Senate baths" by older members, is staffed by five professionals, three of whom provide senators with rubdowns. The salaries of these three senatorial masseurs total $93,000 a year.

Senators and House members frequently "duck out" between votes to either take a swim, soak their bodies in one of the whirlpool baths, or allow themselves to be pounded and massaged. Reporters who frequently see senators rushing to the floor for a vote with their wet hair slicked back know they have been taking a dip in the pool while some dreary debate has been going on. Both gym facilities are located in office buildings adjoining the Capitol and are only a few minutes away by underground subway.

Taxpayers willingly provide their lawmakers with many benefits and privileges to help them perform their duties as representatives of the people. In addition to their $60,662 a year salaries, they receive special tax breaks on their homes, get free trips to their districts, free mailing privileges, cut-rate food in their congressional dining rooms, generous health and pension benefits, free parking, plus many other perks and benefits too numerous to mention. A great many of them are millionaires. Most of them are considered "financially well off" by any standard.

However, I think Americans draw the line at having to pay to have their lawmakers' backs rubbed at their place of work.

Most Americans spend their lives working hard, probably harder than many members of Congress. But they are not provided with free athletic club facilities at their jobs. They do not have free access to their own masseur. And if these congressional facilities appear to be a throwback to the Roman baths enjoyed by patrician senators and other high government officials and noblemen, that is exactly what they are. When I asked a veteran House member how he justified this expenditure of public funds, he answered, "I don't suppose you can rationalize it, at least not to the public." He's right. To the average American—who must scrimp and save to enjoy the simple pleasures of life—this $212,000 annual expenditure is a bummer. The gyms should be closed and the rooms used for additional office space when needed.

PROGRAM 31

Double Dippers — $1 Billion

There are nearly 179,000 double dippers on the federal payroll and that figure is rapidly moving toward the 200,000 mark. Their military pensions while "retired" on the civilian government payroll are adding $1 billion a year to the Pentagon's budget.

Just about everything that can be said about this issue was covered in Chapter XIII in the first half of this book. However, it may be useful to add several of the major findings contained in a 1978 report issued by the Investigations subcommittee of the House Civil Service Committee on this subject:

—During the 38-month period from April, 1972 to June, 1975, the number of military retirees employed as civilians by the federal government increased by 26 percent.

—During this same 38-month period, the number of military retirees employed by the Department of Defense activities increased by 33 percent (from 58,741 to 78,124). (This increase resulted despite the fact total civilian employment at DOD during this same period decreased by 34,000 jobs.)

—Military retirees employed by the federal government as of June 30, 1975, represented approximately 14 percent of all individuals receiving military retired pay. In other words, one out of every seven military retirees was employed by the federal government.

—Although the Dual Compensation Act of 1964 provides for reductions in retired pay for certain military retirees who are employed by the federal government, only about 3.6 percent (5,000) actually have their retired pay reduced as a result of the 1964 act.

—There is little justification for exceptions to the reduction-in-retired-pay provision . . .

—The total cost of military retired pay paid to retirees employed by the federal government as of June 30, 1977, was more than $958 million. (This now surpasses the $1 billion mark.)

—Many former high ranking retired officers employed in full-time federal positions receive inordinately high total compensation (military retired pay plus civilian salary)—24 retired generals, admirals, colonels, and Navy captains received more than $80,000; another 15 received more than the $75,000 salary of the vice president; and an additional 122 received more than the $66,000 salary of the

Cabinet members for whom they work. (More recent figures indicate the number of "big dippers" now exceeds 200.)

—The root problem is early retirement (after only 20 years of service), and dual compensation is a problem created by early retirement.

Double dipping should be stopped. Yet some critics of this practice argue that, even if double dipping were abolished, it would only drive military retirees from the civilian payroll into the private sector and thus little savings would accrue since they would continue to receive their pensions anyway. This may be true to a degree, but many double dippers would choose to remain in their federal jobs even without their pensions. For one thing, many could not find comparable wages and benefits in the private sector, nor the lifetime security of a federal job. Many, too, are working toward a civil service pension to add to their military pension. The answer, obviously, is to combine any phasing out of dual compensation with termination of 20-year retirement from the military. When that is done, this nightmare of waste in military pensions will be brought to an end.

PROGRAM 32

Economic Research Service — $30 Million

If you happen to be thumbing through the Carter administration's fiscal 1980 budget, turn to the proposed requests for the Agriculture Department. On page 379 you will notice the president sought no funds for this agency. He abolished it, right? Wrong. The agency was merely folded into another program at USDA. Its functions continue. Its employes remain at their jobs. The only thing the administration abolished was the Economic Research Service's name.

To see where the program ended up, look at the bottom of page 378. There you will see a new agency called the Economics, Statistics and Cooperatives Service. In fiscal 1978 this agency had outlays budgeted at only $6 million. Suddenly, however, its budget zoomed to $82.7 million in fiscal 1979 and to $87.5 million in fiscal 1980. The reason for the enormous increase was due to the addition of several programs, including ERS and a related agency, the Statistical Reporting Service, which, by the way, was also terminated as a separate budget item. Thus, the administration got rid of, so to speak, two agencies and replaced them with one larger one. And that is how you cut the bureaucracy without really cutting it. Pretty clever, huh?

The Economic Research Service, however, deserved to be abolished, not just shifted to another corner of USDA, because most of what it does is totally unnecessary to American farming.

ERS is the Agriculture Department's research and analysis arm. It employs 534 economists among a total staff of about 1,000 persons. Many of its reports and studies are prepared expressly for various agribusinesses and large commodity and trade associations which gladly accept them free of charge.

Some of ERS' most dispensable reports have been issued through its Food Consumption Demand Analysis and Consumer Interest Program, which became famous for a $113,417 study titled "Mothers' Attitudes toward Cotton and Other Fibers in Children's Lightweight Clothing." After interviewing 2,161 mothers, this report concluded— get ready—that mothers prefer children's clothing *that requires no ironing.* Other studies churned out under this program include:

—Homemakers' Preferences, Uses, and Buying Practices for Selected Noncitrus Fruit and Fruit Products, a Preliminary Summary Report.

199

—Men's Attitudes Toward Cotton and Other Fibers in Selected Clothing Items.

—Consumers' Buying Practices, Uses, and Preferences for Fibers in Retail Piece Goods.

—Consumers' Preferences for Fresh Tomatoes.

—Consumers' Preferences, Uses, and Buying Practices for Selected Vegetables.

These and other studies and market analyses are being done by ERS clearly for the benefit of major food and fiber industries (who would no doubt pay to have them done if they were not being prepared for them at the taxpayers' expense). A survey of nearly 600 ERS reports reveals that they were specifically prepared for, and presented to various industry associations benefiting from the market commodity being analyzed. Thus, a report titled "An Economic View of Soybeans and Food Fats in the 1980s" was presented before the Institute of Shortening and Edible Oils, Inc., while a study titled "Economic Outlook for Edible Vegetable Oils in the U.S." was presented before the Potato Chip Institute. Another study, "Outlook for the Dairy Industry," was prepared for the annual convention of National Milk Producers, while a paper titled "U.S. Exports of Raw Wool and Wool Tops: Recent Trends and Market Implications" was presented to a meeting of the International Wool Textile Organization in Rome.

Some of ERS' work, such as its situation-outlook reports and long-range marketing forecasts, do respond to an important national need in the nation's argicultural output. But much of the data that has gone into these reports has come from the department's survey-making arm, the Statistical Reporting Service alluded to earlier. However, the overall balance of ERS' output reveals an agency that has lost all touch with its original mission, if it had any. Here's a sampling of what ERS has turned out in the past:

—Implications of Population Trends for Quality of Life.

—Quantitative Dimensions of Decline and Stability among Rural Communities.

—Potential Supply and Replacement of Rural and Urban Males of Working Age 20 to 64 for States and Other Areas of the United States, 1970-80 and 1960-70 Decades.

—Percent Nonwhite and Rural Disparity in Nonmetropolitan Cities in the South.

—Changing Retail Activity in Wisconsin Villages: 1939-1954-1970.

—Age Stratification and Value Orientations.

—Age Stratification and Life Attitudes.

—A Look at the Dairy Farm Labor Image.

—Discussion of Social Attitudes, Economic Growth, and Place of Residence.

—Socioeconomic Trends and Nonfarm Demands for Resources in the Tennessee Valley.

—Economic Analysis of the Campground Market in the Northeast.

—Need for Research on Land Policy Issues Associated with Strip Mining.

—Alternatives to the Property Tax for Educational Finance.

—Mobile Home Residents in New Hampshire.

—Spice Trends in the United States.

—The Changing Pattern of Eating Out.

—A List of References for the History of Agriculture in the Midwest, 1840-1900.

—A List of References for the History of the Farmers' Alliance and the Populist Party.

—Books on Agricultural History Published in 1970.

—On-Farm Peanut Drying Justified.

—Potential for Oilseed Sunflowers in the U.S.

—If You're a Cattleman, How Do You Compare with This 'Profile'?

—Teletype Auctioning: Valuable to Canadians, Still Virtually Untried in United States.

—Computer Decision-Making Seen as Aid to Baking.

—Cut Flower Imports: The Impact on the American Market and the Tri-State Area.

—Changing Patterns in the U.S. Carnation Industry.

—The Market for Food Consumed Away from Home: Dollar Value Statistics.

—Demand for Farm Raised Channel Catfish in Supermarkets: Analysis of a Selected Market.

—Rural Zoning in the United States. Analysis of Enabling Legislation.

—Who Owns America's Land? Problems in Preserving the Rural Landscape.

—Outdoor Recreation Resources in the Chicago Metropolitan Area.

—Spain—A Thriving Commerical Customer.

Very few of these studies directly aid the American farmer in any discernible way. They are, however, aiding various industries, commodity giants, and other economic special interests. Said one ERS official, "Industry collects a lot of statistics about itself and we get a lot of statistics from industry." If that is so, let the agribusinesses and trade and commodity associations and institutes provide their own market analyses and surveys.

"If the Economic Research Service were disbanded tomorrow, what would happen to American agriculture?" I once asked an ERS administrator. "Probably nothing," he answered, adding that in the absence of an ERS the nation's agricultural industries would move in to provide most of the data research and marketing analysis necessary to compete in the world's food and fiber markets. Additional demand for research analysis and marketing statistics would no doubt be met by the private sector from which we have seen an enormous rise in independent marketing research and economic study firms throughout the country. "They would continue to have farm economists in private industry who would perform the analysis and forecast functions we are now doing," this ERS official said.

A close examination of ERS shows that most of its work is of marginal importance. It should be put out of business. America's prosperous and powerful agricultural business enterprises should begin paying their own way.

PROGRAM 33

Alaska Railroad — $8 Million

In a message to Congress in 1970 President Nixon said, "It is time for the federal government to get out of the operation and ownership of the Alaska Railroad."

Nixon's suggestion was part of a proposal to abolish or reduce 57 government programs or agencies which he believed were of low priority, in need of basic reform, or just obsolete. The rationale for dropping federal support for the Alaska Railroad could fall into any of these categories.

Operated by the Federal Railroad Administration, the government for years has been giving the 470-mile rail line funds for capital improvements, i.e., buying new cars and locomotives, and maintaining its track. Congress gave the railroad $7.5 million in fiscal 1978, and over $8 million in fiscal 1979. The administration requested another $6.5 million for 1980. The railroad line extends from Seward and Whittier through Anchorage to Fairbanks and includes branch lines to Eielson Air Force Base and to the Matanuska and Suntrana coal fields. The line employs 816 workers whose average salary is $25,700 a year thanks to this federal subsidy. (While the railroad pays its own operating costs from its revenues, its income would obviously be diminished substantially if it had to shell out money from operating funds to pay for capital improvements.)

Alaska is now an oil-rich state, brimming with economic development. The need for maintaining federal ownership of this line has vanished. It must by now be considered an attractive investment and should be sold to private enterprise, possibly to the coal and oil companies there. Barring that possibility, it should be turned over to the state of Alaska.

PROGRAM 34

Economic Development Administration — $2.4 Billion

Think about this for a moment. In the name of improving our economy, this agency has taken billions of dollars away from the private sector—from investors who wished to begin risk capital ventures that would have provided new jobs; from businesses which wanted to expand their operations and their labor force; from ordinary taxpayers who would have boosted the economy by spending this money on new cars, homes, clothes, appliances, furniture, and other consumer goods. Moreover, this agency doesn't care where the money comes from.

It gets it from rich communities as well as poor communities, economically thriving cities as well as chronically depressed areas. Since 1966, the Economic Development Administration has taken over $12 billion out of these sectors of our economy (or, rather, the Congress has done so in EDA's behalf through taxes and borrowing). Then, believing it is really doing the country a favor, EDA returns these funds, in a manner of speaking, to the economy. However, on the return trip a lot of this money is consumed by government salaries and other administrative costs. In fiscal 1980 EDA skimmed $40 million right off the top for salaries and operating costs. As we shall see, a great deal more money is wasted or lost along the way.

EDA was established by Congress in 1965 to reduce persistent and substantial unemployment in economically depressed areas. It has tried to do this by spending these billions on public works grants and loans, and through business development loans and guarantees in economically distressed areas. The idea is "to leverage private sector investments that will create new permanent jobs," according to the government's 1980 budget.

Many questions need to be asked about this program, not the least of which is, How can the private sector be leveraged into investing in anything when so much of its capital is siphoned off by programs like these? The answer is, *it can't.* The economy would have been infinitely better off had the $12 billion been left in economic circulation, because businesses, investors, and consumers would have had use of all of that capital from the beginning instead of settling for what's left over after government drains off what it wants in overhead, planning, research, administrative, consulting, and other costs at the federal, state, and local levels. The government hasn't asked these hard questions because the answers would spell disaster for the future of federal programs like EDA. But then, this is par for the course for government programs. Few, if any, bother to evaluate whether they have been effective in accomplishing their mission.

One little-noticed study, however, done on this program in 1974, showed how wasteful, inefficient, and nonessential EDA really is. The study was called the "Bellmon Report," because Sen. Henry Bellmon (R., Okla.) authored the amendment that led to a six-month review of EDA by the Office of Management and Budget and the Commerce Department, which concluded EDA's activities were "inadequate" in pursuing its stated objectives.

While the program has been considerably enlarged since this study was done, its conclusions still deserve thoughtful reconsideration.

One of the major questions the study asked was whether EDA grants and other assistance had made a significant impact on areas of high unemployment. In 1966 it found 424 areas of the country were eligible for EDA assistance because of their heavy unemployment. In fiscal 1973, 427 areas qualified on the same basis. But of the original 424, a total of 311 still had serious unemployment by 1974. The report declared these figures showed EDA had "made only minimal progress toward the original objective of creating employment in areas of persistent, high unemployment." One of the reasons for its ineffectiveness, the study said, was that EDA's resources were dispersed

> . . . in relatively small amounts to a large number of areas. . . . With but a few exceptions, the amount of assistance to any one area has not been great enough to overcome the economic causes of distress in the areas and, therefore, has not resulted in self-sustaining economic growth sufficient to eliminate the problem.

For example, the study found that about 65 percent of EDA's funding went for government public works projects while only 18 percent went for direct assistance to the private sector. Significantly, it concluded that the private sector was still "the principal determinant" in an area's economic development.

EDA's practice of spreading its resources over thousands of localities, many of them small communities, has in most respects been regarded as a waste of money. "There are relatively few kinds of economic activities which can operate efficiently in such small communities, so the potential for economic development in the communities is relatively small," the study said. An EDA official added:

Too often we've put money into a town when it would be better if the town went away. They're small communities with dwindling populations, one-industry towns with little basis for future economic development. They would be better left, in many instances, to the fate of normal market conditions.

An examination of EDA's spending in recent years confirms that much of what the Bellmon report said then remains true today. In addition to more than $40 million being eaten up in salaries and other overhead costs, another $30 million is spent to just administer loan applications. And this is *only a fraction* of what is consumed by the governmental process each step of the way. In 1978, for instance, EDA gave over $25 million to state and local planning commissions. Most of this money did not find its way into the private sector, but into the nonproductive coffers of local and state governments and their employe's salaries. In 1978 these planning grants included: 199 grants totaling $9.4 million given to multi-county development districts conducting "coordinated economic development programs"; 41 grants totaling $658,050 to enable districts "to provide specialized services to local communities"; 96 grants totaling $11 million to states, metropolitan organizations, cities, and urban counties "to strengthen planning activities."

In fiscal 1979 EDA spent $351 million in economic development assistance programs in an effort to boost investment and expansion by the private sector, but it poured a lopsided $2 billion into government public works programs. As expected, this public works spending was accompanied by an ocean of planning grants which again gave governments at the state, county and local level—in addition to consulting and other nonproductive money-consuming activities—still more opportunity to devour private-sector income. Nearly $35 million was spent in fiscal 1980 for this type of planning assistance to local governmental units. Another $30 million went for "technical assistance."

EDA's spending in fiscal 1980 also included $4 million in economic research and program evaluation, much of which was spent on studies and projects of dubious value. For example, more than $85,000 was spent on an international conference and study program concerning balanced growth in European countries; $125,000 went to fund a student loan intern program; another $125,000 went to the Educational Development Center for another intern program; $9,933 was spent on a panel to review the final draft of a National Science Foundation-OMB task force report; $90,000 went to the

National Center for Public Service for an internship program in the southern states; and $101,000 went to Northeast-Midwest Institute for six research and dissertation projects. Total research and evaluation spending in fiscal 1979 alone amounted to $8 million.

The Carter administration asked that spending for this agency be cut from the $2.4 billion spent in fiscal 1979 to $832 million for fiscal 1980, arguing that the recession had receded and the jobless rate had fallen significantly in the last two years. Nevertheless, even this request, to which the Congress was expected to add additional sums, was still $832 million too much.

What is wrong with this program is the mistaken notion that the state can remove vast capital resources from the economy, sprinkle that money over the national landscape, and then reap some magical economic bonanza. This is not only bad economics, it is wasteful fiscal management at its worst.

In recent years EDA has placed enormous emphasis on public works, because Congress likes the political rewards it can translate at the polls through pork barrel public works spending. EDA poured $3 billion into public works in 1978 and $2 billion in 1979, which represented the lion's share of EDA's spending in both those years. The theory behind this approach has been that public works assistance builds the economic "infrastructure" desired by businesses wishing to locate or expand in a given area. But, as the Bellmon report observed, businesses "have not responded to such indirect incentives." In fact, the report said, many studies have shown that *"direct incentives to the private sector result in a higher return on investment in terms of jobs per dollar than do public works."* That sentence says more about how to deal with depressed areas and persistent unemployment than anything Congress has heard before or since. And the best economic incentives the government can give the private sector to create jobs—permanent jobs, not temporary public works jobs—is to let the market place retain more of its earnings in order to build investment and expansion capital necessary to a healthy economy. There are, of course, other free market avenues open to government to help businesses expand the resources with which to provide needed jobs. EDA, according to the best evaluation available, is not one of them.

PROGRAM 35

Congress' Florist Service — $40,000

If you happen to be walking down a corridor of one of the House and Senate office buildings, your chances are good, on any given day, of seeing the "plant man" pushing his plant-laden cart down the hallway, stopping at offices to make his deliveries. The plants are lush green ivies, ferns, and other tropical varieties. During the months of January through May he also delivers fresh-cut flowers to our lawmakers.

All of this comes from the gardeners at the U.S. Botanic Garden, which is located at the foot of Capitol Hill. Its interior is a peaceful oasis of dense vegetation and quiet pools surrounded by a wide variety of palms, cycads, ferns, cacti, orchids, fruit trees, and other tropical and subtropical plants. It is one of the finest botanical collections in the world and is offered as an educational facility for students, botanists, and floriculturists to study rare and interesting specimens. The tourists love it too. (Unfortunately, Congress can't resist the temptation to exploit every service and benefit it can lay its greedy hands on.)

In 1978 the Botanic Garden supplied congressional offices with more than 3300 plants, regularly replacing those that die or wilt. Floral centerpieces are also supplied—more than one thousand of them a year. Huge tropical palms are also popular in offices and hearing rooms, and for various congressional receptions and other special occasions. All of this is charged off to congressional office allowances, totaling an estimated $40,000 a year.

There has been some effort to curb this expenditure. In 1973 the Botanic Garden was supplying offices with *between 12,000 and 14,000 plants a year*. But this activity is still out of hand. There have been numerous reports that many of these plants are taken home by members of Congress or their staffs. And of course they are replaced as they disappear. Some staff members describe the practice as "well known" and "systematic" in many offices. "It is a ripoff," said one aide.

Many Americans would like to have beautiful plants regularly supplied to them and periodically replaced with freshly potted ones or have their drooping philodendrons cared for by their personal horticulturists. A look at the prices charged for plants nowadays suggests why many taxpayers can't afford such luxuries. Many members of

Congress are calling on us to make sacrifices to help hold down the cost of living. It only seems fair to ask these same congressmen to make similar sacrifices. Their personal florist service should end.

PROGRAM 36

National Science Foundation Low Priority Research —
$100 Million

It goes without saying that the National Science Foundation performs a great deal of valuable research, research which contributes to mankind's wealth of knowledge and to our ability to deal with the many problems of our society. Nonetheless, it is also manifestly true that a great deal of NSF's research funding is being wasted on projects which, by any rational and intelligent judgment, are not of the utmost importance to the health, well-being, and productivity of our nation.

Although we examined a number of NSF grants in Chapter 17, it wouldn't hurt to look at more of this agency's remarkable expenditures. They have included:

—A study of Russian national income for selected benchmark years between 1885 and 1917. *Cost*: $36,736.

—Development of a chronological calendar of Charles Darwin's correspondence between 1822 and 1882. *Cost*: $40,200.

—A study of the emergence of ornithology. *Cost*: $16,800.

—A history of science and polity in France. *Cost*: $76,100.

—An edition of the scientific and technical correspondence and miscellaneous papers of architect Benjamin Latrobe. *Cost*: $67,200.

—A history of the U.S. Synthetic Rubber Industry from 1925 to 1955. *Cost*: $18,601.

—History of the design of automatically controlled machine tools. *Cost*: $25,100.

—A study of the effectiveness of the Occupational Safety and Health Administration's safety standards program. *Cost*: $273,000.

—An assessment of the social consequences of the adoption and use of citizens band radio in the United States. *Cost*: $136,100.

—A study to determine the economic effects, both on consumers and the telephone industry, of changes from "flat rate" to one based on usage of service. *Cost*: $307,200.

—An analysis of the adoption and implementation of Community land use regulations for flood plains areas. *Cost*: $249,070.

—A study of existing literature concerning the impact which labor unions have had in the United States on the introduction of technological change. *Cost*: $81,500.

210

—To produce three films on the behavior of the ring dove, one of which is to be produced for television. *Cost:* $193,000.

—A series of five monthly lecture and debate programs at the Smithsonian Institution dealing with "major and controversial scientific issues." *Cost:* $34,000.

—Research for a compilation of an Atlas of Affective Meanings, based on a worldwide sampling from two dozen communities on their values, attitudes, stereotypes, and beliefs. *Cost:* $123,900.

—A study on gender-determined attributional biases favoring men over women in other cultures. *Cost:* $54,031.

—A study of crowding and its effect on humans. *Cost:* $51,900.

—A study on patterns of facial muscle activity accompanying low-intensity emotional states. *Cost:* $90,000.

—A study of time-use patterns at work and in the home. *Cost:* $85,000.

—An investigation into the nature of interpersonal relationships in heterosexual and male and female homosexual couples. *Cost:* $78,400.

This is not to say that these studies should not be made, or would not contribute to the acquisition of scientific knowledge. The question that must be asked is *whether the government* should be paying for them. And the answer is a decisive no.

There are those who say that the NSF budget must be accepted without question, without criticism. And anyone who violates that rule is considered automatically guilty of the worst sort of yahooism. The great weakness of this kind of intellectual elitism is that it denies that laymen are capable of sensibly evaluating whether certain research projects are worthy of federal funding. It also denies that such research should be required to meet any standard of financial priorities. That is to say, there are those research projects which can yield important human benefits or potentially useful scientific knowledge, and thus should be considered high priorities for what admittedly is a limited pool of public funds. Yet there are obviously other research proposals, as we have seen, whose end product does not meet any conceivable priority.

Indeed, it sometimes appears that NSF gives away money *for virtually any idea*, no matter how esoteric or unrelated it may be to goal-oriented human needs and scientific achievement. It was in this regard that an editorial in *Science Magazine*, titled "Burden of Competitive Grants," pointed out:

> In every competitive [research] program the majority of the proposals are rejected. The rejection rate can vary from 60 percent in some programs to 95 percent in others, but in general, it ranges between 70 percent and 85 percent. Thus, roughly three out of every four proposals failed to obtain funding for the researchers.

Nevertheless, NSF officials have indicated that 48 percent of all proposals submitted to their agency receive federal funding. This led Sen. William Proxmire to ask NSF officials at a hearing, "Doesn't this indicate that we may be giving you too much money?" It does indeed.

Even those within the scientific community are beginning to question NSF's research priorities and the agency's financial impact upon our centers of learning as well as upon this nation's falling productivity. Among them is Dr. Allen Rosenstein, a professor of engineering at UCLA, who looked beyond NSF's spending levels to what its dollars are producing, or—to be more precise—are *not* producing. He presented his thoughts in a paper before the annual meeting of the American Association for the Advancement of Science which was summarized this way by the *Houston Chronicle*:

> American policy makers and educators must realize that while basic scientific research, or knowledge for knowledge's sake may win prestige and awards, it is the expertise of the public-oriented professions that determine a nation's economic and environmental standards.
>
> The dichotomy is well understood in Japan and on the European continent, but has been ignored in the English-speaking countries.
>
> Seeking "academic responsibility" through pure scholarship and encouraged by the influence of the prestigious National Science Foundation, professional schools gradually transformed their faculty makeup and curriculum.
>
> One result of the shift has been that while Japan and the non-English speaking countries of Western Europe are turning out true professionals and rapidly increasing their productivity, the English-speaking countries—Britain, the United States, and Canada—have lagged far behind in productivity improvement.
>
> Thus, while academic folklore insists that the more resources committed to basic research the better, Rosenstein points to the lack of correlation between a nation's basic research ability and its ability in the marketplace.
>
> Data for the past thirty years would indicate that beyond some nominal commitments, further increases in the national basic research budget will adversely affect both the international trade balance and the annual rate of GNP increase (of the United States).

Thus, as Proxmire suggested to NSF officials, the issue is "not simply one of increasing federal funding for R&D, but rather the quality of R&D spending" in the United States. And the quality of much of that R&D, as the litany of research grants reveals, has sadly deteriorated.

Moreover, criticism has also been aimed at NSF's "incestuous," as Sen. Henry Bellmon once described it, relationship with America's major universities and colleges. What NSF's one billion dollar a year funding is doing to our centers of learning, Proxmire noted, is "encouraging research scientists to stay on college campuses and fostering the idea that university research is somehow a more honorable profession than industrial employment," and thus is impeding the movement of technical innovative development into American industry. "Isn't this one way of explaining why a nation that supports 50 percent of the world's research and development is having a terrible productivity problem?" Proxmire stated.

One need only look at our colleges and universities to see what NSF has wrought. A report by the Committee of the National Research Council noted this gradual shift of our nation's best brains from industrial research to academic research. The Council particularly took note of the rapid growth in the number of doctoral scientists and engineers hired in research positions that are "neither post doctoral appointments nor faculty appointments." Indeed, more than 80 percent of doctoral research staff members have worked on federally funded projects, yet nearly 50 percent of faculty researchers received no federal support. Proxmire observed:

> Those statistics indicate that the federal government is creating a new class of university personnel who are supported largely by federal funds but who do not participate in the education of students. If we assume that the primary purpose of a university is teaching, isn't this a disturbing trend?

Indeed it is. And the NSF is behind it.

Is it any wonder, then, that so many academic researchers, anxious to win a piece of NSF's billion dollar pie, are flooding the agency with requests for funding? At least 156 researchers, in fact, have more than one active NSF grant. Many have several grants going at the same time. One researcher had 12 separate NSF grants that totaled over $1 million.

Clearly there is a need for NSF and the academic research community to understand that federal revenues are finite; that there are many competing demands for this money; and that not all scientific proposals are worthy of federal support. This program must make its sacrifices just like any other. But with an average annual growth rate of 8.5 percent since 1970, NSF has hardly been making sacrifices.

The research grants used as examples of unnecessary or low priority research in this chapter as well as in Book I of this work were largely taken from NSF's "biological, behavioral, and social sciences" studies category which was earmarked to receive $172 million in fiscal 1980. At least $100 million could be cut from this NSF program and other low priority research activities. That would still leave this agency with $900 million a year to spend, which by any standard should be enough. Studies like those on lawyers, congressional campaigns, peasant Alpine villages, and the pitfalls of romantic entanglements must end.

PROGRAM 37

National Institute of Building Sciences — $750,000

The National Institute of Building Sciences was created by Congress in 1974 to promote new building technologies and standardized building codes. In reality, however, it is nothing more than an expensively paid government consulting arm.

The Institute was established to eventually become a "self-sufficient" corporation (if one can call these creatures self-sufficient) through federal consulting contracts and other public and private sources. In 1974 Congress gave the Institute $5 million to get started, and it has been feeding the Institute ever since with annual appropriations. In its own words, the Institute's mission is 1) to bring about "a more rationale building regulatory climate," and 2) to encourage "the acceptance of improved technology."

Hardly anyone had heard of this agency until 1978 when this reporter disclosed that its top five officials earned annual salaries of from $75,000 to $47,500. The agency had only 11 employes! Congressional criticism forced the agency to reduce the salaries of its president and vice presidents to $65,000 and $52,000 respectively. But the top salary is still substantially more than the $60,662 paid to senators and congressmen, and virtually as much as that paid to Cabinet secretaries. Even the agency's vice presidents are making as much as Cabinet undersecretaries.

Not surprisingly, most of its budget goes for salaries, travel and other administrative expenses. The rest is spent on studies about solar energy codes and other housing-related subjects which are conducted in conjunction with the Department of Housing and Urban Development. Since all of these studies and research efforts fall within HUD's responsibility anyway, a separate institute is not necessary to handle these tasks, certainly not one with salaries like these.

This was why the Carter administration did not include the Institute's $2 million budget request in its fiscal 1979 budget, nor their budget for the previous year. "They felt it should be part of the HUD budget," said a top Institute official. "They did not see this as an independent operation." (The administration did, however, seek $750,000 for this agency in its fiscal 1980 budget.)

This Institute only *duplicates* the responsibilities assigned to HUD—which has an entire department to handle work like this. The Institute's activities, as well as its big salaries, should be terminated.

215

PROGRAM 38

Military Recreational Facilities — $301 Million

Most Americans would agree that, within reason, necessary recreational facilities should be provided for our servicemen who are stationed for long periods of time in remote and distant military facilities and bases, both here and abroad. Yet like virtually everything else in the government, military recreational facilities have been expanded beyond belief. The Defense Department is spending over $301 million a year to maintain and operate everything from 18-hole country club golf courses to boating marinas. It is an expenditure that should, with perhaps reasonable exceptions, be terminated.

The government spends at least $15.6 million a year to operate more than 660 full-size golf courses, driving ranges, practice greens, and pitch-and-putt courses at more than 280 bases throughout the United States and around the world. According to the GAO, there are more than 300 military golf courses, both nine and 18-hole, and still more being constructed. While in some instances these courses are 500 and even 750 miles from the nearest public or private course, most are located in areas where there are other public courses nearby—in some instances as many as 50 to 69 public courses within a 25-mile radius. For example, there are two 18-hole golf courses at Andrews Air Force Base in Maryland, plus one driving range and three putting greens. The nearest public and private courses are six miles away. In all there are 27 public golf courses within a 25-mile radius of Andrews. There are 51 public courses within a 25-mile radius of the Naval Training Center in Great Lakes, Illinois, which has an 18-hole golf course and a driving range on the facility. There are 69 public courses within easy driving distance of the U.S. Naval Station at Long Beach, California, where there is one 18-hole course, one 9-hole course, one driving range, and two putting greens.

Most of this appropriated money is used for maintenance of the courses and clubhouse facilities plus the salaries of some of the golf course supervisors. At least $20.8 million in nonappropriated funds is also spent to run these courses, but these funds come from fees charged to servicemen and women and other income from special base services. However, they are not enough to cover costs, and Uncle Sam picks up the difference.

And these costs can get pretty hefty. In 1974, the last time a comprehensive study was done on the courses by the GAO, the Army, Navy, and Air Force were spending $6.6 million in additions and improvements to the courses, which included relocating trees, adding lighting and irrigation systems, fairway renovation, and building repair. At least $600,000 of this was provided by taxpayers, the rest came from nonappropriated funds.

In 1978 the Air Force spent nearly $19,000 to replace about 1,400 tons of sand in their sand traps at Lackland Air Force Base's golf course in Texas. This expenditure was brought to the attention of Sen. Proxmire by a couple in the San Antonio area who wrote:

> In 1977, my wife and I earned $14,000 and paid $1,400 in taxes. We hate to see our money being poured into a sand trap.

Later, Proxmire found out that the sand was not simply for replacement of sand that had been eroded by rain, but that the "old sand" had actually been hauled away from the traps before the new sand was delivered. Now that's what I call luxury. I mean, who wants old sand in their traps?

Said Proxmire:

> I have no complaint with maintaining golf courses for our military personnel or even providing new sand for the traps as necessary, as long as it is accomplished with nonappropriated funds and that means not with taxpayer's money.

But the golf courses are only a small part of this $301.4 million recreational expenditure. This money is also being spent to run and maintain stables, boating marinas, bowling alleys, swimming pools, intramural sports, tennis courts, and other activities and facilities.

All of this sports activity is funded under what the Defense Department calls "Morale, Welfare, and Recreation Facilities." It is based on a 1953 DOD policy directive which declared:

> It is the policy of the Department of Defense to promote and to provide a well-rounded morale, welfare, and recreation program to insure the mental and physical well-being of its personnel. Adequate free-time facilities should be provided, operated, and maintained through financial support tendered by the federal government.

This regulation, however, was made back during the Korean War at a time when we drafted men into the armed forces and paid them next to nothing. All of that has changed dramatically. Salaries have sharply increased. Benefits have been broadened. We are not at war. Our servicemen and women are all volunteers. In other words, times have changed, and this directive is dismally outdated.

But more importantly, the policy is wrong because it fails to differentiate between recreational needs at bases in far away locations where there is little to do, and military bases located in heavily populated areas or vacation paradises like Hawaii where there is an abundance of recreational, athletic, and entertainment activities.

There is a need to maintain the morale and enthusiasm of our military men and women, but this does not mean that the military should be given carte blanche to build whatever facilities they want wherever they want them. Even a Defense Department-OMB study recommended that these programs be readjusted "based upon a thorough local evaluation of patron interests and the availability and accessibility of specific off-base (recreational) alternatives."

Wherever possible the military's recreational facilities should be placed on a pay-as-you-go basis. The federal subsidies, in other words, should end. The military servicemen and women who use them, golf courses and all, should be required to pay for their operation and upkeep. In those cases where use by local military personnel is inadequate to support such facilities, they should be opened up to nonmilitary personnel who, through special fees, could help support them. Other options would include providing shuttle busses to local golf courses and other facilities, perhaps even special agreements with local recreational parks and clubs.

The Pentagon's recreational expenditures have been fattened out of all proportion to the military's needs. Except in places where there are no public recreational opportunities for our men and women in uniform, these facilities should be supported by those who use them or else be shut down.

PROGRAM 39

Mexican-United States Defense Commission

This agency was established in 1942 by the presidents of the two countries to coordinate defense preparations in the midst of World War II. Its affairs are now run by a top military official assigned by the Joint Chiefs of Staff.* A Pentagon official says the commission works on "common defense problems."

No one is assigned to the commission full time. Instead, a committee of officers in the Army meets occasionally to discuss mutual issues.

The commission is an outdated military vestige of the last world war and no longer has any usefulness. When I last inquired into this agency in 1975, a Pentagon official said it had been "inactive for I guess the past 15 years. They haven't been a going entity for some time now." When I persisted that they must have some function to perform since they are officially carried as a government agency, he replied, "Oh, socially perhaps." He left me with the distinct impression that this rather vague commission was kept on the books simply to chalk off an occasional luncheon or dinner for military bigwigs.

We maintain strong diplomatic ties with Mexico, and the military attaches of our two countries' embassies can handle whatever defense problems may routinely arise. Moreover, Mexico and the United States are also part of the Organization of American States which can also address defense problems concerning the two countries. There appears to be no compelling reason why this commission should continue to exist. By now, its World War II function should have been fulfilled.

---

*The Pentagon cannot provide any cost figure for this commission because the officer and secretary who handle its minimal affairs also spend their time performing other duties.

PROGRAM 40

Inter-American Defense Board — $1.8 Million

The Inter-American Defense Board serves as the defense arm of the Organization of American States which funds and supervises its activities, although technically the Board is an independent agency. Its mission is to "prepare and recommend measures for the collective defense of the Western Hemisphere."

The Board receives its funding from the OAS which obtains 66 percent of its budget from the United States. The Board's budget is expected to rise to nearly $2 million in 1981.

The Board was founded on March 30, 1942, with the onset of World War II, to defend the Western Hemisphere against the Axis powers. Its president, and its finance and administrative officers are all U.S. Army officers and are paid by the Army. Also, the Board's Counsel of Delegates is paid for by each member country which sends a delegate. Thus, its overall cost to the United States is really more than the $1.8 million that is officially given.

Also included in the Board's activities is the Inter-American Defense College at Fort McNair in Washington, D.C., which provides top-level military officers of member nations with the opportunity for advanced studies in social, political, economic, and military problems.

Once again, these defense preparations could be worked out through other channels, with the Defense Department working directly through our embassies' military attaches and the OAS member countries themselves (there are 19 members in addition to the U.S.). After all, when was the last time South America was invaded by a foreign power? This board is one more expense item we could just as well do without.

PROGRAM 41

Highway Beautification Program — $20.5 Million

The job of removing ugly billboards and junkyards from along our nation's major highways is not one for the federal government. This is a responsibility that quite properly belongs to state and local governments. In most cases, states and communities have laws and agencies which govern the placement and format of signs along their roadways as well as regulations concerning the location of junkyards.

The highway beautification program, administered by the Department of Transportation under the Federal Highway Administration, has spent more than $131 million on this program since 1965. The government pays three-fourths of the cost of purchasing and removing billboards and other signs, with the states picking up the balance. Has it made any headway? Said James McLane, a DOT official:

> It was thought that the whole program could be completed within five to ten years. But at the present rate of funding it will take 109 years at today's costs, and we both know that costs will go up.

By the middle of 1978 this program had removed 95,566 billboards along highways constructed with federal funds. However, according to the government there are another 201,000 signs which still need to be removed. Said McLane, "This means a compliance rate of roughly 30 percent over a 13-year period."

Obviously, the program hasn't been working, in part because Congress has not been enthusiastic about pouring more money into it. In fiscal 1978 Congress approved outlays of $30 million. This was down to $20.5 million in fiscal 1979. And the administration proposed lowering it even further in fiscal 1980 to $15 million. Essentially, this just barely keeps the program going without doing very much to accomplish its mission.

At a time when other more important federal programs deserve higher priority, not to mention the obvious necessity to control spending, this program can and should be phased out of existence. If state control programs and local community sign ordinances aren't working effectively, then concerned citizens should press their local governments to act. In a time of continuing budget deficits, this program sticks out like—well, like an ugly billboard.

PROGRAM 42

Coast Guard Selected Reserve Program — $39 Million

In 1979 President Nixon, presumably with the advice of his top advisers, proposed abolishing the Coast Guard's Reserve program, saying that its termination "would not significantly reduce the overall effectiveness" of the Coast Guard.

While the Guard argues strongly for its retention, the evidence is persuasive that the program could be phased out without actually affecting the Coast Guard's work in any substantive way.

There are 11,500 men and women in the reserve program. After serving two years active duty in the Guard, Coastguard men and women are required to enter the reserves and train one weekend a month, plus two weeks of active duty each year, for which they are paid.

However, the Coast Guard also maintains a Ready Reserve system which has 7,600 volunteers. These men have had four full years of training and experience in the Guard and are kept on a volunteer, nonpaid, standby status. This force would be ready to serve in peacetime or wartime emergencies, despite the termination of the Selected Reserve.

The Selected Reserves are called up only rarely. It takes the Coast Guard a little over a page to list their "achievements," most of which involve manning search and rescue stations at vacation beaches. In one case reservists assisted in the monitoring of a grounded asphalt barge on the Outer Banks of North Carolina. These are all tasks which can and should be handled by the Coast Guard's regular personnel. Its authorized strength is 38,000 strong (excluding reservists), in addition to 6,300 civilian personnel. The Guard's total operating budget is more than $1.5 billion a year. All of this should be enough to handle the Guard's many responsibilities.

This low priority reserve program should be dismantled and placed on a nonpaid standby status, with reservists shifted to the Ready Reserves where they would be available to the Coast Guard for any emergencies.

PROGRAM 43

Chauffeured Limousines — $4.8 Million

At least 175 federal officials in Washington are being driven to and from work in chauffeured government cars, although only 22 of them are entitled to this luxury by law. This is of course a perquisite that top government officials and their subordinates virtually drool over. It is also one of the government's most indefensible and wasteful expenditures.

The cost of government chauffeurs averages about $25,000 per car, although as we shall see some of them make more than the lesser VIPs who may ride in their cars. The average annual operating costs of these immaculate, polished cars is another $2,800. But the 175 people receiving this aristocratic privilege are only a small part of the total number—which also includes ambassadors, counsels, first secretaries, military attaches, chiefs of stations, Agency for International Development officials abroad (who are supposed to be working in behalf of the world's poor), four-star generals, and special security cases. Thus, the yearly cost cited here is a *very conservative* figure at best. Actually, hundreds of government officials both here and abroad are putting on the Ritz with chauffeured automobiles, but the government has never made an attempt to determine their total number or cost.

Meanwhile, we do know that the number of government officials being chauffeured around Washington to meetings, receptions, parties, and to and from their homes each day has grown from 148 to 175 in the last two years. The figures were compiled by that archeconomizer, Sen. Proxmire, who found that the total annual cost for this tax-supported luxury has grown from $3.3 million in 1977 to $4.86 million in 1979.

The worst offender is the Defense Department where 61 officials have chauffeur-driven cars. Twelve officials are regularly driven to and from work, while 49 others are given the privilege when they determine it "essential to the successful accomplishment of their duties for a given day."

Other violators of this elitist practice include the Department of Transportation, where 14 VIPs are chauffeured to and from work. The State Department provides the service to seven of its officials. The Civil Aeronautics Board, a relatively small agency, has four of-

ficials getting the royal treatment, while three Commerce Department officials also receive such services.

Washington's chauffeurs are also among some of the higher-paid
civil servants in the government when their regular salary is combined with the enormous amount of overtime they can earn while
waiting for their bosses to leave some party, or while squiring them
or their spouses around on weekends.

Because of this overtime, at least seven chauffeurs were making
more than $30,000 a year on the federal payroll, with the all-time
earner being the man who drove former HEW Secretary Joseph Califano around. He made up to $38,405. Defense Secretary Harold
Brown's driver made $37,800. The chauffeur for Commerce Secre-
tary Juanita Kreps pulled in nearly $20,000 in overtime to add to his
regular salary of $15,538. Agriculture Secretary Robert Bergland's
chauffeur earned $11,000 in overtime in addition to his $19,064
salary, while the secretary of the Army's driver earned at least
$23,900.

Of the 175 government bigwigs being driven to and from home,
only 22 are allowed by law to use this privilege. They are the president, the vice president, the 13 Cabinet secretaries, the Chief Justice
of the Supreme Court, and the six top leaders of Congress (the Speaker
of the House and the House Republican and Democratic leaders,
the Senate president, plus the Senate Republican and Democratic
leaders).

But as Mike Causey of the *Washington Post* pointed out, the privilege is frequently extended to many others:

> In most departments only the cabinet officers and his or her deputy rate
> 24-hour on-call chauffeur service . . . but cars and drivers are some-
> times lent to lesser officials for pickup and delivery when they have
> been working particularly hard. These are the backseat men and women
> Washington drivers often seen in the evening, studying important-look-
> ing papers and using goosenecked, high-intensity lamps which are very
> much a status symbol in federal carpools.

In these instances, our highly paid chauffeurs can be making more
than the officials they have in their backseats.

Causey goes on to quote an official responsible for automobile
records in one department as saying that it is "not unknown" for
Cabinet officials and other government big shots to "loan" their car
and driver "to the wife or husband for errands, or to drop junior off
to school." The chauffeurs, of course, know all about this practice,
but Causey quotes one driver: " 'I get paid to keep my eyes open

and my mouth shut'. He was on overtime when he made that statement."

Title 31, Section 638a of the U.S. Code says that government automobiles can be used only for "official purposes." And those "official purposes" do not include being driven to and from one's home by a government-provided chauffeur and car. The law excludes only the president, Cabinet secretaries, government doctors on outpatient duty, and officials out on field service where they are long distances from home.

Certainly the president could end this wasteful government activity with a simple order at his weekly Cabinet meeting, or by acting through the Justice Department to uphold the law. While the Congress is not under this law (it only applies to the Executive branch), I would put an end to chauffeur-driven cars for our congressional leaders too. Their election to high office is privilege enough. As representatives of the people and leaders of Congress they do not need such a manifestly unnecessary luxury to enrich their offices.

PROGRAM 44

Federal Election Commission — $8.5 Million

The Federal Election Commission has had a deteriorating influence both upon this nation's political system and the Constitutional right of free speech. Only recently have political scientists and other experts begun to detail the turmoil and injury the FEC has inflicted upon our political process. Its confusing regulations, prejudicial rulings, arbitrary penalties, and inherant conflicts of interest have made this one of the most dangerous and wasteful agencies to be created by Congress in years.

Established under the 1975 Federal Election Campaign Act, the FEC has imposed costly regulatory and legal burdens on candidates for federal office. More importantly, it has seriously diminished the role of the major political parties, chilled traditional grassroots participation, expanded the role of special interests in campaigns, given incumbents an extraordinary advantage over challengers, and substantially hampered, indeed discouraged, third party and other minor party candidacies.

By creating the federal election laws of 1971 (which were subsequently amended by Congress in 1974 and 1976) and then establishing the FEC, Congress sought primarily to curb spiraling campaign costs and rid elections of any corrupting influences. Instead, Congress created a bureaucratic monster that has tried to regulate what is essentially a spontaneous, freewheeling and largely heterogeneous political process upon which the very basis of free speech rests.

Needless to say, Congress' goals have not been achieved. Campaign costs have risen dramatically. And the government has forced Americans into a situation in which anyone who runs for elective office, works in a campaign, directly supports a candidate, or who spends money on their own or in concert with others in opposition or in support of some candidate, may quite easily find themselves in violation of the FEC's entanglement of laws and regulations.

Said the Harvard Institute of Politics' Campaign Finance Study Group:

> In order to enforce the law, the Federal Election Commission has been forced by the logic of its mandate to place extreme burdens upon actors in the political systems. . . . Over-regulation has rapidly begun to emerge as a grave concern in this most sensitive arena of our governmental system.

The Harvard study,* as summarized by *Washington Post* reporter Fred Barbash, "said publicly what many politicians have been saying privately": in many respects, the law "simply has not worked" and in other respects "has produced results opposite those intended."

The Harvard political scientists went on to say that the federal election laws have produced overregulated, underfunded campaigns that have become increasingly dependent on special interest financial support. Moreover, as Barbash reported:

> The laws have further diminished the role of the major political parties in campaigns . . . while at the same time having a chilling effect on minor candidates throughout the country.

The study further found that because candidates have been caught between the $1,000 ceiling on individual contributions and rising campaign costs, they have turned increasingly to business and organized labor political action committees (PACs) for financial support.

"The money flowing through PACs is increasing far more dramatically than is the total amount of money raised by congressional candidates," the Harvard report said. PACs have "increasingly supplanted" other sources of money in politics, and candidates for Congress have become "increasingly dependent" on them. "If one of the original intentions of campaign finance reforms was to limit the appearance of special interests in the political process, the law has, in practice, had the opposite effect."

The study found other distortions were being produced by the federal election laws, such as increased use by wealthy candidates of their own personal resources in campaigns. This in turn has made it harder for ordinary-income people to consider running for federal office, let alone mount an effective campaign.

Equally significant is the fact that the election laws have curbed contributions from the political parties to their own candidates, causing a "further deterioration of their roles," the study said. About 17 percent of funds contributed to congressional candidates came from their party's committees in 1972. This percentage declined to 4.5 percent in 1978.

The study also found that the enormous amount of paperwork generated by the FEC sharply contributed to increased campaign costs, putting a heavy burden on "local party committees, smaller campaigns, new entrants to the political system and candidates from outside the two major parties." These added costs imposed on

*Conducted for the House Administration Committee, July, 1979.

congressional and presidential campaigns—which require auditors, attorneys and other specialists—are derived from the FEC's legal requirement that they disclose the identities of all contributors giving $100 or more to a candidate or political committee. The FEC then audits these reports and disseminates them to the press and public. It issued 25,000 printouts of contributor files in 1978 alone.

It is also the job of this agency to apply the vaguely-worded election laws to thousands of cases requiring differing interpretation and judgements. This in turn has led the FEC into often ludicrous rulings and opinions on such things as whether a well known musician could voluntarily play at a candidate's rally without the value of the star's services being considered an excessive contribution to the candidate; or whether a congressman could send macadamia nuts to his constituents without violating FEC rules; or even whether a New York congressman should include on his credit card that it was paid for and authorized by his reelection committee. In one case the agency ruled that a senator could lease his electric car to his office in Washington but not in his state if he used it in his campaign.

In its attempt to regulate politics and elections the way the government regulates interstate trucking or the communications industry, the FEC's activities often reveal the arbitrary and conflicting way in which they have applied their mandate.

For example, when then-Rep. Edward Koch (D., N.Y.) was running for reelection in 1976 he wanted to issue campaign buttons that read, "Carter-Mondale-Koch." Not the kind of activity, one would think, the government of the United States would be worrying about. But the FEC's 270 employees are given $8.5 million a year to wrestle with such problems. Koch's buttons were financed with private campaign funds supporting his reelection. The law forbade such support for Carter's campaign because he had chosen to accept public financing. Would the Carter-Mondale-Koch buttons violate the law? After weeks of deliberation, the FEC ruled that Koch could keep his buttons.

In another case, the FEC launched an enforcement action against the Central Long Island Tax Reform Immediately Committee (TRIM) which had issued a brochure that criticized a congressman's voting record. The material did not suggest in any way that the congressman be voted out of office. It merely called on constituents to get in touch with the congressman and make their views known. Nevertheless, the FEC ruled it had "reason to believe" TRIM was in violation of federal election laws and voted to take legal action against the group and its chairman. The amount of money spent by TRIM to commit this alleged infringement of the law was only $135. In its first four years the FEC produced more than 130 pages of regulations, many of them arising out of cases like these in which the government really has no business involving itself.

Washington attorney John R. Bolton, an expert on federal election laws, said:

> The commission devotes large amounts of its resources to pursuing the most trivial kinds of violations. It gives considerable attention, for instance, to the so-called non-filers—federal candidates who have failed to register with the commission, failed to file the proper disclosure reports , or failed to establish principal campaign committees, as required by the statute. To date, the commission has instituted over 100 civil suits against non-filers.

In a brilliant analysis* of the FEC in the American Enterprise Institute's journal, *Regulation*, Bolton observed that these nonfilers were not corrupt people but by and large

> . . . third-party or independent candidates, or candidates seeking the nomination of one of the two major parties. They include no incumbents. Only a tiny minority of them win more than a minuscule share of the vote, and their expenses are typically trivial. The FEC has, for instance, instituted civil suits against members of the Socialist Workers party, the Prohibition party, La Raza Unida, and the Communist party.

Remarked former Sen. Eugene McCarthy about the FEC's abundantly trivial activities:

> If you are waiting for an FEC investigation of the link between campaign contributions and the cargo preference bill or a check of bank loans to the Carter campaign, remember that the commission is burdened with more important work.

To this, Bolton added:

> One wonders, however, what kind of example the commission is setting when it proceeds against the least powerful and least popular federal candidates—when, in effect, it is prosecuting the widows and orphans of the political process.

Bolton further points out that the FEC's rulings and opinions are often grossly prejudicial in favor of members of Congress who are, after all, the lords and masters of this obsequious little agency. "One consistent theme in commission pronouncements," he said, "is that

*Bolton, who served as counsel to Sen. James Buckley and former Sen. Eugene McCarthy in their 1976 suit against the Federal Election Campaign Act and its amendments, published this article in the July/August 1978 issue of *Regulation*.

whenever the statute offers the option, the commission rules in favor of incumbents."

For example, members of Congress are in a position to receive useful federally-subsidized research for their campaigns free of charge. Such research is routinely made available to them. On the other hand, challengers must forage for their own campaign research and data wherever they can find it, usually paying for such services. And yet, said Bolton:

> The FEC found it permissible for incumbent members of Congress to use public funds in ways ultimately useful to their re-election efforts (Advisory Opinion [AO] 1976-34). If an employee of a corporation takes a leave of absence from his job to run for federal office and the corporation continues to pay his salary, the corporation has made an illegal contribution (AO 1976-70). Yet when a member of Congress runs for re-election, his salary is paid by the government and lawfully available to him to spend on his campaign. Thus, while incumbents have control over their own income, the FEC is busily restricting what challengers can do with theirs.

"There is undoubtedly considerable pro-incumbent bias inhering in the (FEC) statute itself," Bolton adds. "But the FEC's performance has made the situation even worse."

The FEC's obvious bias in behalf of organized labor has been one of its most egregious sins. In case after case the FEC has been asked to investigate or take action against illegal or doubtful political expenditures by a labor group, but the agency has refused until forced to do so by the courts.

For example, in October, 1976, the National Right to Work Committee filed a complaint asking the FEC to act against the National Education Association Political Action Committee's reverse check-off procedure which collected campaign contributions from member teachers. Under this system, the NEA deducted campaign contributions from teachers' paychecks without their advance approval and then distributed the money to congressional candidates. If members wished their money returned, the NEA said, they could apply to their state or national NEA offices. The FEC saw nothing wrong with this until the Right to Work Committee went into federal court and won a ruling that the check-off system was not only illegal but that the money collected should be refunded. Not only did the FEC fail to impose a penalty on the NEA, it later ruled that none of the congressional recipients of NEA funds (there were 260 of them) would have to return this illegally obtained money.

In another case the FEC refused to act on National Right to Work Committee charges that the AFL-CIO illegally funneled $312,000 in compulsory dues from its general treasury into political campaign funds operated by COPE (Committee on Political Education). The Right to Work Committee obtained a court order forcing the FEC to act, but the agency ended up fining the labor organization only $10,000, leading an AFL-CIO spokesman to happily declare, "We made $302,000."

Compare this to the FEC's handling of another case involving the Gun Owners of America. This group had sought approval from FEC officials about plans concerning financial dealings with two affiliated committees. On the basis of what the FEC told them, the group believed it had clearance to go ahead. Unexpectedly, however, the FEC accused the group of violating the law and slapped them with a record $11,000 fine, even though it was clear that the Gun Owners had made every effort to comply with the law. This, Bolton remarked, "says something about the way the FEC does business."

Administratively, the FEC is a mess. An investigation into its activities by *Washington Post* reporter Barbash, entitled "Chaos at the FEC,"* reported these findings:

—Despite the fact that the FEC regulates a $400 million industry, it had no certified public accountant on its auditing staff.

—The agency has had a personnel turnover rate of 25 percent a year.

—As of April, 1979 the agency still had not completed its audits of four 1976 presidential campaigns.

—The FEC disbanded its investigative staff despite the fact that a sample audit of 1978 congressional races revealed that 40 percent of the campaigns had accepted what the FEC considered "illegal" contributions.

—The FEC didn't finish auditing Carter's primary campaign until March, 1979, two and a half years after it was over.

—Elmo Allen, the chief auditor of that audit, quit after complaining, "I just believe that those people don't know what the hell they're doing." Allen also said some of those who worked on the Carter audit "never had any audit training. We had some very inexperienced people on it."

—Moreover, conflict of interest was evident when the FEC hired Kenneth Gross as an assistant general counsel to advise auditors on

*Washington Post, April 30, 1979.

legal questions, including the Carter audit. Gross came into his job from the Atlanta law firm of Robert Lipshutz, White House counsel and treasurer of Carter's campaign. Said FEC general counsel William Oldaker, "I would think that Lipshutz had something to do" with the hiring of Gross.

Robert Moss, chief counsel for the House Administration Committee which oversees the FEC, said:

> There are severe administrative weaknesses over there. . . . There have just been too many blunders. If a secret vote were taken in Congress today, the FEC would be disbanded.

Added Bolton:

> In the face of the record, it is difficult to justify the commission's continuing to exist in its present form, or to deny that the wisest course would be to reexamine the underlying reason for its existence.

To which the *Washington Post* suggested in an editorial that "perhaps the whole agency" should be abolished and its responsibilities turned over "to someone else with more auditing and enforcement experience—such as the General Accounting Office or the IRS."

Because of the broad range of agencies being examined here, I have only been able to offer a small number of examples of the FEC's many transgressions and excesses. Nonetheless, it is clear that this is an agency that is plunging our political system into a Kafkaesque nightmare of regulatory demands which are slowly burying our political process beneath a morass of conflicting laws, decrees, and accusations. It is an agency that is bloated by over-regulation, a shameful bias in behalf of incumbents, needless bureaucracy, and excessively complex rules and regulations that have baffled legal experts and accountants, as well as the average American wishing to participate in our political system. Instead of opening up that process, as our lawmakers promised, it has been so severely restricted that only a select few—powerful special interests and the wealthy—are prospering from its encroachments.

The federal election laws and this agency have *not* provided our nation with campaign reform. They have heaped bureaucratic supervision and harassment and censorship upon our most fundamental and Constitutionally guaranteed right, the right to freely and vigorously express ourselves within a democratic political process unencumbered by the heavy hand of government. This agency is the epitome of *political control at its worst.* It should be thrown out forthwith before what is left of our free political process is forever smothered in the name of still more "election reform." A simple system of public disclosure of major contributors to a candidate's campaign is all that is needed to keep our political process open, honest, and free.

PROGRAM 45

Government Lobbyists — $24 Million

In 1978 the White House's Office of Management and Budget conducted an examination of 12 Cabinet departments to determine how many government employes are engaged in what has come to be known as "congressional liaison" activities. To its surprise, OMB found there were nearly twice as many people working in this field than they originally suspected. More than 1,000 people from 29 different agencies are assigned to congressional relations. Altogether they cost more than $24 million a year. Some of their salaries are as high as $50,000 annually.

Most of these people are of course nothing more than government lobbyists whose mission in life is to promote their agency's budget among members of Congress. Some of their tactics verge on blackmail. They are an unnecessary component of the federal bureaucracy.

The experience of Rep. John N. Erlenborn (R., Ill.) provides a glimpse into how these lobbyists operate with our money. According to Erlenborn, the Labor Department and the National Endowment for the Humanities sent him letters which said, in effect, "If you vote in favor of our appropriation bill, we'll try to see that some money is sent into your district." Said Erlenborn:

> If a businessman or union representative sent a letter to members of Congress saying that they had enclosed a tentative list of political action committee contributions for re-election campaigns contingent upon a member's vote on a particular issue, there would be outraged calls for a Grand Jury investigation.

In a letter from Joseph Duffey, Chairman of the National Endowment for the Humanities, Erlenborn received this message:

> Please find enclosed a confidential list of institutions in your district which are tentatively scheduled to be awarded Challenge Grants by the National Endowment for the Humanities.
>
> We cannot announce or make these awards until Congress takes final action on the FY 1980 Appropriations Bill. However, *this information about our intent* may be useful to your constituent institutions for planning purposes. (Emphasis added)

According to Erlenborn, on an accompanying sheet there was listed an institution

> . . . in my district which, it is implied, would receive $365,000 if I vote the right way. At the bottom of the attachment there is a warning that this should not be made public because it might not come to pass.

A little while later Erlenborn received a similar offer from the Labor Department. The letter, signed by Nik B. Edes, deputy Under Secretary for Legislation and Intergovernmental relations (read that lobbyist), said in part:

> Please find enclosed the FY 1979 program allocations and FY 1980 preliminary planning estimates for the Private Sector Initiative Program.
>
> The FY 1980 preliminary planning estimates are also based on the assumption that the Congress will act on the President's budget request as proposed.

Erlenborn said the attachment revealed that

> . . . while the 14th District of Illinois is only scheduled to receive about $97,000 in FY 1979, the good people at the Labor Department have seen fit to allocate over $386,000 for FY 1980 to my district.
>
> The implication is clear: "If you vote the right way, we'll try to get some money pumped into your district. We can't guarantee anything, you understand, but we'll try."

These kind of letters to Erlenborn, of course, are typical of similar "offers" and promotional overtures that government lobbyists are making to members of Congress all the time.

Said an aide to a veteran lawmaker:

> These guys will do almost anything to win your vote for their budget or for some bill or amendment important to their department or agency.

Erlenborn said:

> There are laws on the books which prohibit departments and agencies from lobbying members of Congress. We are all aware that this law is winked at and we are lobbied constantly.

But this law didn't stop the Departments of State and Defense and the Arms Control and Disarmament Agency who, according to the General Accounting Office, spent $600,000 in 1978 to push the SALT II Treaty.

The lobbying must stop and the various legislative lobbyists, including $50,000 a year assistant secretaries for legislation, should be dismissed.

PROGRAM 46

HUD's Office of International Affairs — $357,000

This agency's ridiculously wasteful activities were discussed in Book I in the chapters on The Forgotten Agencies and HUD: The $76 Billion Disappointment. It is so obscure that many knowledgeable congressional aides were unaware that the Department of Housing and Urban Development had an agency concerned with "international affairs."

Previous administrations have suggested that this agency's functions belong in the State Department, if they are needed at all. With millions of low-income families existing in slum housing conditions, spending money on studies about the influence of our foreign heritage on American cities and New Towns in the Soviet Union is a criminal waste of money.

The Office of International Affairs has a full-time staff of 13 and an annual budget of $357,000. Anyone who takes the time to read through their literature, including profiles on foreign countries for American businessmen looking for get-rich investment opportunities abroad, will know this is an agency that has little justification for existing.

PROGRAM 47

Selective Service — $9.8 Million

Despite the end of both the draft in 1973 and the registration of young men in 1975, the Selective Service has continued to exist— without a genuine, ongoing mission to perform.

Its funding has dropped dramatically since fiscal 1975 when the agency was being given a budget of $45 million to essentially do nothing—though it had been asked to develop feasible contingency plans for the immediate registration of men in the event of emergency mobilization requirements. That plan has been developed. The question that must be asked now is why must we have an agency of 84 federal employes who no longer have a job to perform?

A 1974 Senate Appropriations Committee report concluded:

The morale and intelligence of the volunteer soldier is high and there are strong indications that our military forces are now both combat-ready and of sufficient strength to meet our military manpower needs.

The committee directed the Selective Service to explore "alternative less costly methods of maintaining a standby draft system, with particular emphasis on the increased use of volunteer registration and processing personnel." The panel said it believed that "an accelerated winding down of the Selective Service System's operations is justified in fiscal year 1975."

That was in 1974. Today there are those in Congress and elsewhere who are pushing for resumption of the military registration system, believing that the nation needs to be prepared to quickly induct men into the armed forces in a national defense emergency. Some argue that a resumption of registration, and indeed the draft, is necessary because the all-volunteer system has not provided needed manpower to keep military personnel at full strength levels. The Defense Department gave the movement toward renewed registration further impetus in 1977 when it changed its time requirement for inducting military personnel in a national emergency. The department's former quota was 100,000 men in 150 days. Now the Pentagon says the requirement should be 100,000 men in 60 days. This change placed further pressure on the Selective System to try to meet the Defense Department's more stringent time schedule, as well as on the Congress to resurrect mandatory registration. By late 1979, legislation had been approved by House and Senate committees to resume the

237

registration of 18-year-old men but the idea was overwhelmingly rejected by the House.

The Selective Service should have been put completely out of business when Congress did away with its reasons for existing. While agreeing there is a need for a standby system to register eligible men in a time of need, this agency is not necessary to fulfill that standby mission. Moreover, the period of time it would take to register the number of men the Defense Department needs to fulfill its manpower schedules for mobilization is nowhere near as long as was previously believed. A study by the Selective Service found that every 18-year-old male in the country could be registered within five days without local draft board lists by employing a network of computers. In a letter to Sen. William S. Cohen (R., Maine), Selective Service Director Robert Shuck said the "preliminary findings" from a test run using computers to register young people who had not signed up

> ... indicate that such a system is quite feasible for accomplishing the input of registrant data quickly and efficiently in an emergency situation as well as during continuous registration.

Shuck said the plan would be able to process draftees within 30 days of a military call up by the Pentagon—half the time required by the military.

It is true that recruitment under the all-volunteer system has fallen in recent years, despite better pay and benefits offered for military service. However, it is also the case that reenlistments have been gradually rising. Recruitments numbered 208,915 in 1975, but fell to 134,425 in 1978. On the other hand, reenlistments went from 71,147 in 1975 to 73,823 in 1978, a 54 percent reenlistment rate for that year. Totals for both new recruits and reenlistments numbered more than 208,000 in 1978.

One of the reasons our all-volunteer system has not fared as well as it could has been the misdirected emphasis on recruiting men over women. The military's recruiting ads and program benefits have focused primarily on male needs and career requirements, while ignoring the large pool of eligible women who could be attracted into the military. We should more vigorously recruit women into the armed forces where I believe they can perform virtually any task, particularly administrative and technical assignments which consume a large portion of the Pentagon's manpower resources. Assigning more of these and other jobs to women would allow the military's more combat-oriented needs to be filled by a larger percentage of available male recruits.

The United States presently has two million men and women in uniform. Add to this our present reserve forces and an increased recruitment level and that should be more than enough to handle military manpower needs for the forseeable future.

The registration of young men should not be resumed. Instead, a computerized or other standby volunteer-run system of registration should be maintained by the Defense Department out of its existing budget. In the event that a true military mobilization occurs, and the nation must resume the draft, the president could be given authority to renew the Selective Service if necessary. Meantime, this agency should be discharged from inactive duty.

PROGRAM 48

Impact Aid To Education, "B" Category — $288 Million

On February 28, 1978, then-HEW Secretary Joseph Califano told a House committee that it was "an annual rite of spring" for the Executive Branch to march up Capitol Hill with a broad proposal to reform impact aid and to march down the Hill in the summer without it (reform). But as the cost of this program rapidly moves toward a $1 billion annual expenditure, the Congress will eventually be forced to seriously consider terminating impact aid to school districts which do not need it.

We discussed impact aid in Chapter XI, but a few more facts and observations are in order. The program originally benefited 512,000 school children in the 1950s whose parents lived and worked on federal installations, primarily military bases, which placed a burden on local schools which had to educate these children. As noted earlier, Congress was persuaded to go beyond impact aid for this narrow category of government workers. Now an estimated 2.4 million of this country's 44 million public school children benefit from impact aid which cost taxpayers $816 million in fiscal 1979.

Few would have any quarrel with the $343 million in impact aid paid to school districts for those students whose parents both live and work on federal property, or federally connected property. Aid to this group of school districts is called "A" category assistance and makes sense.

However, the impact aid which many critics do oppose is the "B" category through which an added $320 million is paid to districts in which the parents of students either live or work on federal or federally connected property, though not both. A position paper issued by the Carter administration on this issue said that all "B" category students

> ... have parents who contribute to local property tax either through their residence or workplace. These families do not place a substantial or unique burden on local school districts. While they do not both live and work on land that contributes to the local property tax base, neither do thousands or other parents throughout the country who commute outside the school district in which they live to work.

Moreover, abolishing aid to "B" category children would not result in any undue loss of school revenue. Out of the approximately 3,500 school districts that would lose their "B" assistance payments, over

240

90 percent would end up losing less than 2.5 percent of their operating budget.

As the administration argued in defense of abolishing this "B" program:

> It now provides large amounts of assistance to districts not actually adversely affected by the presence of federally related activities. For example, children of foreign embassy workers were included in the program. Further, impact aid money goes to communities whether they need it or not. It has been reported that some of the biggest beneficiaries are among the wealthiest school districts in the nation.

But because virtually every congressional district in the country gets some assistance under this program, Congress has refused to reorder its priorities in spite of the fact that many of the poorest school districts in the country get nothing from this program while the richest are reaping millions from it. Indeed, the Congress was even considering expanding the program to include children of postal workers!

Ending most of this "B" category—with the exception of funds for Indian children and some military base school construction money—would save up to $288 million in fiscal 1980 and more than $1.5 billion over the next five years. It is a reform that is long overdue.

PROGRAM 49

HUD's Office of Interstate Land Sales Registration — $1 Million

This agency was created in 1968 after some consumer organizations convinced Congress Americans were being ripped off by unscrupulous land development agents. As in so many similar situations in the past, Congress decided that the transgressions of a relatively few dishonest people demanded that costly government regulations, fees, and paperwork be imposed on honest developers and realtors throughout the nation. The result, of course, has been increased land development and housing costs which have been passed on to the consumer.

The agency provides the public with information from required reports filed by interstate land developers of 50 lots or more. Filing fees are based upon the size of the development. Average fees run about $2500 per development, but can run much higher as we shall see.

The agency, which resides in HUD, also possesses enforcement authority to suspend sales, investigate firms, and seek criminal indictments. It has a total of 86 employes located in Washington and in area offices around the country.

More recently, however, the Office of Interstate Land Sales Registration (OILSR) has moved beyond its "interstate" responsibility and imposed its costly regulations upon intrastate land dealers who do no business beyond the boundaries of their state. This movement to expand its authority has even angered the agency's original sponsors in Congress who have tried, unsuccessfully, to clairfy the law so that its restricted domain will not be exceeded.

The chief aim of the Interstate Land Sales Full Disclosure Act was to eliminate fraudulent land sales practices in "interstate" markets only—cases in which "cheap land" deals ended up bilking buyers who bought land through the mail without an onsite inspection, later finding they had purchased either swamp or desert. Nowhere in the law was any authority ever given over land sales conducted entirely within a state's boundaries. But OILSR broadened its interpretation of the Act to mean that they indeed had authority to regulate intrastate land sales, too.

An all too typical example of their zeal was a Green Bay, Wisconsin, real estate operator who had never sold property interstate in his life but ended up being nailed by OILSR because, they reasoned, "he has advertised in newspapers, used the telephone and made use of the U.S. mails"—all of which they considered part of interstate commerce. True, the realtor did use the telephone and mails as part of his business, but all within the state of Wisconsin. And his advertising consisted of ads in one local newspaper, the *Green Bay Press Gazette.*

In another case a Waukesha, Wisconsin, small businessman was subpoenaed to appear in Washington after he had ignored OILSR's first request to comply with its registration demands.

He wrote back:

> I am at a loss to figure out what is happening to me. My business operations here in Waukesha is a small enterprise consisting of one man, myself. I don't even have a secretary. I have checked with attorneys, savings and loan organizations, other land developers, realtors, and innumerable other laymen. None have had to, nor heard of anyone having to file a subdivision under the Interstate Land Sales Act when it is strictly a small local business.

In numerous cases, OILSR has not only threatened small land sellers, who claimed exemption, with criminal penalties, but demanded that prescribed letters of rescission, written by HUD officials, be sent to all land purchasers. In one instance, a one man sales operation, who had sold a total of seven lots over a three-year period—all within his state—was forced to send such a letter, without adding any explanation of his own, which he now feels hurt his reputation as an honest businessman. Four of the purchasers decided to void the sales, but the developer ended up reselling the lots for an additional $16,000 in profit—an outcome that hardly lived up to this agency's consumer protection claims. After 16 months of legal maneuvering, this developer eventually qualified for an exemption from the law, but not before he had spent several thousand dollars for legal and administrative costs—all of which were passed along in higher land and housing costs for the consumer.

And costs imposed by this regulatory agency can be alarmingly high. Richard Farrer, chairman of the National Association of Realtors' legislative committee, said full OILSR registration "can cost as much as $20,000 and may consume 150 man hours in preparations." William Ingersoll, counsel for the American Land Development Association, said land developers can spend $25,000 to $100,000 on registration, "including legal, accounting and engineering expenses, staff time and other miscellaneous expenses."

Efforts were made in Congress by those who supported the original act to exempt from federal reporting requirements companies who sell at least 95 percent of their land to residents of the same state. Firms selling land to persons who live within a 100-mile radius of the subdivision would also be exempted. Thus far, even that modest modification in the law has failed to receive legislative approval from our lawmakers who are fond of lashing out at "unnecessary and costly federal regulation" in their political speeches back home.

But the sponsors of this amendment aren't going far enough. The agency should be totally dismantled. It is the height of legislative folly to believe that the entire nation must be regulated simply because of a relatively small number of dishonest land speculators and dealers. This agency is costing businesses and consumers many times more than it is allegedly saving consumers who may have been bilked because they did not take prudent steps to assess what they were buying. Moreover, crooked land dealers and speculators are the responsibility of the states, many of whom have land sales agencies of their own. In the more than 10 years this agency has existed, only 16 indictments have been obtained charging 84 persons and companies with violating the law. Hardly an overwhelming record, or one that would indicate there is widespread land fraud requiring a national federal program.

PROGRAM 50

USDA Costs of Inspecting, Classifying, and Grading Cotton and Tobacco — $13.7 Million

The Department of Agriculture—as it does for many agricultural industries—grades, classes, and inspects cotton and tobacco. But while other agricultural industries pay the cost of these government services, the cotton and tobacco industries do not. These costs are paid by the taxpayer.

The annual costs for government grading, classifying and inspecting in fiscal 1978 was $5.6 million for tobacco and $8.1 million for cotton. If payment from these two prosperous industries were recovered by the government, the taxpayer would save a total of $13.7 million a year.

It would seem only fair and equitable that since the poultry, dairy, fruit, vegetable, and grain industries pay the cost of these government inspection services, the cotton and tobacco industries should do the same. But these two special interests have powerful allies in Congress who would fight any effort to abolish this favored subsidy. Even so, abolishing what is an expensive gift to two wealthy and influential agribusinesses would be a nice gift to the American taxpayer.

PROGRAM 51

Military Commissaries and Exchanges — $710 Million

The government is subsidizing supermarkets and department stores to the tune of nearly three-quarters of a billion dollars a year. It is without a doubt one of the most indefensible expenditures in our government.

Most of this money—$566.4 million a year—is being spent to run the military commissaries* where active and retired military officers, their dependents, foreign embassy officers, and their dependents can purchase groceries at discounts of from 20 to 25 percent—all courtesy of the American taxpayer.

In addition, $143.5 million a year is being spent to support military exchanges (department stores). According to the Defense Department's figures, these stores do not pay for themselves as we have been told. At least $82.5 million is being spent annually to transport merchandise to exchanges overseas. Another $61 million a year is spent to pay for utility costs overseas and maintain the exteriors of the buildings.

All told, more than $710 million a year is being spent to operate and maintain the commissaries and exchanges where military officers and retirees can buy everything from radios to porterhouse steaks at substantially reduced prices.

Said Rep. Les Aspin (D., Wis.):

> This is half again as much as we spend on all our National Parks and almost as much as we appropriate for cancer research. I think we have our priorities mixed up. If the services want to run these stores and let their people buy goods at discount rates, that's perfectly proper. But why should the public be expected to subsidize the stores so that cameras and candies can be sold cheaper still?

Aspin also pointed out that while the government is trying to discourage cigarette smoking, the Defense Department is subsidizing the price of cigarettes sold to military personnel, the majority of whom are in their late teens and early twenties. But then, as we saw in the previous chapter, the government has no qualms about providing subsidies to the tobacco industry.

For most Americans who must pinch their pennies and struggle with the increased costs of food and other consumer items, it is the height of absurdity that their taxes should be subsidizing food and

*See Chapter 14 for a more detailed discussion of the commissaries.

other luxury items for our public servants in the military, not to mention retirees who are pulling two incomes: their pension plus their regular salary in second career jobs.

It is criminal to require American taxpayers to come up with $710 million a year out of their earnings to pay for this unnecessary and wasteful fringe benefit. The subsidies should be terminated and the prices at these commissaries and exchanges raised accordingly to pay all their operational costs.

PROGRAM 52

Office of Technology Assessment — $11.2 Million

The Congress of the United States has many research services at its disposal: The Congressional Research Service within the Library of Congress; the General Accounting Office, its auditing and investigating arm; the Congressional Budget Office, which issues a plethora of analyses; and a sea of Washington-based research and technical data firms and organizations who provide Congress with information in testimony, under contract, and through other less formal channels. Nonetheless, in 1972 Congress created yet another research arm, the Office of Technology Assessment, largely as a result of the initiative of a former House member, Emilio Q. Daddario (D., Conn.), who was fond of giving lengthy speeches on technology issues which were so boring that even Daddario's hometown newspapers often wouldn't report them.

When Daddario gave up his seat in an unsuccessful attempt to become governor of his state, his friend, Sen. Edward Kennedy, sponsored a bill to establish this agency within Congress which gave Daddario, who became its first director, an opportunity to pursue his technology passion. But, according to *Science Magazine*, it wasn't long before the agency "was reeling from accusations that it had been politicized" by Kennedy, who served as its first board chairman. Many of OTA's studies and reports, it turned out, concentrated on issues that were of special concern to the Massachusetts Democrat. The views expressed in them were always, of course, right in line with Kennedy's views (or any liberal's, for that matter). Moreover, the magazine reported, under Daddario's directorship OTA's "sense of identity was vague"—about as vague as his speeches.

In its early years few members of Congess could tell you much about OTA. Some didn't even know it existed. The purpose of the agency ostensibly was to provide congressional committees and their members with studies that would "identify the range of probable consequences, social as well as physical, of policy alternatives affecting the uses of technology." The agency was divided into three divisions: Energy, Materials and Global Security; Health and Life Sciences; and Science, Information and Transportation.

In practice the agency's studies have proven to be duplicative, frequently shoddy, not altogether objective, and often ignored. Many of OTA's critics, including Sen. Orrin Hatch of Utah, complained

248

that OTA had "a disturbing pattern of ignoring congressional over-sight and service," running off on its own to become "a sort of Brookings Institution," a reference to the politically liberal Washing-ton-based think tank.

Consider this 1979 assessment of OTA's activities by Sen. James Sasser of Tennessee, chairman of the Senate Legislative Appropria-tions subcommittee, who presented then-OTA Director Russell Pe-terson with a list of critical questions from Sen. Warren Magnuson, chairman of the full Appropriations Committee:

> I am, frankly, troubled by the Office of Technology Assessment. This letter from Chairman Magnuson is just one more example of the type of tenor of questioning I have received from my colleagues and others about the Office of Technology Assessment. Frankly, this recurring question raises doubts in my mind about the need for the Office of Technology Assessment. From time to time I hear that OTA very often duplicates studies conducted by the three other congressional analytical agencies. . . . The accusations are leveled that OTA studies are medi-ocre, and they are not used in the legislative process, but rather, most of them end up in the warehouse gathering dust, as so many government studies do.

Sasser's biting criticisms were right on target and similar to those which have been leveled at OTA for many years. Duplication, however, is the major criticism brought against the agency. For ex-ample, the agency conducted a study about what to do with nuclear waste at the same time that the Tennessee Valley Authority was un-dertaking a $2 million study of its own on disposal of such wastes. Other agencies such as the Department of Energy and the National Science Foundation have performed related studies.

As this sampling of OTA reports shows, many of its studies are in areas where entire federal agencies are performing identical work: An Evaluation of Railroad Safety; The Automobile: It's Driving Us to Think; Enhanced Oil Recovery Potential in the U.S.; The Effects of Nuclear War; A Technology Assessment of Coal Slurry; Drug Bioe-quivalence; Coastal Effects of Offshore Energy Systems; Automatic Train Control in Rail Rapid Transit. All of these are issues being addressed by major departments and agencies of government, in many cases by research consultants working for the government. All of this research, moreover, is made available to the Congress.

To a large degree, OTA has become a consulting finance arm of the Congress—awarding hundreds of contracts each year to com-panies and nonprofit institutions. In fiscal 1978 the agency awarded

354 contracts at a cost of nearly $3 million. The contracts ranged as high as $120,000. Significantly, the vast majority of them were awarded on a sole source basis, meaning that few were put up for competitive bids but were instead given to those companies or organizations OTA officials chose *for whatever reason they wanted*.

It is hard to find a member of Congress who has been influenced by a study by the Office of Technology Assessment. Most members of Congress do very little reading anyway (they have aides who read for them). But poor congressional reading habits notwithstanding, OTA's minimal influence may have more to do with the nature of their reports which often are so technical few members can understand them. The agency was reprimanded for this very reason by the House Appropriations Committee which said:

> ... there seems to be an inordinate amount of technical content in some OTA reports. Technical matter tends to distract the intended primary consumer of OTA information, members of Congress and their staff. OTA should take steps to reduce technical content and concentrate on providing concise findings and recommendations on the impact of technological change.

The committee also chastised OTA for its lack of "coordination of studies by legislative branch agencies," and then proceeded to scold the agency for having large carryover balances from previous years. Indeed, OTA has been notorious for not spending all of its allotted sums. In fiscal 1978 it had almost $1.8 million left over; in fiscal 1979, $1.3 million remained; and in fiscal 1976 nearly $3 million, or 44.4 percent of their funds was still in their account at the end of the fiscal year.

The committee said the carryover balances suggest the agency is getting more money than it needs.

By fiscal 1980 this 140-man agency was asking for a $13.5 million budget, a $2.6 million increase over its previous appropriation. The House Appropriations Committee, however, gave them about what they had spent in fiscal 1979, hardly a ringing endorsement of OTA's activities.

There has been a rapid expansion in recent years in Congress' committees, staffs, and other activities, all of which are costing taxpayers more than $1 billion a year. This expansion produces studies, white papers, and volumes of reports, much of which are never read by anyone, and a great deal of which ends up each week being dumped into a trash vehicle. Platforms line the basements of the House and Senate office buildings on which are stacked cartons of reports and other documents which have been overordered from the Government Printing Office. What all of this means is that there is more research being done in Congress than its 535 members, or their staffs, can possibly digest.

According to *National Journal* reporter Richard E. Cohen, Rep. Adam Benjamin Jr. (D., Ind.), who chairs the House Appropriations subcommittee on legislative matters, said:

> The large growth in each area (of Congress) suggests that committee staff increases may be promoting the overlapping growth of research arms such as the Congressional Research Service, the Office of Technology Assessment, and GAO.

The Office of Technology Assessment is an unnecessary agency of the Congress. If specific technological evaluation and study is needed by any committee, the panels can, when necessary, contract out for their own studies, which many of them do now anyway, or use the vast research resources of the executive branch and the independent agencies. There are, in addition, Congress' other research agencies which have been noted here. Perhaps some techological assessment studies do need to be performed from time to time, but the Congressional Research Service or GAO could be given additional resources to fulfill that need. All of this, in the meantime, should be more than enough to meet the House and Senate's legislative responsibilities.

PROGRAM 53

Minority Business Development Agency — $53 Million

The Minority Business Development Agency is based on the mistaken premise that minorities need counseling from the federal government about how to launch businesses of their own. MBDA was created without congressional legislation by President Nixon in 1969 as part of his "black capitalism" pitch to enlist political support from blacks and other minorities. Congress, unable to vote against anything with "minority" in its name, went along and provided funding for the program which was thrown into the Commerce Department, which has become a bureaucratic receptacle for programs administrations don't know what to do with.

Today this agency, which costs over $53 million a year, is supporting 188 business development organizations around the country whose 1,600 federally-paid employes provide consulting and counseling services for minority businessmen. At its headquarters in Washington MBDA employs an additional 207 workers to oversee the program. (Originally known as the Office of Minority Business Enterprise, the agency was given its present title by the Carter administration in November 1979.)

MBDA has been such an obscure program that for a time in 1978, as I noted in Chapter V, no legislative committee in the Senate was exercising oversight responsibility over it. But then MBDA was only a paltry $50 million program, not something busy senators would want to spend their time worrying about.

After surveying this agency's activities, the Senate Appropriations Committee said in a 1979 report:

> The committee strongly supports assistance to minority businesses as witnessed by our recommendations for the Small Business Administration. However, MBDA has never had legislative authority, and the testimony at the hearing was weak and by no means persuasive of the role of this organization.

Said a Commerce Department official who did not wish to be identified:

> I don't really see it (MBDA) doing that much for minorities. In most cases they don't need counseling, they need capital.

During the committee's fiscal 1980 hearings, Sen. Lowell Weicker of Connecticut, a proponent of merging MBDA into the Small Business Administration, told Commerce Department officials:

> As we know, there has been enormous waste of money in this area.

Here would be an ideal time to both save money and get money to the minorities in a way that will be helpful to them. I can't think of a more important subject, both in light of the failure of the programs as they are now sitting in a disjointed state and in the sense of money floating around totally mismanaged.

Ignoring Weicker's disjointed syntax, his characterization of the money this program is wasting is a correct one. His cure for the problem, however, is not. Merging a bad program into another equally bad program (SBA) does not produce a good program. It is just another way of bureaucratically hiding the problem.

The Minority Business Development Agency, as Nixon's political advisers conceived it, was to give minorities "a piece of the action" by helping them get started through a variety of counseling services. The fact remains, however, that relatively few members of minorities have been truly helped by this program. Not only that, but the government is awash with so many business assistance programs that they are largely duplicating MBDA's purposes—Economic Development Administration, Community Services Administration, the Agriculture Department's Rural Development programs, the Small Business Administration, and programs to channel federal contracts into minority businesses are just a few of the minority self-help programs available. But ask the average small businessman or woman, whatever their race, if the government has done anything tangible to help them. They will tell you everything you would ever want to know about the burden of government taxes, increasing federal paperwork, regulations and inspections, all of which are making the small business an endangered species fighting to survive in an era of large corporate chains, franchises, and conglomerates.

Rather than wasteful programs like MBDA, the government should undertake a more generic approach that can help everyone instead of the lucky few singled out by the federal government. For openers, cutting federal income taxes for small business by 50 percent would do more for small businesses—particularly minorities with little starting capital—than any multi-million dollar program the government might devise. The incentive to work hard and keep a larger share of the fruits of one's labor continues to be the most effective way to encourage business expansion and a healthier economy. America does not need a special business counseling program for a few minorities. It needs a reformed tax system that allows *everyone* to claim a bigger "piece of the action" on their own, no matter what the color of their skins.

PROGRAM 54

National Institute of Education — $86.5 Million

In fiscal 1975 the National Institute of Education confidently asked Congress for a $130 million appropriation, an incredible $55 million increase over its previous year's budget of $75 million. But when the Senate Appropriations Committee saw how NIE had been spending its research funds, the panel voted not to recommend any money at all. It was an extreme action, and one rarely taken by the Appropriations Committee.

In its report to the Senate the Committee said, "The Institute's success in nearly all endeavors it undertook can be considered minimal at best." It went on to note that many "favor the dismantling of NIE and a return of research activities to their appropriate bureaus" in the Office of Education, and suggested that this "may well be the wisest possible course of action."

To say the Appropriations Committee disliked what NIE was doing with the taxpayers' money was putting it mildly. In unusually strong language the committee declared that the Institute's many research projects were "extrinsic to the real needs of our nation's education system." It added that all too often its research concentrated "on a proliferation of research projects covering a much too broad spectrum," and insisted that further funding for NIE was unjustified because it had made no effort to cleanse "marginal, less-productive educational research and development projects" from its R&D portfolio.

The committee's no-more-money decision, unfortunately, did not prevail. The House insisted on continuing the agency and it was budgeted for the following year—though at a level much closer to its previous year's spending.

Today, however, nothing has changed in this program. An examination of NIE's current research spending shows it has not improved in any substantial way. It is still throwing its money into vague, often esoteric research and experimental education projects which have nothing whatsoever to do with the everyday reality of educating our children.

NIE originally grew out of the Bureau of Research, within HEW's Office of Education, but in 1972 was reorganized under its present name. Its mission: To promote "equality of educational opportunity" and to improve "educational practice . . . the process of learning and instruction and the management of educational organizations." To achieve these goals NIE has issued hundreds of millions of dollars in federal grants and contracts to college and university researchers and other educational institutions and agencies for a myriad of projects, studies and experiments. Money is poured into three primary areas: teaching and learning, educational policy and organization, and dissemination and improvement of educational practices.

Here are examples* of what NIE has been spending our money on, and which perhaps show why public education has been failing for so many years despite increasing public financial support:

—Extended Evaluation Training Workshops for Women. Purpose: To study women's opportunities for entry and promotion in the educational fields of evaluation, research and development, and administration. Cost: $15,230.

—Sex Role Attitudes in Young Women and Men: Their Relationships To Plan and Attainments in Education, Occupation, Marriage, and Parenthood. Purpose: To study the overall development of sex roles throughout the country. Cost: $102,127.

—Documentation of the Crisis in Public Education In New Jersey—1975-76. Purpose: To gather facts involved in the debate over educational finance in New Jersey and analyze them. Cost: $54,146.

—Experimental Project for Increasing Participation of Women and Minorities in Education Research and Development: Purpose: To increase the participation of minority individuals in R&D and to upgrade the capability of the Learning and Research and Development Center to recruit minorities. Cost: $89,000.

—Film on Women Facing Mid-Career Changes. Purpose: Half-hour film to discuss the general problems women face going from the household, or when their children grow up, in entering a career decision. Cost: $172,182.

—A study of 1200 students to determine "Why Women Avoid the Study of Mathematics." Cost: $65,975.

—Catalog of Early American Textbook Collection. Purpose: The publication of a catalog of the 18th and 19th century textbook collection in the Educational Research Library. Cost: $34,000.

—Harvard Project Zero: Analysis and Training of Processes and Component Skills in the Arts. Purpose: Improved educational practices in aesthetic perception and production. Cost: $286,017.

—Follow-up of 1000 Project Talent-30-Year-Olds. Purpose: Study

*These examples were extracted from NIE's 1978 project catalogue, "Educational Research in Progress."

of 30-year-olds who remember experiences as secondary school students in 1960, relating the education received to the requirements of the life they wish to live. *Cost*: $211,000.

—Politics, Policy, and Equality in the American South. Purpose: A study of the causes and consequences of educational policies in the American South since 1940. *Cost*: $10,000.

—Parents, Policies, and Political Structure: A Study of Policy-Making and Parental Support in Nonpublic and Public Schools. Purpose: To investigate why parents who select parochial schools for their children do so when free public schools are available. *Cost*: $79,065.

—The Role of Educational Experience in Political Acculturation of Cuban Students. Purpose: To examine the role of educational experience in shaping political values, attitudes, and orientations of Cuban youths in the Miami area. *Cost*: $68,000.

—School Organization. Purpose: To provide a scientific basis for the development of new organizational forms for elementary and secondary schools. *Cost*: $1.5 million.

—Legal History of American Colleges and Universities. Purpose: An analysis of the status in law of American institutions of higher education, as this status has changed from the founding of Harvard College in 1636 to the present day. *Cost*: $80,000.

—Moral Development of Life Outcomes. Purpose: To test the hypothesis that the level of moral judgement attained during late adolescence predicts life outcomes as measured by job status, earned income, job satisfaction, and life satisfaction. *Cost*: $62,000.

—Effects of Social Class Background on the Career Commitment of Women Attending Non-Elite Colleges. Purpose: To find out more about the aspirations and concerns of working class women by examining the relation of parental socioeconomic status to female role conceptions and how this influences educational and occupational aspirations and career commitment. *Cost*: $13,629.

—Overall Conference Planning and Management Services. Purpose: To help NIE hold conferences around the country. *Cost*: $1.7 million.

—Sex and School Board Activity. Purpose: Aimed at exploring differences in manner of operation and educational policy outcome of school boards with varying numbers of female members. *Cost*: $45,000.

—Television Career Awareness Project. Purpose: "To design, develop, produce, broadcast, and evaluate a television series aimed at a national audience of elementary school children and their parents, with the central goal of expanding the career awareness of its viewers. *Cost*: $3.3 million.

—The Nature of a Superintendent's Work. Purpose: Study the work six school superintendents do in the day-to-day performance of their jobs. *Cost*: $27,000.

—Support of the National Commission on Working Women. Purpose: A $200,000 annual grant for two years to establish the Commission under the belief that the average working woman has been neglected by past research which has concentrated on professional women or unemployed welfare recipients. Thus the Commission seeks to provide a national focus on working women.

The federal government is pouring billions of dollars into public education every year and every year the same problems—inadequate schools, poor achievement scores—remain. In many cases they have grown worse. Meanwhile, NIE among other federal agencies has been spending enormous amounts of tax dollars in a vague and unending search for better ways to educate America's youth. Much of this spending, as these studies indicate, is of marginal value. Most of it is flagrantly wasteful.

On the other hand, a few NIE studies do have considerable merit, particularly those dealing with special education for the handicapped and the disadvantaged. However, there is no reason why this far narrower category of research cannot continue within HEW without this agency. The vast majority of NIE's other studies are not going to improve the education of our children. Indeed, this was why the Senate Appropriations Committee found them "extrinsic to the real needs of our nation's education system."

Fortune magazine reported in 1979 that a mathematician had devised a series of arithmetical correlations on federal spending. A 1.0 signified a perfect correlation. A −1.0 signified a perfect negative correlation. And a zero signified no correlation whatsoever. In correlating federal spending on education between 1968 and 1976 and the average verbal scores on the scholastic achievement test, he came up with −0.95. Said William Proxmire, who reported the findings to his colleagues:

> That is about as close to a perfect negative correlation as you will ever come upon in this complex human world of ours. It suggests that the more federal money we pour into education, the dumber our students become. Now I know there are lots of extenuating circumstances, lots of alibis, lots of excuses. But this simple little fact, that the more money

we have poured into these educational programs the worse the results, simply overwhelms all the lame explanations.

The people at NIE no doubt have a lot of explanations. But the questions we must ask both them and members of Congress who approve their funds is why are we spending money on these studies and projects? Do we really need to undertake, as NIE has done, a $99,000 survey on the political attitudes of college professors? Or a $37,000 study of the 1973 New York City School Board Elections? Studies like these by this agency must stop. It should be clear by now that this kind of wasteful research and experimentalization *has done nothing* to improve American public education. If anything, judging by the nation's dismally low student test scores, it has hurt our system of education. NIE should be dismantled. Its money could be more beneficially channeled into improving the educational facilities and tools of our poorest schools.

PROGRAM 55

Institute of Museum Services — $7.8 Million

The Institute of Museum Services was created by Congress in 1976 to provide assistance to museums and other institutions of knowledge through grants and other support services. Both public and private nonprofit institutions are eligible for federal funding from this agency, which strangely enough resides within HEW. The recipients can include aquariums, botanical gardens, planetariums, zoos, nature centers, as well as museums.

Actual funding of this agency began in 1978 when it received an appropriation of $3.7 million for distribution to 259 institutions, plus $89,000 for administrative expenses. Its fiscal 1979 budget rose to $7.8 million. The Carter administration asked for an $11 million budget for fiscal 1980, an almost 40 percent increase over the previous year, and nearly triple the 1978 budget. Its administrative costs have risen to half a million dollars a year, although the agency only employs 14 people. But as do all federal agencies, the Institute has ambitious future plans to gradually enlarge its budget and become a major financial supporter of the nation's museums. Its literature observes that, to assist eligible museums with their minimal basic needs (less than 10 percent of their gross operating costs), IMS "would require funding at the $100 million level."

No one enjoys and appreciates museums more than I do, but there has never been a convincing case made that these institutions—all 7,500 of them at last count—truly need federal assistance. Long before federal funding was made available to them, these institutions managed to grow and survive without assistance from Washington. Moreover, the initial response to the federal dollar was hardly enthusiastic when the program began. Only about 800 originally applied, although IMS officials expected the number to grow substantially as more institutions became aware of the availability of federal aid.

There isn't an organization or institution in our society that could not fashion some argument in behalf of getting federal assistance. The question is whether we must succumb to every demand for our money. Museums and like institutions are established to respond to the cultural and educational needs of the communities and cities in which they reside. If further assistance is needed to support them, it

should come voluntarily from philanthropists, foundations, corporations, and other individual contributors who wish to support these
worthwhile institutions, and, if necessary, from local governments
who know the needs of their communities best.

PROGRAMS 56–58

Law Enforcement Assistance Administration
National Institute of Law Enforcement and Criminal Justice
Office of Juvenile Justice and Delinquency
TOTAL — *$486 Million*

When the Law Enforcement Assistance Administration announced it was awarding a $650,000 contract to find out why people
move more frequently from neighborhoods where the crime rate is
high, the public was told everything it would ever want to know
about this agency's work. I mean, this was like undertaking a study
to determine why every Pope is Catholic. But it shouldn't have come
as a surprise to those who closely followed this agency's activities.
In a little more than a decade LEAA and its component subagencies
have wasted billions of our tax dollars on ridiculous, misdirected
research projects, studies, grants, and other highly questionable expenditures. From the beginning, however, this agency's premise was
suspect: that a federal program in Washington could do anything to
combat crime on the streets of the nation's cities and towns.

Created under the Omnibus Crime Control and Safe Streets Act of
1968, LEAA was largely an emotional and political response to the
rioting and social unrest of the mid-1960s when "law and order"
was the political catch-phrase of the day. LEAA was directed to assist
state and local government in "strengthening and improving law
enforcement at every level" by national assistance.

Numerous members of Congress have been critical of LEAA's programs, including Sen. Joseph Biden of Delaware who warned that
> . . . unless something substantial be done to correct what I believe to
> be the inefficiency of the program and the lack of direction, the program
> would be better eliminated than continued in its present form.

Others, too, have called for its abolition over the years, including
former Attorney General Griffin Bell. It is not hard to see why.

The study of why people move from high crime rate areas was not
an isolated lapse in sanity. Loyola University in Los Angeles, for
example, was given a $293,700 grant to study the need for a loose-
leaf encyclopedia on law enforcement, an undertaking which produced a two-volume report that by any stretch of the imagination
could not be construed to have contributed anything to the fight
against crime.

Former District of Columbia police chief Jerry Wilson received

261

$48,465 to write a book about crime in the District as part of a two-year $163,828 research project intended to survey 10 years of crime fighting in the nation's capital. The agency spent $17,481 to have Press Intelligence Services, a Washington newsclipping service, clip and send it stories about LEAA. Another $32,477 went to an Arlington, Va., visual arts firm to do the art work for a six-volume report of the National Advisory Commission on Criminal Justice Standards. LEAA, which employs over 820 workers, has even paid others to write its own annual reports. One writer received $100,000 to prepare four of the agency's seven annual reports.

In other areas LEAA issued a $541,623 grant "to promote physical fitness in police officers" in which the agency planned to spend an estimated $200,000 of it for an array of exercise equipment and medical devices. Former LEAA Administrator Richard Velde, who publicly acknowledged that "there has been waste in our program," wanted to develop a Dick Tracy-type wristwatch that would allow police officers to obtain a quick reading of their blood pressure, temperature, and pulse while on the go.

Other examples of waste include a $27,000 study to determine why inmates want to escape from prison. The study was apparently supposed to predict which types of prisoners were most likely to try to escape and which were least likely. Exclaimed William Proxmire:

> This study is a crime. And if those responsible for it were tossed in jail, I'll bet they wouldn't need a dime of the taxpayers' money to decide why they wanted to get out.

Still another example was a $2 million prototype police patrol car that was so loaded down with exotic space age equipment and James Bond-type gadgets that LEAA's plans for field testing it were abandoned. In addition to the fact that some of the car's elaborate systems didn't work, an LEAA report warned that since officers

> . . . must hook their radios as well as themselves into the system, rapid ingress and egress, especially under stressful situations, could be hampered by the additional necessary disconnect-connect functions.

Translation: The police could get stuck in the car. The median price of the vehicle would have been nearly $50,000 per automobile, above and beyond the sticker price of the car.

Proxmire, who has made numerous attempts to abolish LEAA, remarked, "Projects like this convince me of the need to continue my efforts."

Over the years enormous sums of LEAA money have gone into the purchase of expensive automobiles and other equipment and weapons as local and state police forces overreacted to this new influx of federal assistance. There has been no evidence that any of it has been effective in combatting crime. Declared Proxmire:

> The police hardware industry has been booming. Sales of radios, helicopters and riot gear have never been better. The consulting business particularly has done exceedingly well. The sad fact about LEAA is that it has encouraged states and local units to be more creative about winning federal grants than about combatting crime.

By virtually every intelligent standard of evaluation the government's premier program to fight crime has been a fiasco. Its grants to state and local law enforcement agencies have, according to one Senate study, been characterized by "inefficiency, waste, maladministration, and in some cases corruption." Moreover, after three separate studies to determine what effect if any LEAA has had on crime, the GAO came up empty-handed. The total number of major crimes committed in the United States (crimes of violence and against property) increased from 6.7 million crimes in 1968 (when LEAA was enacted) to over 10 million in 1977. The rate per 100,000 persons also rose from 3,370 cases in 1968 to 5,055 in 1977.

LEAA's overall performance has been so bad that its appropriations have declined steadily in recent years. (An agency or program has got to be really pitiful before Congress will cut its budget. Congress' natural inclination is to increase the budgets of failing programs, believing that any program's ills can be cured if enough money is poured into it.)

In fiscal 1978 LEAA'S total budget was $724 million. It declined to $723.6 million in fiscal 1979 and thus was not even allowed to keep pace with inflation. An evaluation by the Carter administration led to a draft proposal to abolish the agency, so dismal was an internal report by Carter's reorganization task force. (This suggestion, however, was rejected for political reasons. The agency's grants are, after all, popular with governors and mayors who will take every federal dollar they can lay their hands on.) Instead, the administration opted for a revamping of the agency which Congress undertook in 1979. In the meantime, Carter proposed cutting LEAA's budget to $546.3 million for fiscal 1980, a substantial drop from fiscal 1979.

During Congress' 1979 debate over how much to give the agency, the Senate Budget Committee (not known for its tightfistedness) voted 11-3 to cut the administration's reduced LEAA budget even further, approving an amendment by Sen. Biden to slash the agency down to a flat $400 million, and to keep it at that level through 1984, not even allowing increases for inflation.

In the House, meantime, Rep. Richard Gephardt of Missouri proposed cutting LEAA's authorization to zero and letting it expire after 1983 when funding already in the pipeline would have been expended. "It's time for local jurisdictions to take stock in what they have learned and wean themselves from the federal purse," Gephardt said. The House Budget Committee rejected his sensible suggestion, voting instead to accept Carter's truncated LEAA budget. But in the end Congress even cut that by $60 million, agreeing on a fiscal 1980 budget of $486 million—a figure that not only represented a sharp reduction in LEAA spending but served to emphasize Congress' disappointment in this agency's performance.

The National Institute of Law Enforcement and Criminal Justice, LEAA's research agency, consumes about $32 million of LEAA's overall budget. An 18-month study* of its activities by the National Research Council concluded that "the Institute has not been the catalyst or sponsor of a first rate and significant research program commensurate with either its tasks or resources." The study went on to state that "structural and political constraints have all too often deflected the Institute from its true mission," adding that, unless changes were made, the Institute in its present form is "not likely to become a significant and quality-oriented research agency."

The Council also said that because the Institute was under so many political and administrative demands, it had been "unable to resist pressures that are inappropriate to a research role." In sum, the study said the Institute had not been pursuing its primary mission which was to develop a body of knowledge "that is useful in reducing crime." The examples of LEAA research given at the beginning of this chapter provide ample evidence that the Council's sharp criticisms of the Institute's work were more than justified.

The Office of Juvenile Delinquency was enacted in 1974 and was placed within LEAA, which had been spending over $140 million a year on juvenile delinquency programs anyway. This newest LEAA agency brought along a considerable amount of bureaucratic baggage, including a Coordinating Council on Juvenile Justice and Delinquency Prevention, an Institute of Corrections, and an Advisory Committee for Juvenile Justice and Delinquency Prevention.

*Understanding Crime: An Evaluation of the National Institute of Law Enforcement and Criminal Justice by the National Research Council, Susan O. White and Samuel Kirslov, editors, National Academy of Sciences, Washington, D.C., 1977.

Among its many missions, this Office was to establish temporary shelters and counseling services around the country for runaway youths—hardly a top law enforcement priority, but Congress has to do something with the money we give them. The program was to have started with a budget of $350 million over three years, eventually reaching an annual budget of $150 million by fiscal 1977. President Ford, however, decided that budgetary restraints precluded him from seeking any funding for the agency. This changed with the Carter administration, and its present annual budget is now $100 million, most of which is spent on grants to state and local law enforcement programs. In 1977 the Office underwent reorganization by Congress and became the Office of Juvenile Justice and Delinquency Prevention.

There are a number of things wrong with this program, not the least of which is that it has had a difficult time spending its money. LEAA officials estimated that of the $340 million appropriated for the juvenile delinquency program from 1975 to 1979, only $163 million was expended. In other words, only 47 percent of the total amount of money Congress had made available to this LEAA agency had been spent by the end of fiscal 1979. In 1978 only about 7 percent of the juvenile justice block grants were expended. When asked by Sen. Fritz Hollings of South Carolina, "How does that flow compare with the flow of the other LEAA offices?" an LEAA official said, "It is a littler slower." Other block grant programs expended at a rate of about 20 percent, he said, compared to the 7 percent for juvenile justice block grants. The official added, somewhat apologetically:

We found when you are dealing with a new program, with some very specific elements in a statute, it is hard to spend money right away.

Thus, a relatively small amount of money is actually getting out into the nation's juvenile justice system. It is no wonder, then, that the administration in fiscal 1979 asked for a 50 percent reduction in the juvenile justice program's funding.

Still another major failing surrounding this program is the all-too-evident fact that the government is swamped with programs providing assistance of one kind or another to the nation's youth, all of which impacts upon juvenile problems. A study by a federal interdepartmental council which sought to coordinate competing juvenile delinquency activities in the government found that more than $12 billion was being allocated each year for a broad range of youth development and juvenile delinquency programs.

Moreover, there are more than 100 agencies in the federal government which perform some type of law enforcement mission and many which assist the states and localities in law enforcement matters. In addition, the government spends $377 million a year to house 28,600 offenders in its federal prisons. All of this should be enough.

In the final analysis, though, law enforcement is largely a local and state responsibility anyway. It is not a problem that can be solved from the nation's capital to any successful degree. All of the available evidence suggests the billions of dollars we have poured into LEAA and its subagencies have not been effective in the fight against crime. But considering the fact that the money going into this program accounts for only 4 percent of the total law enforcement funds being spent each year by the states and localities, should we have expected anything more? LEAA should be removed from the force.

PROGRAM 59

Consultants — $1 Billion

The government's total immersion in the multibillion-dollar consulting business was fully covered in Chapter III. However, a few more remarks and one or two suggestions still need to be made.

No one of course knows the full extent to which the government is employing outside consultants of one sort or another. The best available estimate is that the government is spending at least $2 billion a year on a variety of consulting work which includes research and development, analysis, data collection, writing, and program administration to name only a few examples. An enormous amount of this work, as noted earlier, is wasteful, duplicative, or of extremely marginal value.

It is significant that the Senate Appropriations Committee, after surveying the consulting work being done by the massive Department of Health, Education and Welfare, would declare it did not know of a single "instance where a consultant's recommendation has produced a significant program improvement." That is a pretty devastating indictment of this clearly excessive federal activity but it is not an isolated one. It is a complaint I have had repeated to me by numerous congressional committee staffers, GAO investigators, executive branch officials, as well as by some consultants themselves. One successful private economist, who does most of his consulting business with the government, told me:

> An awful lot of what is being sold to the government is junk, just junk. But the government very often will buy anything.

Said another:

> You wouldn't believe the level of material they are buying at the Defense Department. A group of college students could have put some of these reports together.

Having waded through many government reports and studies by consultants of all sizes and capacities, I'm convinced at least half of all these expenditures are a waste of money—and I am being charitable with this estimate. Nonetheless, cutting consulting costs by this much would save at least $1 billion a year and possibly a great deal more, and that wouldn't be a bad start.

There are many ways the government's passion for consultants can be significantly reduced. The president could issue an executive order to all departments and agencies calling upon them to sharply

267

reduce future consulting contracts by at least 50 percent. More effective, however, would be a concerted effort by the appropriations subcommittees of the House and Senate to cut sharply and deeply into every department and agency's research and policy, planning, and evaluation budgets, which are the feeding grounds of the consulting industry.

This is an area of budget-cutting that wouldn't hurt anyone, except the researchers, institutes, organizations, profitmaking corporations, and other special groups, all of whom have richly profited from this government expenditure. The time has come when consulting costs must be sharply restricted and stringently reviewed to insure that consultants are being used only for the highest priorities—government projects and programs that are vitally important to our nation's military preparedness and its social welfare. Everything else must end.

PROGRAM 60
Civil Aeronautics Board — $100.8 Million

In 1975 when I included the Civil Aeronautics Board on my list of federal agencies to be abolished, the CAB had a budget of almost $85 million a year and was hellbent on government regulation of the airline industry, and particularly fond of protecting the major airlines from outside competition. Deciding to add the CAB to my list wasn't difficult. Just one year earlier the agency had rejected an application from a privately-owned British airline firm who proposed flying regularly scheduled flights from New York to London. The airline, Laker Airways, planned to offer low, $125 one-way fares, about one-third the "economy" rate charged by the other airlines at that time. It is difficult today to comprehend how a federal agency created to serve the consumer could have denied Laker Airways' application.*

All of this has changed. Congress now recognizes the CAB unnecessarily forced interstate airline fares up while unregulated (intrastate) airlines were charging substantially lower fares for comparable distances. What followed in 1978 was enactment of legislation that began a phased withdrawal of the CAB from its regulatory practices, and will eventually bring its abolition by 1985. This is all well and good, but the termination of this agency is taking much too long at much too great a cost. Instead of reducing the CAB's budget, it has been going up. This despite the fact that this agency has less to do. The CAB spent $100.8 million in fiscal 1979, and sought $106 million in 1980.

Since 1938 the CAB has been in charge of regulating civil air transportation within the United States and between the U.S. and foreign countries. Its primary mission has included setting rates and fares U.S. and foreign air carriers may charge, and providing subsidies to domestic airlines. But by setting anti-competitive rates for all carriers, the CAB prohibited free competition between airlines and thus forced them into needless and costly activities such as over-competition on minor routes and too frequent scheduling of flights. The result was that planes often flew nearly empty and capital was being wasted. The CAB prevented the airlines from offering the lowest possible fares and instead drove them into competing over the

*Under deregulation Laker was granted CAB approval and its no-frills flights have been one of the success stories of the industry.

number of daily flights one airline offered over another, the number of meal choices and movies offered on flights, and other costly gimmicks which boosted air fares. The consumer was being denied the fruits of vigorous competition: efficient service at the lowest possible price. Air passengers, given no substantive choice, were forced to pay the fares set by the CAB.

Yet even as Congress considered deregulation in 1977, the CAB saw the handwriting on the wall and began to relax some of its regulations. The almost immediate results were of course more competition and lower fares.

Under the 1978 deregulation act the CAB was directed to place "maximum reliance" on increased competition in the industry. Among its chief reforms, the CAB permitted carriers to lower their rates by as much as 50 percent and increase them by up to 5 percent without prior approval from the government. Under the phase-out timetable set by Congress, the agency's regulation over domestic routes was due to expire by the end of 1981. Its authority over domestic fares and rates, plus acquisition and mergers, was to expire by the end of 1982. The CAB as a whole was to go out of business by January 1, 1985. All that would remain would be the local subsidy program which was to be transferred to the Transportation Department. Authority over foreign air transportation was to be shifted to the Justice and Transportation Departments. The mail subsidy program would be taken over by the U.S. Postal Service.

The question that must be asked is why do we need to wait until 1985 to end this agency once and for all? Equally important, why should airline subsidies be continued anyway?

The CAB is spending $72 million a year on airline subsidies, some of it to provide for the transportation of the mail, and some to provide subsidies to carriers offering service to smaller communities. The rationale for subsidizing airlines is that it helps provide air transportation to communities that would otherwise be without such services. But the subsidy also indirectly places the government in competition with other transportation carriers, namely buses and trains, as well as small airline firms that can't compete with government-subsidized airlines. Obviously, if air travel proves unprofitable in a particular area or region, then rail or bus lines in those areas would absorb whatever transportation demands existed, particularly to and from the nearest point where air travel is provided.

The most convincing and authoritative argument against the CAB's subsidies was made by George Eads, author of the *Local Service*

*Airline Experiment,** published by the Brookings Institution. In it, Eads said this:

> The case for a complete end to the "local service experiment" appears to be a strong one. No convincing evidence has been discovered that any substantial benefits accrue to the nation at large from the continued expenditure of federal funds to support local air service. Furthermore, the fact that total passenger originations either remained constant or declined between 1968 and 1969 at 67 percent of the points serviced exclusively by the local service carriers indicates that even the prime beneficiaries of the subsidy—the travelers who fly for considerably less than cost—believe that the value of the service provided is declining. Traffic was static or declined at 71 percent of the exclusively served cities of less than 25,000 population. Even prior to the establishment of the local service carriers and the postwar expansion of the trunk lines, air service was within easy reach of a substantial proportion of the population. As early as 1938, the average population of cities that were not served was only 11,595, and the average distance from the nearest city with air service was only 35 miles. When account is taken of the probable entry of unsubsidized air taxis at many points if the local service carriers suspended service to them, it is quite conceivable that 97 percent of the metropolitan population, that proportion that the local service carriers claimed to be serving in 1969, would still have easy access to scheduled air service even if the local service subsidy were ended.

Since 1978, we have seen CAB deregulation bear the fruits of increased competition and lower air fares and rates. There is no reason, in light of this, why further benefits could not be derived if deregulation were speeded up and the CAB's 847 employes were more efficiently phased out of their jobs. It should not be necessary to wait until 1985 to get rid of the CAB. It is difficult to understand why an agency that is supposedly going out of business should be receiving larger budget appropriations. Indeed, a phasing out of the CAB should produce reductions in its budget.

The government's deregulation of the airline industry was a long-overdue step. All that remains to be done now is the complete termination of the CAB as soon as possible.

---

*"The Impact of Regulations on the Local Service Airline Subsidy," by George Eads, which was drawn from his book, was published by the Joint Economic Committee of Congress in a report entitled "The Economics of Federal Subsidy Programs," Part 6—Transportation Subsidies.

PROGRAM 61

Japan-United States Friendship Commission — $2.4 Million

This commission was enacted by Congress in 1975 and financed out of a U.S. Trust Fund of $30 million which originates from Japanese repayments for U.S. facilities built in Okinawa, which were turned over to Japan, and for other post-war American assistance. Its purpose is "the promotion of scholarly, cultural, and artistic activities between Japan and the U.S.," to "enhance reciprocal people-to-people understanding," and to make "a vital contribution to the prospects for peace, prosperity, and security in Asia."

The commission is composed of 18 Americans from the fields of business, government, and education. Agencies such as the National Endowment for the Arts, the National Education Association, and the Department of Health, Education and Welfare are among those represented on the commission. Basically, the commission gives out grants under four project areas: Japanese Studies (for Americans), American Studies (for Japanese), the Arts (participants from both countries), and Cultural Communication and Public Affairs (for the United States).

Since the commission admits that "traditional areas" of Japanese studies are already adequately funded, it is attempting instead to "educate a broader stratum of American leadership with respect to Japan." This is done, in part, by giving fellowships to professionals in "law, business, journalism, and architecture/urban studies." Other activities include support for "major collections of Japanese books and publications in appropriate libraries located throughout the United States," advanced language training of American graduate students, plus other support involving education, fine arts displays, and cultural exchanges.

The Japanese are a great people and continued cultural, educational, and political interaction with the United States is necessary and valuable. But this commission is not essential to carrying out these worthy objectives. Exchanges of all types continue routinely through State Department and other government bilateral programs. Many private nonprofit organizations as well as individuals in business, the arts, and education participate in and encourage better relations and understanding between the two countries. All of this should be more than adequate.

PROGRAM 62

Bilingual Education Program — $166.9 Million

The Elementary and Secondary Education Act Title VII Bilingual Education Program was enacted by Congress in 1968. Its purpose is to give Hispanic and other students whose dominant language is not English the opportunity to be taught by teachers and materials in their native tongue until they become fluent in our own language. The Congress directed that "demonstration projects" be carried out to test this approach to teaching non-English language children. But by 1977, as David Savage, associate editor of the weekly, *Education U.S.A.*, pointed out, "the bilingual education budget was up to $150 million, and it was still fraudulently called a demonstration program even though nothing was being demonstrated."

By 1980 an estimated 340,000 students were expected to be enrolled in the elementary program and plans were being made to extend bilingual educational services to the college level.

How has the program worked? Pretty poorly, as David Savage suggested in an article in the *Washington Post*:

... the program certainly has not done what it set out to do: demonstrate the value of the bilingual technique. Still, the administration has recommended that the bilingual education budget go up another $15 million, to $174 million (for fiscal 1980).

Said HEW Secretary Joseph Califano in announcing the new budget: "Our inept administration (of the bilingual education program) should not be used as an excuse for cutting it." Maybe not. But in what year—or decade—can we begin to judge the program on its merits?

Savage was not alone in his criticisms of the program. A 1977 study was also done by the American Institutes for Research for the Office of Education which financed and oversaw the program's operation. After examining 38 project sites encompassing 11,500 students, the AIR study concluded that the program has not been very effective. One of its findings, in fact, showed that Hispanic students in the program were gaining less in English reading than other Hispanic students who attended regular classes.

The study said that "in terms of one of the major goals" of the bilingual program—that of having students of limited English-speaking ability achieve competency in the English language—the projects which have been operating four to five years "have not been generally effective."

273

The study continued:

> All in all, there seems little doubt that most of the students in the Title VII projects included in this evaluation generally were not performing in the English language at expected educational levels. This overall level of performance was not a result of large numbers of Spanish monolingual students being in the program. Rather, the majority of the students were classified by their teachers as being bilingual and English monolingual. While their present level of English proficiency suggests that additional instruction in English Language Arts would be necessary to bring these students up to grade level in English proficiency, it is not evident from the current data of the Impact Study that Title VII bilingual education as presently implemented should be considered as the most appropriate approach for those students.

In other words, a large number of the students enrolled in these classes spoke both English and their native tongue, or spoke only English. What they required, according to this study, was additional instruction *in English* language skills, not an elaborate bilingual program.

One of the most disturbing findings concerned what happened to Hispanic students once they had become reasonably versed in English:

> Analyses of the policy of each project with regard to the placement of a Spanish-dominant student once he/she is able to function in school in English showed that by far the majority of the projects were implementing a Spanish maintenance bilingual project.

What this means is that, instead of being moved on to regular classes when they were ready, these students were being continually educated in their Spanish language. Indeed, the study went on to point out that

> ... eighty-six percent of the project directors indicated that once a Spanish-dominant student learns English well enough to function in school he/she remains in the bilingual project. Only 5 percent of the project directors indicated that a Spanish-dominant student is transferred from the project to an English-only classroom with no Spanish language maintenance once he/she learns English well enough to function in school.

Other educators have been equally critical of bilingual programs, believing they have encouraged dependence upon one's native language and thus retarded academic progression in school. The American Institutes for Research study provides a devastating critique of this teaching technique and shows that it has not worked. Students placed in these classes are by and large being forced to rely on their native tongue rather than making them "reach" upward academically for greater proficiency in the language they must master if they are to succeed educationally and job-wise in our society.

Some have argued that the bilingual classes have provided Hispanic students with more self-confidence and a feeling of belonging because they are taught in their own language. However, the study found that "no clear trend" was found which would indicate that participating in the bilingual program brought about an increase in positive attitudes toward school.

In most cases, as the AIR study revealed, the students participating in these bilingual classes only need more help in English language skills—which the public schools *should provide* for them. There are those who come to our public schools knowing no English whatsoever, but as the AIR study points out they are few in number. There is no reason why special English tutoring classes cannot be provided for this relatively small number of children. Meanwhile, the bilingual program should be terminated.

PROGRAM 63

Military Servants — $4.5 Million

Out of a sea of government waste and extravagance there is nothing more outrageous and arrogant than the use of enlisted men by our military brass for their personal servants.

There were more than 1700 military servants being employed in 1973, but Congress—primarily at the insistence of Sen. Proxmire—has gradually trimmed that figure until it is now down to about 300. It is still 300 too many.

The servants, lower ranked enlisted servicemen, are assigned to our highest ranked officers, usually generals, admirals, and the like. Their duties include menial chores such as walking the dog, driving the general's wife around, mowing the lawn, cooking, serving meals, babysitting, grocery shopping, doing laundry, running errands, bartending at parties—all of which are paid for by the taxpayer. The servants earn between $10,000 and $15,000 a year. The usual allotment is one or, at most, two servants for a top brass official. But the heads of the military service academies are assigned three servants and the Joint Chiefs of Staff are given the services of five each, which is the equivalent of $60,000 in free benefits. (At one time there was even a school run by the military in Virginia to train these servants in the proper ways of serving food and announcing visitors but it was shut down, at Proxmire's insistence.) There are laws, of course, which prohibit using enlisted men as servants, but the vaguely worded regulations still allow our servicemen to be used for virtually every imaginable task.

The military makes three overall arguments in defense of this 18th century practice: 1) high-ranking officers have many social responsibilities that come with the job, so it is unfair to expect them to pay to have these chores done; 2) the homes provided for our top brass are old and in frequent need of repair which the servants are needed to do; and 3) it is an age-old military tradition to provide servants for our highest ranked officers.

First, there are many high government officials, including senators, Supreme Court justices, and Cabinet secretaries who have enormous social responsibilities as part of their job, but they are not assigned servants in their homes at the taxpayer's expense.

Second, while it is true that many of these military homes are old, they aren't rundown by any means. Many are graceful colonial and federal period houses that anyone would love to live in. If there are repairs to be made, it would be cheaper to just fix up the houses and dump the servants.

Third, there is a tradition here and it goes back to pre-Civil War days when blacks were used as servants for the military. Prior to World War I, the Navy used Chinese and Filipinos in the Pacific as their manservants and valets. Even today, 98 percent of the Navy's servants are still Filipinos—which many people believe continues an unfortunate racial practice that should have been abandoned many years ago. This is not a tradition that the military should be proud of. It is *aristocratic arrogance at its worst.*

All of this amounts to nothing more than using GIs as domestics for our top brass, who are paid well enough to be able to afford their own servants, if they need them.

When a top Army official once told Appropriations Committee Chairman George Mahon he didn't think the chief of staff should have to rush home after work to mow his lawn, Mahon snapped, "Well, he could hire his own help, like the rest of us."

The practice of using military servicemen as stewards and servants at the taxpayer's expense to perform domestic chores for our top military brass is a travesty. Most Americans cook their own meals, pick up their own laundry, clean their own homes, and drive themselves to and from work. Our military men can do the same. The American taxpayer will gladly pay the taxes needed to maintain our military strength at whatever levels are needed to keep our nation strong and free. But continuation of the present aristocratic practice can only further weaken citizen support for America's already highly criticized military budget. It is an expenditure that must be eliminated.

PROGRAM 64

Youth Conservation Corps — $70 Million

The Youth Conservation Corps may sound good, but if you examine who has benefited from it in relation to those who are among this society's most disadvantaged youths, it becomes readily apparent that this is a misdirected, low priority program that should be shelved.

The Corps, located within the Agriculture Department's Forest Division, provides about eight weeks of summer employment on federal and nonfederal public lands for unemployed youths between the ages of 15 and 18. There were about 38,000 program participants in 1979, but most of them (77 percent) were white and more than one-third of the youths were from middle class families. Eligibility is open to anyone who wishes to apply. As the Carter administration explained in a position paper urging the program's abolition, "It is essentially a public-financed summer camp with pay."

One of the program's chief aims is to develop an appreciation for our nation's resources and environment among young people. The YCC was first established as a three-year pilot program in 1970 and then made permanent in 1974. Has the program raised the level of environmental consciousness of those who have participated? An internal administration white paper on the program said:

> No studies have indicated that long-term improvements in environmental understanding can be imputed to the program. It is quite likely that no improvements would be found given the relatively small gain in test scores between entry and exit from the program.

While some of the projects the youths engage in may be worthwhile, many of them are of dubious value to the public at large and of no value to the environment. The *Washington Post* in the summer of 1979 discovered, for example, that YCC youths were being used to fix up the golf courses at Andrews Air Force Base and to perform landscape work at Vice President Walter Mondale's official residence. An Interior Department (which participates in the program) official conceded, "I don't think the projects at Andrews fit too well, but the road to hell is paved with good intentions."

According to *Post* reporter Mike Sager, the YCC youths over the past two years have:

—Built 10 rain shelters on two golf courses at the air base—courses

278

that are restricted to Defense Department personnel, their dependents, and guests.

—Done landscaping work at Mondale's home on the grounds of the U.S. Naval Observatory.

—Constructed a mile-long, 20-station, jogging and exercise trail for base personnel.

—Erected a 26-by-26-foot, concrete-floored picnic shelter at Andrews and improved the base's picnic areas, tables, and trails.

Essentially, Sager reported, the Defense Department "appears to have found a windfall" in the program, "trading barrack space, dollar-a-day meals, and the cost of materials for free labor and new facilities."

It is no wonder, then, that the Carter administration selected this program for termination in fiscal 1980, arguing:

> It is not needs-oriented. It does not address the high priority needs of unemployed youths. Its contribution to environmental understanding is minor. It is a relatively high cost method of accomplishing work.

The administration sensibly suggested that the money could be better spent on programs targeted to low-income youths who need help far more than white middle-income kids who are among the most employable of our youth population.

This program cost $70 million in fiscal 1979, and it was expected that Congress would keep it going, perhaps at reduced levels, despite the administration's suggestion that it be ended.

PROGRAM 65

Government Advertising — $30 Million

Accurate government-wide figures concerning this activity are difficult to come by. Hard as it may be to believe, the government has no central list of who in the bureaucracy is engaged in media advertising, nor does anyone have accurate, up-to-date figures on what the government is spending annually on advertising. We have to go outside the government to get such figures.

Fortunately, *Advertising Age** conducts a regular survey of government advertising and provides what are widely considered to be the best estimates available. Unfortunately, the figures are two years old. More unfortunately, the totals do not include the government's internal costs of producing these ads—that is, the salaries, benefits, pensions, and other overhead costs of the federal officials who plan them and contract out for their production.

Still, the figures show this to be one of the government's growth programs. According to the authoritative advertising industry journal, government advertising expenditures totaled $128.5 million in 1978, representing an increase of $12.5 million, or a rise of almost 10 percent over the previous year. The magazine also reported that the government has become the nation's *25th largest advertiser* in 1978, up eight notches in the corporate ranking. My own estimate, after talking with GAO experts and other government officials, is that the government is spending a total of at least $200 million on this activity when federal salaries and other administrative costs are factored in.

Nonetheless, in ad contract costs alone the *Advertising Age* figure is substantial, although the lion's share of it—more than $100 million—represents military recruiting ad costs. This, however, is clearly an activity that is vital to the needs of an all-volunteer military force. It is the other areas of government advertising that I find to be often trivial, ineffective, and redundant.

At least 122 federal agencies are into mass-media advertising. Only nine of them are military recruitment programs. The Defense Department must pay for its ads because of the need to reach large prime time audiences. However, other federal agencies are similarly taking out paid advertisements, including the Postal Service, whose budget is more than $6.8 million a year; Amtrak, which spends nearly $10 million annually; Public Broadcasting Service, whose

*See the September 6, 1979, issue.

280

annual ad budget has reached $3 million; and the U.S. Travel Service with a budget of more than $2.1 million a year.

Government agencies issuing public service ads, which the stations run free, include the Departments of Energy, (which has a $1 million ad budget, Interior, Labor, Agriculture, Health, Education and Welfare, Housing and Urban Development, Transportation, the Consumer Product Safety Commission, and the Social Security Administration, among others.

As noted in Chapter 10, a great deal of this "free" advertising is usually broadcast in the wee hours of the morning when few if any listeners or viewers are awake. Thus, there are healthy reasons to question whether the public is getting much benefit from this expenditure of public funds. As to the overall effectiveness of these advertisements, there is *no evidence whatsoever* that *any* of them are achieving their purported objectives. In some cases the ads are produced primarily to promote an agency's public identity.

Government advertising is on the whole a wasteful expenditure of tax dollars and should be drastically cut back, with the exception of recruiting ads and public service announcements concerned with poison control or health-related messages that address a nationally vital problem or danger. There is a potential savings here of $30 million in unnecessary or marginal government advertising which the nation could get along without. These include all those ads (discussed in Chapter 10) about national parks, skiing and skateboard safety, stamp collecting, and other messages delving into areas where the government has no business sticking its nose.

PROGRAMS 66–67

National Endowment for the Arts
National Endowment for the Humanities
TOTAL — $300 Million

These federal agencies are convinced that if their programs were ended, the arts in America would shrivel up and die. They believe that after Congress created them in 1965, they nursed the arts back to health, and brought about an artistic renaissance in the United States. The truth behind this elitist pomposity is that the arts have always been a vibrant and growing part of our national culture, whether in theatre, literature, film, art, sculpture, dance or music. America's primary support and inspiration for the arts comes from where it has always come, the people, not the federal government.

The government shouldn't be in the business of underwriting artists. Art is a uniquely individual activity that is appreciated and defined in a very private and individual way. It means different things to different people. It is something that can only, in the final analysis, be defined by the people who experience it, not by a government agency. What is art to one may be a fraudulent piece of junk to another. The trouble comes when we forget that *only people* can decide what is art and what is not art, what is good art and what is bad art. When the government begins making these decisions through their subsidies then we have lost the freedom that is intrinsic to this most indefinable of human expressions.

Equally important, the government in its present fiscal posture cannot afford to subsidize artists, as cruel as that may seem to artists who, for obvious reasons, are the biggest supporters of these programs. With a $30 billion deficit in fiscal 1980, with people trying to make ends meet in the midst of skyrocketing inflation and burdensome taxation, and with so many other more pressing human needs, these two programs are most certainly among the most dispensable in our government.

A tremendous amount of money has been wasted on these programs, money that could have been put to better uses—providing better health care for our children, better nutrition, decent housing, or improved educational opportunities. The point is that with many Americans still living in squalor, filth and deprivation, how can we defend spending money on activities like these by the National Endowment for the Arts:*

—$10,000 to support a film about employment in the artistic disciplines.

—$10,000 for a 60-minute documentary film about the Pachuco Zootsuiters (a group of Chicano youths in the 1940s).

—$25,000 to support the aesthetic management program for small urban natural-area parks.

—$10,000 to make a film about the mutual support afforded by two black women during their social and economic difficulties.

—$2,000 to support the completion of a lyrical film on the setting and mood of Thoreau's *Walden Pond*.

—$10,000 to support completion of a film entitled "World War II and Me," a personal documentary incorporating film footage shot by a combat cameraman and including a visit with Picasso.

—$7,500 to support a program to plan, produce, perform, and tour an original vaudeville show based on the music, myths, and history of the Pacific Northwest.

—$5,000 to the Feminist Radio Network to support a conference designed to improve the quality of programming by, for, and about women.

—$2,000 to investigate the aesthetic and archival problems of permanently installed photographic murals in public spaces.

—$15,000 to Conservation Foundation, Inc. to support the production of a film which examines issues of aesthetics and visual quality of rural landscapes.

—$2,750 to produce and disseminate a series of audio and video-tapes explaining the use of color poems as a model for the teaching of creative expression in dance, drama, and literature.

—$15,000 to Partners for Livable Places to support a comprehensive recognition program which will give proper credit and stimulus to the nondesign community for imaginative design solutions and creative planning partnerships.

—$380 to Henderson State University in Arkansas for projects concerning the publication of *Proscenium*, a school literary magazine.

—$2,500 for projects related to future publication of a literary magazine in Bolinas, California.

—$10,000 for a new dance work by two Los Angeles artists.

—$10,000 to support an animated film demonstrating animation's

*All of these examples were extracted from NEA's grant catalogue.

ability to concentrate information in a profuse flow of images.

—$3,000 for future publication projects by *Gay Sunshine*, a literary magazine in San Francisco.

—$7,500 to support the completion of a feature length film in which documentary and narrative footage will be intercut to illustrate the relationship of fantasy to life.

—$3,500 to Friends of Books and Comics of San Francisco to support publication of a guide to alternative press media.

—$7,500 to Physics/Consciousness Research Group in San Francisco for continued support of a floating museum.

—$10,000 in "Works of Art in Public Places" category to the San Francisco Art Institute to support a planning project for the redevelopment of the northern waterfront of San Francisco incorporating the expertise of artists, an architect, a psychologist, an art historian, and a sociologist.

—$20,550 to the San Francisco Museum to support the production of a 28-minute training film on the proper care and handling of paintings.

—$15,000 in "City Spirit" category to the San Mateo County Arts Council of California for support of the Council's multicultural task force through an intensive retreat during which a catalytic event and facilitation training will be developed.

—$8,000 to support work in the autobiographic genre, investigating the possibilities of translating environmental context into personal content.

—$10,000 to the District of Columbia Council on Minority Planning and Strategy to support the research, designs, and plans for a tribute to author Alex Haley in six cities in the state of Tennessee.

—$7,250 to Alonzo Crawford of the District of Columbia to support a one-hour docudrama on a 10-year-old boy growing up in a Washington neighborhood.

—$18,500 to the La Jolla, California, Museum of Contemporary Art to support an exhibition of historic and modern prototype chair designs.

—$10,000 for a film focusing on the difficulties of being a black artist.

—$1,500 to the Cultural Council Foundation, Creative Time, Inc., New York, for the sponsorship of a residency program with one artist and four assistants and the creation of a three-mile laser light sculpture called "The Green Lady."

—$1,500 to an artist to design an animated sequence of up to 30 seconds on the spectacolor display system, a computerized electronic lampback matrix (New York Museum of Modern Art).

—$25,000 to support an audience development project aimed at 150,000 union members in western New York.

—$5,000 to Womanrite Theatre Ensemble, Inc., Brooklyn, New York, to support the creation of an original feminist work.

These are only a few examples of thousands of grants awarded by these two agencies. But they are by no means isolated ones. While all of them may be worthwhile artistic works, they are not the kind of activities the federal government should be spending public money on—not while there is poverty, decaying cities, and other unmet national needs.

How do we explain to a family living in a shack in Mississippi whose children must survive on an inadequate diet that it was more important to award a $6,000 grant to a Pittsburgh artist who filmed crepe paper and burning gases being dropped out of two small airplanes? The film was in part made on the Caribbean resort island of St. Maarten where the artist and her husband, who was the cameraman, stayed for one week during one of the worst winters to hit the United States. The woman said it was necessary to do the film there because it was an area that had influenced her development as an artist. The project, according to the grant summary, was supposed to "document on film an event designed to alter an audience's immediate environment for a short period of time." The artists also flew to El Paso, Texas, where they threw four one-mile-long crepe paper rolls from two planes, accompanied by two sky divers. In another scene, skydivers parachuted in Pennsylvania wearing backpacks of glowing gases. The film, which ran about 20 minutes, contained many scenes that showed the artist posing in St. Maarten.

With $300 million a year to give away, it is no wonder that artists with ideas like this are flocking to the Endowments for funding. Michael Straight, former deputy chairman of the Endowment for the Arts, knows, perhaps better than anyone, how their money has been spent. Straight recalled in an article of remembrances* the frantic "last-minute rush to get grants signed and mailed" by the end of the fiscal year when no agency wants to be caught with any surplus funds. As Straight tells his story, one morning in June of 1974 he found a batch of projects on his desk, most of them for $3,000

*Washington Post, August 26, 1979.

fellowship grants, which awaited his signature. "I began to read them, and a few left me perplexed," he said:

—"My project is a series of paintings, 10 to 15 layers of paint deep, consisting entirely of extremely subtle gradations of gray.

—The project I propose will temporarily manipulate the Chicago skyline for the period of one year.

—My project is to introduce taxidermy as a sculpture media by using painted plywood construction, dirt, sand, gravel, and animals to create different environmental situations.

—My project, the Structure of Dry-Fly Fishing, is a complex video artwork on the order of a piece of sculpture.

—I have in mind several pieces involving templates of the curvature of the earth, and of monumental man-made structures. These in-scale templates would be transformed, rolled, folded or somehow distilled in order to give insight to an otherwise vast visual or conceptual order.

—The Porpoise Opera Project is an experimental project intended to function in an oceanarium's porpoise stadium; to make use of existing facilities; and to work with resident porpoises (Bottlenosed Dolphins) in an effort to plan and develop a full-length program or opera to be seen by the public and documented on film."

Now, it is difficult for the average taxpayer to understand how the government would even consider supporting such proposals. But Straight said:

> On reflection, I signed these grants on the ground that the projects had been endorsed by our professional advisers and that they probably would not harm the Endowment.

There were other fellowship grants, however, that Straight said he in good conscience could not sign, though one wonders how they could have received endorsement from peer review panels in the first place. One of them proposed dripping ink from Hayley, Idaho, to Cody, Wyoming. Another involved an artist who wanted to rent a ground-level studio "adjacent to a lush meadow," commune with nature, animals, and his friends, and record the whole blissful experience on video tape. Straight's resistance, unfortunately, was overcome by his superiors. "I was speechless," he said. He still refused to sign the grants, but they were approved anyway.

In the future, however, the Endowment decided it did not want these weird explanations of what the recipients of these fellowships planned to do with their grants. Instead, the Endowment said, it wanted only endorsements from the artists' peers and transparencies of past works.

The fellowships, which can be as much as $7,500 each are being given to "starving artists," according to NEA officials, though I know of no one who claims to have ever seen one of these poor, unfortunate creatures. Poor maybe, but not starving. The money is given out solely to "promote the artist's work." What is done with the money is his or her concern. A trip to Europe to tour the art galleries? Fishing trip? Whatever further's one's artistic career. Not bad, huh?

Clearly, as the foregoing examples suggest, there is an enormous opportunity here for abusive and wasteful use of the taxpayer's money. And this is why the Endowments, as Chicago Tribune reporter Raymond Coffey has written, "have been attracting more criticism and provoking more doubt and disappointment about their operations."

One of the major criticisms being leveled at both Endowments is their apparent politicization. NEA Chairman Livingston Biddle was a longtime aide of Democratic Sen. Claiborne Pell of Rhode Island, who chairs the subcommittee that oversees the Endowment's activities. Biddle also played a major role in their creation and promotion. His appointment was seen as a political payoff to Pell. The chairman of the National Endowment for the Humanities is Joseph Duffey, who along with his wife, Anne Wexler, worked actively in President Carter's 1976 campaign. Among those criticizing this politicization was Straight himself, who said, "the Carter administration made a conscious decision that they would use both Endowments for their own political purposes."

This kind of crass political use of the arts by the government was deviously evident when the National Endowment for the Humanities gave a $45,000 grant for a series of "town meeting" programs on the merits of the Strategic Arms Limitation Treaty (SALT II). Was the Endowment embarrassed by its involvement in so political an issue? Not in the least. Duffey told the Chicago Tribune, according to Coffey, that "he saw no problem with the grant being 'political,' that SALT II is not only political but has a 'historical and philosophical perspective' as well and therefore fits into the humanities." By that twisted rationale, the NEH could involve itself in virtually every piece of legislation that came before Congress.

But NEH* is also busy giving out grants to wealthy doctors, lawyers, and school administrators to attend month-long, vacation-like

*NEH's fiscal 1979 budget totaled $145.2 million.

summer seminars in the country. Under this project, NEH gave out $750,000 one year so that up to 300 professionals could attend these pleasant retreats. The agency not only paid for their transportation and materials but also gave each participant a $1200 stipend. The professionals, according to the NEH, were brought together to help "clarify understanding of the fundamental issues facing modern society and broaden the perspective from which thinking citizens view their professions and society at large." The discussions were strenuous, apparently, because they were limited to only three hours a day. Duffey once remarked that his predecessor had taken a rather "elitist" approach to the agency's activities. Giving well-paid and well-educated professionals special opportunities like this represents the height of social elitism.

One of NEH's most celebrated grants, which received Proxmire's "Golden Fleece" award, gave $2500 to Arlington County, Virginia, to study why people are rude, cheat, and lie on the tennis courts. The grant was made to determine why tennis players hog the courts when others are waiting, why they become irritated when they have to wait, and ways tennis players can solve overcrowding of court facilities.

Other projects funded by the Endowments include a "silent opera" entitled *The Life and Death of Joseph Stalin*, which runs wordlessly and in slow motion for half a day; Tom Eyen's *The Dirtiest Show on Earth*, described as a play of devil-may-care nudity that frolics to a sexual orgy for its dramatic finish; a $17,885 grant to an artist in Santa Fe, New Mexico, for a history on Cheyenne Indian beadwork; a $5,270 grant to the Chicago Historical Society to plan an exhibit on Chicago furniture from 1840 to 1950; and a $3,000 grant to construct "the biggest cowboy boots in the world," 30 feet from toe to heel and 40 feet tall, as a sculptural exhibit in downtown Washington, D.C.

Several years ago Michael Straight remarked, "I look forward to the day when the workingman comes home, opens a can of beer, turns on the television and watches the Metropolitan." It may come as a shock to Mr. Straight, but there are already many working people in America, many with little formal education, who do come home from work, open a can of beer, and put *Turandot* on their stereo. They found the arts long before the National Endowments began doling out their millions.

The dramatic rise in the number of orchestras, art galleries, legitimate theatres, arts exhibits and fairs, chamber music societies, opera houses, and other manifestations of artistic activity and growth in recent years far surpasses the rather limited financial parameters of the National Endowment for the Arts. Had their funds* never existed, this growth would have still taken place because it has drawn its support from the people who support the arts through their patronage. This is ultimately where support for the arts must come.

However, ending these programs does not mean that financial assistance to orchestras, museums, and art galleries cannot be provided by local and state governments who, after all, know and appreciate the needs of their artistic institutions and organizations best. Meanwhile, it must also be underscored that support from businesses and their foundations continues to be a major source of funding for the arts. According to the Business Committee for the Arts, businesses provided more than a quarter of a billion dollars to the arts in 1978, and that figure was expected to be substantially higher in 1979 and 1980. And bear in mind this does not include special financial support from philanthropists, private foundations, and bequests from wealthy estates, which add hundreds of millions of dollars more each year to the support of the arts. All of this, when added to the nation's overall individual support for the arts, amounts to an enormous sum of money, dwarfing all of NEA's work.

Finally, it should be emphasized that, without the Endowments, the federal government would still be generously providing hundreds of millions of dollars for a broad range of projects, services, and endeavors for the arts and humanities, much more in fact than the Endowments do now. For example, the government is presently appropriating $180 million a year to support Public Broadcasting, whose magnificent programming in the arts and humanities reaches millions of people. Additionally, the Smithsonian Institution, which operates more than a half dozen museums and at least half a dozen art galleries, receives $170 million a year in federal support. The National Gallery of Art in Washington added a $70 million addition to its art complex (financed entirely by private funds, by the way) and operates an art exhibit program that serves schools in about 4,000 communities a year. The Smithsonian operates a traveling exhibit program. Additional money is provided to support the arts within the Departments of Commerce and Health, Education and Welfare, among other agencies of government. And of course there is the famed

*NEA's total fiscal 1979 budget totaled $149.5 million.

Kennedy Center and Ford Theater in Washington which are also supported by federal funds. All this, by any standard, should be more than enough.

PROGRAM 68

Office of Consumer Affairs — $1.8 Million

The only thing this agency could do to truly help the consumer is to self-destruct and save us all the $1.8 million a year it is spending largely on itself.

Created by Congress in 1971, the Office of Consumer Affairs, according to the fiscal 1980 budget, advises the Secretary of Health, Education and Welfare, in whose department it resides, as well as other federal agencies on consumer-related policies and programs. It acts as a consumer advocate within the government, testifying before regulatory proceedings and providing a clearinghouse for consumer complaints.

Its director, Esther Peterson, also serves as the special adviser to the president for consumer issues. She supports the cause of the consumer movement primarily by appearing around the country, at government expense, making speeches to demonstrate that the president is a friend of the consumer.

The agency has been involved in other frivolous activities such as running a weekly radio program giving tips on how to cope with inflation, and issuing literature and studies on consumer problems.

The federal government is loaded with agencies and programs that are responsible for looking out for the consumer, including the Food and Drug Administration, the Department of Agriculture, and the Justice Department. Moreover, most of the money being spent by this agency—almost $1.3 million out of its total budget—is consumed by the salaries of its 50 employes, who earn an average of $24,000 a year. Nothing this agency has done over the years justifies its cost to the taxpayers. Consumers would be better off without it.

PROGRAM 69

Interstate Commerce Commission — $80 Million

For more than 90 years the Interstate Commerce Commission has been inflicting costly, complex, and often ludicrous regulations upon the nation's rail, truck, barge, and bus industries. This in turn has added billions of dollars to the cost of everything we buy. By suffocating competition within the transportation industry, the ICC has reduced American productivity, wasted precious operating capital, crippled the railroads, and frozen small businessmen—particularly minorities—out of the interstate trucking markets solely to protect what has become a government-sanctioned trucking cartel. It is, in short, an agency that should have been abolished many years ago.

Even the *New York Times*,* which rarely calls for the abolition of any federal agency, declared in an editorial that it saw "no more reason to regulate trucking than supermarkets." The *Times* added:

> It would be preferable to phase out the ICC altogether, in the way the airline deregulation act dealt with the Civil Aeronautics Board. The federal duty to assure safety could easily be assumed by other agencies.

William Proxmire, among others in Congress, has also called for its abolition, saying:

> . . . there are more whiskers and cobwebs at the ICC than any place in the government. With fierce competition among air, rail, barge, and road transportation, regulation for other than safety purposes has long been unnecessary. The answer is abolition plus strong enforcement of the antitrust laws.

Many problems have plagued the railroad industry over the years, scarce investment capital and poor management being chief among them. Yet the fact remains that the railroads have primarily been the victims of insufferable and prejudicial ICC regulation. An antiquated rate structure and a straightjacket of rules and regulations that has prevented innovation, organizational overhaul, and the movement of capital into profitable lines, has sown the seeds of destruction for the rail carriers.

Such a rate structure for the railroads, concluded UCLA economist George W. Hilton in a brilliant analysis** of the ICC:

> . . . cannot survive in the face of competition, since the rival mode (of

*New York Times, May 29, 1979.
**"What Has the ICC Cost You and Me?" Trains Magazine, Oct., 1972

transportation)—mainly private trucking—becomes the principal alternative open to the shipper, and thus the actual measure of the value of rail service to him.

The effort to preserve the [ICC's] traditional rate structure inevitably results in the loss of some rail traffic to trucking, thereby preventing as full utilization of rail plants as otherwise could occur.

It all began when Congress, in a series of acts between 1887 and 1914, attempted to stop rate wars between the giant railroads and proceeded to set railroad tariffs in which rates were figured on the value of the service, rather than on what it cost to provide that service. Thus, the decline of railroads began as industries sought out competitive alternatives to the railroad, and truck and barge transportation moved to fill their needs. Unfortunately, Congress wasn't content to stop there. It broadened the ICC in 1935 to include regulation of trucks and buses, and, in 1940, of water carriers. Thus, the ICC became the overlord of a noncompetitive industry, producing higher transportation rates, wasted resources, and lower output—all at an increased cost to the economy and, thus, to the public at large.

What the ICC has born, Hilton observed, is a transportation cartel that, like a monopoly,

> . . . generates idleness. In railroading, idleness stems from the nature of the rate regulation, restrictions on exit from unprofitable activities, barriers to diversification, and the bias of regulation to present rail technology.

Thus, as we have seen, the ICC prevented the railroads from amputating miles of underutilized tracks on branch lines that should have been abandoned long ago because they were no longer economically feasible to continue. It forbade lines to raise or lower rates when necessary to remain competitive. It required railroads to ship certain commodities that could have been better handled by other carriers. All of these restrictions have had a destructive effect upon the nation's railroad industry. Many of these unprofitable routes have of course been taken over by the government's rail passenger service, Amtrak, and the U.S. Railroad Administration, the government freight service. Both, however, continue to operate at substantial deficits, despite enormous federal subsidies.

Meanwhile, the railroad is not the only industry being hurt by the ICC's overregulation. Truckers, too, as a result of nonsensical regulatory rules that defy comprehension, suffer from underutilized facilities. Trucks, for example, have been required to make

uneconomical semifilled hauls, empty backhauls, often on round-
about routes that wasted time and fuel.

President Carter complained:

> Too many trucks are rattling back and forth empty on the road today,
> burning up precious diesel fuel, because ICC rules prohibit two-way
> hauling. Some trucking companies can deliver all the ingredients nec-
> essary to make soup to a factory, but are forbidden from hauling soup
> away from the factory. Restrictions like these are symbols of government
> regulations gone wild.

Common carriers have been operating empty backhauls more than
16 percent of the time, according to the *National Journal*. The Grand
Union supermarket chain complained that, because of ICC regulations, its trucks were running empty 40 percent of the time.

Incensed by the ICC's rulemaking madness, the *Times* even discovered that

> . . . any trucker is welcome to go into the business of hauling raisins to
> market, provided they are unprocessed or coated with cinnamon, honey
> or sugar. But if the raisins happen to be the chocolate-covered variety,
> the same trucker has to apply for permission from the ICC—and stand
> a real chance of being turned down.

All of this has perpetrated idleness of transportation resources,
prohibited the most productive and economical mode of transportation (rail) from responding to the incentives of the marketplace,
and resulted in higher costs to industry and, ultimately, the consumer. How much? Stanford University economist Thomas Gale
Moore estimated the additional cost to the public at $10 billion per
year. Hilton has estimated added costs of $6.5 billion per year. On
the average, each American family is said to be paying up to $200
a year more for the cost of everything they purchase because of ICC
regulations.

Who profits from all this? As Hilton pointed out:

> The avidity with which the American Trucking Association fights to
> preserve the present organization of the industry is the best possible
> indication that the major truckers benefit from the cartelization.

Who would gain if the trucking industry's cartel practices were
broken? Hilton's answer:

> In a competitive framework, they (the trucking industry) would be beset
> by rate-cutting railroads . . . and by a vast inflow of independent truck-
> ers, mainly from minority groups, offering basic, cheap service.

An excellent clue to how counterproductive and wasteful the ICC
has become was evident when Congress created both Amtrak and
the U.S. Railroad Administration to take over bankrupt freight and

passenger lines in the northeast and elsewhere. It shouldn't come as any surprise that the Congress didn't want their attempts at running railroads to be under the supervision of the ICC. Not on your life. They knew better, and virtually bypassed the ICC in the day-to-day operations of Amtrak and USRA. Unlike the privately-owned railroads, Amtrak can raise or lower its fares and change its routes at will without ICC approval. The same is generally true for the USRA, where the ICC was given a largely advisory role in its affairs. But Congress still wants the remaining privately-owned railroads to conduct their operations under the ICC's bureaucratic nightmare which our lawmakers insist on continuing. Somehow this incredible double standard escapes most members of Congress.

It is particularly significant that, when the House Interstate Commerce Committee conducted a study of the federal regulatory agencies in 1976 and ranked them according to their effectiveness, "at the bottom" was the ICC. This agency, the committee said, "remains mired in confusion over its appropriate regulatory function." The reason for this may be that, after nearly a century of operation, the ICC no longer has a function to fulfill.

In 1979 President Carter proposed legislation, which had the support of Sen. Edward Kennedy and others in Congress, that would deregulate the ICC. Among other things, the proposal would end restrictions on the types of commodities licensed carriers may haul, stop "backhaul" restrictions, open up interstate licenses and routes to truckers applying for them, remove price-fixing procedures that permit truckers to agree on rates among themselves, and allow truckers within limits to raise and lower rates without prior commission approval.

This is a good step, but it is *not enough*. While the proposal would eradicate some of the worst of ICC's regulatory practices, the rest of its costly and unnecessary machinery, paperwork and rules would remain in place. This in turn would place continued costs and demands upon the transportation industry, and do little to alleviate the problems of the railroad industry, which is in need of drastic deregulation. Government regulation of the transportation industry *has to stop* before there isn't anything left worth regulating—which is virtually what we have confronting us today in the railroad industry.

Perhaps at one time a persuasive case was made in behalf of the government operating the ICC, but that case can no longer be made effectively in the 1980s. A total dismantling of the ICC would allow America's railroads to rehabilitate themselves in a free competitive climate and to compete aggressively and equitably for freight and passenger business. Indeed, the entire transportation industry, with the ICC's passing, could begin to offer the nation cheaper, more efficient, and more productive service.

PROGRAM 70

Office of Small Pox Eradication — $1.2 Million

Small pox disease has been wiped off the face of the earth. Other than a case of small pox reported in the United States in 1963, there hasn't been an outbreak in this country since 1947, when a foreign visitor in New York contracted the disease. Yet the Office of Small Pox Eradication continues to exist within the Center for Disease Control in Atlanta. Its own officials say it should be abolished.

The Office did not actually become an independent unit until 1966. Formerly its functions were located within the Bureau of Epidemology. The 1963 small pox case triggered the establishment of a special small pox unit to make sure that no further outbreaks occurred in the United States.

In 1966 it was decided that a separate office needed to be created to work with the United Nations' World Health Organization and also with the Soviet Union for the worldwide eradication of small pox. The agency worked in West Africa, Sudan, and Indonesia until, by 1976, small pox had been virtually eradicated through vaccinations.

Since that time this agency has been devoting a little more than 5 percent of its time to small pox matters, devoting almost all of its energies to other areas of medical service for the World Health Organization. A large part of what they do now involves studies on nutrition.

Said a top official of the Office, "It does not make sense to continue" the agency, adding that the Office should be reorganized to reflect their nutritional work, or else be totally abolished. According to officials at the Center for Disease Control, the work of this agency, collecting data on nutrition studies, could be easily taken over by the Center for Health Statistics. With so many other life-threatening diseases here and around the world, the resources of this tiny agency, which includes a staff of 51, could be better applied elsewhere.

PROGRAM 71

Advisory Commission on Intergovernmental Relations
— $1.8 Million

The Advisory Commission on Intergovernmental Relations dates back to 1959 during the Eisenhower administration. At that time Congress decided it wanted an agency that would study "points of intergovernmental friction and make recommendations for improving the federal system." This agency has been studying ever since.

The Commission has a staff of 37 employes and an annual budget of $1.8 million, 82 percent of which is spent on salaries and other personnel costs. It also has a 26-member board of advisers made up of representatives from the Executive branch, Congress, the governors, and state and local governments. The Commission's work is broken down into three areas: staff research, policymaking, and implementation of its recommendations.

Most of its work has been in the production of policy reports and studies on federal-state issues and problems. But as its implementation function suggests, a great deal of the Commission's energies have been devoted to lobbying Congress on a wide range of issues through its reports, as well as by more direct methods. The Commission keeps up with legislation on Capitol Hill that impact on local and state governments, and it maintains contact with members of Congress to make sure its positions are known. Those positions usually support continued or increased assistance to the states and localities.

The Commission has conducted studies and adopted recommendations on countercyclical aid, federal compensation to local governments for tax-exempt federal lands, and categorical grant assistance. It has conducted surveys on numerous issues, including one which measured the public's changing attitudes on taxes. The Commission has also proposed reforms that would affect the federal grant system, cigarette bootlegging, crime control, and urban policy. One study completed in late 1979 examined revenue sharing and, predictably, recommended that it be continued. Other studies have included "Trends in Metropolitan America" and "Who Should Pay for Public Schools?"

Most of this work is unnecessary. There are many organizations representing state, local, and county governments, as was pointed out in "Paying the Special Interests," which study these issues and their interrelationships and which make their reports and views known to Congress. Moreover, studies on these issues are often conducted by various agencies within the Executive branch and state governments too. Thus, this is a redundant program that does not fulfill an absolutely vital function for the federal government. The nation could get along quite comfortably without it.

PROGRAM 72
Ethnic Heritage Studies — $2 Million

If anyone needs proof of Congress' inexhaustible ability to think up politically self-indulgent ideas on which to spend the people's money, this program is it. The declared purpose of Ethnic Heritage Studies is to make public school students more aware of their own ethnic heritage as well as the cultural backgrounds and customs of other ethnic groups. The obvious political purpose is to curry favor with ethnic voters back home.

The program, begun in 1974, was located within the U.S. Office of Education's Bureau of School Improvement. It pursues its mission through three functions: curriculum development, training and workshops, and dissemination of materials to educators. The program purportedly furthers ethnic studies through the issuance of— what else?—grants to various public and private nonprofit educational institutions and organizations which operate ethnic studies programs. In 1978 the program awarded more than $2.3 million in grants. In fiscal 1979 it received a budget of $2 million.

An examination of these grants reveals a large number of them are going to colleges and universities for very dubious projects of little or no priority. They include: $39,000 to develop a "Multi-Ethnic Southern Agrarian Heritage—A Model Oral History Curriculum Unit"; $40,000 for a "Heritage of a Plantation Community"; $40,000 for "Appreciation of Ethnic Pluralism in Education for Social Work"; and $22,446 for an "Ozark Ethnic Heritage Studies Project."

This program *makes no sense whatsoever* to anyone who has ever attended a Polish festival in Detroit, an Italian fair in Boston, a German picnic and dance in Milwaukee, a Greek Orthodox church bazaar and food sale in Philadelphia, a Chicano social gathering in Los Angeles, a Mexican fiesta in the southwest, an Indian tribal ceremony in Arizona, a Lithuanian bake sale in Cleveland, or an Albanian wedding in Worcester. We may indeed be a "melting pot," as our schools have taught us, but America is still very heterogeneous in terms of our cultural and ethnic roots, which are still very much alive in this country. And these ethnic traditions are made manifest in countless ways in our schools, churches, neighborhoods, restaurants, as well as through thousands of social, civic, business, and ethnic organizations throughout the nation. This is what makes this program not just superfluous, but disgustingly paternalistic. America's ethnic heritage does not need to be promoted by the federal government.

PROGRAM 73

International Development Association — $1 Billion

How would you like to borrow $1 billion and have 50 years to pay it back interest-free, with a 10-year grace period to boot?

No, these are not the terms of a loan shark organization. They are the conditions under which the World Bank's International Development Association (IDA) has been giving billions of dollars to underdeveloped nations around the world. IDA's only charge to the foreign governments who borrow this money is a three-fourths of one percent charge on the disbursed portion of each loan to cover administrative costs. As they say, it is an offer that you can't refuse.

IDA's funds are provided primarily by 21 major contributing member countries. By far the biggest contributor is the United States, whose annual contribution to IDA's fund has ranged as high as 40 percent.

In 1974 the U.S. pledged $1.5 billion to IDA, planning to spread the payments out over four annual installments of $375 million each from 1976 through 1979. Prior to this, the United States had contributed over $2 billion to IDA. But there were those in Congress who were sharply critical of the way IDA had been using its money. Rep. Clarence Long of Maryland echoed the complaints of his colleagues when he said, "What has disillusioned most of us is the fact that the money has not gone to these poor people." So when the 1974 authorization for IDA's money came to the House floor it was resoundingly rejected, only to be brought back by its sponsors six months later with a sweetener provision attached that allowed Americans to own gold. That was enough to "buy" the requisite number of votes to get it passed.

Since then, Congress has been grudgingly providing the money IDA was promised—nearly $1.3 billion in fiscal 1979 and more than $1 billion in fiscal 1980. These larger amounts were needed to catch up to authorized levels because in previous years Congress had cut appropriations to the World Bank's lending institutions as criticism over this form of foreign aid heightened. IDA is one of six international financial lending institutions being supported by the United States taxpayer. In addition to IDA, created in 1960, there are the World Bank's International Bank for Reconstruction and Development and the International Finance Corporation, plus the Asian Development Bank, the Inter-American Development Bank, and the

302

African Development Fund. Congress appropriated a total of $2.5 billion to these international financial institutions (IFIs) in fiscal 1979, and another $2.7 billion in fiscal 1980 which was part of a foreign assistance package totaling nearly $8 billion.

For a long time IDA's critics have been questioning whether its loans have truly helped the world's poor, or whether the money has instead been helping wealthy landowners, big industrialists, and foreign governments and their banks who have *lent the money out* to other borrowers, and sometimes even other countries, at substantial interest rates, while the poor died in the streets of their cities.

"The problem is, the money is being wasted," declared Rep. C. W. (Bill) Young of Florida. Most of the money "is not being used to accomplish the objective" of helping the world's poor.

Young expressed the feelings of many members of Congress who had read a revealing House report on the activities and management of the World Bank's lending institutions and affiliates which had been prepared by the House Appropriations Committee's investigative staff. The investigators had conducted a 13-month study of the IFIs and issued what members called a "devastating" indictment of their lending practices. Among its charges, the committee found that loan projects being supported were extravagantly overdesigned and badly supervised, that financial auditing of loans was virtually nonexistent, and that the IFIs *were pushing the money* on recipients, who sometimes did not want it.

The investigators said they were told during field visits by project managers and local government officials that there were

> . . . higher levels of funding of certain [building] projects than were deemed necessary, as well as of more elaborate designs than were really needed.

As an example, the report said a community center and swimming pool-gymnasium complex built in a Latin American country with the help of a $44 million International Development Bank urban development loan was more elaborate than anything that might be found "in affluent communities of developed countries."

Another project in an Asian country, funded by a $13 million IDA loan, included a building to house administrative staff for a family-planning program. The project included, the report said,

> . . . excessive amounts for hardware and brick and mortar construction rather than concentration upon the human element necessary in reaching the rural poor in remote sections of the country.

Other projects, the report said, were "likewise overdesigned to con-
form to local traditions." Photographs showed buildings, built to
local government demands, which contained elaborate decorations
and exterior sculpture and design that did not appear to represent a
wise expenditure of money by an impoverished nation.

The report also suggested that many corrupt government officials
and businessmen in recipient countries may be getting rich on these
interest-free loans. The investigators said they were told by a bank
official in one banana republic that

> . . . corruption is rampant throughout the country and could well exist
> in IFI projects. A problem his bank encountered in the sublending is the
> use of loan proceeds for purposes other than intended. *He also advised*
> *that the ruling members of the co-operative operating the banana plan-*
> *tation and probably the governmental officials overseeing the operation*
> *will enrich themselves from the profits with the ordinary workers not*
> *really benefiting from the profits. With the poor growing poorer and IFI*
> *lending never really reaching them, he believes the country is trending*
> *toward revolution.*

The report also quoted one former IFI official who said:

> A lot of money is being spent on new-style projects but there exists no
> real proof that the poorest of the poor are being reached or that the
> long-range goals are being achieved.

The investigators also criticized the IFIs for sloppy oversight of
loan projects, pointing out that, because there has been inadequate
auditing, program officials do not know if there has been overpricing,
skimming of funds, overbuying, nondelivery of materials, and other
irregularities or abuses. "One (World) Bank official commented that
if a project is all or mainly local costs, there is really no way for the
Bank to control or guard satisfactorily against corruption."

What the investigators found out about the IFIs' financial controls
was shocking. There has in fact been no auditing that expressly
looked for corruption or financial irregularities. "The internal auditors do not review the books and records of borrowers and do not
function as a detached central point for investigating alleged
irregularities."

The investigators also accused the banks of making more money
available to these countries than they have been able to usefully
absorb. This in turn has led to the misuse of funds and lack of coordination. This is why the IFIs have made more loan commitments
than they have been able to disburse to the recipient countries. By
1979 the IFIs had cumulatively made $59 billion in loan commit-

ments, but had only disbursed $34.5 billion or 58 percent of that amount.

In minority views attached to the House Appropriations Committee's report accompanying the fiscal 1980 foreign aid funding bill, Reps. Young of Florida, Virginia Smith of Nebraska, and Jack Kemp of New York also noted that the IFIs "are literally pushing projects on countries, with the result that this effort is straining the absorptive capacities of various developing countries." Indeed, the House report supported this contention when it observed:

> Present and former staff members and officials of the IFIs have decried the pressure upon staff to meet annual lending targets with emphasis upon quantity of commitments made annually rather than upon assurance of quality projects.

The three lawmakers also pointed out that an earlier World Bank study had shown that a large number of projects "should not have been presented for approval, as they were not really ready for implementation." This, they noted, backed up the investigators' findings concerning "the rush to commit funds to meet targeted goals before the fiscal year expired."

But by far the strongest criticism leveled at IDA and the other IFIs concerned their dismal record on human rights.

In 1978 IDA approved a $60 million interest-free loan to Vietnam to construct several water projects, completely ignoring Vietnam's military involvement in neighboring Laos and Cambodia and the inhuman treatment of Vietnam refugees who have fled their country to escape its brutally repressive regime. By late 1979, IDA was considering granting six additional loans to Vietnam totaling hundreds of millions of dollars, completely oblivious to that country's forced labor camps, the beatings and torture of its political prisoners, and the plight of the refugee "boat people."

Other human rights violators receiving IDA loans include the Central African Republic, once ruled by the Emperor Bokassa who, among other atrocities, had a group of school children killed because they would not wear the prescribed school uniform. Bokassa earned further notoriety when he spent $20 million on his coronation. Nonetheless, IDA approved a $2.5 million loan to his country.

Is it any wonder, then, that the National Law Center of George Washington University said in an analysis* that lending institutions like IDA

*"World Bank's Power to Consider Human Rights Factors in Loan Decisions."

... seem to be virtually oblivious to global human rights concerns; indeed, there is mounting evidence that their financing operations in some countries undercut the effectiveness of humanitarian pressures for reform.

The Center went on to say that

... by extending loans to human rights violators, the World Bank is providing direct financial assistance to repressive governments and, at the same time, is facilitating their access to more sizable amounts of private capital. Consequently, it is assisting these governments to withstand international economic pressures from other countries and public interest concerns designed to weaken such governments' economic viability and compel them to implement human rights reforms.

One also wonders whether these loans are giving many countries the freedom to divert more of their financial resources into other less desirable programs. For example, at least 40 percent of IDA's loans have gone to India—which, somehow, found the financial resources to develop and explode a nuclear bomb, but apparently doesn't have enough money to feed her own people. Bangladesh, one of the world's most impoverished countries, received a $20 million loan from IDA to build a telecommunications program which included development of microwave, UHF, and VHF systems, regardless of the fact that it has been the victim of widespread famine.

Meanwhile, as noted earlier, recipient countries are taking these loans and sublending the money to their citizens at high rates of interest. The House investigators pointed to one instance in which money was loaned by the IDA to an Asian country for a $28 million dairy project. Interestingly enough, the Asian government official said his country did not wish to have IFI participation in the project "but consented reluctantly because of the need for foreign exchange." In the end, the money was sublent by the local government bank to farmer cooperatives at 11 percent interest, which the government official conceded was "excessive."

Other IDA loans suggest that many of them are not being directed toward the poor but instead are being focused on developing *plantation industries* which profit at the expense of the poor, who are paid "slave labor" wages. For example, a $21 million IDA loan to Sri Lanka went for replanting a high-yielding tea plant which, the World Bank's annual report noted, would result in "a better quality of tea." About 25,000 "estate labor families will benefit from improved housing, water, and health services," the Bank added. It said nothing about whether the money would help the poor to become less poor.

In several poor countries visited by the House investigators, they found there were no development projects designed to reach the rural poor who are without land and living on little income. Among those who have benefited, however, were "relatively prosperous ranchers with well-managed farms" who had increased beef or dairy production markedly through the loans under the projects.

There is also the irony that many of these loans are being used to rebuild railroads and construct power plants, both of which the United States desperately needs.

Also, a great deal of this money is going to pay inflated salaries of World Bank employes who run IDA. More than one-fourth of the Bank's administrative budget is consumed by fringe benefits for employes, 95 percent of whom work in Washington, D.C. At least 40 percent of the Bank employes are paid as much as 57 percent more than U.S. civil servants in similar jobs. Moreover, even though they work and live within the United States, the Bank's foreign employes pay no U.S. income tax. American employes are of course required to pay income tax but are compensated by the Bank for the tax they pay. House investigators discovered that almost 50 percent of the employes who were eligible for this tax reimbursement were in fact given payments in excess of the taxes they had paid. The average overpayment was more than $2,300.

Yet perhaps the strongest argument of all against IDA is that we cannot afford it. Since foreign assistance programs began we have given away $266 billion to various nations of the world. Now, however, we are in severe debt and are even borrowing money from the very countries we gave aid to after World War II. We have to ask ourselves whether it is wise and prudent to be borrowing money at interest rates of up to 10 percent or more in order to loan it out to other nations interest-free.

Canceling U.S. participation in this program would not exactly turn Uncle Sam into Uncle Scrooge. There would still be the World Bank and five other lending institutions which can continue to provide loans to the poorest nations of the world—although the arguments in favor of ending our support of these other IFIs are equally as impressive. Without them the U.S. would still be doling out more than $5.5 billion a year in foreign aid.

In their minority views, Reps. Young, Smith, and Kemp said,

It is our belief that the time has arrived for the United States to substantially reduce the level of financial support for these institutions. The need for development assistance is great throughout the world and the

United States will continue to provide its fair share of this assistance; however, there are a number of other programs which more effectively reach the needs of the poorest of the poor than those of the IFIs.

The criticisms against IDA specifically are so overwhelming, the evidence of its reckless and irresponsible use of our tax dollars so widespread, that this one banking agency alone virtually *begs* to be abolished.

PROGRAM 74
Community Services Administration — $668 Million

In the summer of 1979 a group of black employes from the Community Services Administration, the government's antipoverty agency, asked to meet with me to talk about CSA and its programs. As soon as our meeting began it became apparent that their request had been made out of a feeling of frustration and anger. Frustration that, despite billions of dollars spent on this agency, the plight of the poor had not appreciably improved. Anger that millions of dollars were being wasted each year on programs and projects that did not in any way touch the lives of the poor.

The CSA workers came armed with memorandums and other documents containing lists of contracts to various companies, contractors, consultants, researchers, colleges and universities, and other institutions and groups who make their living off the government's poverty programs. The CSA officials were personally proud of the work they had done within the agency and the job achievement level they had reached after many years. They were earning above-average salaries. They were intelligent and articulate about what was on their minds.

"We are concerned," one of them began, "that the poor aren't getting helped by this money. Look at these contracts. It's these firms who are getting the grants and contracts. They are benefiting from this money. This isn't helping the poor."

Said another CSA employe:

> The whole emphasis on helping the poor is no longer there. Poor people aren't being helped by giving money to buy study after study that will end up on some shelf somewhere. The poor don't need studies. They need jobs. They need income to take care of their families. You don't need a study to understand that.

Picking out one document from the pile on the table before us, another said:

> Look at this one. This outfit received a $360,000 contract to train CSA employes in human rights activities. They trained less than 30 employes and the entire program lasted four days. How could they spend $360,000 to train less than 30 people?

I glanced over the list of CSA contracts for fiscal 1979. It included $901,219 to Mariscal & Co. to provide technical assistance to CSA's Community Development Corporations; $47,304 to the Southwest Program Development Corporation to provide "administrative and management support services"; $104,306 to Mitchell Watkins & Co. for "evaluation of grantees"; $49,460 to a contractor called Solar American for "research on the solar-heated greenhouse industry"; $5,000 to Voice & Vision for a "16 mm. Show"; $18,663 to the Latin American Center to "conduct a symposium and issue a report"; $50,038 to Black Enterprise Magazine for "three ads on CSA's Community Development Corporations"; $167,190 to Louis Berger & Associates for an evaluation of the "National Demonstration Water Projects"; $27,401 to City University of New York for an 18-month assessment of the Comprehensive Employment and Training Act (CETA) program; and $22,270 to Development Associates, Inc. for a verbatim recording and transcript of some town meetings.

There were many more on the contract list but I'll stop here since this kind of spending by CSA was extensively covered in Chapter IX on "The Poverty Business." All of the contracts, however, reflected the same frivolous, vague, directionless spending practices evident in CSA's previous years' activities. There were the same studies on energy, despite an entire Department of Energy doing work in this area. There were contracts to perform administrative and evaluative work for CSA despite the poverty agency's more than 1000 employes and budget of nearly three-fourths of a billion dollars. And there were numerous contracts to many of the same old familiar firms for things like evaluation and "T/A", which stands for technical assistance. CSA buys a lot of evaluation and technical assistance.

The CSA employes told me their agency had become "a dumping ground" for political appointees, that the agency had suffered as a result, that morale there was "very low," and that many employes, like them, now believed that CSA had "lost its way."

Shortly after I had written a lengthy article examining the Community Services Administration and its so-called antipoverty activities and programs, I received a phone call from a Carter administration official who worked in the president's reorganization task force. He asked if I would meet with a group of task force staffers to discuss my impressions and findings on CSA's work. Although my investigation was rather limited compared to their comprehensive examination of the agency, I told them I had found widespread duplication within antipoverty programs, substantial waste on projects that did nothing to elevate the poor, low-priority studies that had no relevance to the needs of the poor, and a program that no longer fulfilled an important need. To my surprise, the reorganization staffers told me they had essentially reached the same conclusions. Moreover, they agreed that the entire agency should be dismantled, with some of its component functions handled by other existing departments and agencies.

Unfortunately, they also told me they could not propose this to the White House because of what they termed the "political realities" involved. Politically, they said, CSA had become a symbol for leaders of minority groups and other political special interests whose support the president needed for reelection. Thus, no matter how bad the program was, there was no way Carter could even consider any suggestion to get rid of it. The discussion ended with a general meeting of minds—that a bad program was wasting the taxes of both rich and poor alike.

I do not think it is necessary to belabor this agency any further than has been done here and in the first half of this book. The Community Services Administration and its regional offices around the country should be eliminated. The wasteful consultant contracts, the vacuous studies, the self-promotional literature, the costly symposiums and workshops, the movie-making, the rank paternalism about poor people—all of it should cease. Except for the program's employes, a number of white-collar consulting companies, a few academic researchers, and several special interest groups, no one will notice its disappearance in Washington.

However, there is no reason why many of the more than 800 local Community Action Programs (CAPs), which CSA supports, cannot continue to survive on their own, perhaps through increased state and local government aid or through the availability of federal contracts and grants to continue specific worthwhile antipoverty projects of their own. Some local community action programs are effective and resourceful, and these no doubt would continue to survive and work in behalf of the poor. Many others, however, are wasteful and even corrupt and should have been folded long ago. They no doubt would perish.

Whatever happens to the local programs, however, the umbrella agency in Washington has proven itself to be far removed from the everyday problems of the poor, as the above programs and projects so painfully make evident.

PROGRAM 75

National Highway Traffic Safety Administration —
$198 Million

The rising human carnage on our nation's highways over the years is the most conclusive evidence one needs to prove this agency has failed to make highway traffic significantly safer.

Between 1967—when this agency began—and 1973, annual highway traffic deaths rose from 52,924 to 55,800. The National Highway Traffic Safety Administration began with an $11.3 million budget. By fiscal 1975 its spending skyrocketed to $170.9 million a year. Yet even though its 1975 budget had grown more than 15 times, the death rate kept climbing at a hideous pace.

Then, in January of 1974, an interesting thing happened. Congress temporarily enacted one simple law that brought about a drastic decrease in highway fatalities. It ordered a national speed limit of 55 miles per hour. (Ironically, the new speed limit was initiated not to save lives but to conserve fuel, which had been in short supply due to the Arab oil embargo.) The National Safety Council said highway deaths that year dropped by an astounding 9,600 lives.*

In other words, all of the millions of tax dollars spent by the government on automotive studies, research, and testing had failed to curb the spiraling death toll. Yet a simple act of Congress that required no costly appropriation or additional bureaucracy had achieved what the National Highway Traffic Safety Administration, with all its millions, could not.

NHTSA Administrator James Gregory declared at the time:

We've found continuously over the last few months since it (the 55 mph limit) has been in effect that we have gotten very close to consistent 20 percent reduction in fatalities on the highway.

Gregory said there were other reasons for the reduced fatalities, including less driving due to the fuel shortage. But the reduction in speed, or what happens when people go at a lower speed, is "the big factor" in reducing fatalities, he said. By September of 1974, both houses of Congress had voted overwhelmingly to make the 55-mile-per-hour speed permanent. The Senate Public Works Committee said the limit had produced "the single most effective improvement in highway safety in recent years."

*According to the Council's statistics, 55,800 people died in 1973 in auto accidents. In 1974, with the 55 mph limit, there were 46,200 deaths.

312

But the effect of the 55 mph limit lasted only so long. States became lax in enforcing it. People began to drive faster as fuel supplies increased. And the death rate began once again to climb.

True, there was a slight continuation of the decline in 1975 when traffic fatalities fell to 44,525 (they hadn't been that low since the early 1960s), but then the increase began again. In 1976 the number of automobile fatalities rose to 45,509. In 1977 they reached 49,510. In 1978 the number increased to 51,500. And by the fall of 1979 the death rate was headed toward a full 2 percent increase over the 1978 total.

All of the foregoing must be weighed against this agency's ongoing programs and costs. For while the death rate on our roads has continued to climb in recent years, so has NHTSA's budget, and by dramatic margins too. By fiscal 1978 the agency was spending nearly $144 million a year. By fiscal 1979 its budget had jumped by an incredible $54 million to almost $200 million a year. The question that must be asked is, What has all the billions of dollars spent on this agency bought, in terms of improved highway safety? The figures appear to say that *it has bought us nothing*. In the last decade, the only really effective initiative to reduce traffic fatalities and accidents has been the 55 mph limit—which this agency had nothing to do with.

Eventually, we must be so bold as to ask whether this agency is worth the money we are pouring into it. This question was touched upon by Joan Claybrook, administrator of the NHTSA, who told the House Appropriations Committee:

> I feel if we do not have improvement to measure the work we do, there is no way we can ever properly evaluate whether these expenditures of funds make a difference.

All the hundreds of millions of dollars this agency has spent on research and development to try to make the automobile accident-proof seems to fly in the face of one impregnable fact that we seem to want to avoid: namely, that *people*, not automobiles, cause accidents. And, by and large, safer drivers are not going to be produced in Washington. They can be trained and encouraged only by a diversity of innovative and highly imaginative programs carried out by the 50 states and their communities and schools.

We can develop the safest car in the world, at enormous costs to taxpayers and consumers, but I doubt very much whether, in the end, it will reduce traffic fatalities. Speed causes accidents and traffic deaths, and elaborate research and development and study by this agency isn't going to do very much to change that.

While it is true that safer cars can help somewhat to cut fatalities and injuries, that is something that the automobile industry can be encouraged to do, I think, without the involvement of direct federal spending—something which I will discuss later in this chapter.

Meanwhile, it is time for Congress to think through some new approaches to the problem of traffic safety. We have to begin asking ourselves, Are we spending hundreds of millions of tax dollars effectively and wisely on this problem? Or are we throwing money away?

Admittedly, as recent legislative history shows, Congress has not exactly been enthused over NHTSA's efforts to outfit cars with passive restraint systems.

The ignition interlock-seat belts, which had to be hooked up before an automobile could be started, were made mandatory in the 1974 car models. They were, however, an instant bomb that had motorists pulling their hair. At the same time the air bags, which balloon out of the dashboard at the instant of impact, were to be required in the 1977 model cars. But the House in August of 1974 voted 339-49 to prohibit the Transportation Department, which funds the NHTSA, from making either the interlock-belt system or the air bag mandatory. Instead, the House approved a bill that would have made either of them optional, beginning with the 1977 model cars. The Senate also voted overwhelmingly to kill the interlock-seat belt, but not the air bag. Compromise legislation was later worked out between the House and Senate in October of 1974 which banned the interlock scheme, but gave the Secretary of Transportation authority to order installation of the air bag unless vetoed by Congress within 60 days.

After many delays and much experimentation, the air bag or some other type of passive restraint system was to be required in all automobiles built after September 1, 1983. Still, the air bag has come under considerable criticism in recent years.

NHTSA claims the air bag can save thousands of lives each year. Others, however, including the American Automobile Association, have in the past argued that the air bags would cost consumers 100 percent more than they would return in safety benefits. An AAA study* showed that, when used either alone or with safety belts, the

*Directed by Dr. Lawrence A. Goldmuntz, former assistant director for civil technology in the White House Office of Science and Technology and onetime executive director of the Federal Council of Science and Technology.

benefits of the bags could never justify the additional cost to motorists. General Motors estimates that the bags could add between $200 and $400 to the cost of a new car.

The AAA study said there was "no evidence" to show that the air bags approach "the known lifesaving capabilities of properly worn belt-harness systems." Moreover, it found that the air bag was primarily effective in frontal crashes, but only marginally effective in side impacts, rollovers, or rear-end and multiple crashes. The AAA study also emphasized that no individual using an American harness was known to have been killed in a crash, other than a collision where the passenger compartment of the vehicle itself was crushed or invaded by some outside object. "In these cases no restraint system would have spared the occupant," the study said.

More recently, the General Accounting Office concluded, in a study it made, that the air bag may be *particularly useless in protecting passengers* in automobiles, particularly small children.

In a 1979 report that was sharply critical of the NHTSA's testing procedures, the GAO said tests had not shown that the air bags would provide the degree of protection expected, nor that they would be worth the costs.

"Results of these (NHTSA) tests support the conclusion that air bags offer potential to save lives and prevent injuries in frontal collisions," the GAO said. "However, the conclusion as to the extent of these benefits . . . was based largely on subjective judgment." The GAO called the agency's air bag tests "a simplified and limited simulation of real crash conditions."

Air bags notwithstanding, this agency is involved in many other programs that deserve further scrutiny. These programs fall within four major areas: traffic and motor vehicle safety programs, highway safety research and development activities, automotive fuel economy and consumer information, and state and community highway safety programs.

The agency's research and development activities have expended vast sums over the years to crash automobiles together to test bumper construction, tires, and other equipment. Millions of dollars have also been spent to study pedestrian and bicycle safety, among other things, as well as to run a mass-media safety campaign, although the agency hasn't the slightest idea whether or not it has been effective.

The agency's state and community highway safety programs essentially provide grants to the states and localities to help finance driver licensing, motor vehicle registration, traffic record-keeping, police traffic services, driver education, automobile inspection, and other state and local vehicle programs. In other words, this represents nothing more than subsidizing the states for programs they have to operate anyway.

Money spent on automotive fuel economy has nothing to do with safety, and duplicates similar activities by the Department of Energy and the Environmental Protection Agency. Nonetheless, the NHTSA spent $788,000 to study consumer behavior towards fuel-efficient vehicles, among other studies in this area.

In perhaps one of its most ridiculous expenditures, the NHTSA spent $120,126 in 1978 to build a low-slung, backward-steering motorcycle that couldn't be ridden. The contract was issued to a California firm to design and test a motorcycle with a low center of gravity that was powered by the front wheel and steered by the back wheel. Agency officials actually believed the design would make the motorcycle safer. Tests showed, however, that the backward motor- cycle was almost impossible to steer. The agency eventually gave up on the costly project but not before they had tried several times to get the contractor to make the concept work.

The bulk of NHTSA's spending can be reduced to two major cat- egories: research and development, and grants to the states. As far as its research programs are concerned, the rising highway death toll over the years speaks for itself. Work on stronger bumpers, improve- ments in windshield glass, the collapsible steering wheel, steel beam guards, and all the rest have not turned the death rate around.

Moreover, while some of these improvements may be fine in and of themselves, it should be pointed out that all of them were devel- oped by automobile manufacturers using federal money. Thus, there is no reason why this type of research and development can't con- tinue but without direct federal spending. Simply provide the auto- motive industry with tax incentives to invest more of its working capital into developing a safer automobile, one that can withstand a greater impact without injury to the occupants. Such incentives might allow a percentage to be deducted from a corporation's tax- able income if a certain portion of its profits were reinvested in R&D safety programs.

As far as the agency's grants to the states are concerned, it seems to me that all federal highway safety aid should be keyed to an incentive formula benefiting those states who reduce highway fatal- ities, with each state receiving a bare minimum to begin with. This approach was used to a limited extent by NHTSA which provided incentive grants to states that had significantly reduced their highway fatality rate.

Such an incentive program should be run completely out of the Federal Highway Administration's budget, which is spending too much money on unnecessary highway construction anyway. Its total trust fund outlays were estimated to exceed $7 billion in fiscal 1980. Since the Federal Highway Administration has been given responsibility for improving state and local highway safety programs through matching grants to the states, there is no reason that a larger portion of its mammoth budget could not be diverted into all state safety programs in lieu of NHTSA's grants. Indeed, what could be more relevant to building highways than the lives lost on them?

Meanwhile, the states, knowing they would have to crack down on speeders and implement tougher traffic programs, or else lose their funds, would no doubt be highly motivated to cut their fatalities. Those states cutting their death toll by a sufficiently significant percentage could be rewarded with special bonus grants.

Other innovations should include mandating that the speed capacity of all new automobiles be restricted to no more than 70 miles per hour. I've never understood why automobiles have to be built to go over 100 miles an hour anyway. Cutting engine capacity on all new and imported cars would sharply reduce speeders over the years and no doubt significantly reduce fatalities on our roads, not to mention what it would do to insurance premiums.

The point is that we need to encourage a multiplicity of approaches to the problem of highway fatalities. We need to reject the stultifying uniformity of ideas that almost always comes out of major federal programs which are never held accountable for their lack of tangible progress or improvement in tackling a problem. In short, this $200 million a year agency, with over 900 federal employes, should have its license taken away for good.

PROGRAMS 76–78

Occupational Safety and Health Administration
National Institute for Occupational Safety and Health
Occupational Safety and Health Review Commission
TOTAL — *$169 Million*

It would be difficult to find another agency in the government that has become as intensely disliked by our business community as OSHA has over the years. Even President Carter has said, "There kind of rises something up in me to resist it and not cooperate with it."

It would also be hard to find another agency that has been the brunt of more surveys and studies which have almost uniformly shown that its efforts have had little if any effect upon reducing work-related accidents.

OSHA was discussed at length in Chapter XV (OSHA:Washington's Most Hated Agency), but there are a few more facts and observations that should be made.

OSHA has drawn up more than 4,000 federal rules and regulations which an army of 1,400 government inspectors arbitrarily inflict upon the nation's businesses, large and small, during more than 100,000 inspections a year. This costs business, and ultimately the American consumer, well over $3 billion a year. Yet despite all this, there is no evidence that worker safety has improved.

Charles L. Schultze, chairman of the Council of Economic advisers under President Carter, has said, "OSHA cannot touch the most important cause of industrial accidents" (employe turnover and inexperience) because it

> . . . neglects these aspects of the problem in favor of a futile attempt to define and enforce those kinds of concrete safety measures that the market can handle much more effectively.

It should also be pointed out that fatality figures in industry had been falling for over three decades before OSHA came on the scene. The rate plunged from 43 deaths per 100,000 workers in 1937 to 17 per 100,000 in 1970. The rate fell even further by 1975, down to 15 per 100,000.

One of the chief reasons OSHA has had no significant impact upon industrial safety is that the great majority of accidents (perhaps as high as 75 to 80 percent) have been the result of worker carelessness and inexperience—something that a 10-fold increase in

OSHA inspectors could not do anything about. Only a greater safety effort and awareness by businessmen and their employes can reduce careless accidents.

In a study for the American Enterprise Institute, Robert Stewart Smith of Cornell University concluded:

> Given the limited potential of a perfectly enforced set of standards and the likelihood that inspectors discover only the most obvious violations, it is perhaps not surprising that the estimated effects on injuries are so small that they cannot be distinguished from zero.

In another AEI study James Robert Chelius of Purdue University examined the injury frequency rate per million manhours in recent decades. Chelius found the index dropped from 17 in 1948 to 11 in 1957. It was only until the 1960s, though, that the rate began to turn upward, jumping to 15 in 1970 which in turn fed the movement to create OSHA.

Chelius argued, however, that the upward trend in the 1960s was based chiefly on the increased number of younger workers in the labor force, the result of the post-World War II baby boom and economic expansion. Inexperienced workers, it has been shown, are the most injury prone in our workforce. Chelius said that once all of these variables were factored in, "it is quite clear that no new problems developed during this period" (when the rate climbed).

It is not surprising, then, that Charles Schultze, as a member of a presidential task force to study OSHA, concluded along with his colleagues in an internal memorandum that OSHA's workplace inspection function should be dismantled. In its place, the memorandum suggested, should be a system of tax incentives and other programs to encourage and promote better worker safety by businesses and labor unions.

This proposal was a sound one and deserves to be resurrected.

I would abolish OSHA's occupational safety program, including its Occupational Safety and Health Review Commission to which aggrieved businesses can appeal. However, I would continue OSHA's worker health responsibilities by merging this part of the agency into the Environmental Protection Agency where it belongs.

In recent years we have seen work-related health catastrophes such as the poisoning of chemical plant workers in the Kepone disaster on Virginia's James River and other tragic cases in which workers have unknowingly ingested or otherwise been exposed to injurious and carcinogenic substances over their working lives at plants and other industrial facilities. This is definitely an area in which the government must play a more expanded role and where it can prevent health-related tragedies from occurring. EPA should be as concerned with substances and pollutants that may be poisoning workers in their workplace as they are with what those same chemicals and emissions may be doing to the environment outside the workplace. As part of this effort I would require EPA to absorb that portion of OSHA's research arm, the National Institute for Occupational Safety and Health, that is concerned with such matters. The rest of OSHA, however, should be abolished.

PROGRAM 79

National Board for the Promotion of Rifle Practice —
$704,000

The National Board for the Promotion of Rifle Practice trains civilians to shoot small caliber military weapons so that in the event of war these gun enthusiasts will be prepared to defend the homeland against enemy invaders. To a large degree, however, it is really a program that provides many happy hours of pleasure for people who just like to go out on a range and shoot.

It is hard to imagine why the government is financing this kind of activity, particularly in time of peace, but it has been doing so since 1903. That was the year when Elihu Root, the Secretary of War, first organized the board. Back then, perhaps, there was a demonstrated need for this kind of government activity—after all, it was a product of the *Department of War*. Today, there is no excuse for the taxpayers financing this type of program.

The Carter administration, to its credit, sought to abolish the board in fiscal 1980, but Congress resisted this effort as it has previous efforts to terminate the agency. In fiscal 1979 Congress provided the board with $375,000 in operating funds which is the only figure usually used to identify its cost. But an additional $329,000 is also appropriated annually for ammunition. Thirty-eight million rounds were given out in 1978 in addition to rifles which are loaned to participating members.

Ignoring Carter's suggestion, Congress approved a total fiscal 1980 budget of $704,000.

Run by the Department of the Army, the board's 14 employes are supervised by an Army colonel who serves as executive director. Among its many activities, the board organizes civilian rifle clubs, arms them, holds national matches each year for military and civilian participants, and gives out trophies, medals, arm patches, and certificates to the best marksmen.

The Defense Department's Civilian Marksmanship Program is nothing more than a subsidy to the National Rifle Association because all participants must be NRA members. About 130,000 persons took part in the program in 1978 through 2,000 affiliated clubs. Many of them were teenage members of the Boy Scouts, YMCAs, police boys clubs, and DeMolay.

Proponents say the program is necessary to interest young men in military service, but this is a rather dubious argument because the Defense Department itself selected the board for termination when it conducted its own zero-based budget review. According to a fact sheet provided by the Office of Management and Budget:

> This activity, while desirable, was not considered to be of high priority or directly related to the combat readiness of our armed forces. The action was taken by the Secretary of Defense during his internal review of the 1980 budget.

Teaching civilians how to shoot, holding national marksmanship contests, and giving out trophies and medals is not something in which our Defense Department should be engaged. Sen. Edward Kennedy has correctly stated that

> . . . federal support of civilian rifle practice is an obsolete anachronism that cannot be justified in our modern society. If there is anything that our enormous military training system has mastered—it has mastered the technique for teaching raw recruits how to shoot. The visible and obvious result of these Pentagon-sponsored shooting matches is to provide a federal subsidy for people who derive recreation, enjoyment and personal satisfaction from the use of firearms.

In other words, this is a program that should be *taken out and shot*.

PROGRAM 80

Small Business Administration — $1.5 Billion

The federal government is littered with costly and ambitious programs and agencies from which only a relatively small number of persons actually benefit. The Small Business Administration is a perfect example of this. Despite the impression conveyed by Congress that tens of billions of dollars in direct loans, loan guarantees, and matching loans are helping the small business community, only a minute number of the nation's small businesses—less than 1 percent—has been helped by this agency.

The SBA has had a long history of fraud, abuse, and waste. Numerous congressional investigations have uncovered widespread mismanagement and political favoritism in the distribution of SBA assistance.

Within the past five years some of SBA's staunchest defenders have been hardpressed to give the agency even passing grades. In 1974 the late Wright Patman of Texas, chairman of the House Banking Committee, said:

> My misgivings over the present and future condition of the Small Business Administration program have given rise to the question of whether the Small Business Administration itself should be abolished. Certainly its continued existence without extensive reform cannot be condoned.

Patman had just finished reading the committee's oversight report on SBA which, he said,

> . . . revealed the existence of self-dealing, favored treatment and shaky if not fraudulent loan practices existing in a number of SBA offices around the country.

The SBA "horror stories" uncovered by the committee and a team of investigators, Patman said, makes it "painfully clear the loan guarantees provide an easy path for corrupt agency officials and irresponsible bankers to waste the resources of the SBA program" on unqualified borrowers at the expense of the taxpayers.

Nonetheless, that year, as in subsequent years, Congress voted to continue the program, hoping that SBA could be patched up and glossed over just enough to keep most taxpayers from knowing what was going on. One Democratic committee member, Frank Annunzio of Illinois, said he voted to report the legislation (extending SBA's authority) out of committee, "not because of the SBA but in spite of it."

In 1974, Congress approved legislation raising SBA's $6 billion lending ceiling to $7.3 billion. Total outlays in fiscal 1975 for salaries, operations, and loans, were set at $444 million. However, by fiscal 1979, SBA, with 4,600 bureaucrats on its payroll, had an annual budget outlay of $1.5 billion. Salaries and other administrative costs were running $200 million a year. SBA's outstanding loan guarantees were over $8.7 billion.

Created by Congress in 1953, SBA's fundamental purpose is to aid and assist the interests of small businesses. Congress expanded that simple goal in recent years with vast loan and loan-guarantee programs to help minority-owned businesses, small government contractors, small business investment companies, and other entrepreneurs, including disaster assistance loans. There are three basic types of loans made by SBA: subsidized bank loans, which are guaranteed by SBA; matching loans, in which both the bank and SBA divide the loan; and direct low-interest loans.

In recent years there has been a great deal of criticism over abuses and mismanagement within SBA's minority assistance programs which I will touch upon in a moment. But let us first examine some of the worst abuses that were brought to light by the House Small Business subcommittee in 1973* which led to further Justice Department investigations and, eventually, prosecutions. What the subcommittee's investigation revealed, among other things, was that SBA regional offices had approved loans and loan guarantees on the basis of favoritism and White House pressure, and that frequently SBA assistance went, not to small struggling businesses, but to large firms and to the rich.

One example involved a former football player who had served as co-chairman of Athletes for Nixon in 1968 and 1972. He obtained SBA approval for guaranteed bank loans totaling $250,000 for his Portsmouth, Virginia, construction firm, even though he had often written bad company checks and had defaulted on building contracts. After the bank refused to make the loans, despite the guarantees, the contractor was given a guaranteed line of credit by SBA in the amount of $110,000 with another bank. Defaulting on his payments again, the contractor was refused any additional money by the banker because, in the latter's words, it would be "pouring money down a rathole."

*Oversight Investigation of the Small Business Administration. Hearings before the Subcommittee on Small Business of the House Banking Committee, Nov. 27, 28, 29, 30, and Dec. 4, 10, 11, 1973.

The contractor then tried to obtain a direct $100,000 SBA loan but was turned down by the regional office despite pressure to approve the loan from the central Washington office. A memo from the SBA district director to another SBA official involved in processing the loan papers stated: "Cassie, please get out papers on McRae [the contractor] as quickly as possible. This is a White House case and the heat is on."

Another example cited by House investigators involved an automotive equipment firm in Springfield, Virginia, whose principal officeholder was the father-in-law of the district director's personal secretary. He obtained a $30,000 direct loan at about half the going market interest rate. Under agency regulations, loans involving SBA employes required prior approval by an ad hoc committee in Washington. However, the loan was not sent to the committee until after it was approved by officials. One of the conditions of such loans, where a possible conflict may exist, is that the SBA employe involved must have nothing to do with processing it. Nonetheless, the secretary in question wrote a memo asking an SBA employe to "go ahead and order the check" for her father-in-law's firm. In addition, the proceeds from the loan were used personally to pay the loan recipient $3,400 based on a $7 per hour rate for repairs he himself made to his own building. Not only that, but he apparently advanced a large amount of money to renovate his building out of his own pocket and then reimbursed himself from the SBA loan, indicating he had enough funds to handle the project without an SBA loan.

In another case SBA approved a disaster loan of $4 million at 1 percent interest over 20 years to the Virginia Electric Power Company. This despite a statement in the loan file from the Washington central office stating that an earlier proposed 10-year maturity term was "excessive for a business which is able to repay the stockholders more than 10 times the amount of the loan in annual dividends."

Yet another example of SBA abuses concerned the Petroleum Engineering Company of Norfolk, Virginia, which sought a $300,000 loan guarantee but was turned down by two SBA loan officers. Despite an attempt by higher officers to get the loan approved, it was turned down again by the same two men. On the day it was finally disapproved for the second time, a revised application was submitted for only $150,000. However, this time the application was not routed to the two loan officers who had rejected it in the first instance but instead went to two other SBA officials, who approved the loan.

One of the most shocking examples of SBA loan-making abuse

involved Joseph Palumbo, a Charlottesville, Virginia, insurance executive and real estate developer and a major stockholder in a Virgin Islands bank who had a net worth of more than $1 million.

The subcommittee was presented with an elaborate chart by investigators showing how Palumbo and a number of companies in which he had holdings and served as an officer applied for a total of more than $11.6 million in loans, lease guarantees, loan guarantees, and contract awards. Not all of these loans were given final approval, it should be noted, and not all of the approved loans were disbursed. Of far more importance, however, was the fact that all of the loan-guarantee applications were approved by the SBA's Richmond office, although they were subsequently either turned down by higher authorities or cancelled after subcommittee investigators uncovered them. Underlying the entire case was the fact that Palumbo was the brother-in-law of the SBA office's district director.

Curtis A. Prins, then the Banking Committee's chief investigator, testified that these and other instances were "not isolated cases. I think we have in our files a large number of cases that involve similar type loans." Prins also reported he had discovered that SBA's files had been "tampered with" to conceal evidence and that it was "not unusual to find documents missing" from the agency's files. "In fact," he said,

> . . . we uncovered several loans that were made where there was not even a loan application in the file. The paperwork is extremely sloppily done, missing and in fact . . . some of the processing down there borders on dereliction of duty.

The investigation centered on SBA's regional office in Richmond, Virginia, but Prins said other SBA offices deserved equal scrutiny, including Milwaukee, Dallas, Casper (Wyoming), Denver, Los Angeles, Albuquerque, Atlanta, Philadelphia, New York, Chicago, Washington, Kansas City, New Orleans, Birmingham, San Francisco, Boston, Baltimore, Miami, San Diego, Wilkes-Barre, and Cleveland. The subcommittee didn't have the time or the resources to continue its investigation into these other cities. To this day we don't know what may have been going on within these other SBA offices.

SBA's efforts to direct loans to minority firms in recent years has similarly been marked by abuse. A great number of loans, investigations have revealed, have gone to firms who installed a token member of a minority as a top officer of their business enterprise in order to qualify for low interest loans or loan guarantees. The firms themselves, however, had no real minority connection whatsoever.

Moreover, Senate hearings in 1978 revealed that very few of the legitimate minority firms receiving SBA aid have survived. In fact, only about 30 out of around 2,400 companies that were given assistance over the last 10 years were definitely known by SBA to exist. Officials told the Senate Small Business Committee that in all, more than 4,000 firms had participated in the decade-old program and 1,650 of them remained in the program. But SBA chief Vernon Weaver testified that of those who had left the program because they were considered "economically viable," only "30-something are in business and doing a good job." Weaver added that there may be others but the agency didn't have any record of them.

An incredulous William Cherkasky, the committee's staff director, replied, "If that's all that still exists, then the whole reason for the program is highly questionable."

The agency came under further attack from the committee when investigators learned that out of a total of $137 million advanced to minority businesses throughout the country, nearly $55 million had not been repaid, $26 million of which was considered long overdue.

Sen. Gaylord Nelson of Wisconsin, chairman of the committee, angrily declared that the agency was overrun by "widespread and extensive mismanagement," pointing out there were numerous cases in which wealthy businessmen were taking advantage of the program.

After listening to even angrier remarks from another committee member, William Proxmire, who vowed to introduce legislation to abolish SBA, Nelson said:

> There is great substance to the criticism my colleague makes. If it cannot be reorganized and administered efficiently and effectively, I will join Sen. Proxmire in a move to abolish the whole shebang and fire all 4,500 employes and get rid of every single SBA office in the United States.

But perhaps one SBA project, more than any other, typifies how wasteful and inept this agency has become. That was a $345,000 loan guarantee to Tom Brokaw, the host of the NBC "Today" show who sought the money to buy a South Dakota radio station under a program whose principal purpose was to assist "minority" businesses. The approved loan guarantee was part of an SBA program to help minorities who wanted to purchase radio and television stations and other media enterprises—an area of government assistance which raises inherent first amendment conflicts concerning federal assistance to purchase private media outlets.

Brokaw, who reputedly earns an annual salary of between $400,000 and $550,000 a year, was, in Proxmire's words, "the last person that a government program to help needy businesses should be subsidizing." Brokaw applied for SBA assistance under the firm name, "Tom Tom Communications," which led SBA, no doubt, to think this was a penniless Indian minority firm. Needless to say, Brokaw and his partner are not minority businessmen.

Other investigations into the SBA have also found that the agency does not have a consistent set of standards as to what size firms shall be given federal aid. The General Accounting Office said:

> Under SBA regulations, size standards should channel assistance to firms competitively disadvantaged by being small. But standards have been developed without apparent consideration of the size of businesses most in need of federal assistance. The standards include virtually all firms in some industries.

Another GAO study also found confusion within the SBA over eligibility criteria. The GAO found that criteria for SBA assistance to small businesses that are owned and controlled by socially or economically disadvantaged persons were "subjective and not applied in a uniform and consistent manner." The study concluded that "some officials emphasize social background while others emphasize economic aspects. Contrary to the required procedures, there is often no indication of how approved applicants have met the eligibility criteria."

Most Americans no doubt believe that an agency called the Small Business Administration is helping the nation's neediest and most disadvantaged businesses. As the cases cited here have shown SBA assistance very often has helped multi-million dollar concerns and wealthy entrepreneurs. An SBA official told me that under the agency's quiltwork criteria, the American Motors Corporation is considered a "small business."

Said one congressional investigator:

> This agency is a waste of money. Its history shows that. But these guys (congressmen) can't bear to part with it. It's their only way of making constituents think they are doing something for the small businessman. And in some cases, it does. But most small business people in the country have never had anything to do with this agency and probably never will.

When he announced he would introduce legislation in 1979 to abolish the SBA, Proxmire said this:

> The Small Business Administration has a history of political favoritism, bad judgement and biased decisions. It has been a repository of patronage and scandals. It has helped only a minute number of small businesses. Since the president wants to cut the budget and Congress

wants to cut the budget and the people of the country want to cut the budget, the SBA, which has lost its way and outlived its usefulness, is the place to start.

Little more needs to be said. Both its defenders and its critics tell the story. What remains difficult to comprehend is why Congress—after several investigations uncovering abuses, corruption, and mismanagement—continues to keep this agency alive. Proxmire is right. It is an agency that has "outlived its usefulness." If Congress wants to help small businesses, the only equitable and effective way is to help them all. And that means a substantial and permanent reduction in the taxes all businesses must pay. With the exception of SBA's disaster loans, which should be moved to the Commerce Department, this agency should be eliminated.

PROGRAM 81

U.S. Parole Commission — $5.4 Million

As the crime rate continues to soar, this agency is not only unessential, it is providing a disservice both to the criminals it has authority to parole as well as to society at large.

Reorganized in 1977 as an independent agency within the Justice Department, the commission has nine commissioners, 40 hearing examiners and a little over 100 administrative employes. Yet increasingly the concept of parole is being questioned by many who have come to believe that the nation's federal criminal code should require that all lawbreakers be given mandatory sentences for their misdeeds without the possibility that their sentences will be later reduced.

Essentially, this is the approach taken in the federal criminal code revision that passed the Senate in 1978 and which would have led to the phasing out of the Parole Commission. Sen. Edward Kennedy, who was responsible for shepherding that bill through the Senate, is among those who thinks we should "start making punishment and imprisonment for violent offenders a certainty." Such an approach, Kennedy said in an article for the *Boston Globe*, is the "most effective way to deter potential offenders from criminal conduct. At the same time, mandatory sentencing keeps the violent offender in jail and off the street."

The Parole Commission has in recent years been attacked from all sides. Some critics have said it has been too soft on criminals, unnecessarily letting them out of prison before they have served their time. Others have blamed the commission for arbitrary decision-making, based not on what the criminal has been convicted of but on other things in his past which had nothing to do with the crime for which he was convicted.

NBC reporter Chris Wallace on the network's "Prime Time Sunday" program cited the case of Jim Smith who was arrested and charged with 12 counts involving falsifying bank records. After plea bargaining, 11 of the counts were dropped. Smith, who had no previous record, was convicted on one charge involving $227.98. He expected to do six months in prison on a five year sentence. The Parole Commission sentenced him to 42 months.

"What happened," Wallace said, "was that the Parole Commission held Smith responsible for every count in the indictment, even though all but one had been dismissed."

Wallace went on to say:

> In reviewing inmates' cases the commission "often ignores the recommendations of judges, of U.S. attorneys and of prison staff and it also ignores plea bargaining. What that means is that a man like Jim Smith reaches an agreement with one arm of the government that he'll be punished on a single charge if the others are dismissed. But then another arm of the government, the Parole Commission, refuses to honor that bargain.

Much of the commission's decision-making can be based on a presentence investigation report (PSI) on the defendant. This report, some probation officers say, can include many things that are not necessarily reliable or substantiated, sometimes even hearsay.

Said a congressional committee staffer whose job it is to oversee the commission's activities:

> We have been extremely dissatisfied with the haphazard way in which the Parole Commission has used any and all information that they can get.

Thus, the Parole Commission, Wallace's investigation found, has ignored inmates' due process, second guessed judges and prosecutors and made decisions based on information that is not always factual. "The commission is only doing what Congress says it can do," he continued. "But, what it is doing disturbs people at every step in the criminal justice process."

The Parole Commission should be phased out of existence. Criminal offenders should from the beginning be certain of one thing: that their actions will lead to a flat sentence from which there will be no parole.

PROGRAM 82

Legal Services Corporation — $300 Million

Those who support this program—a great proportion of whom, not surprisingly, are attorneys—believe that no one can survive in this world without lawyers. The fact that most people go through their entire lives without ever needing legal assistance of any kind leaves such people incredulous. They equate legal services with such things as food, shelter, and health care, the essentials of life which the government quite properly provides for the poor. The need for legal services, however, is another matter altogether, one which has never been shown to be necessary.

The very premise of this program is wrong. Those who support its existence never bother to question whether the poor would prefer to forego this and perhaps other federally-funded services in favor of increased income to spend on what they themselves deem necessities. This is why legal services is government paternalism at its worst. If the poor were given more money, instead of this service, they would no doubt go out and spend it on things they need more, clothing, transportation, rent, fuel, or education—needs that have nothing to do with the legal profession.

This agency does nothing to either improve the grim day-to-day lives of the truly poor, or perhaps more to the point, help them to rise out of their circumstances. Indeed, it assumes the poor will always remain in their disadvantaged state in order to provide employment for a corps of government-paid attorneys who are ready to litigate at the drop of a tort.

In truth, legal services is nothing more than an employment program for lawyers. Writer Stephen Chapman, in an excellent analysis of the program in the *New Republic*,* called it "a Humphrey-Hawkins bill for the legal community." With the nation's law schools churning out thousands of lawyers each year, this program is expected in the coming years to absorb the growing excess of would-be barristers. The Labor Department estimates that by 1985 at least 100,000 lawyers will be unable to find employment in their chosen profession.

Thus, there is, as Chapman points out, a brilliant deviousness behind the entire concept of legal services:

New Republic, September 24, 1977.

While siphoning off some of the overflow from the nation's law schools, the legal services program presents no competitive threat to private attorneys. The point of legal services, after all, is to offer legal counsel to those who wouldn't otherwise purchase it; thus, it doesn't take away clients from other lawyers. The LSC expands the job market for lawyers by furnishing a steady flow of federal money, making its lawyers dependent not on demand from clients but on simple bureaucratic momentum.

Lawyers profit from legal services in other ways. If a poor woman sues her landlord, thanks to the advice of a legal services lawyer, someone has to defend the landlord. The beauty of creating a demand for lawyers by offering them "free" is that for every poverty lawyer who starts or threatens litigation on behalf of a client, at least one more lawyer (and possibly more) will be needed to represent the other side. Even if the legal services lawyer prefers to settle the matter without going to court, the defendant—landlord, businessman, manufacturer, local government or whatever—well may require legal advice about the respective obligations and rights.

As a federally-subsidized job-placement program for the nation's growing force of attorneys, Legal Services started small but is becoming immense. In 1965 the Office of Legal Services was created within the antipoverty program's Office of Economic Opportunity and budgeted at a mere $1.3 million a year. But when Congress turned it into an independent corporation in 1974, Legal Services quickly set about to realize its goal of providing two poverty lawyers for every 10,000 poor people. By 1975 LSC's yearly budget had grown to $90 million, leaped to $157.4 million by 1978, and then zoomed to $261 million in 1979. By fiscal 1980 LSC was asking Congress for a budget of $337.5 million, a massive $67 million increase over the previous year. Congress, however, approved a flat $300 million budget which still represented a $39 million hike over 1979. Its growth is a classic example of a federal program begun by Congress with a budget no one could argue with and then sharply increased over a period of years after the program has all but been forgotten.

Legal Services has reached their goal of two lawyers per 10,000 poor people, but of course it isn't satisfied. Now it wants to double that, insisting that four legal services attorneys per 10,000 poor people is the "absolute minimum" needed. To finance that minimum would cost an estimated $875 million a year.

Meanwhile, an examination of what *is* being spent on this massive and costly program strongly suggests that taxpayers aren't getting much for their money.

Over the past four years about 80 percent of all cases handled by this agency have involved four major types of problems: family-domestic problems, 35 percent; administrative proceedings, 15 percent; consumer complaints, 15 percent; and housing, 15 percent. The remaining 20 percent of the cases falls into the "other" category—which can include a variety of problems.

But an analysis of the underlying figures indicates LSC isn't really reaching that many people.

In 1978 LSC estimated it handled 1.4 million cases for the poor which they numbered anywhere from 30 million to a high of 60 million. If the lower poverty figure is used, that means LSC lawyers reached only 4 percent of the nation's poor. If the higher poverty figure is used (a number that most people would find preposterous) poverty lawyers reached only 2 percent of the nation's poor. Whatever poverty population figure is used, an extremely small number of poor people are actually being touched by this program.

Far more revealing, however, are the agency's own statistics on what actually makes up these 1.4 million "cases." While one may think the bulk of the work of this agency involves a lawyer actually representing poor clients before a court or administrative proceeding of some type, only 20.7 percent of all cases in 1978 involved an appearance in court. More than 30 percent of all cases involved "advice only," while 9.3 percent of all cases involved "referral to another attorney or program." Another 4.8 percent of the cases involved "referral to nonlegal agency." Almost 4 percent of the cases were "handled solely by telephone." And 17 percent involved a "negotiated settlement out of court."

Thus, we can see that Legal Services not only reaches a relatively few number of poor people, but that one-half of those reached get little more than advice. But advice, particularly from lawyers, doesn't come cheap. Nearly 70 percent of LSC's budget is consumed by salaries which can range from a low average of $15,000 up to a high of $35,000 or more a year for Legal Services lawyers.

Meanwhile there is also reason to question the value of the other 50 percent of the cases actually involving legal representation and advocacy as well as other LSC activities being funded by tax dollars. For LSC is deeply involved in a lot more than just providing legal services to the poor. A great deal of their support from the taxpayer has been paying for legal suits against state and municipal governments for a wide range of social and political goals which have nothing to do with improving the lives of the poor. In fact, Legal

Services attorneys have been in the vanguard of "social activist" battles, lobbying in behalf of legislation, working to overturn laws, encouraging rent strikes, boycotts, and aiding partisan political organizations and other political and social causes.

In the legal journal, *Clearinghouse Review*, which is supported by LSC funds, two lawyers who worked for an agency funded by Legal Services told how tax dollars can be used for these types of activities and how they expected further Legal Services funding to support their goals of redistributing wealth in the United States through political and social reform. Authors Alan Rader and Dorothy Lang provided this advice to LSC-financed lobbyists:

> To lobby local government effectively, we will have to learn, for a beginning, the demographics of local politicians' districts, their campaign contributors, their voting records, their staff assistants, the social service facilities and agencies within their districts, and labor, church, and civic groups within their districts.

In a column discussing this article, Phyllis Schlafly wrote:

> These Legal Services lawyers frankly admit that they are working "toward long-range institutional change," that their goals "are explicitly distributive," and that they are developing "broad legislative and administrative advocacy strategies."

But Schlafly asks:

> Is it legal for taxpayer-financed lawyers to lobby for or against specific legislation or referendums? The Legal Services Corporation Act specifically prohibits "advocating, or opposing any ballot measures, initiatives or referendums."

However, the two lawyer-authors advise their colleagues that a loophole in the LSC's law says an attorney "may provide legal advice and representation as an attorney to an eligible client with respect to such client's legal rights."

"So," Schlafly wrote, "under the subterfuge of providing 'advice and representation' to a 'client,' Legal Services Corporation uses our tax dollars for lobbying, media manipulation and politicking for or against ballot measures."

In an editorial on Feb. 3, 1979, the *New Republic* correctly observed that Legal Services was "intended to help the poor when they unavoidably get caught up in the complex legal machinery of modern society—in divorces, disputes with landlords, tussles with the welfare bureaucracy, etc. *But too often legal aid lawyers use poor people as guinea pigs in an attempt to impose through the courts some fanciful middle-class view of social justice.*"

As an example of the kinds of suits LSC is funding, The *New Republic* was particularly distressed over one lawsuit in California against the state university "to stop research aimed at improving agricultural productivity."

The suit by the LSC-funded California Rural Legal Assistance against the University of California was sparked by the university's development of labor-saving farm machinery which, LSC lawyers argued, contributed to agricultural unemployment and the demise of the small family farm.

But as the magazine viewed it:

> To oppose research aimed at increasing productivity is simply insane . . . A life spent stooping to pick fruit under the California sun is not so rewarding that we should rush into court to reserve places in the fields for the children of this generation of farm workers.

Surely the more sensible approach would be to provide job training for displaced farmworkers so that they could pursue more rewarding and perhaps less back-breaking employment. The *New Republic* editorial concluded, "This lawsuit is another example of the misuse of government legal services."

This example, unfortunately, is not an isolated aberration on the part of Legal Services. They also financed the lawsuit by the Passamaquoddy and Penobscot Indian tribes to reclaim two-thirds of the state of Maine, an action that is still being litigated and which will cost that state's citizens millions of dollars. LSC lawyers have also lobbied aggressively against utility rate increases, pushed for income tax reforms, and as we pointed out in Chapter IV, have involved themselves in cases concerning hiring policies, welfare reform, food stamp regulations, student rights, and school discipline problems. Furthermore, Charles Fields, assistant director of national affairs for the American Farm Bureau Federation, has charged that Legal Services lawyers have even helped to organize farm workers' unions in California, Florida, the Midwest, and New Jersey.

Much of this social and political advocacy is performed by various institutes, law centers, nonprofit research organizations, and other public interest groups who receive millions of dollars each year in research funding from LSC.

All of this has led groups like the Farm Bureau to call for abolishing the entire program and replacing it with a system in which the poor would receive vouchers they could use to pay for private lawyers whenever needed.

In his *New Republic* article, Stephen Chapman observed:

The legal services program may be the most extreme example of the paternalism of the American welfare state: denying the poor what they explicitly lack—money—in favor of the goods and services the government thinks they should have, in the amount and proportion it deems appropriate. There is much validity in the libertarian argument that this approach denies the poor both the freedom to decide their own needs and the responsibility, essential to individual independence and self-reliance, to accept the consequences of such decisions.

Chapman goes on to point out that Legal Services lawyers "do not see their role merely as one of supplying a minor necessary service to the occasional poor person." Instead, they see within Legal Services
. . . that the adversary system can be a major implement of social change. This is what conservatives object to most about government legal services. Why should their tax dollars be financing efforts to change government policy in ways they may not approve of? But there are other objections that liberals ought to take more to heart. For the government to make social policy by hiring lawyers to file lawsuits is inefficient and undemocratic. The elaborate adversary proceedings of the legal process are no substitute for debate in an elected forum. The very idea that having masses of lawyers available to them can transform the lives of poor people is an example of the sterility of most current thinking about social welfare. Lawyers, psychologists, and social welfare bureaucrats of every sort are provided in abundance, while money and jobs are withheld.

For Chapman, there are better ways to ensure that the poor have ways of settling their disputes and protecting their rights, such as "eliminating the numerous restrictions that prevent competition among lawyers"—which would result in lower fees and, thus, more affordable services. "An even more substantial and far-reaching answer is to avoid reforms that encourage litigation and to nurture those that help people avoid it, like no-fault insurance, arbitration, and mediation." Expanded access to small claims courts would also help the poor, as well as the general population, deal more efficiently with housing, consumer, and similar types of complaints without the need of an attorney.

This program has grown obscenely within recent years. Much of its growth had been channeled into social and political activism and lawsuits Congress never envisioned, reforms that have not measurably impacted upon the real life struggles of the poor, reforms which should be made in our legislatures, not in our courts by federally-paid lawyers.

LSC didn't get the full $337.5 million it wanted in fiscal 1980. But it is a safe bet that in future years this agency will want more and will get more of our money. Indeed, when former LSC president Thomas Ehrlich was asked about the likelihood that Legal Services would eventually be representing criminal defendants, he said, "Five to 10 years down the road we ought to address the problem."

Legal Services is a program that has been rife with abuse, becoming in recent years a tax-supported agency that has financed legislative lobbying and social and political advocacy. It has become a costly vehicle for political and social crusaders while taxpayers—including the poor—are left to foot the bill.

As we have seen, a relatively tiny number of poor people are touched by this program, for all the millions of dollars that it has spent. It should be abandoned.

PROGRAM 83

Defense Civil Preparedness Program — $100 Million

Over the past 15 years the government has sunk nearly $1.5 billion into civil defense programs in the United States. Yet it would be hard to find anyone who believes that because of this enormous expenditure we are any better protected in the event of a nuclear attack.

Bomb shelters became briefly popular about 20 years ago, particularly when the Cuban missile crisis heated world tensions. There was even a proposal before Congress to appropriate half a billion dollars to implement a nationwide shelter program. The idea, even in the midst of that tense period, was shelved.

The Defense Civil Preparedness Agency, located for years within the Defense Department, was reorganized by President Carter in 1979 and merged into a newly created program—the Federal Emergency Management Agency—with four other disaster emergency programs.

The bulk of the civil defense program's funds are parcelled out through a system of matching grants to the states and localities which support almost 6,000 fulltime and part-time civil defense personnel who maintain a national shelter and civil defense education and training programs. An additional 590 federal employes are based in Washington and in regional offices. Salaries consume more than $31 million a year. Another $3 million annually is spent on supporting materials and some research and development.

The Army Corps of Engineers helps to designate certain buildings for shelters. The civil defense program, however, does not build any shelters.

In many respects, this program is nothing more than another form of government patronage. In many communities the so-called civil defense headquarters is the local police department, fire station, or sheriff's office. With the exception of civil defense directors and personnel on the state and local levels, the vast majority of paid civil defense employes are part-time. For many of them civil defense has become a way of earning extra money. That is why William Proxmire has said, "The shelter programs, the evacuation programs are sterling examples of make-work."

Some of this program's missions, such as those concerned with

339

impending natural disasters, obviously make sense and should be retained in FEMA's other disaster assistance programs.

Meanwhile, the Defense Department spends billions of dollars on advanced warning and detection systems around our borders and throughout the world. And, in the event of a national emergency, mobilization of our military forces would entail carrying out mass evacuation and relocation plans. At one time, perhaps, when the nuclear might of the two major powers had to be delivered in planes and dropped over their targets, there may have been a case for this civil defense effort. But in this nuclear age of long-range missiles and multiple independently-targeted reentry vehicles (MIRVs), there is virtually no place to hide from attack. The best protection today against a nuclear attack is a strong defense.

PROGRAM 84

Overseas Private Investment Corporation

In Port-Au-Prince, Haiti, behind a high stone wall sits the two-century-old Habitation Leclerc, once the resplendent residence of Napoleon's sister, Pauline Leclerc. Now a pleasure dome resort for the wealthy, it offers everything from huge circular mattresses, large sunken baths, and private swimming pools, to a discotheque and all the food and liquor you can consume for $150 a day per couple. "Since the Garden of Eden there has never been a place like Habitation Leclerc . . . elegant, exotic, erotic. Privacy within a lush exciting garden of pleasure," its advertising has boasted.

The owners of the Leclerc hotel were able to open their Caribbean hideaway in 1974 with the help of a $415,000 loan from the U.S. government's Overseas Private Investment Corporation (OPIC).

Congress created OPIC in 1969 to take over and expand upon various insurance and loan-guarantee programs previously run by the Agency for International Development (AID) for U.S. investors abroad. Since that time OPIC has written billions of dollars' worth of policies insuring major American corporations investing in developing countries against the risks of war, expropriation of property, and currency inconvertibility.

In effect, the United States has been subsidizing some of America's biggest corporations to send their capital abroad at a time when unemployment and a money-starved U.S. capital market require just the opposite. The Senate Foreign Relations Committee found that 79 percent of all OPIC-issued insurance was provided to firms on *Fortune*'s list of 500 largest corporations and 50 richest banks.

By far OPIC's biggest function has been its political-risk insurance program which has billions of dollars in outstanding liabilities which the U.S. Treasury would have to honor in the event of heavy claims. OPIC's guaranteed loans and direct loans—like the one made to the Habitation Leclerc—constitute a much smaller share of its overall program.

There is no annual cost given at the top of this chapter because OPIC makes money for the government in the premiums and interest rates it charges its customers, although its income has been relatively small by federal budgetary standards. In fiscal 1978 it brought in $65.4 million. In fiscal 1979 revenues were estimated to run about $42.7 million, with a similar amount expected in fiscal 1980. None-

341

theless, OPIC has been bailed out by Congress in the past and may well be again. In fiscal 1970 Congress appropriated $81.2 million which, according to the Foreign Relations Committee, saved OPIC from having precariously low insurance reserves to draw on in the event of heavy claims. Congress appropriated $25 million in fiscal 1974, but turned down a request for an additional $25 million in fiscal 1975. Since 1969 OPIC has received more than $200 million in congressional appropriations.

OPIC is an unnecessary government program that could end up costing taxpayers billions of dollars. The federal government should not be in the insurance-writing business. In fact, experts maintain that more than 75 percent of investments by American firms in lesser-developed countries are uninsured because the companies say *they don't need* such protection. Furthermore, the great bulk of the corporations receiving this tax-subsidized insurance protection are the giants of U.S. industry and more than financially able to purchase their own insurance from the private sector. Despite the trend to provide a host of government guarantees, loans, and other emoluments for business, the fact remains that business must survive or perish on its own within the free market system. If the risks involved in an investment are so high that a private firm will not insure the investment, then the investment should not be made.

Also, it has never been persuasively demonstrated that investments made under this program are either beneficial to the underdeveloped countries involved or even to the U.S. economy. Top American industrial leaders have testified that there has been no intrinsic requirement that OPIC-insured companies purchase U.S. products as part of their foreign investment expenditures. Testimony has also been heard that OPIC encourages an outward flow of capital from the United States by encouraging industries to invest abroad, and that OPIC, at least in the short run, contributes to a worsening of America's balance-of-payments problem.

The Foreign Relations Committee concluded, in an analysis of OPIC in 1974, that its investment guarantee program was

> . . . at best, only a marginal contributor to the development of the poorer countries of the world and OPIC is only a marginal stimulus to private investment in less developed countries.

In the mid-1970s there was an attempt by Congress to begin a gradual shift of OPIC's insurance functions to private insurance companies, although retaining an open-ended reinsurance commitment by the United States. At the time, Sen. Clifford Case of New Jersey called the plan "unrealistic" because it would not accomplish what many in the Senate wished, total termination of the program. Said Case, "I believe strongly that the only way to terminate the program is to terminate it." Well, OPIC continues to exist. Congress would be well advised to carry out its original intention.

PROGRAM 85

Foreign Claims Settlement Commission — $958,000

Since 1954 the Foreign Claims Settlement Commission has been adjudicating American repayment claims for property seized or destroyed in foreign countries. Now, after more than a quarter of a century of operation, there are not enough remaining claims to warrant a separate agency.

Created when Congress merged the War Claims Commission and the International Claims Commission, this agency receives claims from persons who have incurred losses abroad. After taking the testimony from claimants, the three-member commission renders a decision and then turns over the claims to the Secretary of the Treasury who has the responsibility for making all payments. The funds are sought from the countries in which the losses occurred through negotiated agreements, or by liquidating any of the country's deposits or other property in the United States. The only exception to this would be where prisoners of war are involved and in such cases Congress provides necessary funding for agreed upon claims.

In some cases, however, the U.S. has been unable to reach agreement with certain countries—like East Germany, Cuba, and China—in order to honor claims.

Since the War Claims Act of 1948 the commission says it has received 613,800 war-related claims and has granted in excess of $525 million in approximately 391,000 claims. In claims arising out of the nationalization of property, the commission has approved a total of $2.49 billion to claimants.

The commission is staffed by only 30 fulltime employes. Its three commissioners are each paid $47,500 a year.

The only current claims programs that were ongoing as of 1980 were claims against the German Democratic Republic (East Germany) and those of the Vietnam War prisoners. These, however, are not enough to require keeping this agency alive. Congressional experts long familiar with this agency's activities believe its remaining tasks could be absorbed by the State Department. This is an agency that once served a necessary purpose, but now it is no longer needed.

344

PROGRAM 86

Educational and Cultural Exchange Grants —
$33.1 Million

Over the years the government's educational and cultural exchange program has become a sacred cow. Criticizing it is like accusing the government of spending too much money on cancer research. Nevertheless, one component of that program is worth examining in the cold light of world realities and human priorities.

There is nothing terribly difficult about how this activity operates. It gives out grants to private American contracting agencies and organizations who use the money to finance travel, seminars, symposiums, conferences, sports activities, and other programs both here and abroad.

A review of these grants, however, reveals that there is little if any coherent definition or purpose to this program. Its activities are not only often vague and without direction, but highly elitist as well. Its grants in many respects have largely become a travel subsidy for lawyers, educators, political leaders, journalists, government officials, businessmen, authors, and sports figures.

In many cases federal grants are going to rich trade and professional organizations who are able to support such activities on their own without recourse to the U.S. Treasury. In a large number of cases the grants are subsidizing the operational costs of private organizations who would have to close their doors were it not for these federal payments. Moreover, there appears to be little coordination among these grants, as organizations and groups frequently duplicate each other's work.

Judging from the grants which have been given out in recent years, the International Communications Agency, which runs the program, has been giving its money away to virtually any organization for virtually any purpose.

Here are some examples of where these grants have been going:

—$42,672 to the American Bar Association to conduct a program in the U.S. for members of the legal profession from other countries.

—$83,185 to the International Marketing Institute to carry out "a program of study, travel, consultation, and practical experience in the field of marketing for business executives, government officials, education, and marketing specialists from other countries."

345

—$64,761 to the American Bar Association to conduct two seminars in the U.S. for lawyers and jurists from Latin American countries.

—$396,902 to the American Council of Young Political Leaders to carry out exchange programs for young political leaders between the U.S. and other countries.

—$2,114 to the Association of American Publishers, Inc. to conduct a seminar in the U.S. for leading American and Soviet publishers.

—$4,100 to the Aspen Institute for Humanistic Studies to conduct a conference in the U.S. for business, government, civic and political leaders from foreign countries.

—$59,833 to the University of Arizona to develop and conduct a symposium in the U.S. for Latin American journalists.

—$32,400 to the Brookings Institution to conduct a seminar for East Asian, Pacific, Near Eastern, and South Asian economic specialists.

—$28,600 to Columbia University to develop and conduct a program in the U.S. for Latin American authors.

—$76,550 to the Conference Board, a business-supported organization, to conduct a program "designed to improve the capacity of American corporations to understand and operate in different overseas environments."

—$19,800 to the Festival Foundation, Inc. to help the Foundation "in arranging for the Westminster College Choir to appear at the Festival of Two Worlds in Spoleto, Italy.

—$7,000 to Harvard University to conduct its Trade Union Program.

—$10,602 to Theatre of Latin America, Inc. to conduct a program in the U.S. for Latin American theatre critics and playwrights.

—$23,334 to the U.S. Conference of Mayors to help the Conference "in carrying out a program designed to further mutual understanding between the U.S. and the Soviet Union.

—$18,050 to the U.S. Lawn Tennis Association, Inc. to develop and administer international tennis teaching projects and to send American tennis players to Nigeria to run workshops, clinics, demonstrations, and tournaments.

—$251,569 to the U.S. Youth Council to conduct its International Labor Desk Program "aimed at strengthening relationships between labor programs in the U.S. and those of other countries."

—$39,030 to Friendship Ambassadors Foundation to "conduct an observation and consultation program in the U.S. for international visitors prominent in the media of their home countries.

—$21,544 to Adventure in Education to conduct a teacher-coach athletic tour in the fields of track and basketball in selected countries of the Near East and South Asia.

—$15,000 to the American Forum for International Study, Inc., to carry out a study and travel program in Africa for American educators.

—$3,500 to the Business Council for International Understanding to conduct a seminar in the U.S. for Japanese broadcasting executives.

—$35,000 to the Free Trade Union Institute to conduct a "union-to-union labor exchange program" with Spain.

—$113,200 to the International Management and Development Institute to increase "involvement by the American business community in international corporate citizenship and public affairs programs."

—$141,900 to the Japan Society, Inc. to conduct programs designed to enhance the educational and cultural relationship between the U.S. and Japan.

There are many things wrong with these grants. The funds, for one thing, have benefited only a relatively small number of people for all the hundreds of millions of dollars that have been spent. The conferences, symposiums and other projects often deal with subjects—business relations, sports competition, the media, the law—that are a million light years away from the real problems of the world's disadvantaged populations: hunger, disease, inadequate shelter, and illiteracy. It may be fine that American tennis players, in their sparkling whites and expensive rackets, want to teach Africans how to play tennis, or that someone wants to bring Latin American theatre critics and foreign media stars to the United States, but what does any of this have to do with the more pressing needs of the world's poor? What possible priority could these grants have in those countries where famine is a common occurrence of life? Instead of tennis clinics these countries need health clinics.

Certainly the idea of giving out grants to improve business relations between our country and other nations is a wasteful exercise when we see American and foreign business people competing daily around the world. Meantime, universities and colleges are conducting their own exchange programs. Many government agencies, similarly, are funding travel and exchange-related programs involving a broad range of intellectual disciplines, including the National Science Foundation, the Agency for International Development, and the Smithsonian Institution. And, of course, there are numerous private exchange programs being run by museums, art galleries, research institutes, libraries, foundations, and other institutions both here and abroad.

ICA's budget for all its educational and cultural exchange affairs was $73.4 million in fiscal 1979. The agency requested $85.3 million for the program in fiscal 1980. Thus, ending this $33.1 million in grants would still leave the entire program with between $40 million and $50 million to spend on its other cultural and academic exchange activities.

As long as the United States is in its present state of economic depression and debt, this is surely an expenditure that can be safely dispensed with.

PROGRAM 87

American Battle Monuments Commission — $7.5 Million

The American Battle Monuments Commission, established by Congress in March of 1923, has been responsible for the construction and permanent maintenance of American military cemeteries and memorials abroad as well as several memorials within the United States. The commission has rendered an important and valuable service to the nation by maintaining these resting places and monuments to our honored war dead. But by now it has clearly become unnecessary to have a separate agency fulfilling this task which could be just as easily taken over by the Army.

The commission operates offices in Washington, D.C., where it is headquartered, as well as in Rome, Garches, France, and Manila. With a staff of 388 (most of whom are foreign nationals)—which includes eight Army officers—the commission oversees 23 military cemeteries and 14 monuments and memorials. Since the Army is in charge of all domestic cemeteries, there is no reason why they cannot handle this responsibility as well.

PROGRAM 88

USDA Extension Service — $250 Million

A sure sign of a dying federal program is one in which Congress slowly begins to lower its budget. Since fiscal 1978 that has been the case with the Agriculture Department's Extension Service when the program received $251.7 million. That dropped by only $1 million in fiscal 1979, although in real terms the decrease was much larger due to the rise in inflation. In fiscal 1980 the Carter administration requested a budget of $232.6 million for the agency, a decrease of $18 million over the previous year.

The government's shrinking support for this program is not difficult to understand. In its present state it is an archaic and wasteful bureaucracy that to a large degree has outlived its original purpose as the Agriculture Department's educational and assistance service agency for farmers and rural families.

Ever since the Extension Service's creation by Congress under the Smith-Lever Act of 1914, it has been an unquestioned part of the government's agricultural program. At that time America was largely a rural, agricultural nation. Communications were still relatively primitive. Farmers were physically remote from the centers of government where information could be obtained. Travel was still slow. Therefore, it made sense to establish a county by county network of Extension Service offices which are now run by 17,000 professional staffers and supported by the technical and research services of the land-grant colleges. Funding for the offices comes through a 40-60 matching grant formula, with the federal government paying 40 percent and the states and counties paying the balance.

Unfortunately, despite many decades of existence, the Extension program has never been critically evaluated by Congress. Lawmakers have followed the maxim that, if it worked in 1914, it will work in the 1980s. But a great deal has changed in the last 65 years. This agency is providing services that are no longer needed in many areas of the country where farming has all but disappeared. There are county Extension offices operating in Manhattan, Boston, Detroit, Chicago, Los Angeles, and other urban areas where a farmer is someone people only see on television.

Congress must begin asking whether in today's highly mechanized, technological farming industry many of the Extension Service's programs are still relevant in the 1980s and beyond. There

350

may have been a time when this program's home economics, nutrition, and youth programs were needed to make up for poor education in remote areas of our country. But the Extension Service's "homemaking" programs are now as out-of-date in our mass media age as the horse-drawn plow. Rural consumers and homemakers receive more information about home economics, nutrition, and related subjects from television, newspapers, magazines, books, and other sources than the Extension Service could hope to provide if its staff were tripled.

The Service's 4-H program was and continues to be an exemplary organization aimed at developing farming skills, agricultural careers, and leadership among our youth. Still, much of the program's activities are being addressed through public education programs. True, with the nation's declining farm population there is a need to encourage careers in farming, but this can be done just as effectively by an independent 4-H organization.

Let me strongly emphasize that I do not mean to suggest that the Extension Service should be totally abolished. What Congress needs to do is to reevaluate what portion of the Extension Service program is worth preserving and what is no longer useful to American agriculture. Certainly it is no longer necessary in this modern day and age to maintain an agricultural outpost in every county in the country.

As was pointed out in Chapter VIII ("Where Are the Farmers?"), the Extension offices have become involved in many activities that anyone would be hard put to defend. For example, issuing advice and educational materials on lawn care, ornamental plants and shrubs, and other backyard gardening problems is something the federal government should not be providing. Not with the private sector producing a mountain of information on these and other subjects for homeowners. When I last looked, county agents were annually devoting more than 500 man-years to dealing with "lawns, home gardens, and house plants" and were planning to expand this service.

These and other Extension Service programs *need to be eliminated*. Congress could start by phasing out the Extension Service as it is presently constituted. In its place there is a need for a more modest but more highly focused program that is geared solely to helping the American farmer and related agricultural problems. Everything else should be dismantled.

PROGRAM 89

HUD Urban Development Action Grants — $675 Million

The government is giving out these grants under the pretext they are needed to stimulate rich and powerful corporations and banks to build office complexes, shopping malls, factories, hotels, movie theaters, and other privately-owned properties. The Urban Development Action Grants (UDAG) represents one of the most wasteful and unnecessary expenditures of our tax dollars. Yet members of Congress are convinced that somehow this money, which is taken out of the private sector, can be usefully returned to the economy to stimulate private investment in areas where businesses would not ordinarily wish to invest.

The grants, as envisioned by Congress, were to be awarded to local governments to revitalize communities where a declining population had produced a dwindling tax base and poverty-torn neighborhoods. The primary purpose behind these grants is to stimulate new or increased investment and thus provide jobs and economic expansion. Local governments can use these grants to leverage private investment in their areas. In other words, the grant is to serve as a spur to private investment, not come afterward when the project is a foregone conclusion.

UDAG, a concept developed under the Carter administration, was established by Congress in 1977 at an authorized spending level of $400 million a year. Totally sold on the political benefits of Washington's being able to hand out still more grants to counties and municipalities, Carter asked Congress to boost UDAG's annual budget by an incredible $275 million in fiscal 1980. Knowing their states and districts also stood to benefit, and appreciating the political reward they stand to gain, our lawmakers quickly agreed to the increase (despite disturbing evidence that this program is not what it is cracked up to be).

What has been happening is that grants have been awarded under the guise of stimulating building projects when, in truth, the projects in many instances were to be built anyway, regardless of the availability of federal funds.

In an analysis of 18 sample UDAG grants, the GAO found four that were highly questionable. Two of them were approved "without any substantial commitment of private resources." One grant was "apparently not needed to stimulate private investment." And the fourth "primarily benefited a private firm." Other grants have similarly raised questions as to their value and effectiveness.

A case in point concerned a joint announcement in 1978 by the governor of Georgia, George Busbee, and Proctor and Gamble Company that a subsidiary planned to build a $200 million pulp mill in Montezuma, a small Georgia community of fewer than 4,000 people. At the time of the announcement the company had purchased the building site and signed a contract to begin construction. Indeed, it wasn't until six days after the announcement that Montezuma filed an application for a $5.8 million UDAG grant to build bypass roads that would serve the pulp mill. But, since the subsidiary had already committed itself to the project, HUD was advised by its representative in Atlanta to turn down the grant application. Area HUD economist Bette A. Jimerson wrote in a March 1978 memorandum that the company planned to build the mill "whether or not this application is approved." Jimerson advised HUD that the building project "does not need the boost of a UDAG application to make it either desirable or competitive." Incredibly, HUD approved the grant anyway and Proctor and Gamble's subsidiary received their bypass roads.

In another case, the city of Corning, N.Y., successfully applied for a $1.8 million UDAG grant to improve access roads and storm sewers as part of a $16.3 million project by Corning Glass works to construct a new headquarters. The new private investment stimulated by the grant amounted to only $50,000, according to the GAO, a minute fraction of the public funds involved. Was Corning's building plans contingent upon the grant? Hardly. The city didn't file an application for the grant until 10 months after the company was committed to the new building. Rep. L. H. Fountain of North Carolina, chairman of the House Intergovernmental Relations subcommittee that held hearings on the GAO's report, found it "extremely difficult . . . to draw a conclusion that the UDAG grant influenced" Corning's decision to build. Fountain noted that the company had "very close ties" to the city, was the "dominant taxpayer," and that Corning was the home of the company's founding family.

Meanwhile, the Montezuma grant, according to the GAO, *stimulated no new investment.* It was, Fountain said, "tantamount to additional revenue sharing money for the state of Georgia."

In another case, the GAO found that a $6.8 million UDAG grant to Cincinnati for construction of an industrial park failed to stimulate any private investment, tax revenues or additional employment. Although HUD had predicted that the grant would produce nearly $40 million in new private investment, the GAO found it had produced nothing.

Contrary to HUD's criteria that UDAG grants are to be used as leverage to encourage private businesses to build or otherwise invest in depressed areas, the GAO found that UDAG grants have been made without any private commitment.

"Two of the grants we examined, involving a total of $1.25 million of UDAG funds, did not involve any strong private financial commitment," the GAO said. The grants were made to Binghamton, New York, and Detroit, Michigan.

In the case of an $8 million grant awarded to Boston, the GAO said its review

> ... indicated that the UDAG funds were not needed to stimulate new or increased private investment. The development was, in fact, one to which the city and a private developer were already strongly committed.

The grant was to be used to build an underground parking garage that was said to be necessary to entice the developer into building an adjacent 500-room hotel. "In discussing this grant with HUD's headquarters office reviewer," the GAO said, "we learned that the primary reason the funds were granted was to relieve the city of Boston's tax burden." This of course *totally violates* all HUD criteria for issuing these grants. What has been happening is that the grants have been used to bail out cities for the cost of providing needed public facilities necessary to building expansion.

Concluded the GAO in the Boston case:

> We view the use of UDAG funds in this particular instance as highly questionable. We do not believe it is consistent with the program's stated intent of stimulating new economic development activity.

In some cases these grants are directly benefiting private companies and investors. In one case the GAO questioned a UDAG grant to Dowagiac, Michigan, which it said "benefits primarily a private business rather than the community." Dowagiac officials announced on Aug. 2, 1978, that the city would receive a $35,000 HUD grant to help rebuild a movie house that had been destroyed in a fire. The GAO said:

> It appears to us that this theater could well have been an economically viable activity that could have been financed without federal assistance.

It was the only movie theater within a 20-mile radius.

The GAO's findings, along with other published reports, reveal that UDAG grants are being used for purposes other than those Congress intended. The money is being awarded for projects that were proceeding ahead in any event. In many cases these projects are located in downtown areas, not necessarily in depressed neighborhoods in need of redevelopment and jobs. The GAO study also indicates that HUD has often overstated the amount of private investment to be generated by the grants which in a number of cases turned out to be zero. Additionally, many of the companies benefiting from these grants are huge corporations and major state banks that have no intention of building anywhere else but in their home areas whether UDAG grants are received or not.

Moreover, this is clearly a program that is wide open to political abuse. Grants can be used to reward one's friends and punish one's enemies. Thus, it may not be surprising that poor records have been kept on grant distribution. The GAO said one of its findings was that

... documentation currently maintained on the UDAG program is seriously deficient. The 18 project files that we examined did not identify adequately the reasons for funding certain projects or withholding funds from others or how reviewers' concerns and criticisms of the projects were ultimately resolved.

The government is not helping distressed local economies with this program. Most of the building that has been done in our nation's communities is not based on the availability of UDAG grants, but on a myriad of other factors that impact on whether or not an investment will be profitable. By mounting this program—which is removing *nearly three-quarters of a billion dollars* a year from the economy—the government is depleting scarce investment capital which will result in less building, fewer jobs, declining productivity, and slower economic expansion for our cities and towns.

And if you are waiting for HUD to conduct a study of these grants to see how they are affecting the poorest and the most depressed areas of our country, don't hold your breath. There is absolutely no evidence, nor will there be, that this kind of program is going to make the poor any less poor, or our communities economically healthy. This is a bad idea that should be junked. Eventually, one hopes, Congress will learn that it has goofed, but not before billions of tax dollars have been thrown into a wasteful and unproductive program.

PROGRAM 90

Capitol Police — $5.5 Million

The nation's Capitol is swarming with police. They guard the doorways of every committee and subcommittee hearing and meeting, give directions to lost tourists, keep subway cars waiting for tardy senators and congressmen, prevent visitors from taking reserved parking places belonging to congressional employes, check purses and packages of all persons entering the building, process the photo-identification cards issued to reporters covering Congress, patrol the grounds, sidewalks, and corridors, and stop traffic so a rushing congressman can cross the street against the light.

Like everything else in Congress over the years, the Capitol police force has grown out of all proportion to any need for law enforcement protection. There are now about 1200 officers on the force, more than the entire state highway patrol for Ohio or Florida, larger even than the police forces of Atlanta, Buffalo, San Antonio or San Diego, to name only a few. It is little wonder, then, that Capitol Police Chief James Powell says, "Some members of Congress think we have too many police officers."

The budget for this pistol-packing army is more than $22 million a year.

The Capitol police began its expansion shortly after Puerto Rican nationalists shot at members of Congress from the House gallery in 1954. Since the Senate and House disagreed about establishing a professional police force, Congress began borrowing from the District of Columbia police while building up their regular ranks. At that time 10 Metropolitan police officers were "loaned" to the Hill's force to bring leadership and "experience" to its ranks. Twenty-five years later the number on loan stands at 29, all of which costs nearly $1.3 million a year. This is because the Congress reimburses the District government for the salaries of the loaned officers, plus a 61.4 percent surcharge for retirement benefits. That brings the total cost for each loaned policeman to $42,100 in comparison to the average cost for Capitol Hill police officers of $18,263. In fact, Chief Powell himself has been "on loan" from the District police since 1958.

The Capitol is overloaded with police, many of whom stand around office corridors doing nothing. Their budget can be pruned at least 25 percent. Part of that cutback should include the "loaned" D.C.

police officers. The rest of the reduction should be made in the force's regular ranks.

If special emergencies should arise, the Capitol police can always be supplemented from the sizeable ranks of the District of Columbia police. Meanwhile, it is ludicrous for Congress to be maintaining a police force *larger than the forces of some of our bigger cities*.

PROGRAMS 91–92

*Franklin Delano Roosevelt Memorial Commission —
$25,000*

Commission of Fine Arts — $263,000

The Franklin Delano Roosevelt Memorial Commission was established in 1955 to develop plans for a permanent memorial to FDR. Its unsuccessful search for a suitable monument has been marked by endless dispute and bickering. By the end of 1979 no memorial had been erected, despite the expenditure of hundreds of thousands of dollars over a quarter of a century.

There is evidence that FDR informed close friends he did not want a monument erected in his honor. His son, James Roosevelt, once told the commission the Roosevelt family did not like the plans they had been considering and believed a garden area "in the nature of an arboretum of principal American trees" would be a more suitable memorial than the costly, and ugly, concrete monuments being considered. Roosevelt also told the commission that if it could not reach agreement by 1965, it should be disbanded. Needless to say, the commission ignored all of his suggestions.

There are already a number of memorials to FDR, not the least of which is the federally-supported Franklin D. Roosevelt Library in Hyde Park, N.Y. A small stone monument was also placed on Pennsylvania Avenue in Washington in his honor. Plans for a monument to FDR should be abandoned and the Roosevelt Memorial Commission should be abolished forthwith. It has been a waste of the taxpayers' money.

The Commission of Fine Arts was created in 1910 to advise the president and the Congress on matters relating to art and architecture within the nation's capital. Its initial legislation authorized the seven-member body to advise the government on statues, fountains and monuments within the District of Columbia when requested.

Since monuments and memorials are so infrequently erected in Washington, keeping a fulltime commission is wasteful. The commission members serve without pay, but the agency has a paid staff of seven. Their total annual budget is $263,000 a year.

Over the years the commission's work has included the architectural design of new and refurbished government buildings in the city as well as the ongoing revitalization of historic Georgetown. It is right and important to have a body of artistic and architectural experts and historians to review and approve such building endeavors in the nation's capital. But there is no reason why this commission cannot continue to meet as it has on a periodic basis to review and evaluate various projects and proposals when called upon and to render its judgments as an informal advisory panel. Such occasional advice, however, would certainly not require a fulltime staff and a budget of more than a quarter of a million dollars a year.

PROGRAM 93

Council on Environmental Quality and Office of
Environmental Quality — $3 Million

These types of White House advisory offices and councils are created to give the president access to his own independent resources for policy review and program development. But they have in recent years become largely political and public relations devices.

They were particularly popular in the Nixon administration. For a while it seemed that for every major government department there was a special council of independent advisers in the Nixon White House. Such councils gave the appearance that the White House was giving special priority to certain issues—issues that affected powerful interest groups. So the Council of Environmental Quality was created in 1969 by Nixon in the midst of the environmental movement's rise to power. Despite a housecleaning exercise by the incoming Carter administration which swept several similar agencies out of the White House bureaucracy, this council was preserved.

The council consists of three members appointed by the president with the advice and consent of the Senate. The Office of Environmental Quality provides the staff for the council which assists and advises the president on issues related to the national environment. Both bodies are administered by a single organization.

The House Appropriations Committee said the council's only significant activity is "to prepare the annual environmental quality report of the president summarizing major developments of the past year." The council is also

> ... continually concerned with review and policy direction of environmental considerations in federal programs and is actively involved in recommending policies to protect and improve the quality of human surroundings in a broad spectrum of activities.

Maintaining a $3 million a year council to write an annual report for the president that summarizes the "major (environmental) developments of the past year" is a waste of money, particularly when so much is already being spent by the government on environmental protection. In fiscal 1979 the government spent $4.2 billion to run the Environmental Protection Agency.

The council should be folded into EPA. Surely with all that money someone can be found in EPA to write the president's annual report on the environment. EPA is, after all, an agency of the Executive branch administered by the president and his subordinates. The chief executive can at any time call upon EPA's vast resources to provide him with a wealth of information, advice, analysis, and policy and program review.

Don't be fooled by these types of agencies. Many White House councils and offices are *nothing more than political patronage devices*. They are also intended to convey the impression that the president is so deeply concerned with certain problems and issues that he is bringing the government's program right into the White House where he can keep an eye on things. Getting rid of this council should be the start of cleaning out similar White House agencies that only duplicate what is already being reviewed and analyzed in other Executive branch departments and agencies.

PROGRAM 94

Smithsonian Special Foreign Currency Program —
$4.3 Million

Whenever I think of this program I am reminded of a picture of a mother in India holding her naked child, his bony, listless body all but emaciated. While hundreds of millions of people throughout the world are suffering from malnutrition, hunger, and disease, the Smithsonian Institution's Museum Programs and Related Research activities are financing projects like the "Anatomical and Ecological Study of the Indian Whistling Duck" in some of the poorest countries in the world. How many children in India would the $6,000 spent on this study have fed? How many could have been medically treated with the $70,000 spent on studying wild boars in Pakistan? Or the $2,000 spent to examine the Comparative Population Dynamics of Competitively Exclusive Lizard Species? Or the $11,540 for A Biochemical Investigation of *Rana esculenta*, A Bisexual Frog of Possible Hybrid Origin? Be patient, little children. The ducks in India must come first.

There are many research and study projects like these being financed under the auspices of the Smithsonian. Grants are awarded to American colleges and universities and others to undertake research projects in countries where the United States holds excess foreign currencies. The currency is derived from the sale of U.S. agricultural commodities through the food for peace program (Public Law 480) for which the United States is paid in non-controvertible local currencies. The U.S. has normal requirements for this money— such as the operation of its embassies in these countries—but sometimes there is an excess of this currency that our government cannot use. This money is given out in the form of scientific and cultural grants by the Smithsonian as well as by several other federal departments. Any U.S. institution of high learning or researcher is eligible to apply for these grants. Selections of recipients are made by an independent board of scholars. The grants are paid in the currency of the foreign country in which the research work is being carried out. There are four areas in which grants are awarded: 1) Archeology, 2) Systematic and Environmental Biology, 3) Astrophysics and Earth Sciences, and 4) Museum Programs.

There are five excess countries: Burma, Egypt, Guinea, India, and Pakistan, although Egypt was expected to leave the list because her

362

high rate of inflation had effectively ended any excess currency in the country.

The Smithsonian spent $3.6 million equivalent in excess currencies on this program in fiscal 1978 and nearly $4.3 million in fiscal 1979. Over $5 million was budgeted for fiscal 1980.

A provision in Public Law 480 states that these foreign currencies may be used to

> ... collect, collate, translate, abstract, and disseminate scientific and technological information and conduct research and support scientific activities overseas including programs and projects of scientific cooperation between the United States and other countries such as coordinated research against diseases common to all of mankind or unique to individual regions of the globe, and promote and support programs of medical and scientific research, cultural and educational development, family planning, health, nutrition, and sanitation.

Thus, the Smithsonian is doing nothing more with this money than Congress has authorized in the broadest language possible. The scope of this provision is so typical of Congress. Rather than concentrate this money on a few worthy and vital goals, Congress couldn't resist spending the money on virtually everything under the sun.

Some of the Smithsonian's grants are going to highly worthy programs involving important archeological discoveries and preservation projects. However, most of its excess currency has gone into wasteful, low priority research in countries where there is a serious need for the essentials of life, such as food and medical care.

In the past, this money has been spent on such projects as a "Revised List of the Mediterranean Fishes of Israel"; the "Semen of the Ceylon Elephant"; "Vermeulenia—a New Genus of Orchids"; "Recovery of a Spotbill Duck in U.S.S.R."; "Sponges of Red Sea Origin on the Mediterranean Coast of Israel"; "A Review of the Recovery Data Obtained by the Bombay Natural History Society's Bird Migration Project"; "Studying Skulls in Egypt"; "The Excavation of Two Glass Factory Sites in Western Israel"; "A Red Sea Grouper Caught on the Mediterranean Coast of Israel"; and "Cytological Studies of Pacific Land Snails."

A review of the Smithsonian's 1979 spending projects suggests that this excess currency is still being squandered on similarly low-priority projects. Here are some examples:

—$47,590 to prepare a catalog on the art objects in the new Luxor Museum of Ancient Egyptian Art as well as designing and writing label information.

—$6,078 for the "Editing and translation of Ali ibn-Ridwan's *On the Prevention of Bodily Ills in Egypt*, dealing with epidemic diseases and historical background of health conditions in eleventh century Egypt."

—$20,000 for the publication of "a comprehensive body of literature on the 4500-year-old cities of the Indus civilization."

—$253,271 for the travel expenses of American participants to the Xth International Congress of Anthropological and Ethnological Sciences in India and other conferences convened in connection with that meeting.

—$6,364 for an "ethnographic film study of a nomadic herding society, Pashtoon people of Afghanistan, some of whom have settled in India."

—$14,463 to conduct an "initial survey of cross-cultural folk traditions using folk puppets to promote international understanding among diverse cultures of Africa and Asia."

—$30,988 for "a search for Paleocene and Eocene (55-65 million years old) fossil mammals in Pakistan."

—$61,500 for "a search for fossils of small and large animals in Pakistan."

—$73,917 for "studies of smelting sites preserved from ancient times to locate the sources of copper ore and examine the techniques of early mining and smelting."

Some of these projects no doubt deserve financial support from our great educational institutions and foundations, but *not from the federal government*. The excess currencies should be withdrawn from the Smithsonian's use. Congress should sharply narrow the uses to which these excess currencies can be put by the government, focusing solely on absolutely vital world priorities in countries of unbelievable poverty. Those priorities should obviously include projects related to health, nutrition, sanitation, and family planning. Federal funding for studies on the Indian Whistling Duck, the trips to international anthropological conventions, and puppet shows must await some future time when more pressing needs have been satisfactorily alleviated.

PROGRAM 95

Consumer Product Safety Commission — $40.6 Million

This agency is a perfect example of the "rubber room syndrome" that has become so symptomatic of the government's mania for consumer protection. Carried to its illogical conclusions, the Consumer Product Safety Commission believes that if it promulgates enough rules, regulations and standards, most major injuries in our everyday life can be prevented. To believe this is to believe in the tooth fairy. The history of this $40 million-a-year bureaucracy provides ample proof of its ineffectiveness and irrelevance to real consumer needs.

Created by Congress in 1973 as an independent regulatory agency, the Commission has been a case book example of excessive federal regulation. Congress established the Commission to pull together a hodgepodge of federal consumer protection programs that had been scattered over the bureaucracy: the Poison Prevention Packaging Act, administered by the Food and Drug Administration; the Federal Hazardous Substances Act, implemented by HEW; the Flammable Fabrics Act, carried out by the Federal Trade Commission and the Commerce Department; and the Refrigerator Safety Act, also placed under Commerce (although this act hasn't been enforced in years). Charged with "reducing unreasonable risks of injury associated with consumer products," the Commission was authorized to issue mandatory safety standards for products, ban unsafe products from the marketplace, oversee recalls of dangerous products, and where possible to encourage voluntary safety standards by industry. The agency was also authorized to implement a program of information and education for the consumer on product hazards, conduct research, and gather injury data.

Even some of the Commission's staunchest proponents concede that the program has been "just a disaster," as one congressional committee counsel put it. Instead of concentrating on a narrow range of products where there is potential to reduce a large number of injuries, the Commission spread its regulatory net over everything. Thus, it has concerned itself with products from skateboards to television antennas. It has instructed skiers to tighten their bindings and to keep their ski equipment in tip-top shape while on the slopes. It has lectured mothers on how to care for their infants in the nursery. It has advised people on the do's and don't's of bicycling. It has

365

cautioned users about the risks of swimming pool slides. It is, in short, *government paternalism gone berserk*.

The Commission's efforts at issuing mandatory standards have been among its chief failures. Between 1973 and 1976 it issued only three standards concerning swimming pool slides, matchbooks, and miniature Christmas tree lights. The courts threw out the swimming pool slide standards, and overturned parts of the matchbook standards. The tree lights standards won out, but they, like the pool slides and the matchbooks, were responsible for a relatively tiny number of accidents.

Equally humiliating has been the Commission's ridiculous attempts to make the powermower safer by coming up with a device that would automatically shut off the engine each time the mower came to a halt. There are an estimated 80 million people in the United States who use powermowers, according to the Outdoor Equipment Institute. The Commission estimates that 62,000 people injure themselves with powermowers each year. That is eight hundredths of one percent of the number of people who use powermowers, an infinitesimal number. Moreover, the number of injuries by powermowers has been dropping, declining from sixth place on the list of the nation's most dangerous products in 1977 to 10th place in 1978 without the Commission's having done anything. Ignoring for the moment the number of coronaries this device will cause among people forced to jerk the starter cord every time the machine turns off, this proposal would raise the price of powermowers by as much as $100 or more. (But maybe that's what the Commission has in mind—to drive up the price so high that people can afford only manual lawnmowers.)

The extent to which the Commission has sought to impose its "rubber room syndrome" on the nation is not only ludicrous, it is insane. Because of the number of fires begun by a few careless smokers who fall asleep on chairs and sofas holding lighted cigarettes, the Commission is considering the development of mandatory standards for nonflammable upholstery. In other words, because of a relatively small number of careless people, the entire nation will be forced to purchase furniture made with government-licensed nonflammable upholstery. This will not only drive up the cost of furniture for consumers, it will no doubt severely limit the types and varieties of fabrics that would be available. The Commission also requires that carpets and rugs meet certain flammability standards which in turn has added to their cost.

As long as there have been playgrounds, children have hurt themselves on them. The Commission says that about 75,000 children require some sort of hospital treatment for injuries received on the playground, usually for stitches or X-rays for possible fractures or broken bones. Yet because of a relatively few injuries, especially when one considers there are 40 million children between the ages of one and 12 in our country, the Commission was considering standards to reduce the risk of falls or being hit by moving equipment.

When asked to point out the Commission's major accomplishments, a congressional supporter of the agency named bike standards, noting that, because of the Commission's actions, "pedals are not as sharp as they once were and chain guards now protect bikers." From what? Why, from getting their trousers caught in the bike's chain. Even so, there are no figures to show that bike accidents have been appreciably reduced because of this agency's activities. Most bike-related accidents result either from carelessness by the users or from motor vehicle traffic. Indeed, the Commission's own figures show that of the five products most often involved in injuries in 1978, bikes continue to head the list. The other four most dangerous products are stairs, football and related equipment, baseball and related equipment, and playground equipment.

Has the Commission had any really successful accomplishments? The agency touts the child-proof cap on medicines as one of the nation's major safety reforms, but in truth this was developed under the Poison Prevention Packaging Act *before* the Commission was established by Congress. Others have pointed to the agency's recall of hair dryers whose components contained asbestos, a cancer-causing substance. However, this product's hazard was brought to the public's attention by a Washington television station, not by the Commission. In fact, the agency knew about the asbestos hazard a year before the station's disclosure, but the CPSC said that because of its relatively small budget, it couldn't conduct the necessary tests. Hair dryers didn't fit into their priorities.

The Commission has also been concerned with toys and the potential injury some of them can cause. But some of the CPSC's efforts have unnecessarily harmed toy manufacturers.

A case in point was Ed Sohmers, general manager of Marlin Toy Products, Inc., a Wisconsin firm that found one of its toys cited as unsafe by the U.S. Food and Drug Administration. The FDA said the toy, a plastic ball that contained colored pellets, was unsafe because children could swallow them if the ball broke open. Marlin has been marketing the toy since 1962 and had never received a complaint.

The company nonetheless recalled the toy at a cost of $95,000 and removed the potentially harmful pellets. But that wasn't the end of its problems. As soon as the Commission began operation in 1973 it issued a list of banned toys, and the Marlin toy was on it. Despite the company's protests, the agency refused to recall the 250,000 copies of the list it had distributed to thousands of toy stores around the country. Not "just to take one or two toys off the list," as a CPSC official put it. (Note that the Commission was applying a little cost-benefit evaluation in *its own* behalf, something it wouldn't dream of doing in behalf of businesses and consumers who must bear the costs of their regulatory activities.)

Marlin's toy business dropped sharply. With $1.2 million in losses, it had to lay off almost all of its 85 workers, many of whom were handicapped. Sohmers wrote more than 700 letters to try to obtain legislative approval that would let him sue for damages. He spent weeks and $15,000 putting together the documentation needed to prove its losses. Eventually, the company went out of business.

Remember the government's drive to make children's sleepwear nonflammable? The Commerce Department, which originally administered the Flammable Fabrics Act, forced the garment industry in the late 1960s to meet a flammability standard that was so strict only one flame retardant chemical on the market met its specifications. Its name was TRIS. Clothing producers begged Washington to give them more time to develop alternative flame retardants, but the Commerce Department pressed its demands. Years later, it was learned that TRIS was carcinogenic and that children could get cancer either by sucking the material, or absorbing it through their skin. The garments were taken off the market by the CPSC at great cost to manufacturers, costs which all consumers had to pay in higher prices. Another flame retardant was approved by the Commission, but consumer groups say that this chemical is also carcinogenic. The upshot of the government's mismanaged efforts is that many mothers, confused and frightened by the government's regulations, are putting their youngsters in untreated longjohns or other nontreated garments at night and thus escaping the government's experimentation with their children. But the government continues to insist that chemical-drenched sleepwear be manufactured for our young. In 1979 the Commission was in the process of clarifying its definitions of sleepwear covered by its standards because "there has in the past been confusion as to what garments are included."

Since 1973 virtually all of the Commission's efforts have been ineffective in reducing product-related accidents. In most cases the accidents in question have nothing to do with the product itself. The accidents are almost always caused through carelessness or inexperience. Government can, and has, forced manufacturers to modify certain products but in most cases this has only made the product more expensive while doing little if anything to curb accidents.

Raked over the coals in recent years by congressional oversight committees for squandering its money on such trivial matters as swimming pool slides, the Commission has all but abandoned its efforts to impose mandatory standards on industry. Instead, the agency is trying to find alternative ways of accomplishing its mission through the development of approved voluntary standards that the CPSC can monitor. Said one congressional committee official charged with overseeing this agency:

> If it doesn't work, then I would say they are a likely candidate for sunset (abolishment). Congress has told them that they have three more years. If we can't see some improvement, we'll find another way to do it.

As was pointed out earlier, a sure sign a federal program is dying is a reduction or status quo in its funding. The CPSC is dying. In fiscal 1977 the agency received a budget of $39.8 million. In 1978 Congress gave them $40.5 million. In fiscal 1979 that figure crept up to $42.9 million, but then dropped again in fiscal 1980 to $40.6 million. These budgets hardly represent a vote of confidence by the Congress. In fact, the figures represent an even sharper reduction because the agency isn't being kept abreast of inflation. As far as Congress is concerned, this agency is going nowhere.

It would be cruel and unusual punishment to let this commission linger any longer. Its work, in the words of one top level committee aide, has been "an embarrassment." Said another:

> Look, nothing the Congress has created in the last 10 years has succeeded. The LEAA is a disaster. The Energy Department is inept. They've all been failures. The CPSC is a good example of what has been happening.

Commission officials are always fond of saying that their agency is at "a crossroads" in its history and that success is just beyond the next fiscal year. An exasperated Sen. Proxmire told CPSC officials at their fiscal 1979 budget hearings:

> Unfortunately . . . your agency seems to always be at the crossroads.

Last year we were told about the impressive results your reorganization and priority setting would produce. The year before that Commissioner Simpson told us that if CPSC could set priorities and stick to them, you could do twice as much work on the same budget. And we are constantly told that with just a few million more dollars the Commission can perform as it was meant to do.

But we keep pouring the dollars into your agency and very little seems to come out the other end in the way of standards or injury reductions.

The House Interstate Commerce Committee's 1976 report on federal regulatory agencies was equally unkind in its review of the commission's work:

Its performance to date has been disappointing. The agency has fumbled over arranging its priorities, run into complex problems in seeking to maximize public participation, and delayed launching an effective enforcement program.

The CPSC should be put out of its misery. The government is trying to prevent what cannot be prevented. Nothing the federal government does in Washington or requires of manufacturers is going to prevent someone from falling off a bike, taking a tumble on the ski slopes, falling down stairs, or slipping off a swing on the playground. It is the height of naivete to think otherwise. The commission should be abolished and the respective consumer safety acts within its jurisdiction should be divided up among appropriate agencies to be applied on a far narrower scope but, one hopes, in a more effective and realistic way. The government could, for starters, seek to encourage broader voluntary safety standards among industries who, after all, are just as eager to avoid costly lawsuits as anyone else.

PROGRAM 96

Department of Education

In September of 1979 the Congress, against the editorial advice of virtually every major newspaper in the country as well as the American Federation of Teachers, voted to establish a $14.2 billion Department of Education. It was the 12th department to be created by the government and the second department to be created within the first three years of the Carter administration.*

Its creation represents one of the most blatant political payoffs of recent times. When Jimmy Carter was running for President in 1976 he promised the National Education Association (NEA), the nation's largest teacher's union, that if he were elected, he would support legislation to establish a Cabinet-level Department of Education, just for them. Carter got NEA's support that year and won the organization's "paid on delivery" endorsement again just days after the administration successfully pushed the Department of Education bill through Congress. It was support that Carter, whose public standing had dwindled to almost nonexistent levels, needed desperately in the fall of 1979. The payoff was no secret. Throughout consideration of the bill virtually every published account mentioned Carter's promise and the likelihood that NEA would vote to endorse the president for re-election in 1980, if he succeeded in getting their bill signed into law.

NEA's bill passed, but not by much in the House where it won by only 14 votes on final passage. A vote on an earlier version had passed the House by only four votes.

In the end it was sold to lawmakers on the flimsiest of grounds, with the major argument being that breaking up the Department of Health, Education and Welfare (now called the Department of Health and Human Services) and combining its education activities with related programs from other agencies would eliminate duplication and fragmentation, saving taxpayers millions of dollars. How much of a savings? The Office of Management and Budget figured the consolidation would save—brace yourself—between $15 million and $19 million. Now bear in mind that while $19 million is nothing to sneeze at, it is hardly much against a $548 billion budget. Moreover, the transition costs alone for this department were put at $10 million. Thus, we were really talking about a savings of $5 million

*The Department of Energy was established in 1977.

371

to $9 million (The transition estimates were ridiculously low, and were expected to be far above that figure once all of the relocation, office furnishings, and other reorganizational changes had taken place).

Proponents argued that no new employes would be added, and that some would even be eliminated. Such, however, will not be the case, because the mere establishment of this new department required a new secretary, assistant secretaries, undersecretaries, assistant undersecretaries, and deputy assistant undersecretaries, plus additional support staff. The department also demanded regional offices, larger office space, new stationary and paperwork, cars, drivers, personnel offices, and a wide range of other bureaucratic machinery to run its affairs. An amendment was added to the legislation to force a modest cut in its 18,000 employes within one year, but the bureaucracy knows how to circumvent such things. Officials can merely hire consultants to handle work these employes were doing. *Not a dollar* will be saved.

Thus, the major argument that reorganization of the government's educational activities will save money is patently fraudulent. The administration predicted in the long run that $100 million would be saved. But this figure appeared to have been pulled out of thin air. Most members of Congress knew it to be fraudulent. They're not that dumb. They know how government works.

A veteran Washington reporter who covered the bill from beginning to end said:

> Of course it's going to end up costing more. A department by its very nature requires many more people to run it because of its superstructure. There are certain administrative functions HEW handled for the Office of Education, such as personnel, that the new department will probably have to handle on its own. All of this takes more people and more money.

There are other reasons why this department will be costlier than its original components. When budget time rolls around, a department is able to exert more clout in pressing for larger funding from Congress than can smaller agencies. It carries a bureaucratic momentum and muscle all its own. Since it no longer has to compete with health and welfare, as it did under HEW, the new department will be able to exert the full brunt of the education lobby in its behalf upon the Congress. Make no mistake about it, the principal reason the NEA and the administration wanted to elevate the Office of Education to a fullfledged department was to give it the political power and prestige to seek bigger budget increases for federal educational programs.

As *Washington Post* reporter Spencer Rich noted in his story on final congressional approval of the bill establishing the new behemoth, Carter's arguments for the department "included enhanced prestige for education in having a department and cabinet spokesman all its own . . ." That, to a large degree, was what the NEA lobby sought. That is what many special interests seek. The question is whether it is wise to establish Cabinet-level departments solely for special interests.

That question has been convincingly answered by virtually every government reorganization commission over the past 30 years. The Hoover Commission of 1949, the Heineman Commission of 1967, the Ash Council of 1971 all concluded that federal departments should be created to serve general purposes, while strongly *rejecting* the idea of establishing departments that serve narrow constituencies.

That was why Reps. Benjamin Rosenthal, John Conyers, Henry Waxman and Ted Weiss stated in dissenting views on the bill:

> While the concept of a general purpose department is difficult to define precisely, it does suggest that departments should have as their objective the achievement of certain national policies, not merely the maintenance of relatively narrow grant programs. It also suggests that the Secretary of a Cabinet-level Department should not be faced with a single set of interest groups, but rather should have a sufficient number of competing interest groups so that he is not unduly influenced by any single pressure group.

The lawmakers asked:

> If the educators have their own department, will the medical profession also demand a department of its own? And the remnant, the social welfare and income maintenance groups, would, by default, have their own department. It is not unreasonable to assume that by deciding to establish a Department of Education, Congress is really deciding on three new Departments, not one.

Indeed, for a number of years welfare rights groups have pushed for a separate Department of Welfare as have other constituencies.

When Congress decided to consolidate related programs and agencies into the Departments of Transportation, Housing and Urban Development, and Energy, the same arguments were used: namely, that consolidation would lead to greater efficiency and lower costs; that the departments would in the long run be cheaper than the sum of their parts. The rapidly rising budgets of these three departments—which collectively account for more than $34 billion a year—is proof positive that such departmentalization guarantees that government will continue to grow larger and more costly. The real cure for duplication is to eliminate those programs and agencies whose work overlaps other programs and agencies, not to consolidate them into one bureaucratic pot.

Moreover, on the question of consolidation of related programs, the Department of Education is particularly fraudulent because it does not encompass several major school programs, including veterans' educational programs, job training programs, and Head Start, the preschool assistance program. These were left out because sponsors of the bill feared they would lose the votes of lawmakers beholden to other constituency groups who did not wish to see their pet programs disturbed from their existing locations within the government.

Virtually every major newspaper in the country, including the *Washington Post* and the *New York Times*, opposed the creation of this department, calling it unnecessary, wasteful, and a political payoff to the administration in return for NEA support.

Said the *Post*:

> The creation of this department is a response, by both the president and the Congress, to one specific organization, the National Education Association. The NEA represents many, but not all, of the people who are employed by public school systems. It is always questionable policy to establish a large public agency whose constituency is the same people whose work that agency oversees. The NEA is, for example, adamantly opposed to any systematic attempt to measure the quality of the education that schools provide. The NEA's opposition to standardized testing, of either students or their teachers, has become increasingly explicit in recent years.

Public education in this country has continued to decline for more than a decade, despite substantial increases in public funds for school costs and vast programs involving educational experimentalization. Federal education dollars in the last 17 years have gone from $1.2 billion in 1962 to $8 billion in 1979 (in constant 1972 dollars). But student achievement levels under public education have been consistently falling. Scholastic Aptitude Tests of college-bound high school seniors in 1979 dropped two points, to 427, in the average verbal scores and fell one point, to 467, in the average mathematics scores. An 800 is the highest score possible. In 1968 the average verbal score was 466 and the mathematics average was 492.

No savings is given at the head of this chapter, because there is no way of knowing precisely how many layers of bureaucracy have been added to existing educational programs and agencies brought under this department.

Surrounding the government's educational programs with more bureaucratic trappings and a morass of Cabinet-level officials is not the way to improve them. As the SAT and other student test scores continue to plunge downward, we must begin holding our educational programs accountable. Instead of rewarding an inept system of federal aid to education with the added prestige of having its own department, we should begin questioning whether unworkable programs and agencies should be reorganized or abolished. This newly-created department *should be dismantled* and its respective educational programs and agencies returned to their previous places in the government. Then Congress should undertake a major reexamination of every dollar we presently spend on education with an eye to throwing out bad programs and strengthening those that work.

PROGRAM 97

Maritime Administration — $491 Million

The Maritime Administration was established in 1936 to "promote a strong U.S. Merchant Marine for the water bourne carriage of U.S. foreign and domestic commerce and to serve as an aid to national defense." Today, however, this agency is no longer needed to insure that America has the shipping resources to export and import U.S. goods and thus protect our national security.

Long known as the sugar daddy of the U.S. merchant marine, this agency annually pours hundreds of millions of dollars in subsidies into shipbuilding, shipping operations, training of shipping crews, shipping research and development, and marketing and insurance programs—all to benefit the nation's private sea-going transport companies. Many of these subsidized lines are highly profitable and provide their shareholders with regular dividends and their employes with handsome salaries. One of them is Moore McCormack Inc. which reported total sales and revenues in 1978 of $351.6 million. The company's before tax income was $44 million for the year. Their cargo-liner services enjoyed an operating profit of 28 percent. Their bulk transportation services had a 30 percent profit, according to the firm's 1978 annual report. Nonetheless, in addition to these profits, Moore McCormack had 10 cargo vessels subsidized at a rate of $27 million for the year.

Let's take a look at this agency's major activities.

MarAd issues "construction differential subsidies" to shipbuilders in an effort to make the costs of building ships in this country competitive with cheaper vessels in foreign nations. But as we shall see, countries such as Japan and Korea can still build ships at substantially less cost than that of U.S.-subsidized vessels.

In 1978 there were 48 new merchant marine vessels being built. Their total contract value was $3.1 billion. Of the 48 ships, 24 were built with federal subsidies. Twenty-two of the remaining 24 were financed by federal loan guarantees. The combined construction costs of the 24 subsidized vessels amounted to $1.7 billion—of which $552 million was paid or subsidized by the government.

Loan guarantees totaled $430.7 million for 1978, covering 275 vessels. The agency has guaranteed over $4 billion in loans.

There are 745 ships in the U.S. Merchant Marine, of which 532 are actively in operation. Of this total, *only* 186 vessels are receiving operational subsidies. To qualify for operating subsidy payments, the ships must operate in "essential foreign trade," must agree to prescribed routes, and must hire only American citizens for its crews.

MarAd paid $300 million in operating subsidies in 1978 to American shipping companies. Part of this subsidy has supported the shipment of grain to the Soviet Union. In 1978 alone, 58 vessels carrying grain to the USSR received subsidy payments totaling $7.5 million.

Over a 41-year period, from 1937 to 1978, total operating subsidies to shipping lines have exceeded $5 billion, $127.3 million of which has supported Soviet trade.

More than $8 billion was spent on shipbuilding and operating subsidies during this period.

MarAd also supports the state and federal merchant marine academies that train our nation's seamen. These include the U.S. Merchant Marine Academy at Kingsport, New York, and six state merchant marine academies. In fiscal 1979 MarAd gave the U.S. Academy over $17 million to run the school. State schools received over $5 million.

MarAd also spends about $17 million a year on research and development programs for the maritime industry. This money is primarily aimed at improving ship operations and shipbuilding.

Among a range of other services, the agency provides war risk insurance when it decides that conventional insurance is not reasonably available. It also conducts a marketing development program, making contact with policymaking officials overseas to promote commerce, and it initiates studies on such things as port and terminal operations.

Yet despite MarAd's enormous subsidies and related programs over the years, it has failed to stem our merchant marine's precipitous decline. The United States is now ranked 11th out of 15 major merchant fleets in the world. Compared to this country's 532 active ships, Liberia has 2,627 vessels registered under its flag—although most are "flags of convenience" vessels registered in that country solely for tax purposes. It hasn't always been this way. Prior to and after World War II, the United States had the largest merchant marine fleet in the world. However, after the war the government began selling off most of its ships, though a large number of them, the so-called ghost fleet, still remain mothballed and could be returned to active service.

It is not necessary to go into the details of the maritime industry's downfall. What should be clear by now to everyone is that the industry has not been improved by this agency's vast system of subsidies.

One of the major problems is the enormous cost of ship construction in this country in comparison to other nations. Robert Calkins, a maritime policy expert, notes:

> The root of the problem is that the operating and construction costs of American ships are higher than those of any other major maritime nation whereas the productivity of American and foreign flag ships are approximately equal.

Other problems further aggravate the industry. Over the years the government's maritime laws have placed more and more restrictions and prohibitions on U.S. shipping. For example, shippers are required to purchase their capital equipment in the United States and not abroad where it is cheaper. This is not true in other maritime countries.

Congressman Pete McCloskey of California, one of the few members of Congress who has been critical of the Maritime Administration, has called its subsidy program "a failure." McCloskey stated that

> . . . more than once, by the American shipowners who are required to operate ships that are constructed with construction subsidies, the program has been characterized as an albatross about their necks.

In 1979, when he tried unsuccessfully to cut $70 million from MarAd's subsidies, McCloskey said:

> There continues to be a trend which causes ship operating companies receiving operating differential subsidies to bear heavier and heavier burdens of supporting the shipbuilding industry. In a healthy industry, such a result might be of little concern; however, the state of the operating differential subsidized industry today is far from healthy. Two companies have gone bankrupt; three others operated at a loss last year. . . . five subsidized line companies are not operating in a state to attract new capital.

Significantly, McCloskey told the House, the one company that was making money and considering expanding its operations was Sea Land, which was building its ships *overseas* at 50 percent less than the firm would have to pay in the United States.

In a letter to McCloskey, Sea Land told why they built their ships abroad:

> The D-9 class vessels were contracted for $30 million each in a fixed dollar contract. Our ship construction department estimates that U.S. construction costs are about $80 million per vessel. The differential is

$50 million; but section 502 of the 1936 Act permits a maximum subsidy of 50 percent of the U.S. cost or $40 million.

Therefore, even with a 50 percent construction differential subsidy, our company would have paid a penalty of about $120 million to get later delivery of 12 ships from yards with little or no experience in building the required machinery plants. In addition, there would have been a further penalty of a delay of about 12 months in starting the service. Added to that, the sequence of delivery from American yards would have been at least every 90 days versus every 30 days.

If one is looking for more reasons for merchant marine decline, McCloskey offers this example involving Pacific Far East Lines, which in 1978 went broke:

One of the reasons Pacific Far East Lines stated to our committee that they went into bankruptcy was because the union on the west coast forced them to carry a crew of 40 on the ship where the Coast Guard manning level was 22.

Similar size ships in New Orleans, McCloskey added, "carry a crew of 32, 10 above the minimum level for safety purposes," yet still manage to turn a profit.

Pacific Far East Lines was forced by the union to "featherbed" and to carry a crew "well above 50 percent over the safety level." In fact, McCloskey said,

. . . a crew of 40 is 25 percent higher than the crew that that same ship was carrying out of gulf coast ports. Where the rub comes is that those eight additional crew members are paid for by taxpayers of the United States through an operating differential subsidy, this year about $250 million.

To have the taxpayers pay for more crew than is necessary to safely and profitably run a ship is "an outrage," McCloskey told his colleagues. Unfortunately, his amendment to correct this was defeated when shipping and steel interests teamed up against him in the House.

Many maritime specialists have pointed to the federal requirement that U.S. ships and labor must come from domestic markets as the principal reason for the industry's troubles. John G. Kilgour, in his book *The U.S. Merchant Marine National Maritime Policy and Industrial Relations*,* said:

The fundamental problem is an effective requirement that its factors of production (ships and labor) be purchased in high-cost domestic markets. The effect of this requirement has been to burden the industry with extremely high equipment and operating costs and to prevent it from adopting the latest and most efficient technology.

*Praeger Publishers, New York, 1975.

Once again we see that the heavy hand of government regulation is largely responsible for the decline of an American industry. This, however, is not the fault of this agency, but the Maritime Commission which was established to regulate the shipping industry.

The argument can no longer be made that we have not poured enough money into this industry. Indeed, as Gerald Jantscher observed in his book *Bread Upon The Waters: Federal Aids to the Maritime Industries**:

> No industry in the United States has a longer history of aid from the federal government than the ship-operating and shipbuilding industries.

Jantscher's study dismisses the traditional arguments that federal aid to the maritime industry is vitally important to maintaining a healthy American economy and easing our balance of payments.

To put it bluntly, the economic rationale for continued maritime assistance, Jantscher said, is

> . . . not very credible. Whatever force it had depends largely on the assumption that the resources employed in the shipping and shipbuilding industries would lie idle in the absence of the maritime aids . . . The scanty evidence available suggests that U.S. shipbuilders have difficulty securing and retaining the labor they need to build all the merchant ships their customers have ordered, hence that their activity, like that of most enterprises, reduces output elsewhere in the economy.

As for the U.S. balance of payments argument, Jantscher said:

> The U.S. maritime industries are dwarfs in the American economy. Their effect on the U.S. balance of payments is much smaller than that of many other industries.

Jantscher added that, if federal subsidies were to be paid to every industry whose operations produced as large a balance of payments benefit as that produced by the operations of the maritime industries, dozens of industries "would immediately be entitled to public assistance."

Jantscher also finds the national security rationale in behalf of MarAd to be somewhat shaky.

"We are sometimes told," he said, "that much of the nation's overseas commerce must move in U.S. flag vessels if the nation's security is to be protected. Exactly how the nation's security is threatened when foreign flag vessels carry our commerce has never been properly explained . . ."

Still, no matter how reasonable the national security argument may seem

*Brookings Institution, Washington, D.C., 1975.

. . . at a time when commercial relations between nations are becoming more acrimonious, it will not withstand scrutiny. There is no danger today that the world's shipowners could effectively combine to boycott a single nation's commerce—especially the commerce of the world's largest trading nation. The merchant shipping industry is too fragmented; the industry's resources are too mobile; ships are too easily built. Moreover, most of the major maritime nations are allies of the United States and their governments would be sure to disapprove participation by their nationals in any such embargo. If one distant day circumstances change and the possibility of a shipping boycott against this country no longer seems fanciful, there will be ample time to decide how the United States ought to respond and to consider less costly— and possibly more effective—ways of meeting the threat than expanding the U.S. flag merchant marine.

What is chiefly wrong with the current maritime program, Jantscher said, is that its goal of creating a competitive U.S. flag fleet is the wrong goal. He believes that the program should be redesigned so that its primary mission would be national security, which he takes pains to separate from economic security—which the program's supporters argue is intertwined with our national defense posture.

"In my opinion," Jantscher wrote, "the economic security of the United States is not much jeopardized" now by our reliance on foreign flag vessels to move the bulk of our foreign commerce.

The self-serving arguments in behalf of the Maritime Administration *by the special interests who benefit from its endless subsidies* should be dismissed out of hand. Our merchant marine under existing federal rules and laws is a dying industry that this agency believes can be kept alive through enormous transfusions of federal aid. And for what? To keep a costly yet deteriorating U.S. merchant marine industry barely on its feet? To provide subsidies to lines that are already quite profitable? This is *sheer folly* when the goods America needs can be shipped far more cheaply through foreign flag vessels. If American shipping companies can operate more profitably by flying "flags of convenience" under other nations, let them. If U.S. shipping companies can save substantial sums of capital by buying their ships and other equipment abroad, they should be allowed to do so. This will allow American shipping companies to take advantage of substantially lower capital costs which in turn will mean lower prices for American consumers as well as higher profits for American shippers.

The time has come to mothball this agency and release its 1,384 employes. Its shipbuilding and operational subsidies, the market development and insurance activities, the research projects and studies must end.

In its place, as Jantscher suggested, Congress should undertake a major reevaluation of America's shipbuilding and shipping industries, focusing on this industry's impact on our future national security needs. Such an evaluation, he wisely concludes, should be conducted by an independent commission

> . . . composed of men without prior experience in maritime affairs. . . . They should be instructed to evaluate even the basic premises underlying the national security argument and to draw whatever conclusions for maritime policy that their study warrants. They should determine whether reasons of security require that any portion of the nation's peacetime foreign commerce should travel aboard U.S. flag vessels; and if they find such reasons, should justify them scrupulously.

Such a commission, I would add, should consider other ideas that do not involve direct government assistance of the maritime industry, including tax write-offs and complete deregulation, except for safety requirements.

In the end, Jantscher said, "The program will no doubt be smaller." One hopes so. But I am inclined to go much further than that. After a thorough examination of this nation's shipping resources, I suspect we'll find that no program—at least in peacetime—is needed at all.

PROGRAM 98

Federal Trade Commission — $65 Million

Since 1915 the Federal Trade Commission has been investigating and regulating American business. The FTC began modestly, concerned at first with monopolistic practices. But over the years Congress has broadened the Commission's scope and authority to the point where virtually no economic activity seems beyond its reach. Now 1,700 FTC bureaucrats, including 600 lawyers, are trying to regulate everything from health spas to used car dealers.

For decades this agency has been worshipped as one of the government's sacred cows. It existed because it has, seemingly, always existed. Big business had to be controlled by government, we were told. And as business grew, the FTC's power and sweep grew with it. Senator Harrison Schmitt of New Mexico has called the FTC "the second most powerful legislature in the country." The agency, Schmitt said, now

... claims the power to declare any commercial act to be "unfair," regardless of state law, and thereby to amend all state statutes and reverse all state cases that may be inconsistent with its declaration.

Accompanying the FTC's growth over the years has been an increasingly adversary attitude by government that all too often has been intent on punishing business through excessive regulation and civil penalties for largely negligible violations.

Today, however, many thoughtful economic and political thinkers of varying ideological persuasions are beginning to question this agency's value. As the inflationary costs of federal regulations upon the business community, and ultimately upon consumers, are increasingly being realized, the FTC doesn't seem quite so sacred anymore. Even some of its most loyal supporters in Congress who once took this agency for granted, are now angrily challenging its regulatory initiatives. Certainly such questioning of the FTC's role and responsibilities is long overdue. And it leads—as we shall see—to one inescapable question: Why on earth has Congress let this agency exist for so long?

The FTC has three main divisions. The Bureau of Competition, under the 1914 Clayton Act, has responsibility for enforcing our antitrust laws. The Clayton Act gave the FTC the power to combat restraint of trade practices, monopolies, and corporate mergers that lessen competition. This division has a yearly budget of $32 million.

The Bureau of Consumer Protection, with a budget of $30 million, investigates and litigates deceptive or unfair practices harmful to the consumer, and seeks to inform the consumer through educational programs.

The FTC's third division, the Bureau of Economics, undertakes studies and research into business practices and structure. Under a budget of $6 million, it conducts a massive data collection program that demands costly and time-consuming business reports on a quarterly basis. A multitude of surveys and questionnaires extract information from 9,000 manufacturers, 5,000 trade organizations, and over 1,000 mining industries. Other areas of research and analysis deal with market structure and specific industry-wide investigations.

The rhetoric surrounding this agency must have been written by a Madison Avenue specialist. Who can argue with an agency that is "aimed at reducing prices to consumers and limiting the effects of inflation, and fostering and preserving competition and the free enterprise system," and at the same time wants to eliminate "unfair or deceptive practices which preclude full and fair functioning of the marketplace"?

But although the language of the FTC's intent may sound angelic, the reality of its actions is not. For the FTC has been an ineffective and largely destructive instrument of government, kept alive solely because Congress wants to maintain a token agency that appears to be doing something about higher prices and unfair business practices. But the truth is that the FTC has done nothing to significantly curb inflation. To the contrary, it has contributed to inflation. True, the FTC may be able to point to a rule or regulation here or there that may have limited prices for a few products or services, but the indisputable fact remains that consumer prices have soared despite all of its studies, subpoenas, surveys, rules and regulations, civil penalties, and court actions.

What this agency has given us is simply this: It has forced litigation and regulations primarily upon small businesses, often concerning itself with either trivial matters that pose no threat to anyone, or problems better left to industry or the states. Its major actions against large industries have been costly, time-consuming, bureaucratic safaris that have resulted in wasted tax dollars, and sapped companies of untold millions in compliance and defense costs. In the end, these FTC-induced costs are passed on the consumer whom the FTC is charged with protecting.

In recent years a number of studies have critically examined the

FTC's activities. One of the best was written by Alan Stone, a lawyer with the FTC for eight years, who painstakingly dissected the agency's work in his book *Economic Regulation and the Public Interest*.*

In that book Stone surveyed the agency's numerous faults, noting that critics have found the FTC's "misallocation of resources" to be among its worst offenses. Thus, as Stone observed, critics have charged the FTC with squandering resources on minor matters, while failing to take action on matters of substantial importance to consumers. The cases brought by the FTC have dealt on the whole with petty matters and minor infractions, mostly linked with small firms in highly competitive industries. Similarly, in the field of consumer deception the agency has been accused of "devoting inordinate attention to trivia and little to the deceits practiced by large firms advertising in mass media." Its activities have become so ludicrous that an American Bar Association study found the FTC

> ... issued complaints attacking the failure to disclose on labels that "navy shoes" were not made by the Navy, that flies were imported, that Indian trinkets were not manufactured by American Indians and that "Havana" cigars were not made entirely of Cuban tobacco.

The bulk of the FTC's actions have not been aimed at huge and uncontrolled conglomerates, as its lofty rhetoric would have us believe, but at heavily competitive industries, composed of relatively small businesses: used car dealers, funeral homes, and toy manufacturers. And contrary to its mission, the actual effect of the FTC's activities has been to reduce competition. Said Stone:

> Industries with many small competitors cannot regulate themselves as effectively as those with few firms. A small competitor is the most likely to trigger a price war or initiate some other program of vigorous competition, ending the system of self-regulation. Many industries are incapable of self-regulation because of the large number of viable competitors they contain; these industries are unable to cope with or restrain "price cutters" or "aggressive merchandisers" or firms that introduce new marketing or distribution techniques. And the FTC devotes considerable effort to restricting competition in these intensely competitive industries. In 1959, for example, anti-monopoly cases absorbed 60 percent of the FTC's manpower and money—and in many of these cases the FTC was using its authority to produce conditions that simulated industry self-regulation and prevented intense competition.

The FTC is a classic example of an agency that has been given an epic mission to perform—in this case regulation of the nation's businesses—but relatively little resources to fulfill its enormous task.

*Cornell University Press, Ithaca, New York, 1977.

Congress has made it clear over many years that it does not intend to match the FTC's exuberant rhetorical promises with cold hard budgetary support.

Still, the FTC tries to act big, spraying its authority squid-like over a vast jurisdiction. Yet for all its bravado, only a relatively small percentage of its actions over the years have been pursued with any seriousness.

An audit of the FTC by the General Accounting Office, according to Stone, stated that 97 percent of [the FTC's] cases "never got beyond the stage of initial investigations, and in more than 60 percent of those formally investigated, no charges are brought." Significantly, the GAO said "the vast majority of cases are against small businesses, and involve relatively unimportant minor details or technical violations of the law."

Have the FTC's actions in any way improved the operation of our economy or reduced inflation? Stone's answer:

> It has gone on some fishing expeditions, and occasionally it has come up with a big catch. But . . . the impact upon the national economy of FTC action in these areas has been minimal. The agency's decisions on collusive practices have had no discernible effect on inflation. Nor do its decisions on exclusionary practices appear to have had much effect on the well-being of business units in the aggregate, which respond primarily to changes in such factors as the availability of money, the rate of cost increases, and demand. Because of the nature of its regulatory process, the FTC has largely failed both the proponents of competition and the proponents of stability.

Under the Moss-Magnuson Act, one of the FTC's primary weapons is the promulgation of Trade Regulation Rules (TRR) that place prohibitions and restrictions on industries it decrees are deceiving or ripping off consumers. After an investigation, a proposed rule is drafted, public hearings are held, testimony is taken, expert witnesses are heard, and the Commission then decides on a final TRR. This procedure, however, can take many years before the Commission finally acts. The whole debate can also end up in the courts where cases have languished for a decade or more before an ultimate resolution. The cost of all this, obviously, is born by taxpayers and consumers alike.

The funeral business is a case in point. After a year-long investigation, the FTC in 1973 issued a report that concluded this $6.4 billion industry needed federal regulation. The report said it found funeral parlors that took advantage of grieving customers by selling them more expensive funerals; that undertakers were found to be embalming without approval; and that caskets were being required for cremation.

Let's examine the FTC's criteria in this case. The funeral business hardly personifies corporate America. If anything, it is the epitome of the small business, with the industry composed of more than 22,000 funeral homes across the country. Furthermore, funerals are not something consumers purchase frequently. Only half the population has ever had to purchase one. One-fourth the population has never had to pay for a funeral. More importantly, the prices of funerals have remained largely constant in recent years.

There is no doubt that the practices cited by the FTC have occurred and probably still do. There are unscrupulous businessmen in every profession, just as there are unscrupulous government employes. But because of the infractions of a few, must we impose costly federal regulations on the entire industry?

And make no mistake, these regulations will cost more. For example, one of the FTC's draft proposals would require price itemization. Yet when itemization was ordered in New Jersey, it resulted in increased funeral costs. Congressman Martin Russo of Illinois said that "with forced itemization the 'package funeral' could eventually disappear. This would be economically harmful to lower-income groups."

The FTC steadfastly maintained their regulations would add little if any cost to funerals, but Dr. Vanderlyn Pine, in a cost study submitted to the White House Council on Wage and Price Stability, concluded the FTC's proposal would cost consumers an additional $50 million a year.

Many members of Congress were bewildered by the FTC's action against the funeral industry. Congressman Joseph Early of Massachusetts, who believes the Commission should focus its energies on a few major areas of consumer demand such as food, told FTC officials at a House Appropriations Committee hearing:

> I have been in government 18 years. I have never had a complaint in my district on abuses by funeral homes. Now you people are going to make all sorts of rules, or set a rule, and it is going to affect an abuser in some city.

Meantime, Early said, "all the undertakers in my community of a half million people" will come under the FTC's regulatory umbrella. "Does that alarm you? Does it concern you?" he asked FTC Chairman Michael Pertschuk.

Early went on to tell Pertschuk that although he had never had "one comment" about funeral costs:

> I get hundreds of calls weekly on abuses at the food market. What am I supposed to tell the guy? "No, Mrs. Jones, we are not working on that yet. We are on funerals."

Perhaps the FTC's *preeminent act of paternalism* has been its proposed ban on broadcast advertising aimed at children.

Directed by Congress to insure truthfulness in advertising, the FTC has proposed what is perhaps the most sweeping invasion of first amendment rights of broadcasters and advertisers. Under the commission's proposals, parents need no longer be concerned with toys, foods or other products their children may be exposed to by television. The federal government would step in and remove this parental responsibility by banning all children's advertising during program times when youngsters are likely to be watching. Toy commercials could not be advertised unless they met with prior approval of the Commission. No advertisements aimed at children under eight years of age would be allowed. (Here the FTC mysteriously presumes that a seven-year-old is not intelligent enough to understand that the advertiser is trying to sell a product that his parents may or may not wish to buy.) The FTC believes manufacturers and broadcasters have been taking unfair advantage of children who, they fear, will subject parents to unrelenting pressure to buy what is shown on television. Government, the FTC argues, has a responsibility to protect the parent from this.

But the FTC doesn't stop there in its zealous campaign to insulate us from all decision-making in our lives. Other proposed advertising bans would prohibit broadcasters from advertising diet drinks, some chewing gums, and certain toothpastes and mouthwashes containing saccharin, unless manufacturers aired a commercial focusing solely on the health hazards of saccharin products. Advertisements for over-the-counter drugs and antacid products also could not be made, under the FTC's proposed rules, unless the ads were accompanied by language written by the Food and Drug Administration. What all this means, said Vincent Wasilewski, president of the National Association of Broadcasters, is that the government could dictate "the exact language to be used" in drug advertising. The proposed rule would make it "an 'unfair trade practice' to use words in advertising which had not been approved by the FDA."

The FTC has also proposed that ads would not be able to make any nutrient claims on the air unless they were accompanied by a description of the nutrient composition and value of the food to insure that it met the government's recommended daily allowances for vitamins and minerals.

All of this suggests that the FTC has succumbed to the politics of absurdity. Have we come this far as a nation that we need the United States government to dictate when children's toys and other products can and cannot be advertised? Will the government be banning ads for decoder rings, McDonaldland drinking glasses, and Sesame Street rubber ducks for similar reasons? And are parents to be denied the right to watch such programming with their children? Wouldn't they benefit from knowing what toys are on the market so they can make intelligent consumer decisions of their own?

Furthermore, there is the impossibility of banning ads aimed at children when a multiplicity of age groups may be watching. The American Enterprise Institute's magazine, *Regulation*, pointed out that "young children rarely, if ever, constitute a majority of the audience for any television program."

"As for economic issues," the magazine said,

> . . . one consequence of a ban or strict limitations on the number and frequency of television advertisements directed to young children would be a decline in revenue for children's television programming.

The FTC's involvement in this entire area is government paternalism at its most reprehensible. It represents a major attack on an important component of our rights to free speech. When the government can dictate language for Alka-Seltzer and mouthwash ads, when it can decide what types of ads will appear on radio and television and at what times of the day, then the entire foundation of our economic freedom to advertise will be shattered.

Note, too, that under this twisted approach to truth in advertising, the government decides what is deceptive and the accused must prove otherwise. Professor Yale Brozen of the University of Chicago remembers the case several years ago when the FTC, charging deception, forced the makers of Zerex antifreeze to stop advertisements showing their product stopped radiator leaks. Several years later the FTC admitted the ads were in fact accurate, but by then the damage had been done.

Like the charges against Zerex, the FTC unilaterally decides what is deceptive, conducting a trial by press release, and demanding that the advertisers run ads admitting the deceptions, Brozen said. The burden of proving innocence

... is left to the advertiser, if he can survive the trial by accusation and publicity—a complete turnabout from our judicial system in which an accused is regarded as innocent until proved guilty.

The public's perception of FTC regulatory proceedings is that they are totally objective seekers of truth. That perception is a myth. The FTC is a highly subjective, prejudicial bureaucracy that gives one the impression they have already made up their mind before the rulemaking proceeding starts. That kind of bias, which often comes directly from the top, shocked U.S. District Court Judge Gerhard Gesell, who ruled that Chairman Pertschuk could no longer participate in the consideration of the advertising ban proposals because of his flagrant bias in the case. Judge Gesell disqualified Pertschuk because of his use of "conclusory statements of fact, his emotional use of derogatory terms of characterizations and his affirmative efforts to propagate his settled views."

Evidence of this antibusiness bias has been particularly evident in the agency's public participation program through which the FTC gives millions of dollars in grants to private organizations, many of whom are openly hostile to business. While the FTC sprinkles a few grants among business and trade groups to give the appearance of fair play, the overwhelming majority of the funds go to a multitude of public interest law firms, consumer organizations, and other social advocacy groups and political organizations such as the Americans for Democratic Action (which is discussed in "Paying the Special Interests").

These grants are to go only to organizations representing interests that would not otherwise be fully presented in a rulemaking proceeding, according to the FTC. The rationale is that these interests cannot afford to present their views before the FTC while big business has ample resources to do so. This funding, however, pays for much more than the simple presentation of a group's views before the commission. The grants can also support an organization's secretarial and staff salaries, attorneys fees, travel, and other operational expenses. They can also pay for expert witness fees, surveys and polls, research and other types of professional analysis. The work is often subcontracted out by the grantees, but the funds frequently pay for in-house employes to do what they would be doing for their organization or employer anyway, regardless of their participation in an FTC proceeding. Thus, the grants are in many respects a subsidy for the ongoing operations of these organizations.

Groups getting this FTC money include Consumers Union; the

Arkansas Community Organization for Reform Now; the Consumers Cooperative of Berkely, Inc.; the National Consumer Law Center, Inc.; California Citizens Action Group; the National Consumers League; the New York Public Interest Research Group, a Ralph Nader spin-off organization; the Consumer Federation of America; the National Consumers Congress; San Francisco Consumer Action; Center for Public Representation; and Consumer Action Now, among many others.

One former public interest lawyer said:

> The FTC will tell you the grants are solely to help these groups present their case to the commission, but in reality this money is often used to subsidize organizations who found their traditional sources of private funding have dried up. So they have turned to the government and the FTC as a willing supporter of their causes.

"And isn't it a coincidence" the attorney continued, "that most of the groups getting FTC public participation money just happen to support the FTC's position in these cases." It should also come as no surprise that the largest chunk of this FTC funding is consumed by attorneys fees—lawyers who either work in-house for some of the larger recipient organizations or attorneys in private practice. According to the FTC, 44 percent of the public participation grants are paying attorneys fees and related legal expenses.

A portion of these grants are also paying for public opinion polls and other types of surveys of consumers and other groups. Some House members were incredulous during the agency's fiscal 1980 appropriations hearings that a portion of this funding has been paying for poll taking and surveys. Asked a somewhat surprised Congressman Jack Hightower of Texas, "We are buying the results of polls? Is that what some of this money is used for?" It is indeed.

The FTC's Bureau of Economics, its research and analysis arm, provides further documentation of the millions of dollars being wasted by this agency on inane studies and research projects. Many of the bureau's grants and contracts defy comprehension. But the FTC makes sure it spreads its money around to a myriad of private researchers, college professors, law firms, consultants, and other well-paid white collar groups and companies. A great many of these contracts are duplicative. Some encroach upon work being done by other federal agencies. Others suggest that the government doesn't have anything better to do with our money and wants to quickly spend it to avoid an embarrassing surplus at the end of the fiscal year.

Here are examples of what the FTC has been doing with your

money. And while you read them, ask yourself how does any of this help the consumer?

—$41,900 for a survey on the effectiveness of corrective advertising for Listerine.

—$1,925 for an analysis of children's television viewing and formulation of remedies in children's advertising rulemaking.

—$25,000 to provide computerized data on children's television viewing in various market areas.

—$14,800 to study network programming and advertising practices.

—$19,000 for a survey of households to determine the products eaten by children as snacks.

—$3,200 for an analysis of the effects of television advertising on black children.

—$20,000 for the production and distribution of public service radio announcements aimed at consumers.

—$15,000 for the production of a 30-second counter advertisement on the concept of a balanced breakfast.

—$3,900 for consumer testing of two Fleischman margarine print advertisements.

—$4,500 for a study of children's perception of television advertising.

—$5,150 for a study of the effects of television commercials on children.

—$2,500 for the presentation of a 25-hour course on effective writing within the agency.

—$100,000 to conduct reviews and in-depth studies of the Japanese and Western European automobile industries.

—$900 to study risk analysis of the ready to eat cereal industry.

—$2,700 for another study on the effect of television advertising on black children.

—$1,750 for a study on children's perception of television advertising.

—$15,500 for an analysis of a task force on Women's Business Owners.

—$3,000 to prepare an FTC workshop for women.

—$2,200 for the presentation of an FTC workshop for women.

—$6,000 for a written analysis of the effect of children's advertising.

—$3,250 to conduct between 15-20 interviews concerning consumer problems of the elderly.

—$3,400 in expert witness fees for a dentist to testify on the decay effect caused by sugar consumption.

—$13,000 for a study to assess the effects of regulation and price discrimination in the trucking industry.

—$9,500 for a study and analysis of advertising designed for children's viewing.

—$4,800 for public relations work in preparation for an FTC workshop for women.

—$1,000 for an analysis of the industrial gas industry.

—$59,484 for a study assessing the economic performance of the trucking industry.

—$14,500 for a study examining the effects of televised stimuli on children's understanding of proper nutrition.

—$9,400 for an analysis of surveys on consumer problem reception and design of complaint-handling procedures.

—$27,000 for research and development of an overview to be presented at a Media Symposium.

—$50,000 to conduct a survey of consumer perceptions of warnings in a television advertisement.

—$7,850 for a study of the social and cultural basis of current price competition in the real estate industry.

—$3,500 for a study of children's perceptions of television advertising.

—$9,120 to provide a special report on 60 publications concerning Readership of Cigarette Advertising.

—$20,900 to conduct a survey on the genericness of the trademark Formica in the public's mind.

—$15,428 to conduct a survey of 2,000 nutrition and health professionals on the effect of televised food advertising on children's food choices.

—$790 to conduct a seminar on "Women in Business."

—$22,700 for a study on unfairness and deception resulting from use of advertising practices in toy commercials.

—$11,060 for an analysis of children's knowledge of nutrition at various development stages.

—$1,500 for an analysis of the impact on television advertising on—you guessed it—children.

—$3,500 to review and analyze children's perceptions of characters in advertising.

—$14,000 for a research project to determine the impact of television advertising on pre-school children.

—$7,270 to analyze children's television viewing patterns.

—$70,700 for a survey concerning smoking among teenagers and adults.

—$4,000 for an analysis of Piaget's theory of children's cognitive development.

—$4,800 to a newspaper clipping service for a monthly reading and clipping fee.

—$3,000 to interview persons with a first hand knowledge of the cost of television programming.

—$5,880 for an analysis of food intake records of children.

—$6,500 for the creation and production of two radio commercials.

—$3,500 for the purchase of scripts and video tapes of television advertisements.

—$3,000 for a follow-up telephone census on the three-day cooling-off rule for door-to-door sales.

—$8,000 for three videotaped studies of children playing with toys featured in three television advertisements to focus on the toys' performance capabilities.

—$5,150 for a study of children in two metropolitan areas to determine whether a toy company's television commercial for the "Star Hawk/Star Team" toys communicates to children that the toys in this line are sold separately.

—$6,800 for the rental of a room and facilities for the Bureau of Competition's Media Symposium.

—$52,700 for the purchase and mailing of cigarettes used for testing (Advertising Practices).

—$1,200 to prepare a report concerning the barriers which affect women in starting their own business.

The above is just a small sampling of the FTC's fiscal 1978 and 1979 program contracts, but it vividly illustrates that this agency is researching subjects and conducting projects that are a million light-years away from the real problems and everyday concerns of most Americans.

When FTC officials said they were merely doing what Congress authorized them to do, Congressman Early replied:

> Maybe Congress was wrong. Tell me where the public is getting a better shake because of the FTC? Where in the food market? What has your agency done to give my constituents a better shake in the marketplace, other than establishing studies and those types of things? Why do we have to pay all this money to get these (studies)?

Early's question is an appropriate one and long overdue. The answer is, *we don't*. These expenditures won't contribute one iota to the economic or nutritional well-being of a single American. In fact, an FTC employe who is familiar with many of these FTC contracts privately admitted to me, "A lot of them are a waste of time and money." Similarly, a knowledgeable congressional committee staffer who has closely examined FTC spending, added:

> Many of these contracts have little if any impact upon our daily lives. But Congress gave them this mandate to deal in these things and they are doing nothing more than what we asked them to do.

During the House Appropriations Committee's questioning of FTC officials about the agency's work, a top Commission official described the FTC's budget as a "little pittance." Now, granted $65 million is small change in comparison to the federal budget, but the real cost of this agency is what it inflicts on businesses as well as consumers. This of course is not a subject the FTC is eager to address. You will never see this agency funding a study to determine how much their own regulatory practices have cost the business community and the nation as a whole.

The FTC usually argues that what they spend in behalf of the consumer is small when compared to what business spends to counter FTC actions. For example, the Commission said its rulemaking proceeding on children's advertising cost less than $1.2 million a year, while industries opposing the agency's proposals may spend an estimated $15-$30 million to fight the rules. Once again, because of the FTC's actions, consumers will end up footing the bill.

One of the largest industry-wide investigations ever undertaken by the government is the FTC's probe of the automobile industry which was begun in 1975. The FTC defended this rather vague investigation by saying it merely wished "to determine where the potential areas for anticompetitive practices and structures are in the automobile industry." In the process the FTC asked the industry's automakers to provide the government with private data and records going back as many as 30 years, requiring thousands of nonproductive man-hours to produce a mountain of paperwork.

General Motors, Chrysler, and the American Motors Corporation took their complaints into court where during oral arguments over what the FTC was looking for, an FTC attorney admitted the Commission did not suspect automakers were guilty of any violations of law. They were merely, the lawyer confessed, on "a fishing expedition" to comb the industry's records. If they came up with some dirt, fine.

If not, the FTC would move on to something else—presumably the fishing industry.

What will the FTC's epic auto industry investigation end up costing you and me? The Commission budgeted $1.4 million for the investigation in fiscal 1980. But the big three auto companies estimated the cost of complying with the FTC's subpoena could run as high as $200 million. A motion by the Ford Motor Company that the FTC's subpoenas be squashed resulted in the agency cutting its data requests in half. This of course indicated the FTC didn't need as much information as it had asked for in the first place. Yet even half of the FTC's demands will still be terribly costly to the industry as well as to the consumer. In 1978 General Motors estimated that it spent $1.6 billion complying with federal, state and local government regulations. And this excluded taxes and the cost of government-mandated hardware added to GM cars.

The GAO has estimated that total annual federal regulatory costs directly born by consumers are around $60 billion, while President Ford's Council of Economic Advisers set the price tag of direct and indirect regulatory costs at $130 billion. It has been computed that federal regulations have added at least another $600 to the price of automobiles.

With American automakers in a constant struggle with foreign imports, as well as the unpredictable rise and fall of the auto market due to changing economic conditions and energy-related factors, the FTC's costly "fishing expedition" placed one more unnecessary and harmful burden on the industry's back. (This was strange action by the government when one considers that in 1979 Chrysler was facing bankruptcy and fighting for its very survival.)

The FTC's actions in this case *will do nothing* to bring auto prices down or to improve competition. Indeed, its actions will surely lead to rising prices and probably less competition. Clearly, the FTC's efforts here have hurt the consumer in every way possible.

It is little wonder, then, that when the FTC's fiscal 1980 appropriations bill wound its way through the House Appropriations Committee, members tentatively decided to add a string of severely restrictive amendments that would have forced the agency to its knees—ceasing all investigations into the auto and oil industries and forbidding further action in a number of major trade regulation rule proceedings, including the television advertising ban, used cars, funerals, and over-the-counter drugs.

The prohibitions were never formally adopted, but they served to dramatize how incensed members of Congress have become over the FTC's somewhat bizarre adventures. Yet that was only half of the agency's problems with Congress. By late 1979 the FTC's authorization—which gives the FTC statutory authority to carry out its functions—had been tied up for an unprecedented three years in a House-Senate fight over whether FTC regulations should be subjected to a one-house congressional veto. The one-house veto is a legislative oversight tool rarely used by Congress, in this case to harness an agency whose actions have all too frequently exceeded what Congress had in mind when they enacted it.

By early 1980, final action had not yet been taken on the FTC's reauthorization bill. But whatever the outcome, the FTC was thoroughly shaken by the experience of facing near-termination.

Congress has in the past fought over a myriad of specific FTC cases, disliking some while applauding others. Rarely, however, has any member bothered to evaluate the Commission's entire program against any consistent cost-benefit standard to determine if the nation has been getting its moneysworth. My own belief is that we have not. We are being taken, and taken badly.

In the final chapter of his book, Stone discussed the impact of government regulation on the consumer and concluded that the agency, along with other federal regulatory programs, has not only been ineffective, but also incredibly costly to our nation. Said Stone:

> I have never found a convincingly calculated estimate of total regulatory costs passed on to consumers, but guesstimates are frighteningly high. The Goodyear Tire and Rubber Company announced, for example, that it expended $30 million in 1974 in complying with federal and state regulations. If we assume that regulatory costs represent the same percentage of sales for the top 500 manufacturing firms as for Goodyear (.0057), total regulatory costs for this group of firms alone were in excess of $4.75 billion in 1974. While we have no way of knowing what proportion of the total is passed on to consumers, it seems probable that most is. Thus, while the sum arrived at is clearly suspect as an accurate calculation of the private-sector costs of regulation to consumers, it suggests that the total amount is quite substantial and raises two specific questions: Are the purported benefits from regulation worth the direct costs? And if they are, can these benefits be realized through the process of regulation? My conclusion . . . is that, on balance, the kind of business regulation we now have is not and cannot be an effective instrument for the promotion of public values.

Contrary to those who continue to worship this aging sacred cow, the Federal Trade Commission is a supremely unnecessary and wasteful federal agency that the nation can no longer afford. The FTC's meddling paternalism over breakfast cereals, after school snacks, children's TV ads, aspirins, and mouthwashes must end. If any drugs or food products in any way pose a threat to our citizens, the Food and Drug Administration or the Agriculture Department can deal with it. All that should remain of this agency is the continuation of a vigorous but fair implementation and enforcement of the anti-trust laws within the Justice Department. Everything else should be swept out.

PROGRAM 99

Amtrak — $899 Million

For decades the government forbad railroads from cutting unprofitable and underutilized passenger lines. Ratemaking and other major decisions had to be sanctioned by the government. Railroads were told what to do and when to do it. Because of this crushing regulation, rail service in America began to die. Then in 1970 Congress in a desperate attempt to "save the railroads" established the National Railroad Passenger Corporation, otherwise known as Amtrak, to take over the mess it had created. Ten years later the rail passenger business was still hovering near death.

Congress established Amtrak fully convinced that failing rail lines could be made profitable once more, if only enough of our money was poured into them. After over $4 billion and a decade of experimentation, the result is now painfully obvious. In practically every respect Amtrak has been a costly and colossal failure. The evidence, documented in countless reports and studies, is there for all to see.

At the beginning of 1979 the Transportation Department made a major study of Amtrak's operations. That study contained these startling findings:

—An estimated 75 percent of all intercity travelers and commuters used the train 35 years ago. Today Amtrak carries less than three-tenths of 1 percent of the nation's intercity travelers. If its ridership were tripled, the railroads would serve only one intercity traveler in a hundred.

—Some of Amtrak's major passenger trains averaged a mere 25 passengers on any given day in 1978.

—It will cost taxpayers about $6 billion in continued operating subsidies over the next five years if Amtrak is continued.

—Amtrak is less energy-efficient than the automobile. It would have to average more than 140 passengers on its trains in order to be competitive with the automobile for energy use (measured in passenger miles per gallon) and more than 400 people to compete with the bus.

—Taxpayers are now paying nearly twice as much as an Amtrak rider for each passenger ticket. For every 59 cents a rider pays for a ticket, the government must shell out another $1.

In a position paper on the subject, the Carter administration said:

Given such an extensive subsidy, it would in many cases be cheaper for the government and more energy efficient for everyone if the government gave—free of charge—airline or bus tickets to these Amtrak passengers.

Amtrak's annual deficits have been incredible. None of its routes have been able to cover operating costs—including the heavily traveled Northeast Corridor. Its operating deficit totaled $153.5 million in fiscal 1972. By fiscal 1977 it had more than tripled, reaching an estimated $521.6 million. By 1978 Amtrak's deficit for the year was $578 million—representing about $2 in tax subsidies for every $1 in fares. By fiscal 1979 Congress had authorized a total subsidy of $755 million to cover Amtrak's costs. Annual subsidies are now nearing the $1 billion mark.

The degree to which taxpayers are called upon to make up these enormous deficits is stunning. A study by the American Conservative Union's Education and Research Institute* (ERI) found:

Of the $44 cost of an average Amtrak ride, the passenger pays little more than $16, while the taxpayers pay nearly $28. Despite congressional intentions, in other words, the taxpayer now pays nearly two-thirds of Amtrak's costs.

Congressman Ron Paul of Texas pointed out that a bus ticket between Milwaukee and Chicago "costs $5.50 versus a tax subsidy on Amtrak of about seven times as much," which prompted Sen. Russell Long of Louisiana to wonder why the government was trying to persuade people "to leave a taxpaying organization, the bus company, and ride on a tax-eating organization, Amtrak?"

Overall, federal subsidies represent 63 percent of Amtrak's costs. Compare this to airline subsidies, which total only 5 percent, or intercity buses, whose subsidies are even less (actually, when road-use taxes and other levies paid by buses are figured in, they receive no net subsidy at all).

A study prepared for the National Transportation Policy Study Commission said that even if every seat on every Amtrak train were filled, Amtrak would continue to lose $100 million a year. The commission's report said:

The only major difference between past and present rail operations since the coming of Amtrak is that subsidies are now covered by the government rather than by the privately owned railroads . . . ; a complete network of intercity rail passenger services cannot be operated in the U.S. on a for-profit basis.

*Published by AEI in Washington, D.C., Sept. 17, 1979, by Dolores Davies, David Williams, and Walter Olson.

It should also be pointed out that public support for Amtrak has been sparse. A 1977 Transportation Department survey showed only 18 percent of those polled supported any expansion of Amtrak's services, while 71 percent said it made "no difference" to them if Amtrak was either continued or abolished.

However, Amtrak supporters still maintain that while it may not be profitable, the government should continue supporting it because, of all other modes of transportation, Amtrak is the cleanest and most energy efficient.

Both arguments, though, are disputed by most reputable studies on the subject. A 1978 GAO report stated:

> The trains on all 11 routes reviewed consumed more energy in fiscal year 1977 than would have been consumed if every passenger had used an automobile . . . While only slight increases in ridership would have made some routes such as Seattle/Portland more fuel efficient than automobiles, others like the Washington/Cincinnati route would need to triple or quadruple ridership to meet or exceed auto fuel efficiency.

A Transportation Department study said Amtrak's Floridian line "used more fuel in fiscal year 1976 than if everyone had traveled by automobile and the mail had been carried by truck." And a 1979 Congressional Budget Office study said:

> Outside the Northeast Corridor, the nation would save energy if no rail service were operated. Trains could use considerably less energy per passenger-mile than at present if they made use of new, more efficient equipment and were able to attract enough passengers to operate cars more nearly filled.

But the CBO concluded that by the time these improvements could be realized, cars will have become more efficient in their use of fuel, partly in response to fuel economy standards set by the government.

ERI's study also found that Amtrak was "only about half" as energy-efficient on the average as an intercity bus. In fact, outside the Northeast Corridor Amtrak consumes "even more energy per passenger-mile than an automobile." The Department of Energy in 1977 said that the average intercity bus consumed 1192 BTU's per passenger mile, compared to passenger trains which consumed 4433 BTU's.

The ERI study said:

> If Amtrak ran only its best, most efficient trains at near maximum passenger loads, it would indeed consume far less energy. Unfortunately, Amtrak's ridership falls considerably short of maximum passenger capacity. And most of its equipment is outmoded: the average Amtrak locomotive is 10 years old. As a result Amtrak pollutes much more per

passenger-mile than it would given better equipment and higher load factors. Amtrak, on the average, does have a lower pollution rate per passenger-mile than the airplane and the automobile, but it pollutes more than its true competitor, the intercity bus.

The ERI study also dispelled another argument, namely that rail passenger service is crucial to the nation's rural areas. ERI found that "buses provide much more extensive service to rural areas than do passenger trains."

A number of factors have contributed to the decline of the railroads since the mid-1800s when Congress chartered the first transcontinental railroad and issued government land grants and other special favors to boost rail travel and thus encourage American growth and expansion. But, shortly after the turn of the century, the government began to turn against the railroads. A rash of antirailroad legislation that fixed minimum rates and placed other restrictions on the industry began the movement to cheaper forms of transportation. Government-sponsored union work rules also forced unnecessary and costly labor demands on rail lines. And, in some instances, poor management was also a factor.

The railroad was king as long as it was the cheapest and principal means of passenger transportation. But the rapid availability of the automobile changed all that. Government poured billions into highway construction and the car became a cheap and easy way to travel. (More than five out of six American households now own a car.) Air travel—supported by massive federal aviation subsidies—also offered faster and increasingly cheaper transportation, and to most of the railroad's destinations.

All of this contributed to the decline of rail passenger travel. But *government regulation, more than anything else,* was the predominant reason for the inability of the railroads to adapt to these changes. Unprofitable rail lines, which in a free and healthy business climate would have been cut, were forced to continue under the iron hand of regulation. Ironically, when Amtrak was created in 1970 Congress wanted to have as little as possible to do with the ICC's regulatory rituals. After years of preventing the railroads from dismantling little-used and deteriorating lines, Amtrak's first move was to cut the total number of passenger trains from 547 to 243.

Faced with a $1 billion annual subsidy within the next three years, the Carter administration in 1979 proposed amputating 43 percent of Amtrak's least profitable rail lines. However, Congress, ruled by conflicting self-interests, could bear to part with only 20 percent of the system—a relatively modest cut in an enormously unprofitable and wasteful enterprise.

In the final analysis, Amtrak is a massive boondoggle. The government should never have gotten into the business of running rail passenger lines. By its very nature, Washington is *uniquely unqualified* to make hard, business-minded decisions. Too many bureaucrats, congressmen, and committee chairmen have too many special constituencies to satisfy. But it is never too late to learn from our mistakes and to save billions of dollars in further losses of tax revenues.

First, we should begin by recognizing that America neither needs nor can support a national rail passenger system. However, there are areas where the railroad can play a useful and profitable role, where potential markets can be persuaded to take the train if conveniently offered at a competitive fare. But only the private sector can accomplish this, and only in a free and unregulated economic environment.

Amtrak's subsidies should be terminated and its equipment and rail properties sold at auction to the highest bidder. In most of its operations Amtrak owns only the trains and other equipment, but not the railroad lines which belong to their original owners for whom Amtrak runs the trains and pays the bills. The only exception is the Northeast Corridor (Washington to New York to Boston) where Amtrak owns the whole business. All of it should be sold off, either to the lines' owners, or to other prospective buyers.

Second, the railroad industry must be totally deregulated, except for safety requirements. Tax incentives should be enacted for passenger railroads to make this capital-starved, endangered species attractive to new investors. And the government should also reform railroad labor laws to ease inequitable and unfair labor practices which unnecessarily raise the costs of railroad operations.

Spending nearly $1 billion a year in tax subsidies to keep passenger trains running in areas of the country where passengers account for only a miniscule number of people is a waste of our tax resources. Complete removal of the government from the rail passenger business would, in the long run, be the cheapest and most efficient way of providing rail transportation to those places in America that need, want, and can support such services.

PROGRAM 100
Council on Wage and Price Stability — $5.9 Million

This agency has one primary mission to fulfill, and that is to reduce inflation. In this respect it has been an utter failure.

Established on August 20, 1974 under President Ford, the Council actually replaced President Nixon's Cost of Living Council which had been disbanded four months earlier. In 1975 Congress gave the Council new powers to subpoena business data, including the breakdown of prices and other costs for each product line companies make or sell.

The Council resides within the White House office complex where it is easily susceptible to the pressures any administration is likely to exert on an agency dealing with such a politically volatile subject as inflation.

The Council's primary function consists of administering voluntary wage and price guidelines which the country, theoretically, is supposed to adhere to but of course rarely if ever does.

In an attempt to achieve compliance with its program, the Council monitors wage and price increases within the private sector, as well as certain government actions whose impact could be inflationary, and identifies those exceeding the guidelines. At times, however, the government becomes impatient when the economy does not obey the guidelines. Nixon, for instance, instituted wage and price controls with very disruptive results. President Carter threatened to punish those who violated his so-called voluntary guidelines by denying federal contracts and procurement to them. But the General Accounting Office declared the use of federal purchasing power to punish anyone who declined to obey the guidelines was illegal.

Everyone by now realizes that voluntary guidelines do not, indeed cannot work. All the wage-price monitoring in the world is not going to make a dent in this stubborn and seemingly insoluble problem.

When the Council announced a 7 percent wage-price guideline in late 1978, inflation was averaging more than 9 percent for the year. The rate of inflation in 1979 was running about 13 percent, the worst in many years.

The Council is essentially an attempt at a quick-fix cure for a deeply serious economic problem. No serious economist believes an agency of less than 200 people, through guidelines, monitoring, or even jawboning, can to any significant degree affect the rate of inflation one way or the other. Inflation is caused by much broader problems which the Council does not and in fact cannot address. To a large degree it is caused by too many dollars being released into the economy. This leads to devaluation of the dollar and thus to inflation. The Council, from its very beginning, has been a public relations gimmick to persuade people that the government is trying to do something about inflation without dealing with its root causes. An office is created in the White House, people are hired, a determined "inflation-fighter" is named to head the operation, and a lot of data, reports, testimony, decrees, and paperwork are issued to make it appear that something meaningful is being done. The truth is that nothing effective has been done by this largely impotent and miniscule agency.

Inflation is a problem that can only be dealt with by government in a broad fiscal and monetary way. It requires actions by the Federal Reserve Board, as we saw in the fall of 1979, to tighten the available money supply. It also requires leaner budgets by the Executive branch and Congress to curb spending which is the single most aggravating cause of inflation. And while we are on that subject, the place to start cutting the budget would be to abolish this agency.